Life and Loss in the Shadow of the Holocaust

A family's recently discovered correspondence provides the inspiration for this fascinating and deeply moving account of Jewish family life before, during, and after the Holocaust. Rebecca Boehling and Uta Larkey reveal how the Kaufmann–Steinberg family was pulled apart under the Nazi regime and dispersed over three continents. The family's unique eight-way correspondence across two generations brings into sharp focus the dilemma of Jews in Nazi Germany facing the painful decisions of when, if, and to where they should emigrate. The authors capture the family members' fluctuating emotions of hope, optimism, resignation and despair, as well as the day-to-day concerns, experiences and dynamics of family life despite increasing persecution and impending deportation. Headed by two sisters who were among the first female business owners in Essen, the family was far from conventional, and their story contributes new dimensions to our understanding of Jewish life in Germany and in exile during these dark years.

REBECCA BOEHLING is Professor of History and Director of the Dresher Center for the Humanities at the University of Maryland Baltimore County.

UTA LARKEY is Associate Professor of German Studies at Goucher College, Baltimore, Maryland.

Life and Loss in the Shadow of the Holocaust

A Jewish Family's Untold Story

Rebecca Boehling
and
Uta Larkey

CAMBRIDGE
UNIVERSITY PRESS

CAMBRIDGE UNIVERSITY PRESS
Cambridge, New York, Melbourne, Madrid, Cape Town,
Singapore, São Paulo, Delhi, Tokyo, Mexico City

Cambridge University Press
The Edinburgh Building, Cambridge CB2 8RU, UK

Published in the United States of America by Cambridge University Press, New York

www.cambridge.org
Information on this title: www.cambridge.org/9780521899918

First published 2011

Printed in the United Kingdom at the University Press, Cambridge

A catalog record for this publication is available from the British Library

ISBN 978-0-521-89991-8 Hardback

To the memory of Selma and Henny

CONTENTS

FIGURES

ACKNOWLEDGMENTS

A book project of this type is not possible without the support of numerous individuals and institutions, some whose support is more direct and tangible while others, no less important, play a behind-the-scenes role. There are of course a number of people who fall into both categories. As co-authors who split and shared various research and writing responsibilities we each have some people and institutions we want to thank in particular, but also several who have helped both of us.

This book would not have been possible without the initiative that Marianne Steinberg Ostrand took in saving all those hundreds of letters and other documents, and that her daughter, Suzanne Ostrand-Rosenberg (Sue), took in deciding neither to dispose of them nor simply to keep them to herself. Unfortunately, we never got to meet Nanna, as her friends and family called her, but in many ways we feel we have gotten to know her. Her diaries and her many, many letters and documents form the core of our collection. Nanna's husband, Arnold, also shared with us what he could about his own memories, as well as what he recalled from stories Nanna had told him. Sue, their daughter, has been extremely generous with her time. Whether helping with the copying of the letters and images, answering yet more questions, or bringing out family photograph albums and, together with the authors, explaining yet one more time who is who and figuring out together where and when a picture might have been taken, she has always been ready and willing to help. Had Sue not shared with her cousins in Israel and Chile the brief narrative focused on Marianne that Rebecca's graduate student, Deborah Gayle, wrote, the source base would have been considerably less rich and balanced. We are also grateful to Marianne's son, Tom, for sharing with us numerous memories and stories he recalled his parents telling. We also owe Alicia Frohmann, Lotti's daughter, and Michael Keynan, her son, considerable gratitude for the time and energy they put into searching for, sorting through and sending us Lotti's letters and photographs, and for their willingness to meet with us and be interviewed on several occasions. Gideon Sella, Kurt's son, not only took the time to photograph letters his parents had saved in Tel Aviv and to meet with us on multiple occasions but also shared with us the artistic work he has done over the last few years, as he worked through the family memories and stories, spoken and unspoken, and the impressions that the many letters made upon him. We are grateful to him for allowing us to use a photograph of part of his work for our cover.

We also would like to thank Selma and Henny's nephew, Ernest Kaufman, the only close Kaufmann relative of that generation still alive who actually knew Selma and Henny. He was willing to reminisce about his aunts and his memories of sharing a room with Onkel Hermann, when in the mid 1930s he lived briefly with the Kaufmann–Steinberg family. Considerably younger than his cousins, Kurt, Lotti and Nanna, Ernest was a fount of information about the extended Kaufmann family, his father's many sisters and their children. His contributions have added considerable texture to our portrayal of family relationships. On the Steinberg side of the family, we are grateful to Marianne Bachrach Luedeking, who shared her understanding of family relationships and memories, including attending the weddings of both Lotti and Nanna.

The access that was granted us at various archives and libraries in the United States, Israel and Germany was invaluable. The list of institutions to which we owe our gratitude includes: the Center for Advanced Holocaust Studies at the US Holocaust Memorial Museum, in particular Ann Millin and Jürgen Matthäus, the Alte Synagoge Archives and the Stadtarchiv in Essen, the Nordrhein-Westfälisches Hauptstaatsarchiv in Düsseldorf, the Thüringisches Hauptstaatsarchiv in Weimar, the NS-Dokumentationszentrum and the Germania Judaica Library in Cologne, the Institut für Stadtgeschichte, Frankfurt am Main, the Leo Baeck Institute in Berlin and New York, Yad Vashem, Stiftung Gedenkstätten Buchenwald and Mittelbau-Dora and the archives at Terezín Memorial (Theresienstadt). We are especially grateful to the Leo Baeck Institute in New York, which awarded us a joint David Baumgardt Memorial Fellowship, and to Frank Mecklenburg in particular. For the opportunity to present our work-in-progress, we would like to thank Yad Vashem, the Holocaust Education Foundation, Franklin and Marshall College, the German Studies Association and the New York Area German Women's History Group, the Upper Keys Jewish Community Center, Goucher College and the Department of History at the University of Maryland, Baltimore County (UMBC).

Producing this book would not have been possible without the transcription assistance with Selma's early handwritten letters that we received from Jutta Georgi. Our editor at Cambridge University Press, Michael Watson, has been incredibly supportive and patient as he shepherded this project through its many stages. Our special thanks go to him and the Cambridge University Press staff. We would also like to thank the anonymous readers who first recommended publication and those who graciously reviewed the semi-final manuscript. Whatever shortcomings the final manuscript may have are of course our own.

The authors

Rebecca Boehling would like to thank the following individuals in particular for their assistance to her during her research trips in Germany: Martina Strehlen at the Alte Synagoge Archives, Essen and Jutta Vonrüden-Ferner at the Stadtarchiv Essen, Barbara Becker-Jákli and Martin Scherpenstein at the National Socialist Documentation Center, Cologne and Angela Genger at the Mahn- und Gedenkstätte der Landeshauptstadt Düsseldorf. Their willingness to share their expertise, both in person and on-line, was invaluable.

I also wish to acknowledge the research efforts of two individuals in particular, whose work provided a initial start to our further research. Deborah Gayle, my former Masters student, not only copied and set up an initial database for the first set of letters but also researched and wrote the narrative, "A German-Jewish Family's Odyssey through the Holocaust." She approached this research not only with scholarly diligence and a desire to complete the requirements for her Master of Arts but also out of her own genuine interest in this compelling family story. Hans-Jürgen Schreiber, a local historian in Essen, who established contact with the Steinberg siblings and/or their spouses in the 1990s as he began researching the history of the Jews of

Altenessen, graciously provided Rebecca Boehling in 2005 with a tour of Essen and copies of a 1994 unpublished manuscript and various draft essays. To Herr Schreiber go my special thanks.

UMBC has generously provided support for my research trips to Germany. John Jeffries, in particular, who has been very supportive of my work on this project from the days when he was my department chair, and a member of Deborah Gayle's Masters committee, to his current role as my Dean of the College of Arts, Humanities and Social Sciences at UMBC, also deserves special mention. On a more personal level, there are many colleagues and friends who provided their advice and support through this writing process. There are too many to name them all, but I would like to single out: the New York area German Women's History Group, Annette Aronowicz, Gloria Avner, Renate Bridenthal, Anne Chamberlain, Irene Kacandes, Marion Kaplan, Florence Martin, Michele Osherow, Mark Roseman and Calla Thompson. I would like to thank the husband of my co-author, Ed Larkey, who graciously provided meals and computer help as his wife, Uta, and I kept working and working and working. Finally, I would like to thank my own husband, Mark Lipkus, for his encouragement and for accepting how the priority of writing this book often put his and our plans, especially as a commuting couple, on hold.

Rebecca Boehling

Uta Larkey would like to thank Goucher College for supporting this book project, in particular for my research trips to Israel and to Theresienstadt and for allowing me to share my work. I am very grateful to my colleagues in the Department of Modern Languages, Literatures and Cultures, in particular to my dear friend and colleague Florence Martin. I truly appreciate her encouragement and inspiration.

I am grateful to Steve Salzberg and Jenifer Rudick Zunikoff, who teach the Oral History on the Holocaust course with me. They have contributed to my deeper understanding of memory and commemoration in our work with Baltimore-area Holocaust survivors and Goucher students. One of the remarkable survivors who has become a good friend over the years is Leo Bretholz. I thank him for inspiring the next generations in grappling with the legacy of the Holocaust and for his generosity in time and spirit.

Several archivists in Germany, Israel and the Czech Republic have contributed to this book, located and sent me important documents, often following up with a helpful e-mail exchange. I would like to thank in particular Harry Stein from the Stiftung Gedenkstätten Buchenwald and Mittelbau-Dora, Frank Boblenz from the Thüringisches Hauptstaatsarchiv Weimar, Gabriele Mierzwa from the Museum und Historisches Archiv (VMM) of the MAN company, Yaacov Lozowick, the former head archivist at Yad Vashem, and Tomás Fedorovic from the archive at the Terezín Memorial.

I especially thank Theresienstadt historian Anna Hajkova for sharing her work with me and helping me gain a better understanding of the circumstances surrounding the early deportations from Germany to Theresienstadt. I am also indebted to Doris Bergen, Jeff Peck and Claudia Schoppmann, who have been very supportive of my research over the years and provided many insights and new perspectives.

My semester as a scholar-in-residence at the Hadassah Brandeis Institute (HBI) was a very inspirational and rewarding experience. It provided the opportunity to further my research and engage in enriching scholarly discussions on the project, "Families, Children and the Holocaust." I would like to thank in particular project director Joanna Michlic and HBI director Shulamit Reinharz, and the helpful staff at HBI. I am also very grateful to Robert Beachy and Soheila Ghaussy for reading my chapters and for their encouragement and critique.

Finally, I want to thank my husband, Ed Larkey, for his love, patience and unwavering belief in me, and my son, Adam, for bringing so much joy into my life.

Uta Larkey

Kaufmann family tree

Isaak Kaufmann (1824–84) m. 1867 Caroline Vassenberg (1843–87)

Julie Kaufmann (1868–1932) m. Leopold Roer (1854–1938)

Gustav Kaufmann (1869–71)

Bertha Kaufmann (1870–1942) m. Max Lachs (1862–1934)

Selma Kaufmann (1871–1942) m. Alex Steinberg (1866–1933)

Amalie Kaufmann (1872–3)

Emma Kaufmann (1874–1942)

Henriette Kaufmann (1875–1942)

Paula Kaufmann (1876–1931) m. Karl Kaufmann (1870–1944)

Leopold Heumann (1876–1942) m. Thekla Kaufmann (1883–1942)

Siegfried Kaufmann (1880–94)

Karola Heumann (1908–?) m. Salo Weindling

Hilde Heumann (1910–?) m. Fred Horns

Otto Kaufmann (1919–2003) m. Ruth Markus

Rudi Kaufmann (1912–44)

Allfonse Manuel m. Lina Kaufmann (1909–?)

Arnold Oesterreicher (1911–2004) (name changed to Ostrand)

Thomas Ostrand (1944–present)

Else Roer (1890–1942) m. Fritz (Fred) Marcus

Leo Kaufmann (1878–1942) m. Mina Menko (1919–2009)

Lotte Kaufmann (1914–present)

Fritz Kaufmann (1906–?) m. Paula Winter

Marianne Steinberg Ostrand (1911–2002) m.

Suzanne Ostrand-Rosenberg (1948–present)

Ernst Kaufmann (name changed to Ernest Kaufman) (1920–present) m. Adele

Ernst Kaufmann (1905–?)

Charlotte (Lotti) Steinberg Frohmann (1908–2003) m. 1st Hans Kaiser-Blüth (1906–80)

2nd Heiner Frohmann (1903–65)

Michael (Kaiser-Blüth) Keynan (1939–present)

Alicia Frohmann (1951–present)

Moritz Kaufmann (1903–44) m. Bertl Anfänger

Kurt Steinberg (name changed to Sella) (1906–69) m. Hanna Levy Sella (1910–2003)

Miryam (Steinberg) Sella Shomrat (1942–present)

Gideon (Steinberg) Sella (1945–present)

Lina Lachs (1897–1946) m. Fritz Levi (1894–?)

Martha Lachs (1899–1942) m. Walter Haase (1892–1942)

Fritz Lachs (1902–58) m. Erna Hoch-Städter (1908–?)

Richard Lachs (1895–1975) m. Johanna Leven (1896–?)

Ernst Roer (1896–1944) m. Toni Spier (1903–44)

Toni Roer (1903–?) m. Richard Rothschild (1896–?)

Eugen Roer (1897–?)

Siegfried Roer (1899–1918)

Lotte Heymann (Meiningen)

Selma Roer (1894–?) m. Oskar Eschelbacher (1894–?)

Steinberg family tree

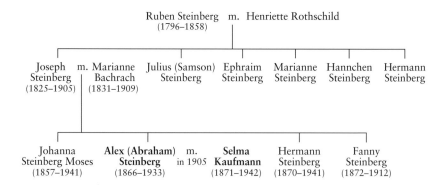

Ruben Steinberg m. Henriette Rothschild
(1796–1858)

Joseph m. Marianne   Julius (Samson)   Ephraim   Marianne   Hannchen   Hermann
Steinberg   Bachrach   Steinberg   Steinberg   Steinberg   Steinberg   Steinberg
(1825–1905) (1831–1909)

Johanna   Alex (Abraham) m.   Selma   Hermann   Fanny
Steinberg Moses   Steinberg   in 1905 Kaufmann   Steinberg   Steinberg
(1857–1941)   (1866–1933)   (1871–1942)   (1870–1941) (1872–1912)

Bachrach family tree

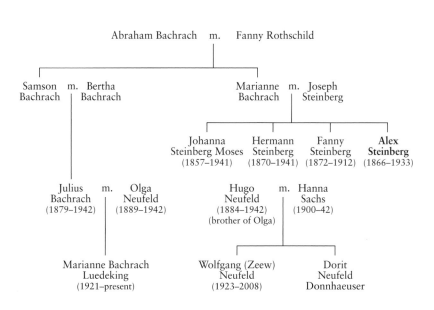

1 INTRODUCTION

Marianne Steinberg Ostrand often talked to her children as they were growing up in New Jersey about her happy memories of her youth and young adult life in the 1930s in Germany. Especially when she brought out old family photograph albums she would reminisce about her various sports awards in school, her skiing adventures and bicycle trips with friends. She told stories about the good times she had swimming, dancing and playing tennis, often with her older siblings, Kurt and Lotti, and their, mostly non-Jewish, friends. She described how her family had celebrated Jewish holidays with neighbors from down the street in Altenessen, outside Essen. She always reminded her own children, Tom and Sue, of the birthdays of her mother and beloved Tante (Aunt) Henny. Marianne and her siblings had come to think of these two women collectively as their parents. Marianne, Kurt and Lotti did have a loving father, but he had become seriously ill in the aftermath of World War I, before the children were even teenagers. Yet Marianne did not dwell on memories of her father's debilitating illness; nor did she draw attention to how quickly her mother, Selma, seemed to age in her photographs, especially in the 1930s and 1940s.

Marianne only occasionally talked about what life had been like for her and her family under the Nazis. She rarely mentioned any specifics about the impact on the family of the economic boycott of Jewish businesses. She did not regale her children with any details about having been called to Nazi Party headquarters not long after the Nazis came to power or her brother's 1938 arrest in Frankfurt am Main and his incarceration in the Buchenwald concentration camp.

Marianne's young children, although curious, sensed it was best not to ask many questions.

Marianne had always been one to save things. But she had experienced so many disruptions and moves in her life that no one close to her even considered that she might have preserved many, many letters, postcards, diaries and photographs, even dried leaves and flowers from her life in Germany, Britain, Switzerland and her first years in the United States before, during and following World War II. Yet this is precisely what she did. In 1986, shortly after she had retired as a physician, Marianne donated a handful of 1940s postcards, letters and photographs to the archives of the Leo Baeck Institute for the Study of the History and Culture of German-Speaking Jewry in New York. But this was only a minute portion of what she had saved from the 1930s and 1940s.

In 2002 Marianne's daughter, Sue, found some 200 wartime family letters, neatly bundled up, in her parents' house in Columbia, Maryland as she prepared to put their house up for sale. Sue recognized that the letters must have belonged to her mother, but by then Marianne was 91 and so ridden with Alzheimer's that she could provide no answers to the many questions Sue had about the letters. Over the course of the next year, as Sue unpacked various boxes, she discovered packets of many more letters, including a few family letters written during the Weimar Republic, and many letters to and from Marianne between the 1920s and 1939, as well as after World War II, including considerable correspondence between her parents. Sue's father had some vague idea that his wife, Marianne, had saved letters, but he had no idea of the volume of what his wife had preserved. Sue recognized in the letters and on the saved envelopes the names of most of the writers of the letters, including her mother's mother, Selma Steinberg and Selma's younger sister, Henny Kaufmann. These two sisters had lived together almost their entire lives, except for several years when they and their eight siblings as orphans were sent to live with various relatives across the region of the Rhineland. Sue also recognized the occasional note from her mother's uncle, Onkel Hermann, whose World War I German blanket her mother had passed down to her. Sue eventually realized that her mother had actually saved more than twice the number of letters than the initial packet of 200 wartime letters she had found. Most of the letters in this collection were to and from Marianne's mother and her aunt, Henny, and Marianne's two older siblings, Kurt and Lotti.

Most of the letters were in German and were handwritten, but during the war German-language letters could provoke censors in Palestine and in the United States and cause even more delays in mail delivery. Thus, during the war the siblings often typed letters to each other in a rather awkward English. Sue found the handwritten German letters, especially those from Selma and Henny and the occasional short notes from Onkel Hermann and other extended family members, difficult to read. Sue's family, unlike those of her cousins who grew up in Palestine/Israel and Argentina, had not spoken German at home, and the German-language skills Sue had acquired in school, decades earlier, were somewhat rusty. After reading several of the letters in English and struggling through a few in handwritten German, Sue wanted to know more about her family. But she needed more historical background and an understanding of the extended family to grasp all the references. She suspected, nevertheless, that these letters held a story of historical value to others beyond herself and her own family.

Wondering what to do with the letters, Sue, a biology professor at UMBC, was directed by colleagues to Rebecca Boehling, the professor in twentieth-century German history at her university. Rebecca matched Sue up with her Holocaust Studies graduate student, Deborah Gayle, a trained archivist. Deborah carefully organized the first group of 200 wartime letters with an eye toward preparing a short family narrative, at least on the basis of the fifty English-language letters she could read. The informative Masters project Deborah wrote centered on Marianne. It contextualized the letters that Marianne and her siblings wrote in English to each other during the war, as well as conversations with Marianne's daughter, Sue.[1]

It was Deborah Gayle's narrative that Sue then shared with her cousins in Chile and Israel, the children of her mother's deceased siblings, Lotti and Kurt, all of whom now wanted to know more, particularly about the story told in the German letters and written to and from the older generation in Germany. Getting this brief taste of their family's history provoked a flurry of activity among the cousins across three continents. Old boxes in various closets and storage rooms were opened and sorted through. Sue's successive discoveries brought together a collection of over 450 family letters her mother had saved. Sue's cousins in Israel and Chile found and sent Sue copies of another 100 or so related letters that their parents, Kurt and Lotti, had saved before, during and after the war. After the realization that some later letters, especially those connected to restitution and trips back to postwar Germany, might shed light on still unanswered questions, at least fifty more letters from the 1950s and 1960s were made available from the various collections: the Ostrand collection in Columbia, Maryland, the Frohmann collection in Santiago, Chile and the Keynan and Sella collections in Tel Aviv, Israel.

Sue and her cousins now hoped this aggregate collection of over 600 letters might provide the basis for a full-fledged history of their family in the 1930s and 1940s. When they approached Rebecca about writing their family's history, she was both excited and conflicted about taking on such a large, but very compelling, project. She welcomed the offer of her colleague at nearby Goucher College, Uta Larkey, who was teaching German and Jewish Studies and Holocaust-related film and literature courses, to co-author a history of the Kaufmann–Steinberg family. Together, at the end of 2003, we embarked on this project.

We quickly grasped how remarkable it was that this correspondence included Marianne's letters to her mother and aunt in Germany, letters that typically did not survive the war. Wanting a record for herself of what she had sent, especially since postal delays were notoriously long during the war, Marianne (or Nanna, as those close to her called her) had made carbon copies when she wrote her wartime letters. She had also saved a diary from the late 1920s until 1933 and a diary-like notebook she had kept from 1933 until 1941.

The wartime letters between Marianne and her siblings, who were by then already in safe havens though still very worried about the older generation left behind, provide an interesting and unusual glimpse into family dynamics in the midst of immigration and rescue attempts. The texture and content of the hundreds of letters written in German, their native tongue, especially those to and from their mother and aunt in Germany on the eve of the Holocaust, tell a complex and layered story of loving and painful family relations, and of immigration and rescue attempts. Most of this five-way (eight-way including eventually the children's spouses) correspondence is extant; it provides the *raison d'être* of this book. The vast majority of the letters were written in German. All quotations from letters originally written in English are designated as such in the endnotes. The translations of the German letters, the diaries, interviews and other documents are our own.[2]

Realizing early on that the breadth of this source base was unique but expecting the sources to tell a rather typical German-Jewish family story, we were surprised to detect so many ways in which this family's history differed from traditional portrayals of assimilated German Jews in the late nineteenth and early twentieth centuries. For example, the Kaufmanns were Orthodox Jews well into Selma and Henny's generation, whereas the Steinbergs were Reform Jews. The Kaufmann–Steinbergs considered themselves an observant Jewish family (at least Selma and Henny did), keeping kosher in their own way in a small suburb with few Jews and often without easy access to a kosher butcher. They walked miles back home after attending services Friday evening before opening their store for business on Saturday morning. The family belonged to a Reform synagogue community in Essen proper, in which the seating, as decided upon by the congregation on the eve of World War I, was segregated by gender. Growing up, most of the Steinberg children's friends were not Jews, but they were frequent guests in each other's homes. In terms of assimilation and Gentile–Jewish relations, at least until the Third Reich, the Kaufmann–Steinbergs do not fit neatly into easy categories. The Kaufmann–Steinberg family also challenges our expectations with regards to gender roles. For example, the two Kaufmann sisters, Selma and Henny, founded one of the first female-owned businesses in the industrial city of Essen in the early 1900s. Then, after World War I these two women managed to raise two daughters and a son and have them educated as a doctor, a dentist and a lawyer, respectively, during the Great Depression. Selma's husband, Alex, never recovered from the Spanish influenza he contracted in 1919, dying just after the Nazis came to power in Germany. The children thereafter occasionally referred collectively to their mother Selma and Tante Henny as their "parents." It was the daughters who emigrated first, primarily for professional reasons, and the son who left Nazi Germany last. Yet rather than simply label this family atypical on the basis of gender roles, assimilation and religious practices, this family history challenges much of what has been portrayed as typical of German Jewry in the early twentieth century as more of a simplistic trope than a reality.[3]

In some ways this family's experiences in Germany, as told in the letters, resonate with other German family experiences we read of in social histories, memoirs and biographies, both before and after 1933. The Kaufmann–Steinberg letters often deal with daily life: illness, courtship, marriage, pregnancy, employment and financial concerns, friends, even fashion. Much of this could equally well be representative of Gentiles, at least prior to the Nazis' rise to power, at which point this family's "everyday events" are overshadowed by anti-Jewish social, economic and political restrictions and ultimately by questions of whether to stay in or leave Nazi Germany. Including the family's history prior to the Third Reich allows us to contrast their experiences and perceptions before and after 1933.

Early on we decided to approach this as a collective family biography. Biographical researchers need to find the right balance in the relationship between the subject and the context and to deconstruct the subjective mythology inherent in many of the sources. We have tried to parse the role of individual identity versus the comparative significance of the subject(s) and, in doing so, to evaluate what is unique versus typical.[4] Biographers are sometimes prone to present a continuous and coherent, even linear life trajectory of their subject. Yet twentieth-century German-Jewish history, in which the reality of historical discontinuities prevails, make linear life trajectories much less common. Indeed, the Kaufmann–Steinberg family story is one of transience and change. Unlike a prosopography, which investigates the common characteristics of a historical group, and in which the individual biographies may become largely untraceable, this family history intentionally explores both the individual lives and the dynamic interaction between the individuals within the family. The balance we strike between the family history and the broader context definitely favors the family, whose experiences and fate must be understood in the context of Jewish life in Germany and the potential for emigration/immigration, as well as the threat of deportation during the Third Reich.

Our approach contextualizes this particular family's place within the German-Jewish experience, both chronologically and topically. Chapter 2 sketches the historical background for the German-Jewish experience from the early stages of Jewish emancipation in the mid-nineteenth century up through the Weimar Republic (1918–33). Against this backdrop we trace the personal tragedies and social mobility experienced by three generations of the Kaufmann–Steinberg family. Chapters 3 through 5 create portraits of individual family members, each chapter exploring different aspects of the Jewish experience in pre-war Nazi Germany. Chapter 3 looks at economic boycotts and "Aryanization" through the lens of Selma and Henny and their drygoods store, the Geschwister Kaufmann. Chapter 4 investigates the personal and professional roadblocks experienced by Marianne and Lotti, a physician and a dentist respectively. Both daughters ultimately chose to leave Germany because of the impact of anti-Jewish legislation on their professional lives and personal futures. In Chapter 5 the attention turns to Kurt, the one Steinberg sibling who was able to work in his field of law during the Nazi regime, albeit only within the Jewish community. Kurt, as the only son and the family member most affected by the November Pogrom of 1938 (Kristallnacht), was compelled to leave Germany under the threat of being sent once again to a concentration camp. New beginnings and life in Palestine are the main theme of Chapter 6. In the concluding two chapters we juxtapose our discoveries about the various family members' wartime experiences with the family's own postwar revelations. The Epilogue (Chapter 9) centers on the family's attempts to come to terms with the past.

All of our chapters, in varying degrees, allow the voices and the perspectives of the individual members of the family to resonate as we present their story and analyze particular family dynamics. We decided we could achieve this best by selecting relatively short excerpts of the correspondence to cite and choosing other parts to paraphrase or synthesize. We also mined postwar written and oral testimonies given by the three children and one of their spouses, a diary and a diary-like notebook, and other historical and family documents, such as those related to restitution. In order to sustain a strong and consistent narrative we limited the number of long, extended excerpts from the letters, quoting at length only when the issue raised was of critical importance to a decision being considered or a personal relationship or to the fate of an individual or when the language and/or sentiment is strikingly revealing.

Alexandra Garbarini's book, *Numbered Days: Diaries and the Holocaust*, on diary-writing during the Holocaust, provides a basis of comparison and a theoretical framework from which to consider letters and diaries as forms of contemporaneous communication.[5] Our source base includes two diaries from one of the daughters, spanning from the late 1920s to the early 1940s. They furnished us with access to both spontaneous and reflective analyses and concerns that one was less likely to share with others. Yet letters can also provide a unique opportunity to capture the moment, the dynamics of interaction and communication, the choice of words and of subjects, self-censorship and the process of decision-making. Unlike diaries, which are usually an introspective testament, letters convey an inner monologue addressed to another person in monologue/dialogue form. Depending on the intended recipient and his/her relationship to the writer, the dialogue and even the inner monologue might still contain the same factual information, but the ways in which the information is framed differ. From these letters we get not only snap or still shots but actual moving pictures of the family dynamics.

Family letters provide a glimpse into each individual family member's understanding of the historical events that play havoc with their lives and their futures. The Kaufmann–Steinberg family letters illuminate the process of each person deciding when and if he or she should leave Germany, THE crucial question for German Jews during the Third Reich. As primary sources, letters can expose the day-to-day fluctuating emotions of hope, optimism, resignation and despair, emotions that are often buried and/or forgotten in memoirs, which are sometimes tainted with hindsight.

We recognize that letters do not always convey emotional introspection or even an accurate relaying of daily or historical events, but they can contain spontaneous expressions of a person's stream of consciousness. At other times they are carefully constructed and reflected accounts, reports and/or descriptions of personal experiences, domestic and local events told as part of a conscious dialogue and/or to elicit a response. Depending on who the particular addressee is, certain omissions, distortions or even provocations may occur, and therefore letters cannot be taken at face value. In the case of the Kaufmann–Steinberg family, when letters increasingly came to replace direct personal contact as the temporal and geographic distance between the family members grew, the human dynamic and the breadth and depth of their bonds, mutual understanding and intimacy were significantly reduced.

Besides the letters and the two diaries themselves we have made considerable use of primary and secondary sources to ground the narrative. Our interviews with Selma and Henny's grandchildren, as well as other relatives now in their 80s, have helped us to fill in missing details and confirm and/or challenge our own presumptions and speculations. On several occasions we visited sites of the family's history, not just to conduct research in the archives but also to trace the steps of the Kaufmann–Steinberg family members, visit their old neighborhood and schools and the site of their former synagogue, and talk to current residents and local historians. Family photograph collections and personal papers, in addition to interviews Marianne and Lotti gave long after the war and our own interviews with family members, have all helped to explain references in the letters and to close gaps in the chronology of events. For example, when the correspondence on the surface appears to ignore key events in Nazi Germany, we are careful to analyze what role censorship might have played in what is being omitted or circumscribed and to note how certain events and family dynamics might affect one's choice of topics in a particular letter. This is especially important as many parts of the Kaufmann–Steinberg family correspondence, not unlike other family letters sent to and from Nazi Germany, are written in a coded language.

We have grounded the correspondence in its specific historical and geographic setting, interpreting and analyzing how the external events surrounding the individual family members affected their personal life decisions and determined what they wrote, or avoided writing, in their letters. As authors we have set the stories told in the letters against the backdrop of anti-Jewish legislation in Nazi Germany and the daily challenges and uncertain futures faced by German Jews first in Germany and then in exile in various lands. This context derives from extensive historical scholarship on the economic, political, social and cultural changes in the lives of Jews in early twentieth-century Germany, including the steadily increasing stages of persecution that Jews experienced during the Third Reich, as well as on the German-Jewish exile experience in the United States, Palestine and, to a lesser extent, Argentina, the primary sites of interest for the Kaufmann–Steinberg family's immigration. Eyewitness accounts from other German Jews describing their experiences under the Nazis and during the Holocaust and in exile, as well as documents in various German, US and Israeli archives that deal with specific events and developments in Essen, Frankfurt am Main, Cologne, the Buchenwald concentration camp and Theresienstadt, have further allowed us to draw a more complete picture of the experiences of the various members of the family.

In tracing the family's history we have benefitted from a number of local and regional histories of Jews in Nazi Germany, many written in German, and published since 2000. In English we have relied on excellent works on the German-Jewish experience before and during the Holocaust, including Marion Kaplan's *Between Dignity and Despair: Jewish Life in Nazi Germany*, with its focus on Jewish daily life during the Third Reich.[6] The United States Holocaust Memorial Museum (USHMM) has provided a tremendous English-language primary resource by publishing in 2010 the first volume in its translated source collection series, *Jewish Responses to Persecution*, which encompasses the years 1933 to 1938 in Germany.[7] Our collective-biography approach, however, is neither that of a historical synthesis nor of a translated primary-source collection.

Unlike our collective biography, a number of other works in English published in the last decade focus on one individual within a family, such as Mark Roseman's *The Past in Hiding*, a probing analysis of the history and memory of a young German-Jewish woman, Marianne Ellenbogen, born in the 1920s, who survived the war and the Holocaust in hiding.[8] There is also David Clay Large's story of Max Schohl, who together with his family struggled through Europe to escape the war and what is now known as the Holocaust.[9] Armin and Renate Schmid explore the tragic story of the immigration attempts of the Frühauf family in the aptly titled *Lost in a Labyrinth of Red Tape*.[10] Our book also examines obstacles to immigration, but explicitly with an eye to the attempts of the various family members who had already emigrated to try to help those remaining in Germany find a place to emigrate to. Martin Doerry's biography of Lilli Jahn uses an approach comparable in some ways to what we have done, integrating into a narrative Jahn's letters and those of her young children. Yet the Jahn family's situation differed considerably from that of the Kaufmann–Steinbergs. Lilli Jahn's children's father was Gentile, making the children less vulnerable to anti-Jewish persecution, and the letter exchange between Lilli and her young children was not in any way an adult exchange.[11] Nevertheless, these authors' works, which all use letters as part of their primary source base, have helped us conceptualize this Kaufmann–Steinberg family history.[12]

Others have approached large collections of Holocaust-era letters differently. For example, the compelling volume edited by Richard Hollander, Christopher Browning and Nechama Tec, *Every*

Day Lasts a Year: A Jewish Family's Correspondence from Poland, combines narrative chapters with chapters of consecutive letters, all to one individual, Joseph Hollander.[13] Unlike this volume of letters from a Polish-Jewish family to Joseph, their son/brother/uncle, we have the fortune of having all sides of a family correspondence, a true exchange among two generations of a German-Jewish family.

The letters, especially during the war, did not always arrive in the chronological sequence of when they were written or sent. Given postal delays and the complications of letters crossing two and sometimes three continents, re-creating who knew what when and who was responding to what when was a crucial part of our research and re-telling of this story. Having all sides of this Kaufmann–Steinberg exchange in these remarkable collections across three continents uniquely allows us to tell a complex family story before and during the Third Reich. As the situation in Germany worsened for Jews, and direct communication in or out of Germany became even more difficult, fears over what no news might mean for the fate of their loved ones set all the Kaufmann–Steinbergs on edge. The wartime letters reveal the siblings' very human recriminations, toward themselves and each other. Finally, the postwar correspondence makes possible the exploration of the experience of the Holocaust legacy and the impact of immigration and exile on this family.

Our particular narrative of this family's history provides unique insights into gendered, intergenerational and exile experiences and rescue attempts from various sites of safe haven. An especially intriguing gender aspect of this family is that the women in both generations find themselves taking care of and/or helping to financially support debilitated male family members, often in dire professional situations. These women seem rarely to question their roles as providers for the family. Interestingly, one of the daughters and Kurt's wife, Hanna, occasionally have male nicknames, Nuckel and Hannes respectively. These nicknames may well reflect tendencies within some of the youth and women's movements in the 1920s and early 1930s, but one would not even know of the use of the nicknames had it not been for these letters.

While considering questions of inter- and intragenerational dynamics, gender and professional and national identity, we analyze the correspondence of two generations of a German-Jewish family as they try to live normal lives, or at least write as if their lives were normal. The letter exchange renders an account of mutual concern and love of the "parents" and of the children for each other, as well as the sibling tensions that predictably emerge as the children grow physically and emotionally apart while no longer having the presence of their "parents" to help mediate their sibling relationships. As the question of leaving Germany becomes more and more crucial for the older generation from 1939 on, the younger generation is caught between, on the one hand, building financial and professional security and, on the other, pursuing increasingly difficult emigration and immigration procedures to persuade their mother Selma and Tante Henny to immigrate to their respective countries. The letters, diaries and archival records allow us to trace Selma and Henny's steps toward emigration/immigration, as well as their children's attempts to rescue them, as the children navigate their own way toward new national identities. The increasingly infrequent communication once the war begins and then the deafening silence from their "parents" feed the children's individual sense of powerlessness, on the one hand, and expressions of recrimination toward each other, on the other.

These family letters allow us to reconstruct agonizing family decisions, obstructionist emigration and immigration procedures, and gender-specific coping strategies. More than anything, however, trawling through these letters to write a history of this family has helped us to elucidate the lives of women like Selma and Henny, innocent victims of a brutal regime, and their children, heroic in their own right, as they set up new lives in completely foreign lands, while continually trying to re-unite the generations.

2 GERMAN-JEWISH LIVES FROM EMANCIPATION THROUGH THE WEIMAR REPUBLIC

The roots of the Kaufmann–Steinberg family in Germany reach back at least three centuries. Over the course of the eighteenth and nineteenth centuries earlier generations of the two families had experienced the various phases of progress toward and obstacles to Jewish emancipation, and the gradual progression toward Jewish integration into Gentile German society. The two sisters, Selma (born 1871) and Henny (born 1875), whose lives and family are at the center of this book, were members of both the first generation of Germans to be born into a united German nation state and of German Jews to have full civil and political rights, although as women Selma and Henny did not enjoy the right to vote or eligibility for public office until the beginning of the Weimar Republic (1918–33), by which time they both were already in their 40s.

Most German Jews welcomed citizenship rights as well as the achievement of German national unification in 1871. Yet most Jews also found blending into Gentile society within a framework that safeguarded Jewish identity fraught with difficulties. The new German empire (1871–1918) expected Jewish citizens to abandon their separate status in order to play a role in the larger polity, yet most Jews also wanted to retain and sustain certain aspects of their Jewish identity.[1] An individual's Jewish identity was defined partly by his or her level of religious observance as well as by secular beliefs.

The first half of the nineteenth century saw the emergence of a Jewish Reform movement in Germany that fused Enlightenment philosophy, cosmopolitanism and *Bildung*, a German concept combining education, culture, cultivation and self-improvement, with a relatively secular understanding of Jewish history and new approaches to Jewish theology.[2] This Jewish Reform movement, or Liberal Judaism as it is called in Germany, discarded various aspects of the practice of Judaism it considered only vestigial, such as dietary laws. It also emulated many aspects of Christian worship with the introduction of sermons, choir singing and, at least in some Liberal synagogues, mixed seating of the sexes during services.[3]

Since the Middle Ages local Jewish communities (*Gemeinden*) across the German states had legal status as "corporations." Each community exercised certain decentralized functions of self-government, including administering its synagogues, cemeteries, schools and various cultural institutions. The community acted as the official representative of Jews to the Gentile world, including paying "corporate" taxes to non-Jewish authorities. In Imperial Germany the local Jewish community retained its legal corporate status but was now regarded as more of a traditional religious community, made up of various Jewish congregations in those cities with larger numbers of Jews.[4] It was from this unified Jewish community, in which Liberal Jews formed a majority in Imperial Germany, that numerous Orthodox Jews, who feared that their religious values would be compromised by what had rapidly become a Liberal majority among German Jews, seceded.[5]

Not all traditional or Orthodox German Jews were prepared to separate themselves from the larger corporate community or to forsake the financial benefits of membership that stemmed from retaining their legal status as part of the recognized Jewish community.[6] Among Orthodox Jews, whose numbers approximated at most 20 percent of all Jews in Germany in 1900, some chose to stay within the general Jewish community as adherents to neo-Orthodoxy.[7] Still other Jews advocated a compromise between Reform and neo-Orthodoxy, a Conservative Judaism, but also stayed within the larger general Jewish community (*Gemeinde*).[8] From what we can extrapolate about the Kaufmann family, Selma and Henny's parents' generation was among the neo-Orthodox who remained within the Jewish community.[9]

Numerous Kaufmann family characteristics were typical of nineteenth-century Orthodox Jews, including the fact that Isaak Kaufmann (1824–84) and his wife Caroline (1843–87) brought eleven children into the world within some seventeen years of marriage, that he was almost twenty years her senior, and that they both came from and lived in rural areas (in the Rhineland).[10] Two of the children died as infants, but the remaining nine received a rather religious upbringing.[11] Yet as historian Steven Lowenstein reminds us, little is known about individual religious beliefs among rural German Jews in the nineteenth century. We do know there was little Jewish religious training in rural areas; visiting rabbis or other teachers assigned to large regions might visit a community once or twice a year.[12] At least two of the eight Kaufmann children who survived into adulthood remained Orthodox all their lives, Emma (born 1874), and Leo (born 1878), the only son to survive into adulthood.[13] Their rural Rhineland Jewish community of Schiefbahn, near Krefeld, maintained a mikveh, where Jewish women took ritual baths. This was the case for well over half of the Jewish communities in Germany at the time.[14] Indicative of the significance of the mikveh for Caroline and her daughters is the fact that Selma kept and passed on a photograph of this Schiefbahn mikveh to her own daughter.[15] Schiefbahn did not have its own synagogue until 1890, but, typical of many small rural communities, local Jews came together for religious services in a communal prayer room.[16]

The Kaufmann children's upbringing may have well been typical for rural Jews, but most Jews in Imperial Germany lived in urban areas, where Reform or Liberal Judaism predominated, alongside a rise in secularism and intermarriage, even conversion. Whether rural or urban, the majority of German Jews in the post-emancipation era, and particularly after Germany was unified in 1871, continued to identify themselves as Jews at some level while remaining committed to Germanness (*Deutschtum*) as an overarching national and cultural identity.[17] The Rhineland, the Prussian province that was their homeland, was already in the 1830s more supportive of Jewish emancipation than most other parts of Prussia, or the other German states.[18] Jews achieved an exceptionally fast economic mobility in Germany, one that surpassed and began earlier than the rest of the German population.[19] This was especially true in the Rhineland, where economic dynamism already in the 1830s encouraged the acceptance of Jews as equal members of society.[20] The support exhibited by their Gentile neighbors enhanced nineteenth-century Jewish Rhinelanders' sense of belonging to the Rhineland and, after the wars of national unification, to Imperial Germany.

German Jews' attempts at integration into Imperial German society varied from a willingness to adopt what they considered German culture, in other words, to acculturate or to melt, at least in many ways, into the majority, to efforts to assimilate fully.[21] How successful Jews were at integrating into German society depended to a large extent on how willing German Gentile society was to accept them. This in turn was affected by political and economic circumstances. By the second half of the nineteenth century Jews were increasingly linked to modernity and liberalism, the ideology of their emancipation, which also championed parliamentarianism, capitalism and industrialization.[22] Although Imperial Germany's rulers fought against political liberalism, most welcomed economic liberalism and Jews' contributions to German industrialization. By 1870 nearly 80 percent of all Jews belonged, at least in terms of wealth, to the middle class in Germany, and nearly 60 percent belonged in upper-income brackets.[23] This economic success occurred very quickly in the 1850s and 1860s, the period of Germany's industrial take-off.[24] It was in 1867, in the midst of an economic upswing and the Prussian wars of unification, that 43-year-old Isaak Kaufmann and 24-year-old Caroline Vassenberg had married and settled in Schiefbahn, a village between Mönchengladbach to the south, Krefeld to the north and Düsseldorf to the east in the Rhine Province. Six years after their wedding the economic boom came to an abrupt halt.

A depression began in 1873 with numerous bank failures, only two years after Germany was unified. The depression followed Prussia's 1871 defeat of France. An unexpectedly quick flow of French reparation payments had provoked German (over)speculation, and the boom turned into a bust. The depression, which continued intermittently until 1896, led many Germans to question economic liberalism. By this time German Jews' occupational structure was much more heavily concentrated in commerce and trade than that of the general population.[25]

This connection with commerce and trade may have been positive in periods of economic growth like the 1850s and 1860s, but in periods of economic slump and crisis Jews were often scapegoated as the cause of economic problems. Anti-Jewish sentiments rose as capitalism's limits were exposed. During the 1873–96 depression long-standing stereotypes about Jews reappeared alongside a new pseudo-scientific racial anti-Semitism that implied that Jewish conversion to Christianity, long the purported intention behind Christian anti-Semitic measures, was no longer the solution to the "Jewish problem." This new anti-Semitism, which incorporated new racial theories into Christian cultural and economic stereotypes about Jews, found its way into mainstream party politics as social anxieties wrought by the depression grew.[26] Social Darwinism and eugenics theories helped justify racism and neo-imperialist expansion. At the same time a more militant German nationalism directed itself against internal ethnic minorities, such as Poles, and even those Germans whose loyalties were presumed to be divided and thus easily cast into the category of "other," those not considered genuinely German, namely Jews, socialists and Catholics.[27]

No extant personal records indicate whether the Kaufmann family experienced any specific anti-Jewish insults or injury during this depression. But Jews collectively and as individuals bore the brunt of this anti-liberal, often anti-capitalist backlash, in particular because of their association with commercial capitalism and liberal politics.[28] Like those of most German families of the time, the Kaufmann family finances would have suffered, especially as the family's size continued to grow, even as Isaak reached his late 50s. Isaak Kaufmann was a trader (*Handelsmann*) by profession.[29] It is not clear what he traded in, although possibly horses or cattle,[30] but his identification as a trader rather than as a merchant (*Grosshändler* or *Geschäftsinhaber*) implies he conducted small-scale transactions, probably as a middle-man for someone else's business. The family's socio-economic status, especially given its large size, was likely lower middle class rather than solidly middle class. Given their rural background and limited formal education they would not have been part of the cultivated middle class, or *Bildungsbürgertum*.

Isaak died after being kicked in the head by a horse in 1884 at the age of 59, leaving his 41-year-old wife with nine children, the youngest barely a year old. Caroline herself died three years later, due to complications following an appendectomy conducted by the village doctor in the family kitchen.[31] The circumstances of their parents' deaths in such rapid succession surely scarred their children. The remarkable generosity and tenderness that the two daughters, Selma and Henny, showed later toward the children suggests that, if anything, they overcompensated for their having been orphaned by committing themselves completely to them.

After their mother's death in 1887 the Kaufmann children were separated and sent to live with various relatives throughout the Rhineland, mostly around the district of Düren, between Aachen and Cologne. There is little indication that anything other than family linens and a few personal or religious keepsakes were passed on to the children. Proceeds from whatever property that might have existed may well have been passed on to family members who stepped in to help the orphaned children. It was important to the extended family that the children continue to be raised as Orthodox Jews, and apparently they all were. When a particular cousin, whom some family members did not consider very observant, offered to take in one of the children, the extended family protested and prevented this cousin from raising any of the Kaufmann children. Isaak and Caroline's next-to-youngest child, Siegfried, died at the age of 14 in 1894, but the other eight survived well into adulthood.[32]

Selma, the fourth-oldest child, who was 15 when she lost her mother, was sent to live with her uncle, Julius Kaufmann, in the city of Duisburg (with a population of nearly 100,000), where she was apprenticed and learned his trade in his retail clothing store.[33] Jews in Germany were more strongly represented in the textile industry than in any other trade, both in terms of manufacturing ready-made clothing and in the wholesale and retail trade, so it is not surprising that various members of the Kaufmann family learned the textile retail trade.[34] Once Selma had completed her apprenticeship she got a position in Bochum, some 20 miles northeast of Duisburg, where she remained until 1902. Selma's younger sister Henriette, better known as Henny, was only 11 when her mother died, and she was sent to live with other relatives. They also made sure she learned a trade, apparently textile retail, as well. After saving money earned while working in various shops, Selma and Henny found their way in 1902 to Altenessen, a suburb of Essen, 8 miles southwest of Bochum. (See Figure 2.1.) There, in a three-story building, they rented a second-floor flat together and leased the downstairs of the same building on a commercial street near the center of this small town. They set up shop, selling manufactured goods, mostly clothing, in their shop, named the "Geschwister Kaufmann" (Siblings Kaufmann).[35] (See Figure 2.2.) By then the depression was over and the prospects for their new business were good. Although it was exceptional at this time for two single women, at the ages of 31 and 27, without the support of either

Figure 2.1 Selma and Henny, 1902

parents or families of means, or husbands for that matter, to start their own business, Selma and Henny did so. In fact at that time less than 20 percent of Jewish women in Germany were gainfully employed. Among those that were, many worked in family businesses.[36] As small-business owners, Selma and Henny must have encountered both anti-Jewish and sexist prejudices, yet they did not let this discourage them. German Jews, like these two enterprising young women, felt themselves a part of Germany, with rights and opportunities to make their mark. They must have been rather successful, because both in the

Figure 2.2 Selma with Kurt and Lotti, and Henny with two employees in front of the Geschwister Kaufmann store, Altenessen, 1912

1905 and again in the 1908 editions of the Altenessen address book their store listing included not only the store's address and telephone number but also a good-sized advertisement.[37] The sisters also advertised in various other local community publications, including that of a Catholic miners' club.[38] That they could afford to own a telephone and to publicize widely attests to their business acumen as well as to their self-confidence as businesswomen.

There is no indication that the Kaufmann family had ever been particularly political, but that changed somewhat once Alexander Steinberg entered into the family through his marriage to Selma in 1905. Alex Steinberg was one of the founding members of the Rhineland Central Association of German Citizens of the Jewish Faith (Centralverein deutscher Staatsbürger jüdischen Glaubens – hereafter simply Centralverein) branch in Essen, when it was established in 1903.[39] The Centralverein had been founded in Berlin in 1893 to engage in a defensive campaign against anti-Semitism and to reassert Jewish loyalty to Germany and liberalism. It actively sought a German-Jewish symbiosis that would further acculturate Jews into German society while defending the legal rights of Jews in Germany. Intended to attract Jews of all political orientations and religious directions, it did draw mass support from many German Jews, with regional branches established across Germany and a membership of over 60,000 within a quarter of a century. It quickly became the largest and most representative Jewish organization in Germany.[40]

The approach taken by the Centralverein to resist anti-Semitism but for Jews to remain committed Germans did not satisfy all Jews in Germany. Some interpreted the growth of anti-Semitism at the end of the century as a sign of the failure of emancipation and became increasingly unwilling to fight for their recognition as Germans. Instead, they turned to Jewish nationalism, or the ideology of political Zionism, with its yearning for a Jewish national homeland, a return to Zion, the Land of Israel. Unlike in Eastern Europe, Zionism did not find significant resonance among Jews in Germany, at least not until the end of World War I, when the appeal of emigration to Palestine and of political Zionism increased considerably among German Jews. In fact, at the turn of the century German Zionists were more concerned with bettering the lives of Eastern European Jews, whose numbers in Germany rose dramatically as a result of persecution in the Russian empire in particular, than on settling in Palestine.[41]

Following a wave of vicious pogroms in Russia, the influx of Eastern European Jews or *Ostjuden* into Germany in the late nineteenth century complicated the already complex panoply of Jewish religious and political alignments in Germany. A significant number of these Eastern European Jewish immigrants were Orthodox. Their influx helped offset the decline in religious observance as well as the rise in conversions among German Jews at the turn of the century. The percentage of Eastern European Jews who ascribed to Zionism was also higher than that of German Jews, so this influx gave a boost to the Zionist movement in Germany, which tended to be rather secular in its approach to Judaism. Nevertheless, most Orthodox Jews, whether Eastern European or German, opposed Zionism because of its secular, Jewish nationalist orientation.[42] Although the Kaufmanns were Orthodox, at least until the twentieth century, neither they nor the newest member of Selma and Henny's household, Alex Steinberg, were drawn in the least to Zionism.

As a leader of the Centralverein in Essen, Alex overtly asserted the rights of German Jews and never questioned his German national identity or his Jewish religion. Known as Alexander or Alex for short, but also by the Hebrew name of Abraham, Alex Steinberg was a grain merchant.[43] Alex, who always proudly identified himself as a Hanoverian, was born into the Kingdom of Hanover in 1866, just before it was annexed by Prussia. Hanover, with its historic ties to Great Britain, was a liberal area whose inhabitants possessed a certain wariness of Prussia but an increasingly strong commitment to the German nation after 1871. Alex was the second-born of four children, and the oldest son. His solidly bourgeois parents had a small but successful department store in Gronau, a small town less than 6 miles from the border with Holland. In hopes of studying philology, Alex graduated from the humanistic college-preparatory high school (*Gymnasium*) in nearby Hildesheim. His father, however, wanted his oldest son to go into business. This he did, running a grain business and eventually moving to Bochum in 1899 at the age of 33.[44] Yet Alex's orientation was definitely toward education and humanism, thus embodying the *Bildungsbürgertum*. Alex passed these values on to his and Selma's children, all of whom would complete university and postgraduate studies and enter into either the legal or medical profession.

It was in Bochum sometime between 1899 and 1902 that Selma and Alex's lives began to intertwine. Selma worked in Bochum from sometime in the 1890s until her 1902 move to Altenessen.[45] Bochum's population at the time included over 1,000 Jews, but this constituted less than 0.3 percent of the city's population. Compared with rural Schiefbahn or even Duisburg, Bochum was more urban and had a Reform synagogue, as well as an Orthodox synagogue, which served an exclusively Polish-Jewish congregation. Alex, unlike Selma, had been raised in the Jewish Reform tradition. In Bochum, if Selma wished to attend services with fellow German Jews she would have been compelled to do so at the Reform synagogue. It was perhaps there that Alex and she met.[46] Already by the mid 1890s Selma had probably begun her transition away from the religious orthodoxy of her childhood.

Three years after leaving Bochum, Selma, now 34 years old, married 39-year-old Alex Steinberg. (See Figure 2.3.) Alex, whose father had apparently passed away quite recently, moved the 9 miles from Bochum to live with his new family and to continue his grain trade business from his new home in Altenessen. Once Alex and Selma married, Alex joined his wife and Henny's household in their flat one floor up from the sisters' store. Selma's Onkel Julius, who had helped raise her and teach her the retail textile trade in Duisburg, served as a witness at the civil ceremony. The second witness was a Gentile neighbor

Figure 2.3 Wedding picture of Selma and Alex, Altenessen,
15 September 1905

from down the street in Altenessen, Adolf Holzgreve, the owner of a
transport company, who may well have worked together with Alex in
transporting grain.[47] The Holzgreves and Steinbergs remained close,
with Adolf soon moving into a flat on the top floor of the same building as the Kaufmann–Steinberg family.[48] Indicative of many middle-
class German Jews at the time, especially of the Reform tradition, Alex
reached out across religious boundaries and, like his wife and sister-in-
law, had numerous social and business relationships with Gentiles. Of
course, Altenessen with its population of some 40,000 people had only
a handful of Jewish families – twenty-five individuals to be exact, in
1905.[49] Selma, Henny and Alex apparently did socialize with Gentiles
as well as with Jews.[50]

For her generation, Selma married rather late in life and in
quick progression had three children: first a son, Kurt, in 1906, then
two daughters, Charlotte or Lotti in 1908 and Marianne or Nanna in
1911. By the time her youngest was born, Selma was nearly 40 years

old. Just as they did in their business, Selma and Henny now also shared many responsibilities with raising the children. The family did have domestic help, including a nanny when the children were small, a maid and once a week a laundress, in addition to the one or two hired shop helpers in the sisters' store.[51] But in many ways this was a three-parent family, at least until Alex became seriously ill following World War I. Once Selma married, Henny, as the single person in their partnership, was listed as the shop owner. Alex was listed as the owner of his grain business, at least until 1915.[52] In practice, Selma and Henny were co-owners of their store before, during and after Selma's marriage.

When Altenessen was incorporated into Essen in 1915, the store had to compete more directly with other larger textile and dry goods shops in Essen proper. Unlike their advertisements in the small Altenessen address books, Selma and Henny did not place any large advertisements in the much larger Essen address book, which presumably would have cost more and in which they would have been one of dozens of dry goods stores rather than one of two or three in Altenessen.[53] Yet the sisters managed to make a living from the business. In the midst of wartime food shortages and the total mobilization of the economy, the German government took over all grain provisioning. Thus, Alex was compelled to give up his grain business and started working in the Geschwister Kaufmann shop.[54] From 1915 on the store was the family's sole source of income.

Henny and Selma spent most of their time in Altenessen minding their store and maintaining the household. Once Alex and Selma began having children it became more difficult for the women to get away. Selma and Henny went into Essen for both social and business reasons, but often one at a time. The two sisters shared a single theater subscription, taking turns going to a play while the other sister closed up the shop. Alex, on the other hand, went into Essen more routinely between his work with the Centralverein and, until 1915, his grain business. Henny, Selma and Alex Steinberg, and later the children, too, took the trolley into Essen proper on Friday to attend services at the Essen Synagogue at the Steeler Tor (Gate) and then afterwards walked some 4 miles to reach home.[55] (See Figure 2.4.)

Although the absolute number of Jews in Essen had increased throughout the nineteenth century, their percentage in the population declined considerably from 4 percent at its peak in the 1830s to

Figure 2.4 Essen synagogue at the Steeler Tor (Gate)

0.9 percent, or 2,839 Jews out of a population of 294, 653 in 1910. This proportionate reduction of the Jewish population in Essen occurred because of the relative demographic decline of the Jewish population in Germany due to smaller families with fewer births compared with those of their Gentile counterparts. Thus, the Jewish population was an aging population relative to the German population as a whole. The percentage of Jews was even smaller, 0.57 percent in 1910, if one counted both the city of Essen and its surrounding county, which until its incorporation in 1915 included Altenessen. The vast majority of

Jews in early twentieth-century Germany lived in cities and not in suburban or rural areas.[56] In 1910 the membership list of the Essen synagogue community included 535 adult men. Only men counted as members, even in this Liberal community at the time. The social composition of this male membership was strongly middle class and upper middle class, typical of that of German Jews of Imperial Germany as a whole.[57]

Essen did not have its own rabbi until 1894, only a few years prior to Selma and Henny's arrival there.[58] The elementary school teacher, Moses Blumenfeld, led Essen's Jewish services from the 1840s until 1894. He had moved the community toward liberalism in the 1850s and 1860s, when organ music and a choir were added to the service. Blumenfeld emphasized ethical values of Jews over rituals. Dr. Solomon Samuel, Essen's first rabbi, also advocated Liberal Judaism, including German-language prayers, directives and sermons as a routine part of the service, while downplaying the Talmud's prescriptions and ceremonial laws, including kashrut dietary restrictions and Sabbath observance rules, as alien and outmoded.[59]

The Kaufmann–Steinberg family's religious practices reflect a mixture of the neo-Orthodoxy in which Selma and Henny had been raised and Alex's liberalism, as well as Rabbi Samuel's Reform teachings. The Liberal Essen synagogue, which the Kaufmann–Steinberg family attended, served both the city and the surrounding region. By the time the Kaufmann sisters and later Alex and his brother Hermann had joined the Essen Jewish community, it had outgrown its 13- by 19-square-meter synagogue. In 1903 the city of Essen sold a villa property at cost to the Jewish community so that it might build a much larger and more centrally located new synagogue at the Steeler Tor, only 200 meters from the city hall in downtown Essen. The new Reform synagogue could seat 1,400 people during services. Indicative of the economic and political integration of the Jewish community in Essen, the lord mayor and various Gentile city dignitaries participated in the dedication of the new synagogue, alongside the lawyer Max Abel, the head of the original Essen group of the Centralverein and Rabbi Samuels.[60]

When the community moved into the new building at the Steeler Tor in 1913,[61] the women, with the support of the men, opted for segregated upstairs seating, separate from the men.[62] Other characteristics typical of Liberal communities prevailed, however, such as the organ and the mixed choir. During their regular synagogue attendance, Alex Steinberg wore a top hat and sat in a special reserved seat downstairs alongside his brother Hermann when he was in town, while Selma and Henny and the children sat in reserved seats in the women's section in the balcony.[63]

This Essen synagogue housed two communities: a Liberal one in the main or large synagogue, with its entrance on the Steeler Tor proper, and a much smaller Orthodox community, both German and Eastern European, on the lower level, with a side entrance in the adjoining Alfredi-Strasse. The latter held its services in a special prayer room on the lower level of the building, which was sometimes referred to as the weekday synagogue, presumably because of the daily services held by the Orthodox community there.[64] One of Selma and Henny's second cousins, Moritz Schweizer, who was born in 1900, worked as the general counsel for the entire synagogue community in the 1930s and was a member of this Orthodox community. He had a particularly close relationship to Selma and Henny and the Steinberg children. Religious differences did not prevent the extended family members from remaining close their entire lives.[65]

In 1988 Marianne described her family's religious orientation at home as more like Conservative Judaism in the United States.[66] Before and during World War I the family kept kosher, eating only kosher meat, which they got from Essen.[67] But after the war and the onset of Alex's illness they were not able to travel as easily to Essen to the kosher butcher. Selma and Henny thus boiled the meats they bought from a local Gentile butcher and maintained what they considered their own form of keeping kosher. Whereas in 1988 the older daughter, Lotti, recalled that the family did not eat pork and ate bread with only cheese if away from home, the younger daughter, Marianne, remembered that the family did occasionally have sliced ham coldcuts.[68] While Selma and Henny kept the Geschwister Kaufmann shop open on Saturdays, they sometimes walked 4 miles home from the synagogue after services, especially on high holidays like Yom Kippur.[69] Of all the Kaufmann siblings, Selma and Henny were the only ones who worked on Saturdays, a fact duly noted by their other more observant siblings.[70]

Family members often visited each other. (See Figure 2.5.) On Selma and Henny's side of the family, their brother Leo lived in Drove, some 55 miles southwest of Altenessen, and maintained an Orthodox

Figure 2.5 The Kaufmann sisters (from left): Thekla, Selma, Henny, Emma, January 1928

household, often hosting family visits from his seven sisters and their families. Yet Selma and Henny lived furthest away from Drove and worked Monday through Saturday, so it was less common for them to join together on family occasions. Leo's son Ernst did come and stay several months with the Kaufmann–Steinberg family when he began an apprenticeship in Essen in the mid 1930s, but he went home to Drove each weekend and returned with kosher food from his more observant family.[71]

There were considerably fewer Steinbergs in the immediate family, especially since Alex's father, mother and younger sister Fanny all died between 1905 and 1912. Oddly enough, both his mother and his sister Fanny died on separate occasions when visiting Alex and his family in Altenessen. The Steinberg children, Kurt, Lotti and Marianne, thus had no real memories of these Steinberg relatives. In contrast, Alex's younger brother Hermann, an unmarried traveling salesman for a silk firm in Krefeld, was a frequent house guest, a kind, generous and fun-loving uncle to the children. Alex's only other sibling, his 10-years-older sister Johanna, was married and had a daughter, but lived relatively far away in Kassel in Hesse, more than 100 miles from Essen. In Plettenberg, some 40 miles away, Alex's cousin Julius Bachrach had married into the large extended Neufeld family with several children, who became favorite playmates for the Steinberg children.[72]

On Jewish high holidays the Kaufmann–Steinberg family celebrated and went to the Essen synagogue together with Onkel Hermann and their Jewish neighbors who lived just down the street, the Loewensteins.[73] Although the age difference prevented the children of the two families from ever being playmates, the older Loewensteins watched out for the Steinbergs and encouraged the children to visit the toy section of their store.[74] The geographic proximity and the shared religious practices made it easier for these neighbors to celebrate holidays together than for the Kaufmann–Steinberg family to celebrate with the extended Kaufmann family.

The experience of World War I and its aftermath marked a significant turning-point for Germans, including the Kaufmann–Steinberg family. World War I provided German Jews with an opportunity to show their commitment to the Fatherland, and the vast majority did so. Already on the first day of the war, 1 August 1914, the Centralverein, in which Alex was so active, lent its support to the German cause and called on all Jews to do the same.[75] Alex's brother Hermann, despite being in his mid 40s, fought in the war. He brought home his army blanket, treating it as a special memento of the war and a sign of his German patriotism. Two decades after the war he ceremoniously presented his treasured blanket to his youngest niece, Marianne, when she traveled overseas.[76] Alex was ineligible to serve, not because he was in his late 40s already when the war began, but because he had major vision problems. On the Kaufmann side of the family, Selma lost her cousin Gustav in the war.[77]

Rabbis, like Christian clergy, held prayer services for German victory behind the front lines. But as the chances for a clear-cut German victory waned and scapegoats were sought, Jewish loyalty to the Kaiser was called into question. In 1916, in response to charges that Jews were shirking their responsibility to serve, the German government conducted a "Jew census" of Jewish soldiers to see how many German Jews were actually serving.[78] The so-called Jew census was never published, but its mere existence provoked denunciations of

Jews as "shirkers." Later studies published in 1922 showed that the Jewish contribution to the war effort in terms of numbers of soldiers killed and wounded was disproportionately high, that in fact 12,000 Jews had died for their country. Although the Centralverein chairman asked Jews to remain silent on the issue of the "Jew census" for the sake of the Fatherland, the Frankfurt Centralverein and the liberal *Frankfurter Zeitung* protested it in numerous editorials.[79]

When Britain's Balfour Declaration of 1917 promised that the British would "view with favour the establishment in Palestine of a national home for the Jewish people," Zionists in Germany became targets of anti-Semitic invective as if they had moved over to the Entente side.[80] This was despite the fact that German Zionists quite publicly refrained from siding with the Entente Powers and continued to show support for the German war effort. As German defensive nationalism grew, this anti-Zionism was easily broadened against Jews generically. This, however, did not dissuade Jewish veterans from forming the Imperial Union of Jewish Front Soldiers (Reichsbund jüdischer Frontsoldaten) to emphasize their Jewish wartime patriotism, and perhaps convinced them even more of the necessity to wear their patriotism publicly.[81]

In 1915, after Alex was forced to give up his business, he joined his wife and sister-in-law in theirs. A few years before the war, the family had bought a piece of property on the same street, just a little further down on the other side. Their intention was to build a structure that would house both the store and the entire family, but this was not to be.[82] In 1915 the Geschwister Kaufmann underwent several changes: the store had more competition from other, larger textile and dry goods shops because of Altenessen's incorporation into Essen, and Alex started working alongside the two sisters. The family's finances now depended totally on the store's revenues.

Germany's defeat in World War I brought with it territorial losses, financial and military penalties, occupation and international blame for the war at a time that few Germans were prepared for defeat and most were still expecting rewards, if not spoils of war. This further fed defensive nationalism, which in turn fostered xenophobia, racism and anti-Semitism. During the republican government in Germany from November 1918 until January 1933, known as the Weimar Republic, Jews increasingly were singled out and scapegoated, along with socialists, communists and feminists. The conservative military leadership considered such Germans politically suspect and responsible for the otherwise inexplicable defeat, even claiming they had stabbed Germany's soldiers in the back. While the war and defeat fueled anti-Jewish sentiment, the fact that German Jews experienced enhanced prominence and integration into Weimar political and cultural life also provoked antagonism. The association of a number of Jews with the new republic that had come to power in the midst of defeat and had signed the "dictated peace" of the Versailles Treaty provided more grist to the mill of anti-Jewish resentment.[83]

All three Steinberg children were in school by the time the war ended, each attending the local Jewish elementary school (*Volksschule*). The family, like other German families across the country, endured rationing and food shortages during World War I, but these experiences did not mar their adult memories of their childhood.[84] The birth of the Weimar Republic came in the midst of German surrender and the 1918–19 revolution, which in turn sparked a right-wing counter-revolution, lasting throughout the early 1920s and making an impact on the Kaufmann–Steinberg family. Alex joined the local citizens' militia in Essen to help preserve order in the streets at night during the unrest of the 1918–19 revolution.[85] At age 9 Marianne was scheduled to go into Essen to take her high-school entrance exams for the Luisenschule *Gymnasium* in the midst of the 1920 Kapp Putsch, a right-wing attempt to overthrow the new Weimar Republic. Because there was considerable turmoil in Essen near the school, the director of the Luisenschule called Marianne's parents and suggested she go ahead and take the entrance exams at the boys' *Gymnasium* in Altenessen, where her brother Kurt was a pupil. Somewhat flustered at being the only girl taking the test there, Marianne nevertheless passed the entrance exams and went on to attend the Luisenschule, joining her older sister Lotti there and getting to know Lotti's friends, in particular Lotti's best friend, Herta Poth. Marianne herself was so popular in high school that her classmates elected her their class representative.[86]

Because of Alex's progressively debilitating disease, the children's memory of their father was often of his sitting in an armchair being read to by their mother. For years Selma had read the local *Essener Volkszeitung* to her husband, who had already begun to lose his sight prior to World War I. In fact, a favorite family picture was a photo of an intent, yet somewhat fatigued, Selma reading the newspaper to Alex, while he, dressed in suit, vest and tie in his armchair,

Figure 2.6 Alex and Selma at home, 1929

sat and listened attentively.[87] (See Figure 2.6.) Although a loving presence, Alex already at age 53 was unable to be the active father he would have needed to be to keep up with his athletic children, who ranged in age from 8 to 13 when their father first became ill. As the disease progressed, Alex went from the routine of at least dressing in order to spend the day in his armchair to become increasingly confined to his bed.[88]

Although always hospitable and welcoming to the children's friends, almost all of whom were Gentile, as no Jewish children their age lived close by, Selma and Henny were preoccupied with running the store and taking care of Alex. In the midst of the difficult conditions surrounding the French occupation of the Ruhr following Germany's default on its war reparations in 1923, Selma and Henny arranged for Marianne to stay with their nephew Eugen Roer and his wife Lotti in Meiningen in eastern Germany (Thuringia). They sent Lotti away to a children's camp and Kurt off with Onkel Hermann to Gronau. Although they missed them terribly they wanted to spare the children the tensions between the French troops and the civilian population. They wrote the children news of home, of the unbelievable inflation rates, with a pound of meat costing 1.5 million Marks

Figure 2.7 Kurt's bar mitzvah, 1919

and potatoes between 80,000 and 90,000 Marks a pound, and of the fact that they were now selling aprons for 4 million Marks. They wrote that they were losing their help, who sought refuge outside the area, and who they feared might not return. Yet they did not want to worry them and were careful to treat their evacuation as if it were a vacation, closing their letters to each *Ruhrkind* or Ruhr Valley child with such expressions as: "And for the rest I wish you lots of fun and relaxation" and "Amuse yourself ... you have lots of vacation ahead of you."[89]

Selma and Henny, and to whatever extent possible Alex, and his brother Hermann, who was a frequent overnight guest, managed to create a nurturing and supportive family life for the children. (See Figure 2.7.) They made sure the children were able to participate in various sports, including tennis and swimming and taking bicycling tours through the region. Kurt played on a soccer team in Altenessen, and both he and his sister Marianne played on the bat ball (*Schlagball*) team in their schools.[90] At times Selma worried that her youngest spent too much time reading and not enough time outside playing, yet Marianne probably became the most athletic of the three children.[91]

In 1919 the new Weimar constitution gave Jewish communities legal and fiscal equality with the established Christian Churches. Berlin quickly became the unparalleled center for Jewish culture in Europe. Although seen by many Jews as a problematic sign of integration, intermarriage rates rose relative to the number of Jewish marriages overall, and more Jews held public office than ever before.[92] Yet for those who, like the three Steinberg children, grew up during the pre-Great Depression years of the Weimar Republic, Weimar Germany must have seemed to offer numerous opportunities for educated and professional Jews. Five of the nine Nobel prizes won by German citizens during the Weimar Republic went to Jewish scientists, two for medicine and three for physics, including one to Albert Einstein. Bestselling literature included works by Jewish authors Jakob Wassermann, Stefan Zweig, Franz Werfel and Lion Feuchtwanger.[93]

Yet these contributions and the prominence of certain Jews only served to link Jews with a democratic order that never won popular favor owing to its association with the Versailles Treaty, political instability, cultural modernity and economic chaos (early post-World War I hyperinflation, followed by tenuous stabilization in the mid 1920s, and then the Great Depression in 1929). Jews found themselves at the center of the radical Right's critique, blamed for defeat and for undermining the German economy, politics and culture. But most German Jews, like the members of the Kaufmann–Steinberg family, clung to liberalism and Enlightenment values as the basis for German-Jewish identity during the Weimar Republic, hoping that through education and anti-defamation German society would remain, or become, an amicable homeland.[94]

The demographic picture did not look rosy after the war; the rise in life expectancy and a falling birth rate created an "aging problem" in Germany due to the loss of young and middle-aged men in World War I. The German-Jewish population in particular was shrinking and aging. During the Weimar Republic it was affected by an increase in Jewish emigration, communal secession and a rise in conversion rates. Whereas the size of the Jewish community in Germany had reached a numeric high of over 615,000 in 1910, it was down to 564,000 in 1925 and to 503,000 in 1933.[95] By 1925 one-third of all German Jews were over 45, as compared with a quarter of all Gentiles. The 1933 census showed that 9 percent of all Gentiles in Germany were under school age, whereas only 5 percent of all Jews in Germany were this young.[96]

It is perhaps therefore not surprising that all three Steinberg children had a preponderance of Gentile friends while growing up in Altenessen and Essen. Marianne was the only Jewish girl in her all-girls high-school graduation class, although Lotti, her 3-years-older sister, had had two Jewish classmates in her graduation class. Both sisters, when interviewed in their 70s, described their childhoods, and especially their time at the Luisenschule, as happy and devoid of anti-Semitic incidents. Once they headed off to university, Marianne, whose studies began during the Great Depression and the collapse of the Weimar Republic, dated mostly other Jews. Lotti, on the other hand, who had completed her university studies just as the Nazis were coming to power, had had at least as many Gentile as Jewish boyfriends while she was a student. All three Steinberg siblings kept up old school friendships from Essen and traveled in mixed circles in their various academic settings.[97]

Kurt, Lotti and Marianne all did very well in school, reflecting the values of the *Bildungsbürgertum* that their father had taught them. Unlike their parents, who had remained relatively close to their original homes even as they learned their trades and began their business lives, Kurt, Lotti and Marianne all transferred frequently from one university to another, experiencing different regions in Germany and traveling as much as possible. Sometimes they attended the same university, becoming acquainted with the community of friends of their siblings and, in the case of Lotti and Marianne, even rooming together in Würzburg and Kiel. The children were able to lead relatively carefree student lives thanks to Selma and Henny's hard-earned income, along with intermittent contributions from Alex's brother Hermann and, at least until they were forced to repay them, government-sponsored merit scholarships.[98] Marianne originally planned to study law, because her beloved brother Kurt, who was completing his legal training as she was about to graduate from high-school, wanted her to practice law with him. Yet Marianne was so affected by her visit to a children's hospital during her high school graduation trip that she switched her plans to studying medicine.[99] Initially unsure of her specialization, she found herself increasingly drawn to gynecology and obstetrics. Lotti studied dentistry and went on to write a doctoral dissertation in ear, nose and throat medicine.[100]

While Jews constituted less than 1 percent of the German population, 4 percent of all university students during the Weimar Republic were Jews.[101] Jewish women students were even more over-represented among the student population than were Jewish students overall.[102] The Weimar Republic saw a significant rise in the number of Jews entering into free professions: by 1933 16.2 percent of Germany's lawyers, 10 percent of its doctors, 8.6 percent of its dentists, 5 percent of its writers and 2.6 percent of its university professors.[103] The long-term effects of emancipation and freedom of occupation paid off for that generation of German Jews, like the Steinberg children, who were drawn toward the values of the *Bildungsbürgertum*. The social openness that characterized much of urban German culture during the Weimar Republic helped facilitate this rapid professionalization. The Steinberg children were quite representative of this trend, and Selma and Alex, Henny and Onkel Hermann were very proud of the children's accomplishments.

In the 1920s and even early on during the Great Depression, the children's occasional letters or postcards to their parents and Tante Henny or to each other while away at university or traveling during semester breaks indicate a certain *joie de vivre*. Selma and Henny, on the other hand, were mostly homebound between running the store and providing care to Alex. Although the two sisters maintained good social relations with their neighbors, Jewish and Gentile alike, they must have counted the days until their children returned home for weekend or holiday or semester break visits. Selma and Henny, whom the children increasingly referred to, together with their father Alex, as "our parents" even prior to Alex's death, seemed in their children's eyes to maintain good spirits despite Alex's gradual paralysis.

The children's relatively happy-go-lucky lives underwent a dramatic change, however, after mid 1931. In early 1930, Lotti, studying in Munich, attended various *Fasching* (pre-Lenten Mardi Gras-like dances in Germany) balls, without any sign of economic concerns. For Marianne's nineteenth birthday that year Lotti sent her sister a dress and wrote Nanna of the overall joy she felt in her life, quoting Schiller's *Aesthetic Letters* to her.[104] A year later, Lotti spent a semester in Berlin. Her description of her activities in Berlin, such as visiting the city's finest café, the Café Kranzler, and hosting her Plettenberg relatives, Onkel Julius and Tante Olga, who took her out shopping for a new coat, indicates that she needed to watch her finances but still lived relatively carefree. Lotti sent her sister birthday wishes for her twentieth birthday in February 1931, advising her: "Most of all I wish that you take advantage of this time to enjoy everything good and not to concern yourself so much with tomorrow. If the moment appears to you grand and favorable, then seize it."[105]

During that same winter semester in Berlin Lotti also became increasingly aware of both social class injustice and women's rights. Lotti shared with her sister her excitement over attending a gathering sponsored by the feminist, pacifist organization, the Women's International League for Peace and Freedom (WILPF), on the pros and cons of legalizing abortion. She enthusiastically described to her medical student sister the "fabulous women doctors" and a protégé of the sexologist Magnus Hirschfeld who spoke on behalf of legalization. She critically portrayed their "less fabulous" opponents who spoke, including "the morally pure, true German, National Socialists," or Nazis, who condemned "today's women for being too depraved, pleasure-craving and lazy to bear children."[106]

Yet barely half a year later, the tone and content of Lotti's concerns had changed. She was now preparing for exams in Kiel and wrote Nanna that she would not have enough money to feed herself for more than two weeks and thus would have to come home. She pleaded with her sister to see if she could arrange for either more money or food packages to be sent to her from home. She also bewailed the situation back at home: "Father's condition, which has become so bad again, is so sad. If only something could be done! The most terrible thing is to see how much Mother's physical state is suffering under the strain. And when you realize that it is made so much worse by lack of money, you want to tear out your hair."[107] The in-home nursing care they had intermittently had for Alex had stopped coming, apparently because the family could no longer afford to pay for it.[108]

Kurt had written his two sisters in May 1931, while on a visit at home in Altenessen, about their father's miserable condition and his own sense of powerlessness: "Whoever is on watch at night literally has not even a minute's peace. Then there's the constant screaming ... I am incapable of doing even the smallest thing. One lives under constant stress." Kurt also complained of not having been able to get temporary work during his semester break. He remarked upon having seen one of his sisters' Luisenschule friends, Herta Poth, who had just gotten a job and finally seemed transformed from her depressed state. Further evidence of the effects of the Great Depression was Kurt's mention that their friends and neighbors, the Loewensteins, had finally closed up shop completely.[109]

Kurt, the oldest and the only son, was by far the most serious and perhaps in some ways the child most affected by his father's illness; he was 13 when his father contracted the disease. Marianne, who was only 8 when her father became ill, could not, as an adult in her 70s, picture her father except as an invalid.[110] Marianne and Lotti did not feel the same sense of gendered responsibility as Kurt did, as the only other male in the household. The daughters expressed their concerns about their father's condition more often in terms of the effects on their mother and aunt than on their father per se. In a traditionally gendered way Kurt expressed his frustration at his impotence in being able to fix the situation, while his sisters were more inclined to express sympathy and concern for their mother and anger over the lack of money that deprived her of the help she needed. (See Figure 2.8.)

A letter Selma wrote to her daughters in May 1931 is particularly revealing of her own transformation. Although only a handful of letters from Selma exist prior to 1931, a marked difference in tone is detectable in this May 1931 letter. Selma wrote: "Father is doing very poorly again at the moment. He is terribly restless ... but even the strong sleeping pills are not having an effect on him. It's a harsh fate, which has been meted out to him and which affects all of us." Selma goes on to encourage her daughters to take advantage of their youth while they can: "But enjoy your youth, as long as you can and to the extent our modest circumstances allow. The seriousness and bitterness of life come early enough."[111]

Tante Henny, who rarely directly criticized anyone, expressed, however indirectly, her own occasional annoyance with people or situations in her letters to the children. She wrote her nieces in May 1931 of a family trip some of her sisters and their children took, noting how glad they all were when her sister, Emma, left the group early to return home and how well she, Henny, could understand their relief.[112] Emma and Henny were just a year apart in age and were the only children who had never married, yet they were not emotionally close. Emma, who was not mentioned often in either Selma's or Henny's letters prior to 1939, was portrayed as a rather difficult personality if she was mentioned at all.[113]

Figure 2.8 Family portrait (from left): Selma, Lotti, Alex, Kurt, Marianne 1929

Even in the midst of their own drama with Alex's spells at home, the focus of most of Selma and Henny's correspondence with the children was on the children themselves. Selma, in particular, worried about them when they were so often away from home and she could not be with them. Both Lotti and Marianne ended up in the hospital with infections in their wisdom teeth in December 1931. To cheer up her daughters Selma described the antics of their housecat, Petra, and described to them what they could look forward to in the food packages she had sent, regretting that they were not yet able to eat. Protective mother that she was, she wrote Nanna that she kept the news of her hospitalization secret from Kurt, so as not to worry him about his little sister while he was at home studying.[114]

Fortunately for Selma and Henny, Alex's behavior changed in the late summer of 1932. Alex, who apparently had developed meningitis, went from an extreme of sleeplessness and screaming to sleeping up to twenty-two hours in one stretch. Selma worried about this excess sleeping but also welcomed the relief it brought. Henny and she took the time to encourage Lotti as she prepared to take her final set of exams. Kurt, who was home to celebrate his birthday before heading off to work with a youth organization of the Centralverein in Hamm in Westphalia, also wished Lotti luck with her exams. He mentioned that he would be in the midst of his own doctoral exams in half a year's time. With a slight note of brotherly recrimination, Kurt concluded his letter to Lotti: "In case it eases your conscience: You weren't the only one who forgot my birthday. Even Onkel Hermann forgot."[115]

One was expected to remember a family member's birthday. Whenever they could, the children came home to celebrate them. Selma, Alex and Lotti all had birthdays within the same week in November and celebrated them together on the Sunday of that week as a major family event. Of course, not wanting to make anyone else in the family feel they were not equally important, much to-do was also made about Marianne's birthday in February and Kurt's in September. Many of the saved letters between family members when the children were away at university were written on the occasion of family members' birthdays.

In November 1932 Henny sent Lotti birthday wishes after having spent a whirlwind trip over the previous week visiting her various sisters, Emma, Berta und Jülchen. Both the oldest Kaufmann siblings, Julie (age 64), or Jülchen, and 62-year-old Berta were ill. Jülchen had a tumor, and it was not yet known if it was malignant or not, although within weeks Julie died. Despite her worries about her sister, Henny wrote almost wistfully to Lotti about how quiet their household would soon be with Kurt in Hamm and Nanna about to leave to study in Innsbruck, Austria: "Provided Herr Papa is not too restless, we may be re-visiting our single years."[116] The prospect of welcome quiet and calm would not last long, however. In November 1932, outside the confines of the family's home and the sisters' shop in Altenessen, political unrest was growing. Directly next door to them, on the corner of Karlsplatz, the Kaufmann–Steinberg family had new neighbors: the local Altenessen branch of the Nazi Party.[117]

3 LOSING ONE'S BUSINESS AND CITIZENSHIP: THE GESCHWISTER KAUFMANN, 1933–1938

The year 1933 was a dramatic one on many levels for the Kaufmann–Steinberg family, the older generation in particular. Alex, Selma's husband, died at noon on 6 June 1933. His death ended years of suffering but added to his family's gloom as the Nazis consolidated their power in Germany. (See Figure 3.1.) Although medically there was little that could be done for Alex, Selma had patiently provided her husband with vigilant and loving care. While continuing to assist her 58-year-old sister Henny with running the store on the first floor, 62-year-old Selma trekked up the stairs regularly to check on her husband in their bedroom of their second-floor flat.[1]

The two sisters, Selma and Henny, while adjusting to the void left by Alex's passing, could not allow themselves simply to grieve and retreat from daily life. As early as March 1933 a number of Jewish retail stores as well as larger department stores in Essen, as in other cities in this industrial region, had to shut down temporarily while burly members of the Nazis' paramilitary organization, the SA or storm-troopers, dressed in brown uniforms and thus known as Brownshirts, posted themselves outside entrances. These storm-troopers intimidated the Jewish owners and potential customers and warned that real "Germans buy in German stores."[2] As a Jewish-owned small retail textile and dry goods store in Altenessen, a part of Essen with only 56 Jewish residents out of a population of 43,000, Selma and Henny's store was easily targeted for economic and social persecution from local Nazi officials.[3] Nazis paraded down the street in front of their store at 434 Altenessener Strasse. (See Figure 3.2.) From the windows

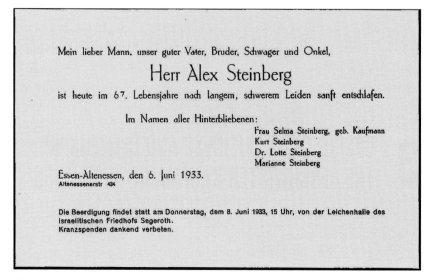

Mein lieber Mann, unser guter Vater, Bruder, Schwager und Onkel,

Herr Alex Steinberg

ist heute im 67. Lebensjahre nach langem, schwerem Leiden sanft entschlafen.

Im Namen aller Hinterbliebenen:

Frau Selma Steinberg, geb. Kaufmann
Kurt Steinberg
Dr. Lotte Steinberg
Marianne Steinberg

Essen-Altenessen, den 6. Juni 1933.
Altenessenerstr 434

Die Beerdigung findet statt am Donnerstag, dem 8. Juni 1933, 15 Uhr, von der Leichenhalle des Israelitischen Friedhofs Segeroth.
Kranzspenden dankend verbeten.

Figure 3.1 Alex's death announcement

Figure 3.2 Nazi parade in front of the site of the vacated Geschwister Kaufmann store and residence, Altenessen

in their second-floor flat above the store the family could not avoid seeing this intimidating display of paramilitary marching. Although incorporated into Essen in 1915, in 1933 Altenessen still very much had the flavor of a small town. The Geschwister Kaufmann store was one of the three oldest Jewish-owned shops in Altenessen and, although small, did not go unnoticed by local Nazi Party officials, whose offices were located directly next door.[4]

Starting with the economic boycott of Jewish businesses that began on 1 April 1933, Nazi economic practices toward the Jews were full of contradictory motives and results. Policies like the boycott were intended not only to intimidate but also to draw attention to the prosperity of many Jews in Germany. In conjunction with anti-Jewish stereotypes about usury and greed and Nazi propaganda about Jews' economic exploitation of good-hearted Germans, the boycott was used as a means to incite resentment and envy among non-Jewish Germans. This boycott had to be officially called off because it provoked international protests and counter-boycotts, which in turn threatened the German economy. It also hurt non-Jewish businesses with ties to Jewish ones, resulting in backtracking on the boycott, at least with regard to larger enterprises.[5]

What historians have termed a "silent boycott" occurred after the April 1933 boycott officially came to an end. This "silent boycott" was accompanied by the continued posting of SA storm-troopers in front of many Jewish storefronts. This intimidation tactic was easily practiced at the Geschwister Kaufmann store, since Nazi Party activists, including SA storm-troopers, came and went routinely next door. While numerous former patrons of Jewish-owned businesses did "silently" change their shopping habits, they did so in response to Nazi activists who barked threats from loudspeakers, posted and distributed inflammatory leaflets, and took photographs of shoppers entering Jewish-owned stores. Jewish store owners and their employees were also intimidated by intermittent surveillance of their mail and phone calls.[6] Although some Germans simply followed their old habits and shopping routines or overtly remained loyal to their familiar shops and businesses, such methods of intimidation eventually took their toll on Jewish shops, including that of the Geschwister Kaufmann.[7]

Discriminatory economic policies were intended to convince Jews that they could not survive financially and should leave Germany. Systematic impoverishment was a key tactic in the Nazis' official party policy of trying to get Jews to leave Germany. Yet some German economists, even some with close ties to the Nazi regime, worried about the potential impact of the loss of Jews' contribution to the German economy. As early as April 1933 "Aryan" clauses,[8] which the Nazis instituted and/or encouraged to exclude and isolate Jews, restricted Jewish participation in the civil service and in many professions and associations.[9] A year after the Nazis came to power, the newly appointed economics minister, Hjalmar Schacht, made certain that none of the "Aryan" clauses would apply to the commercial or industrial sectors of the economy. Schacht, although fully supporting the idea of stripping Jews of their citizenship and various other rights, always had an eye to the short- and long-term effects of restrictions on Jews on the German economy. Schacht thus sheltered prosperous owners of certain Jewish enterprises, at least as long as their businesses and any of their international trade partners continued to be seen as a financial asset for the Third Reich.[10] The early mixed economic messages of the regime, and its encouragement of the success of some Jewish enterprises, convinced especially older Jewish business people that they could outlast the Nazi regime.[11] Such Jewish business owners were unwilling to turn their backs on their property, which they still had hopes of retaining, at least during the early years of the regime. In this regard officials in Schacht's economics ministry were working against the regime's official "racial" goal of expediting Jewish emigration.

The contradictions inherent in Nazi policies toward Jews become even more obvious when one considers the ever-increasing financial penalties placed on Jews who emigrated. The Nazis hoped that the 25 percent Reich Flight Tax (*Reichsfluchtsteuer*) would facilitate the regime's confiscation of Jewish emigrants' property without discouraging Jews from leaving.[12] This tax on assets over 200,000 RM had been introduced in 1931 to prevent capital flight before the Nazis came to power, but under the Nazis the cap was lowered to include anyone with assets over 50,000 RM. Emigrants also faced an additional payment, known as an emigration fee or Disagio on the transfer of capital and eventually also on property for personal use taken out of the country. This Disagio was a fee based on a percentage of the last estimated tax value of Jews' property. Those hoping to emigrate had to deposit their money in RM in special blocked accounts. These "blocked accounts" were held at the German Gold Discount Bank, a subdivision of the Reichsbank. This fee was then taken directly out of the emigrant's blocked account.[13] The fee, originally set at 20 percent, was, as of August 1934, imposed at a rate of 65 percent of the value of the funds and valuables that emigrants transferred out of the country. The regime increased this rate steadily until at the time of the outbreak of the war it was 96 percent.[14] In this way Jews and opponents of the Nazi regime whom the regime wanted to emigrate faced an ever-increasing number of taxes and fees if they did decide to emigrate.

Having to give up their wealth to the Reich Flight Tax and then later the considerably higher Disagio fee made the cost of emigrating seem, for many Jews in Germany, too high.

With regard to the effect of these taxes and fees on even middle-class German-Jewish emigration, the economic historian Avraham Barkai contends:

> *Until 1938 a middle-class Jew with a certain amount*
> *of assets either had to have some money stashed away*
> *abroad or be possessed of a considerable degree of*
> *farsightedness in order to make the difficult decision to*
> *emigrate. Most had neither, so they stayed on – while*
> *the younger and less affluent, who had greater resultant*
> *mobility, chose to leave.*[15]

Choosing to leave did not guarantee one a place to which to emigrate. Having sufficient transferable assets and/or being relatively young and healthy and having sought-after skills in a new host country increased the likelihood of an emigrant getting an immigration visa. Host countries felt more confident that immigrants arriving with assets would succeed financially and thus pose less risk of becoming a public burden. German Jews of means who had decided to emigrate in the early years of the Third Reich often would have been able to take many of their assets with them, assets that would have helped them secure a place to which to emigrate.[16] Yet the less vulnerable German Jews felt, the more likely they were, especially if they were older, to wait and see.[17] Jews who remained in pre-war Nazi Germany, even owners of large and successful enterprises with international trade partners, were by the late 1930s likely to have been forced out of work or business or into selling their property below market value, thus losing many of their assets.[18] By 1939 most German Jews still remaining in the country, which was over half the number that had been there in 1933, did not have sufficient assets left to secure their emigration and immigration. Most of them lost not only their assets but, because they were unable to escape Nazi Germany, also eventually their lives.

By the late 1930s, years after Schacht was no longer economics minister and after Hermann Göring's Four Year Plan for rearmament was almost complete, Nazi economic policies more consistently focused on moving all Jewish-owned property into "Aryan" hands.

Jews in Germany, whether they tried to emigrate or not, had by the eve of World War II few private means left at their disposal. This was the cumulative effect of various Nazi impoverishment measures. These measures included not only "Aryanization," or forcing Jews to sell their property to "Aryans" at considerably below-market prices, and the long-term effect of official and "silent" boycotts of Jewish businesses. There was also a steadily increasing array of other Nazi policies that facilitated the seizure of private property, such as bank accounts, precious metals and jewelry, securities, real estate, household items and books. Jews in Germany were increasingly robbed of all their private means thanks to a combination of confiscation decrees, special taxes and blocked bank accounts.[19] The experiences of the Geschwister Kaufmann during the Third Reich illustrate the impact of such policies, as well as that of exploitative personal practices by "Aryans," fully backed by Nazi policies.

At first Selma and Henny's textile store, the Geschwister Kaufmann, as a well-integrated part of the Altenessen small business community, had managed to weather the April 1933 boycott and, for a while, also the "silent" boycott. But over time the placards on their street instructing potential shoppers not to buy from Jews and the SA men posted specifically in front of their storefront intimidated passers-by and persuaded more and more of their regular clientele to shop elsewhere. Yet, at least temporarily, the continued patronage of non-Jewish individual friends, neighbors and regular customers who resisted the intimidating presence of the SA posts served to reassure the sisters that their business could prevail. For example, their neighbor, Frau Sellmann, continued regularly to patronize the store and visit with her neighbors, the Kaufmann sisters, there. Frau Sellmann owned a confectionary closeby and was a daily visitor to the sisters' store, sometimes to buy but always to chat. Selma and Henny had long supported the Sellmann confectionary, buying delicacies for special occasions. Reciprocating, Frau Sellmann bought linens and clothing and accessories as Christmas presents from the Geschwister Kaufmann's shop not only for her own employees at the confectionary but also for those at the bakery and grocery wholesale company her family owned.[20]

Henny was clearly moved by her neighbor Frau Sellmann's personal loyalty despite Nazi pressure. Henny wrote her niece Lotti in 1935 that Frau Sellmann "still came into the store every day and chatted despite the Nazis, whom she refused to let stop her."[21] Given the prominence of the Sellmann family, the local Nazi SA storm-troopers were probably more wary of harassing this particular customer. But precisely such people of prominence could exercise their influence in ways that helped offset discrimination and harassment, at least for a while and at least on a community level.

Another non-Jewish neighbor, Bertie Holzgreve, also from a successful Altenessen business family,[22] recalled to Lotti after the war how she had found it despicable that the SA storm-trooper posted in front of Lotti's family store entrance had tried to prevent her from entering. Holzgreve described how she had told off the SA storm-trooper, stressing to him that she had the right to go anywhere she wanted.[23] Bertie Holzgreve's letter to Lotti about her unwillingness to bow to SA pressure was written at a time when many postwar Germans were being questioned about their complicity in the Nazi regime as part of the occupying Allies' denazification process. Lotti, however, did not question Holzgreve's motives in writing this letter, a letter that Lotti described as "wunderschön."[24] Notwithstanding individual anecdotes, such as those of Frau Sellmann and Bertie Holzgreve, most of the store's patrons eventually bowed to pressure and chose to stop shopping at the Geschwister Kaufmann store.

The Kaufmann sisters found themselves in late 1934 increasingly unable to keep their business afloat; they had to stop making payments to the store's creditors. Kurt and Marianne came to their mother and aunt's aid, and with, in Marianne's words, "a lot of excitement, work and worry" the store got back, however gingerly, on its feet.[25] This type of event served as a wake-up call for many younger Jews. Because they were less encumbered in terms of family responsibilities and property or businesses, younger Jews might more easily imagine uprooting themselves and emigrating.

Many factors influenced whether and when Jews decided to try to leave Germany or continued to hope to be able to wait out the Nazi regime: age and/or stage in one's life, profession, gender, and marital and socio-economic status, and whether one might be able to retain one's assets. Other variables included one's level of assimilation, views on Zionism, political opinions and/or party affiliations, and the extent of one's family roots and networks of support within Germany. Whether one encountered personal roadblocks or felt sheltered from the ever-changing restrictions placed on Jews in general affected one's perspective on the need to emigrate. Furthermore, whether one had dependants and whether they were willing or able to emigrate were also factors in decisions about emigration.

For older Jews, whose roots were deeper and for whom the stakes were higher, decisions to stay or leave were influenced by their own experiences with the ebb and flow of political crises and economic fluctuations, and often by their expectation that in Germany the rule of law would ultimately prevail. Members of all age groups were influenced by the immigration choices of others within and outside their age cohort. But Jews over 60 were more likely to have to take into consideration their own current and prospective health concerns and their responsibilities for other, older family members. Older German Jews usually found it more difficult to take the active step of leaving rather than the more passive stance of staying.

An important consideration in Jews' decisions to leave or stay in Germany in these early years of the regime was the strong attachment of many German Jews to Germany as their homeland, especially those older Jews with memories of the democratic changes from Imperial Germany to the Weimar Republic, changes that involved the increasing social and political integration of Jews. Although the Nazis' policy of promoting the segregation and isolation of Jews was a bitter pill to a family like the Steinbergs, these restrictions, like the economic policies of discrimination, emerged gradually and could well have seemed temporary.

In 1933 this older German-Jewish generation's sense of German identity and their confidence in the German state, and in the German people as a whole, remained unshaken, even as their wariness of the practices of the new regime grew. As the situation worsened for Jews even the Centralverein gradually changed its stance toward emigration, and toward Zionism in particular. Subjected to increasing pressures from the Nazi government, the Centralverein also changed its course.[26] As the national chair of the Centralverein, Ernst Herzfeld, who, like Kurt's father Alex Steinberg, had been a founding member of the Essen branch of the Centralverein, stated in 1937: "We as non-Zionists acknowledge that Zionism is an important source of Jewish strength ... But we do not share its outlook as it is too narrowly focused on Palestine."[27] After years of debating the need for emigration from Germany the Centralverein leadership realized in 1936–7 the necessity of advocating emigration. Since Palestine had become one of the primary emigration destinations, also for non-Zionists, the Centralverein had changed its perspective on Zionism.[28]

Neither emigration nor immigration were simple matters of moving for Jews in Germany. Emigration was predicated on paying certain fees and being granted exit visas to leave Germany, as well as entry visas for immigration, and on securing the means to reach those sites and to set up a new existence once that relocation occurred. Already in the aftermath of the Great Depression and before the Nazis came to power in late January 1933 many countries had become more restrictive about immigration. So although one could receive permission to leave Germany, emigration was costly, and it was not easy to reach a safe haven in which to relocate. The availability of places to go limited the options even for those of means. There were fewer and fewer countries with doors open to Jewish immigrants.[29] At a time when Jews desperately wanted to escape Nazi Germany, countries such as the United States were tightening restrictions, trying to prevent masses of refugees from immigrating to their countries.[30]

In 1933 younger Jews with few family responsibilities were the first to consider leaving Germany, especially after it became increasingly difficult for Jews to complete their education, practice their professions or continue on a path to social mobility. The older Steinberg daughter, Lotti, completed her training as a dentist just as the Nazis were coming to power and thus as a Jew faced considerable professional obstacles. She married in late March 1935 and emigrated a few months later to Palestine with her wealthy Zionist husband, Hans Kaiser-Blüth. Seeing Lotti marry well and knowing she would be able to work in her profession in Palestine must have helped offset the sadness Selma and Henny felt over Lotti moving so far away. They also had hopes of seeing her before too long.

The legislation known as the Nuremberg Laws, first announced in September 1935 and then expanded and elaborated upon in the following two months, made considerable inroads into Jews' sense of German national identity, even for Jews from traditionally assimilated families like the Kaufmann–Steinberg family. Nazi Germany used the two main components of the laws, the Reich Citizenship Law and the Law for the Protection of German Blood and Honor, to define and segregate Jews according to supposed racial categories. The scope and explicit racism of the laws marked a significant change from the previous discriminatory laws restricting the employment and rights of non-Aryans. The regime's racial theorists categorized individuals as being of "German blood" and thus "Aryan," or of "Jewish blood" based on the declared religious affiliation of one's grandparents. Non-Aryans then became merely subjects of the state (*Staatsangehörige*), whereas those deemed to be of "German blood" and thus "Aryan" continued to be regarded as citizens of the Reich (*Reichsbürger*) with full political rights, at least full relative to the arbitrariness of the Nazi regime. Not only were citizenship rights determined by the Nazi pseudo-science of race and "blood" (lineage) on which these laws were based, but another part of these laws was intended to protect "German blood and honor." Marriage and extramarital relations between Germans and Jews were prohibited, and Jews were banned from flying the German flag.[31]

Although the Nuremberg Laws came as an insult to German Jews, many imagined that such measures would not last. The notion of being able to hold out seemed to characterize, at least until 1938, the perspective of most members of the older generation of German Jews, including Henny, Selma and her brother-in-law, Hermann, and Lotti's in-laws, the Kaiser-Blüths. Julius Kaiser-Blüth, Hans' father, was typical of older, wealthy Jews who were convinced they would be able to hold out during what they saw as temporary Nazi discrimination against certain Jews, presumably other than themselves. In the summer of 1936 Lotti overheard her still-prosperous father-in-law, Julius, during his visit to Palestine, comment to another German Jew who had abandoned his big department store in Berlin in order to emigrate to Palestine that "he [Julius] would not be able to sleep at night if his money were outside of Germany."[32] Even in 1938 after the Nazis had forced the Kaiser-Blüths to sell their factory in Cologne, and after the November Pogrom Lotti's in-laws did not consider emigration. A perplexed Lotti lamented: "We just do not understand the attitude of Hans' parents. I am afraid that they still do not grasp the severity of the situation ... And Father Julius still thinks that he invests wisely when he gives his money to Herr Hitler."[33]

The older generation of Jews in Germany had lived through Imperial Germany (1871–1918) and the Weimar Republic (1918–33) and had contrasted their experiences in Germany with the stories of Eastern European pogroms in the late nineteenth and early twentieth centuries. European Jews in general knew that periods of persecution came and went, but most older German Jews felt at home in Germany and assumed that this unpleasant phase of Nazi rule would not last long. The younger generation, on the other hand, was more directly affected by the lack of opportunities to complete their education and/ or practice their professions in Germany. They were more inclined to start preparing themselves for a new life in a new land.[34] Older Jews found the prospect of turning their back on their roots and history, and possibly loved ones, much more difficult. Starting over in a new country, regardless of the extent of one's wealth, demanded energy and courage, good health and optimism, and a willingness to look forward rather than back, all traits more characteristic of youth than of those over 40.

Hermann, Selma and Henny assumed for years that if they kept a low profile during the Nazi regime they would be safe. Selma, loving and generous as always, even warned her children's Gentile friends in the early years of the Third Reich not to compromise themselves by being seen with Jews, although many of those with whom they maintained contact in Altenessen refused to heed this warning. For example, when Fritz Werner, a former classmate of Lotti's, telephoned and asked if he might join Selma and Lotti as they were about to leave their flat to take a Sunday walk through the neighborhood Kaiserpark, Selma warned Fritz that because they were well known as Jews in Altenessen he should avoid the danger of getting in trouble with the Nazis by being seen in public with them. Fritz, however, insisted. He told them that as long as they would permit him to join them he would accompany them on their walk now and in the future. This he did.[35] But individual friendships between Jews and non-Jews did not suffice in the long term to protect German Jews from the effects of the Nazi regime's policies of discrimination and persecution. As Marion Kaplan has pointed out, simple acts of decency and courage could provide Jews with a false sense of optimism about the number of "good Germans" and the dangers they faced.[36]

A year after the store's late 1934 financial restructuring, Henny, then 60 years old, became seriously ill with uterine cancer.[37] She exhibited courage and stalwartness while hospitalized for over six weeks in the spring of 1936, but her illness and its impact on their business worries took a heavy toll on both the sisters. Having one of the two sisters out of commission for months made it increasingly difficult for Selma to continue to run the store. Now there was no one else to step in. Lotti had already emigrated, Marianne was busy

Figure 3.3 Family outing on the Ruhr (from left): Kurt, Ernst Kaufmann, Onkel Hermann, Selma, 1936

with her studies and Kurt was working full-time at the Centralverein office in Essen. The timing was especially bad: the weeks leading up to Easter were typically one of the busiest times for a dry goods store like theirs.[38] Adding to their workload, the sisters had to let go the young German women who intermittently helped out in their home and in the store. The 1935 Nuremberg Laws included a provision that prohibited Jews from employing women of "German blood" under the age of 45 in their households.[39] The combination of the steady loss of customers, the lack of help, and Henny's surgery and recuperation made it increasingly difficult for the Geschwister Kaufmann store to survive. Fortunately Henny did recover,[40] but the store never did.

Despite their health and financial concerns, in 1936 the sisters invited Ernst Kaufmann, their 16-year-old nephew, the son of their only brother, Leo, to live with them. Ernst was from Düren, some 55 miles away, and needed to complete an apprenticeship as a mechanic in the area. (See Figure 3.3.) Selma and Henny graciously offered to let young Ernst share Kurt's old room that Onkel Hermann used when he was in town. Ernest, as he later called himself, remembered Selma as a loving mother hen. He recalled that Henny had treated everyone that he, or his Steinberg cousins, had brought into the house like family.[41]

He well understood why all three Steinberg children regarded Henny as their second mother.[42]

Family photographs from the 1930s all display Henny and particularly Selma looking much older than their years. Henny's photographs do not betray her worries and frequent health concerns. Selma's photographs, on the other hand, more characteristically evoke a sense of wariness, and weariness as well. From all accounts, no matter what their own physical or emotional worries, Selma and Henny reached out to help family and friends alike.

In October 1936 Selma and Henny began making preparations to close the doors of their store forever. They publicized the store closing sale, noting the "incredibly reduced prices on all their wares," which included bed linens, sewing notions and clothing, such as women's stockings and underwear, gloves, sweaters, caps, workers' overalls and boys' trousers.[43] The leaflets they distributed announced that their extreme price reductions would allow them to meet the legally prescribed deadline to clear out the store's contents once the sale began on 3 November 1936.[44] (See Figure 3.4.) The years Selma and Henny had spent acquiring their store's inventory, laboring over decisions about which fine linens to stock, over the colors and sturdiness of basic hand and dish towels, over how and what to set up in their displays, now seemingly overnight became memories of another life and existence. Being forced to give up the business that had been their life's work together had to have been terribly painful for Selma and Henny. The few days they had to clear the store of all its contents left little time for nostalgia. Marianne noted triumphantly once the liquidation sale was over that they had been "able to sell all the wares in the course of the sale."[45] Her naïve comment overlooks what this loss represented to her mother and aunt.

Closing down the Geschwister Kaufmann store did not just mean a loss of income and a way of life to Selma and Henny. Since 1902 they had rented both the commercial space on the ground floor and the second-floor flat in the three-story building. Once they closed the store they needed to move out of the building altogether. They left behind the flat in which the two sisters had lived since 1902, where they had raised, together with Alex, the three children. Their new home was a smaller, and presumably less expensive, but more modern flat in Essen proper. Marianne was relieved over what she described as her mother and aunt's "retirement" and move to Essen proper: "We are all happy.

Figure 3.4 Flyer for store closing sale, 1936

The flat is pretty and comfortable and also totally electric. Our dear folks (*Herrschaften*) will now finally come to their fully deserved but far-too-long postponed rest. Dear God, keep them healthy!"[46]

From the perspective of a 25-year-old daughter worrying that her elders' life was too hard and that they should have it made easier with modern conveniences and retirement, these changes may all have seemed positive. But the store closing and move at the end of 1936 surely provoked mixed emotions in Selma and Henny. Their move into Essen was into much smaller quarters in an unfamiliar neighborhood and, as they would eventually find out, under the control of an anti-Semitic landlady. Of course, life had also recently changed for them in Altenessen, as it had for Jews all over Germany. Altenessen's Jewish population, already only 0.7 percent of the total population on the eve of Hitler's appointment as chancellor, was by November 1935 down over two-thirds to 0.2 percent of the population; in Essen proper the Jewish population had also sunk, although only by a quarter, from 1 percent to 0.75 percent in that same three-year period.[47] These demographic changes were a result of both the internal migration of Jews toward urban areas within Germany as well as emigration. The smaller apartment in Essen, two bedrooms and a sitting-room as opposed to the four bedrooms, a combination living/dining-room and a parlor they had had in Altenessen, may well have represented a rent saving for them. It was also much closer to their synagogue and to Kurt's rented flat. Marianne chose to see the store closing and her "parents'" move into Essen optimistically, which perhaps her mother and her aunt tried to do as well, whether more to reassure the children or themselves.

Once the store was liquidated, Henny and Selma, who for so long had supported themselves and the family through their own labors, now had to rethink how they would cover their expenses. Kurt, who from 1934 until 1938 worked first as the assistant legal counsel in Essen and then as general counsel in Frankfurt am Main for the Centralverein, did provide them some help with their finances. They also had some savings and whatever profits they had earned from the store closing sale, as well as two pieces of property that could be sold if necessary.

Like Selma and Henny, many Jewish owners of small businesses were forced to shut down or sell their businesses in the mid-1930s. To the extent that Economics Minister Schacht had pushed for restraint concerning the economic persecution of the Jews, these calls were no longer heard after 1936, when Schacht's primary role in the economy was taken over by Hermann Göring.[48] Göring's Four Year Plan, introduced in 1936 to step up militarization and prepare for war, did not in the least concern itself with protecting the role of Jews in the German economy. By 1937, when Schacht was officially removed from office, the policy of "Aryanization" was well underway in many parts of Germany.[49]

By the spring of 1937 Henny's health had improved; her cancer was in remission. Selma felt confident enough about her sister's health to leave her alone in Essen while she traveled to Palestine to visit her daughter and son-in-law. But this was intended as a visit only, an indication of the lack of urgency Jews like Selma felt about leaving Germany.[50] Neither before nor during her visit in Palestine did Selma apply for the visa that might have converted her trip from a visit to a resettlement. While in Palestine Selma had to have an emergency appendectomy, which required a long recovery period. Her incapacitation must have colored her visit and certainly limited her activities. We know little more about this trip other than a mention of Selma and Lotti's return from Palestine in a late September 1937 entry in Marianne's Notebook and in a 1938 letter from Selma, and a few postcards and photographs of Selma on the ship and sitting in Lotti and Hans' flat in Tel Aviv. There were no concrete discussions about Selma's potential emigration to Palestine at this time, although this would change.

When Selma did return to Germany Lotti accompanied her. They stopped to rest for a few days in Italy before returning together for a reunion with the rest of the family in Essen. Selma's return with Lotti to Essen in late September was cause for a family celebration.[51] Henny was of course very glad to see her sister, from whom she had rarely been separated for more than a few days at a time since 1902. Selma's youngest child, Marianne, who had returned from Switzerland to Germany to complete an internship in Cologne, was able to come home to Essen to visit for several days. Kurt was there, too, still living and working in Essen, although a few months later he would move to Frankfurt am Main. Onkel Hermann stayed overnight, having made his way back to Essen from Krefeld for this special reunion with his niece Lotti, whom he and the rest of the family had not seen since her departure for Palestine more than two years before. Despite the long journey and Selma's recent recovery from the appendectomy, Selma must have been thrilled to have had this bittersweet, all-too-short moment with all her loved ones together with her.

This brief family reunion with all their children together could not disguise the fact that the family was about to become even more dispersed. When Marianne had gone abroad for several months at a time to work in 1933 and early 1934 and to pursue her medical studies in 1936, her mother and Tante Henny had missed her terribly. By early 1938, with her year-long internship soon coming to a close and with no prospects of getting her German medical license, Selma and Henny had no doubts that she too would soon be emigrating. Realizing their youngest daughter would be leaving Germany all alone was a particularly painful prospect for both Selma and Henny. But they also knew that Marianne's emigration was for the best.

The situation in Germany was getting worse for Jews. The Nazi government issued decrees in early 1938 that accelerated the process of eliminating Jews from the German economy and from German schools. Jews were denied access to government relief for the poor. Decrees in summer 1938 also forced Jews who had German names to adopt the middle names of "Israel" for men and "Sara" for women to help the Nazis identify Jews more easily.[52] All the members of the Kaufmann–Steinberg family would have had to adopt these middle names. Having lost their citizenship rights already in 1935 and their business not long thereafter, now another part of their identity was under siege. Indeed, they realized, it was time for their youngest to find a better homeland where she could work in her profession and have political rights and access to economic mobility.

Selma and Henny wrote Nanna, as they often called Marianne, on 21 June 1938, only hours after she had left Essen. Their second cousin, Moritz Schweizer, accompanied her on the train. They wanted her to have letters waiting for her on the ship, which departed for New York on the 23rd from Rotterdam. The advice, well wishes and blessings they sent her indicate the panoply of emotions Selma and Henny felt as their children were scattered across continents. Selma in particular had understood how important becoming a doctor was to her daughter and had helped sway Marianne to choose an emigration destination that would hold out the most promise for her professionally. Selma also thought that Marianne's establishing herself as a physician would make it more likely that all the family would be able to afford to emigrate and eventually be reunited. In this parting letter, Selma told her youngest child: "Take these words to escort you in your new life, in another part of the world. All the best for you, my dear, courageous creature! A good journey, safe crossing and a wonderful, free life with fulfilling work in your profession. My thoughts are totally with you, my dear one." In a prayer that she described as her maternal blessing, Selma asked "'the eternal one' to bless and watch over you, to show you the way and give you peace." Henny was too overwrought to write much beyond wishing Marianne a happy journey and a happy life. She closed her letter to Marianne with "all the rest would have to be said without words" and then signed off "tenderly."⁵³

Selma wrote Marianne quite frequently, trying to disguise her own worries and sadness behind words of domestic advice, hope and praise. On 24 June, just after Marianne's ship had departed, Selma wrote: "It is so still and lonely here at our place; I often think the house is closing in on me ... I keep remembering things that we forgot [to pack]; I wanted to give you a couple of freshly washed tablecloths and two plates. Now you'll have to buy plates there if you need them and remember to wash one or two tablecloths in hot water."⁵⁴ Two weeks later a bereft Selma tried to cope with the fact that she was no longer able to play a routine maternal role for her daughter or able to share in her experiences in any timely or direct way: "By the time you get this letter you will have had all sorts of new experiences and your good friends there will be able to advise you and stand by you as much as possible."⁵⁵

Selma's own extended family reached out to her and Henny to try to help them through their sadness of having to say goodbye to their youngest child. Lotti's mother-in-law, Flora Kaiser-Blüth, in Cologne and Olga Bachrach, the wife of Alex's first cousin Julius, who lived in Plettenberg, both insisted that Selma and Henny come to visit. Selma wrote Nanna about how kind they were being to her.⁵⁶ Olga could well fathom what this was like, since she had been working on getting her own younger daughter, also named Marianne, a visa to the United States since 1936, when her daughter was only 17. Olga would not say goodbye to her own daughter Marianne Bachrach until early 1939, but she was already anticipating the pain of parting as she tried to comfort Selma.⁵⁷

Selma wrote cryptically on 24 June 1938 about her worries concerning Onkel Hermann, who had not yet arrived in Essen that evening. She worried how he would be when he got back to Essen from Krefeld and whether he would have "certain paperwork."⁵⁸ Selma's letter of 30 June 1938 made it clear to Marianne that Onkel Hermann was being terminated from his position as a salesman for a Jewish-owned firm which was about to be "Aryanized." Interestingly enough, Selma explained his termination with "his lagging sales success, his external appearance, his shaky posture ... none of which recommended him as a traveling salesman." Selma claimed they all, except Onkel Hermann himself, could see this coming. Yet Selma was also outraged at how Onkel Hermann had been dismissed from the silk company for which he had worked as a salesperson for over forty years, a company "to which he had dedicated his life's work and all his energy." Selma could not hold back her shock at the treatment accorded her brother-in-law, describing it as undeserving of "a house servant employed for less than half a year." As an outraged Selma decried:

> They should have handled this in a more upright manner, called him in and then discussed with him how his employment just could not be continued. They must have thought he would resign after they had been sending other salesmen to some of his best customers. Now Kurt needs to step in and whether that will serve any purpose is most questionable to me.[59]

Selma should have realized that the Jewish-owned silk company where Onkel Hermann had worked for so long was being "Aryanized," but perhaps she intentionally avoided mentioning this in her letter to Marianne. At times Jewish owners would remain in place in name only while a firm was being taken over by non-Jews. Apparently Onkel Hermann had not had the best of relationships with his boss, Herr Simon, and this, in combination with his age and business performance, may have been what Selma and he initially interpreted as the primary cause of his termination.[60] Henny wrote Marianne that Onkel Hermann wished he had gone on the ship with her.[61]

Making use of the expertise he had acquired in helping Jews get whatever economic compensation and legal rights they had left in his work at the Centralverein, Kurt went to Krefeld on Onkel Hermann's behalf to try to seek redress for his abrupt dismissal. Kurt's letter of 22 July 1938 makes it clear that all Jewish employees of the firm were being dismissed because the company was being "Aryanized," forcibly sold at well below market value to "Aryans." Onkel Hermann received the smallest compensation he could legally be granted for the time between his dismissal notice and the earliest date of his termination. Onkel Hermann's emotional response to his employers when he received the news of his dismissal had, according to Kurt, only made things worse.[62] In the past Onkel Hermann had made frequent contributions to the family's income, including helping the children while

Figure 3.5 Onkel Hermann with housecat Petra and kittens

they completed their university studies, but now the prospect of any significant contribution toward family expenses dimmed.

Increasingly depressed and seeming to age overnight, an unemployed Hermann moved in full-time with the two sisters, to Henny's dismay in particular. (See Figure 3.5.) Although Henny had recovered from her uterine cancer in 1936, she was now suffering from chronic arthritis that seemed to get worse at about the same time that Hermann moved in for good.[63] Later that summer of 1938 Hermann's continued financial contributions, apparently from his savings, to his older sister Johanna in Kassel, further worried the family.[64] Selma and Henny were concerned both about his judgment as well as the looming threat that he would become a financial and physical burden. This man, who had been very beloved as the humorous and playful uncle/brother-in-law, had quickly become, now that he had lost his professional identity and income, moody and unpredictable at best, and often rude and inconsiderate toward Selma and Henny.[65]

The financial burden Selma and Henny endured by having to support a three-person household was relieved somewhat in 1938 and

1939 by the sale of two properties. One was the property in Altenessen, located diagonally across the street from the store, and the other in Gronau, outside Hanover, which Alex's parents had owned. However, the amount the family received from both these sales reflects the disadvantages they suffered as Jews conducting business in a Germany where the economy and property were becoming increasingly and quite consciously "Aryanized." In 1938 yet more decrees were issued to further prepare the way for the confiscation of Jewish property in Germany.[66] Apparent in these two sales are the impact of "Aryanization" and the willingness of acquaintances to snap up Jews' property at considerably less than market value.

Selma felt compelled in mid 1938, a year and a half after her sister and she had moved into a smaller apartment in Essen, to sell the property across the street from where they had rented their store and apartment. World War I and then Alex's illness had prevented the dream of building the family a house there from ever becoming reality. The family had spent many hours there, picking berries and enjoying the flowers in the garden, and it was not easy for them to part with it.[67]

The letter that Selma wrote her daughter Marianne about the sale of this property to a neighbor on 16 July 1938, shortly after her daughter had emigrated to the United States, does not betray any coercion or sense of resentment that the new buyer had exploited her with the price he paid. Yet there is a sense of regret and sadness about what might have been and an attempt to justify to her daughter, one of the presumed heirs to the property, why the property could not have stayed in the family's hands. Clearly Selma was disappointed; she wrote Marianne the very next day after the closing about the sale, indicating she had sold it for 1,000 RM under its value as last determined for tax assessment purposes, its unit value (*Einheitswert*). She mentioned that Marianne would know how high that assessed value was, but that although it had not ever materialized into the house of which Alex had dreamed and also had never earned them any money, she was very relieved not to have to cover the expenses associated with it any more. She continued: "We desperately need the interest [on the money from the sale] for our household and now we have the 25 Marks for taxes, which it cost us every month, at our disposal." She then went into great detail about how the sale had come about, referring to the fact that Marianne would have remembered what the unit value of the property was and that this same man had previously made an offer for the property, although also clearly censoring what she wrote. Selma delineated for her daughter the story of how the sale transpired:

> Fourteen days ago, the dentist from the floor below us called for me and told me he had spoken with Kr., whom he knows well, about the property, and Kr. asked him to tell me that I should call him, which I did from right there. He then told me that I should make him a reasonable offer, then something could happen on this. You indeed know that he previously had said that he had thought about 8,000, which was not at all worthy of discussion. We arranged for him to come here the following Sunday. I asked Eugen to come over, because he understands things like this so much better than I do, but it was not at all necessary.[68] When I insisted on the unit value, he offered a thousand less. It was his lucky number and he would not retreat from it. I didn't want to be petty and we came to agree to this price very quickly. He is definitely not petty and very attractive in appearance, absolutely generous. After the formal act at the notary's office we went into the garden, and I showed him then where that was. He was thrilled that his children would be able to play around there. There were also all sorts of berries on the vines...

Selma went on to describe rather romantically and nostalgically the lovely flowers and the natural wildness of the lot. Then, returning to her more practical side, she wrote:

> Well, we have had this piece of property for about 30 years, since 1909. We have had many pleasant hours of relaxation there, but it has cost us, alone in taxes, too much money. I once calculated, since just the acceptance of the purchase offer [Auflassung] – 2,790 Marks. Now I am very happy that it has been taken care of so well and smoothly. I have just written the realtor that he should return to me the property boundary records. I have neither heard nor seen anything from him.[69]

Whether Selma had actively sought out Herr Kr. (Krell) or had openly had the property on the market is unclear, but Krell was and had been clearly interested in it for a while and apparently had initially made far too low an offer. Herr Krell owned a department store in the area and would have known Selma and Henny through their store. Selma probably wanted to have her nephew Eugen present because of his business experience. Her son, Kurt, neither a businessman nor a property owner, was at this point already living in Frankfurt am Main, working as the head legal counsel for the Centralverein there.

But here the Steinberg children's postwar restitution documents tell another part of the story. On 29 June 1951 the restitution court in West Germany reached a decision, at the children's behest, involving compensation to be paid to them as Selma's heirs for the property in Altenessen. The purchaser of the property, Herr Krell, agreed to pay Selma's heirs a total of 6,300 DM (Deutschmarks), the equivalent of 63,000 RM. Herr Krell was still the owner of the property in 1951 during the restitution proceedings and was identified as the owner of the department store Kaufhaus W. Krell in Altenessen.[70] This is considerably more than the 1,000 RM difference less than the unit value Selma wrote about and provides a sense of how values were presumably underestimated for Jewish property so that "Aryans" could more easily take ownership of them. The Essen city address books add to the story: Herr Krell had owned a department store in Essen proper when he bought Selma's property. He did not develop this land, but instead moved a dry goods business into the downstairs of the building with the local Nazi Party headquarters, next door to where Selma and Henny had lived and had their store. After setting up this Altenessen business he was so successful that he was able to open up a third business in Essen prior to the war.[71] He had not driven Selma and Henny out of business, but he profited considerably by the void their store had left in the immediate neighborhood and managed to expand further, perhaps at someone else's expense.

Both Kurt and Lotti wrote Marianne in late summer 1938 about the sale of the property in very positive terms. Lotti wrote how glad she was that the property affair had been decided so positively.[72] Kurt contrasted Onkel Hermann's dismissal and poor severance pay with the sale of the Altenessen property when he wrote: "As a certain 'compensation' we have succeeded in selling the Altenessen property. The interest on the money will be necessary for our 'old folks'" lives."[73] So although the price for the property was hardly a fair one, relative to the times and the predicament of the older generation, without employment and increasingly without property, the sale was celebrated. The family members were relieved that there would be money in the bank and interest being earned to support Selma and Henny and Onkel Hermann, "our old folks," as the children increasingly called the three collectively. The children saw this as a silver lining in a cloudy Germany where a secure future for Jews, especially older Jews, seemed to be increasingly unlikely.

The second property that they were also trying to sell and that helped further to secure the older generation's financial situation was the large Steinberg family-owned building in Gronau, outside Hanover, where Alex's parents and siblings had lived and had their small department store. Selma as Alex's heir and Alex's two siblings, Hermann and Johanna, divided the proceeds from the sale of their parents' house in Gronau. The agreed price was 15,000 RM. But, as part of their policy to impoverish Jews further, the Nazi regime by then had new regulations that required a large percentage of this sum to go to the German state rather than to the Jewish sellers.[74] The buyer of this Gronau property, their commercial tenant, Herr Reising, was able to take advantage of the fact that the sellers, Selma, Hermann and Johanna, were Jewish and paid them far below market value for the property.[75] The buyer was forced as a result of the restitution case in the 1950s to pay compensation of 6,274 DM (Deutschmarks), the equivalent of 62,740 RM to the Steinberg children, as the sole Steinberg heirs, because he had underpaid by over 80 percent, paying only 15,000 RM for the Gronau house rather than the estimated market value of over 77,000 RM.[76]

As the family was trying to sell these two properties Kurt began seriously to consider emigration, although he waited a while to share this news with his family. Lotti's departure in mid 1935 occurred while Selma and Henny still had their store and were both healthy, and before the Nuremberg Laws removed their German citizenship. But by the time Marianne left in mid 1938 their personal and financial situations had changed considerably, many mostly younger friends and relatives either having already left or seriously considering leaving. Older people were more likely to have concerns with their health and the responsibility for loved ones. Selma clearly could not imagine leaving behind her sister and life-long companion, Henny, when she finally did begin to write Marianne about the possibility of emigrating in the fall of 1938. Within a month of Kurt's registering for immigration to the United States and letting his "parents" know he had done so, Selma decided it was time for her to take similar action for herself, her sister and Onkel Hermann as well.[77]

Several international events also influenced Selma's decision to act when she did. First, there was the Evian Conference in July 1938, which President Franklin D. Roosevelt (FDR) had called in the aftermath of the March 1938 German annexation (*Anschluss*) of Austria, when some 200,000 more Central European Jews might join the flood of prospective German Jewish refugees. FDR called in particular on European and Latin American countries to help make possible the immigration and resettlement of Jewish refugees from Germany and Austria, although few countries were willing to welcome an increase of Jewish refugees.[78] Then in August there were heightened tensions and fears of war surrounding the Sudetenland crisis, which resulted in the Munich Conference and England, France and Italy's acceptance of Germany's takeover of this part of the then Czechoslovakia. Selma reported at the time with great relief to Marianne: "Thank God the difficult and worrisome days have finally passed. The whole world breathes a sigh of relief since war could be avoided. It would have been too terrible."[79] Remembering all too well World War I and its aftermath, this older generation was particularly worried about the prospect of another war.

Selma's realistic concern for the future, especially now that her children were all either out of or about to leave Germany, led her to the US consulate in Stuttgart, where on 20 October 1938 she registered herself and the two other family members for whom she felt responsible, Henny and Onkel Hermann.[80] They received the registration numbers 31691–92–93. The trip from Essen to the Stuttgart consulate would not have been an easy one for an older Jewish woman alone. In addition to a long train ride, Jewish travelers at the time had to endure various forms of discrimination. An eyewitness recalled: "Almost without exception, the restaurants and hotels there [in Stuttgart] were forced by the local Party authorities to refuse accommodation to Jews."[81] Selma avoided having to spend the night in Stuttgart and instead traveled to Kreuzau, where she attended the funeral of Leopold Roer, the husband of her deceased older sister, Julie, and then on to Frankfurt am Main, where she saw Kurt, and finally to Cologne to visit Lotti's in-laws, the Kaiser-Blüths.

Henny suffered at the time not only with chronic arthritis but also other ailments, which would soon be diagnosed as a renal tumor. On some level Selma must have realized that Henny's second bout of cancer and her other health problems would probably make it impossible for Henny to leave. Yet she did register all three of them, holding out hope that, by the time her own and her sister and brother-in-law's numbers eventually would be called, somehow their health would allow them all to emigrate.

When Selma applied for their visas to the United States in the fall of 1938, their registration numbers were so high that they were unlikely to be able to immigrate for several years. Only once their numbers came up would they need to provide affidavits from financial sponsors who could prove they could guarantee their economic well-being once they did immigrate. It was often more difficult for older persons who were not wealthy to find sponsors abroad who might vouch for their financial well-being. This was especially true once there were more restrictions on Jews taking money and property out of Germany. The prospects for Jews who had limited access to material means abroad or to employment in a new country with a different language and culture were slim indeed. Few immigrants were able to save quickly to bring over family members soon after their arrival. Selma, however, had faith that her children would have acquired sufficient funds or have also found sponsors by then who could provide affidavits.

In October 1938 when Selma registered herself, Henny and Onkel Hermann for immigration to the United States, Lotti and Nanna in their new homelands certainly wanted and expected that they would all eventually be reunited with their "old folks." But none of the children felt that there was any urgent need in October 1938 to focus their efforts on getting their "old folks" out of Germany. The family in Germany, Palestine and the United States was more concerned with getting Kurt into safety and were glad to learn he had registered already on 1 September 1938 for immigration to the United States. The proceeds from the family's property sales, along with the relative calm in Germany and the recent avoidance of war with the Munich Conference, created the illusion of a relatively secure holding pattern in which Selma, Henny and Onkel Hermann would be safe to wait in Germany until the children could get fully settled and adjusted to their new lives.

4 PROFESSIONAL ROADBLOCKS AND PERSONAL DETOURS: LOTTI AND MARIANNE, 1933–1938

Unlike the situation for many older German Jews with established careers, the professional and personal hopes and dreams of many young German Jews were shaken, if not shattered, already within months of the Nazis' coming to power in 1933. The factors that would increasingly convince younger Jews in particular that they could not remain in Germany usually involved professional and economic roadblocks, which multiplied steadily from the spring of 1933 onward. Outspoken anti-Nazis, both Jews and non-Jews, often encountered physical intimidation and violence at the hands of Nazi activists already in 1933, if not in the Great Depression years before Hitler was appointed chancellor. Young anti-Nazi Jewish activists, who found themselves particularly targeted, often fled Nazi Germany early on, but they were the exception among German Jews. Jews of all ages throughout Germany felt the impact of the Nazis' coming to power, yet many naturally took a wait-and-see approach. Nazi rule varied from place to place and even person to person, certainly at least until 1935, when the Nuremberg Laws placed concrete restrictions on all Jews and on interactions between Jews and so-called Aryans.

Both the political situation in Nazi Germany and Alex Steinberg's imminent death in the spring of 1933 compelled the youngest Steinberg child, Marianne, to return closer to home to study at the University of Düsseldorf instead of going off to Innsbruck as she had planned.[1] Stressing that "the current political situation overshadows everything else," Marianne expressed relief two weeks after her father's death: "Father's passing came at just the right time: he is now spared both further suffering and these times."[2]

The 22-year-old Marianne reacted to the new regime and what it seemed to hold for her own fate and that of other Jews by writing in the last pages of the diary she had kept since she was a teenager:

> So much, seemingly without end, has happened in these last four months. We had the election of 5 March, shortly after the Reichstag fire, which brought the confirmation of Hitler as chancellor and his national uprising. The consequences: Germany's awakening, the persecution of Marxists and Jews. To describe all of this in detail is impossible. I believe everything will stay in my head without my having to write it down.
>
> As to my own personal fate ... my studies and my life up to now, that will be determined by the fate of German Jewry, in particular of the young and coming generation. Our right to live and to earn a living has been denied in this new Germany ... Can one even say "Jewish student" today? If under [German university] student one includes all the rights and obligations that the term student implies, then my expression "Jewish student" no longer is correct. Because here in Germany our rights and duties have been taken away. We no longer belong to the German student body. According to the Führer's stipulations we here in Düsseldorf can only take our seats after all the Aryans have found their places.[3]

As a medical student and prospective physician, Marianne was well aware that the political had become personal. Already in April 1933 all "non-Aryan" doctors were barred from working at clinics and hospitals that accepted state-supported health insurance from patients, and those that were not already affiliated with the insurance program could not join.[4] Since the vast majority of Germans were covered by state-supported health insurance, which paid physicians directly for patients' medical care, German-Jewish medical students were all but closed out of their chosen profession. This legal measure was accompanied by a "quiet boycott" against Jewish physicians and "a campaign of intimidation among patients," with the result that more than half of all Jewish doctors felt compelled to abandon their profession by mid 1933.[5] Because Marianne had already passed the equivalent of her medical school qualifying exams in 1932,[6] she was not vulnerable to the April 1933 quota restrictions on the admission of Jewish students into medical studies.[7] But despite being allowed to continue her medical studies, her prospects of actually becoming a doctor in Germany were already dim. Although there was no way she could have known this in 1933, later decrees prevented any Jews from receiving their German medical licenses, even if they completed all their training and passed all their exams. In fact, a decree issued on 25 July 1938 withdrew licenses from Jewish physicians altogether and restricted the practices of Jewish doctors to the treatment of Jewish patients.[8]

Marianne also worried about the future of her family. The Nazis' spring 1933 economic boycott of Jewish businesses did not bode well for her mother and aunt, or for Onkel Hermann. Nanna knew her brother and sister were also facing professional roadblocks.[9] It was not only governmental policies that restricted non-Aryans from entering into legal or medical practice in 1933: professional groups increasingly decided on their own initiative to exclude Jews from membership. During the Third Reich both regime policy and regime-sanctioned populist actions combined to push German Jews out of professional practice in Germany.[10] This also had an impact on all the Steinberg siblings.

Although her brother Kurt eventually would find work in the spring of 1934 within the Jewish community,[11] Marianne was also worried about her older sister.[12] Lotti had passed her state exams in dentistry in December 1932 at the University of Würzburg and completed her degree in March 1933. This was fortunately before Jews were excluded from taking medical and dental licensing exams.[13] As an indication of the quality of her work, Lotti's doctoral advisor, Dr. Max Meyer, had her thesis published in the *Springer Archive for Ear, Nose and Throat Medicine*.[14] Marianne's fears that Lotti would not find a position were justified. Although her younger sister still expressed confidence in late 1933 that Lotti would persevere and "land on her feet," Lotti was never able to pursue her dream of opening her own practice in Germany.[15] Anti-Jewish legislation beginning in 1933 made it difficult at first, and later impossible, for a recently licensed Jewish dentist such as Lotti to find regular employment.[16]

We know from Marianne's Diary entry of 6 June 1933 that Lotti's prospects were tenuous at best: "After passing the state exam with good grades and earning her dental degree, Lotti is looking for a job ... If she could find a Jewish dentist who could use a substitute or an assistant, she would be incredibly lucky. A Christian colleague won't and can't take her."[17]

In mid June 1933, at this critical personal and political juncture following her father's death and the Nazis' consolidation of power, Marianne compared her own and her siblings' predicament with that of her mother, her Tante Henny and her Onkel Hermann. Marianne was relieved that her elders were safely "at least so far ... already set in their professions." Recognizing in mid 1933 that her family's circumstances were not unique, Marianne quipped: "These are the material concerns ... exemplified by the Steinberg family, which is a typical Jewish family in Germany in 1933 ... even with regard to the occupation of the children and parents." Marianne felt that it was far too commonplace for German-Jewish parents to be employed in business while their children were academically trained. She regretted that so few German Jews were employed in the handicrafts or agriculture, occupations that improved one's chances of obtaining immigration certificates to the British mandate of Palestine.[18] Although Marianne was not seriously considering emigration from Germany at this point, she did keep herself informed about immigration options, including the most sought-after professions in Palestine.

Zionist organizations actively sought out young Jews with handicrafts or agricultural training and experience, or even provided young Jews with training, in order to develop a Jewish homeland in Palestine. The rise of the Nazis caused a growing number of young German Jews to turn to Palestine for a possible future. Various training centers or *hachsharah* had sprung up as early as the 1920s throughout Germany to prepare Jews for *aliyah*, or emigration to the Holy Land.[19] In Palestine, and in other less-industrialized countries such as Argentina, into which many German-Jewish refugees from the Nazis sought to and did immigrate, there was limited demand for academically trained young people.[20] Since the beginning of the Depression in late 1929, the Nazi Party had been increasingly successful in channeling the political aggressions and economic frustrations of the distressed "Aryan" middle class and unemployed university graduates toward not only Jewish store owners but also Jewish doctors, dentists and lawyers, as well as law and medical students.[21] Marianne, aware of this growing resentment and how it increasingly targeted Jews like herself and her family, wished as early as 1933 that her family and she were in a situation that would make it easier for them to settle outside of Germany, if need be.[22]

All three Steinberg children experienced the Nazi regime in their day-to-day lives. In Essen soon after the Nazis came to power in 1933 Lotti had an incident with a former school acquaintance who, as he always had, came to sit down next to her on the streetcar. She asked him to move because the Nazi Party insignia he was wearing made her uncomfortable. He did not seem to understand the reasons for her discomfort, remarking: "But, Lotti, that has nothing to do with you." She responded that "it had everything to do with [her]." Apparently this former classmate had just become a member of the Nazi Party and did not yet connect its anti-Semitic ideology with his personal acquaintances.[23]

Marianne, already in mid 1933, had a run-in herself with the new Nazi regime and knew of several frightening encounters of acquaintances and relatives, which made the possible need to flee Germany not stray far from her mind. She received a letter during her semester break asking her to come to the local Nazi Party headquarters in Altenessen. Although she was treated politely there and never knew exactly why she had been asked to appear, her family's fears that she might not return are indicative of how vulnerable Jews in Germany felt already within months of the Nazis' coming to power.[24] Her second cousin, Moritz Schweizer, who, as general counsel to the Essen synagogue community, was in a very exposed Jewish position, was arrested on 19 April 1933, apparently for no reason other than to intimidate him, and then fortunately released.[25]

Through her boyfriend Edgar Meyer and his brother Alfred, who had practiced dentistry in Barmen, some 25 miles northwest of Düsseldorf, Marianne knew of the violent physical threat that the Nazis could and did pose to Jews in Germany. In the spring of 1933 the SA had murdered Alfred; his body was later found in a burlap sack in a reservoir.[26] Edgar, whom she described in her Diary in 1932 as a communist and a bit of a rabble-rouser,[27] had had his life threatened by the SA when he attended his brother's funeral.[28] On that Friday evening, 30 June 1933, Marianne knew her recently widowed mother was disappointed that she was not returning home, but her plans to visit Alfred's grave now that she had recently moved to Düsseldorf took precedence. Marianne felt torn between the normalcy of spending Shabbat at her family home and her desire to pay her respects to this victim of the Nazi regime on behalf of her boyfriend Edgar, who could not risk visiting his brother's grave himself.[29] Alfred's murder and the threats against Edgar were stark reminders of how much danger existed already during the first few months of the Third Reich.[30] Edgar had no concrete plans to emigrate, despite the recent threat to his life.[31] In fact in early July 1933 Edgar was trying to convince Marianne to return to finish her studies in Würzburg, where he lived. But in early August Marianne clandestinely helped get him to Essen, aiding him in illegally crossing over to Belgium, where he sought refuge with two cousins. From there Edgar made his way to France, where he would live in exile in Tours.[32] Edgar was one of some 30,000 German refugees who in 1933 crossed the border into France, and one of approximately 37–45,000 German Jews and 10,000 Gentiles who fled Germany that first year of the Nazi regime.[33]

Marianne soon felt the effect of Nazi policies directly. On 11 July 1933 she learned that her merit-based German scholarship was being revoked.[34] She had only received notification of being awarded the stipend on 16 March, after having been invited into the same student honor society that had inducted her brother during his studies. She had been told she had received this award because "of her willingness to place her life-long work in the service of the German Volk."[35] The new Nazi-led government set up a special commission in the late spring to determine before the new summer semester began which of the recipients of these scholarships were "non-Aryan." These students were not to be granted any further scholarship money and would be held liable for repaying whatever amount they had already received. Marianne was informed that "because of her non-Aryan lineage" she could no longer belong to this select "German student body" and was now deemed unworthy of monetary support. Not only would she be denied the promised funds for the upcoming semester, but she had to return 307 RM, half the amount she had already been allotted of the promised total.[36]

Throughout the late summer of 1933 and especially after Edgar's departure Marianne increasingly used her Diary to describe her existential angst about being Jewish in Germany and the narrowing of options for young Jews in particular. But she was careful not

to risk mentioning anything, even in her Diary, about Edgar's departure. On the first evening of Rosh Hashanah, 21 September 1933, she
reflected on the dualism of German-Jewish identity while ruminating
about the future:

> We are German Jews. We, not just I am a German Jew.
> That means we are a community of people who live in
> a country for whom that country is a homeland, our
> economic, cultural and intellectual foundation. We are
> Germans, but also Jews. We live in Germany, in the
> Diaspora. With this admission we are faced with a logical
> path laid out before us: to congregate together towards the
> true path homeward. And if we can't all go to Palestine for
> whatever different reasons – I can't be a physician there
> and would have to be a Chaluz [Pioneer] – then at least we
> should inwardly return to our Jewishness. And that we can
> do in any country. We now know once again with whom
> we belong, our grounding... I am a Jew, we are Jews.[37]

It was at this point, after encountering this stark reality of exclusion
and discrimination as a student, that Marianne made arrangements
via an English friend, Doris Meakin, whom she had recently met in
Germany in early 1933, to live and work in Britain.[38] Marianne found
it unpalatable, and financially unviable, to continue at a German university. In Cardiff and London Marianne worked for various English-
Jewish families as a cook, maid and nanny in order to finance her
stay.[39] It was not easy for Marianne to adjust to working for Jewish
families she did not consider her cultural, intellectual or even social-
class equals. She was certainly less than enamored of the British middle-
class provincial life she was thrown into in Cardiff. She lamented: "I
have been yearning for Germany on many occasions since being here,
especially missing the traditional good German taste."[40] Yet she knew
that life back in Germany would not represent a real cure for her discontent: "What should I do, dear God?" she wrote, wondering what
life would be like "without my profession, my work, my medicine."[41]
Letters from her sister and her loved ones at home, her mother, Tante
Henny and Onkel Hermann, helped keep her spirits up.[42]

Once Marianne left Cardiff and moved to London in the late
fall of 1933, she was much happier.[43] There she worked for Jewish

families whom she found to be "more of a German and intellectual type."[44] The family she worked for who impressed her most were active Zionists, Dr. Lauterbach and his wife, although this fact sparked her curiosity rather than struck an emotional or ideological chord.[45]

In December 1933, three months after arriving in England, Marianne debated whether to take advantage of an International Student Service scholarship to study in Bristol or Edinburgh, or to complete a two-year course at an agriculture school for girls in Nahalal in Palestine, which the Lauterbachs offered to arrange through the Women's International Zionist Organization (WIZO).[46] She was not even tempted by the scholarship offer from WIZO.[47] At the end of February 1934 she wrote Ramona Goodman, a WIZO representative and an acquaintance of the Lauterbachs, to decline the scholarship, indicating that she thought she might return to Germany to complete her studies and take her German state exams in medicine. Goodman applauded Marianne's decision to return to Germany for two years to complete her studies and wrote: "What will happen in two years' time, I cannot say; but if I can in any way help you then, I shall do so. We need women like you in Palestine!"[48]

One of Marianne's academic mentors from Düsseldorf, Prof. Dr. Albert Eckstein, wrote her on 6 December 1933 to say that, although she could not be licensed to practice medicine, he thought she could get a doctoral degree in Germany. He recommended that if she did not have the funds to support herself in Germany, she should consider completing all her studies in England. But he advised her against going to Palestine, unless she were a committed Zionist and willing, he added, somewhat tongue in cheek, either to be an agricultural worker or to marry and start a family with an agricultural worker.[49] Marianne grappled with her anger and alienation over what the Nazis were doing to German Jews and yet felt pulled toward Germany not only to return to her family but also because of her strong attachment to her homeland and her German identity.[50]

Marianne could also join her boyfriend, Edgar, in Tours. Edgar had promised Marianne that she could continue studying medicine if she came there. But she feared doing so would mean giving up going into medicine and becoming "simply a wife and mother." Marianne hesitated about moving to France, realizing she would have to repeat her university qualifying exams and various courses to be admitted to university in France and then probably would have to beg for scholarship funding. She wanted to avoid a "future [that] would be totally uncertain and without Germany!"[51]

Still in London on her twenty-third birthday, 2 February 1934, a homesick Marianne surrounded herself with an enlarged photograph of her parents and an assortment of family birthday letters and wrapped gifts, including a train ticket to Tours from Edgar. She looked forward to returning home, where she could discuss all her options with her loved ones.[52] Looking back, some fifty-five years later, on her 1934 decision to return to Germany, Marianne concluded: "I felt I wanted to return to my family in Germany to be with them in those difficult times, continue my studies and see what the future would bring us Jews in the country of our birth. I – as most other Jews – did not know yet what was in store for us."[53]

Following all her homesickness while in England, Marianne quickly felt disillusioned about being back in Germany:

> *There is no longer a sense of being at home. One is totally removed from everything, totally on one's own and detached from the things that used to preoccupy us ...*
> *What shall I do? It remains eternally distressing. Study here further? With never-ending sacrifices use the last Pfennig [penny] to go to Palestine? Go to Tours to Edgar, who has improved himself – intrepid fellow – and is earning 10,000 francs a month in a business where he's employed? I am so happy that I have him now. Otherwise I would see myself as too lonely and purposeless.*[54]

Her Notebook entries indicate the typical worries of a young woman student in her early 20s trying to make decisions about her future, feeling torn between the push and pull of family ties, career and romantic involvements on the one hand and on the other the extraordinary dilemma of a young German Jew in the 1930s trying to guess what choices to make, while so many political and economic circumstances were beyond her control. Marianne recognized that in the midst of so many uncontrollable circumstances she could at least lose the weight she had put on while she was so unhappy in Cardiff: "It's good that despite everything I'm still concerned with my looks."[55]

Lotti, in the meantime, faced various roadblocks in her professional as well as her personal life. Although she was fully qualified

as a dentist after receiving her degree, Lotti was able only to substitute for other dentists intermittently and work as their assistant,
earning minimal pay. The situation in Germany would only get worse
for Jewish professionals. Lotti briefly worked for dentists in Erlangen
and Hanover. She substituted in Cologne for colleagues when they
went on vacation or were temporarily unable to treat their patients. In
November 1933 Dr. Rolf Barmé of Cologne, a Jewish dentist whom
Lotti had assisted previously, offered her a job. But then, three days
before she was supposed to work in his practice again, he withdrew
his offer "due to lack of patients."[56] The gradual decline in the number
of patients at this Jewish dentist's practice following the April 1933
official boycott of Jewish businesses made him worry that his practice
could not sustain another dentist. At the beginning of 1934 Lotti was
apparently able to assist at his practice again for a few months as a
"volunteer assistant," the only employment she could secure that was
even modestly remunerated. Apparently Lotti earned only 25 RM a
month, a salary comparable to that of a receptionist.[57]

So many Jewish dentists were having trouble staying in business in Germany that a special agency was formed in 1934 to help
re-train dentists as dental technicians. The number of Jewish dentists
declined in Germany in the first three years of the regime from 1,150 in
1933 to 750 in 1936.[58] Then, on 13 February 1935, all Jewish dentists
were prohibited from participating in the health insurance system.[59]
This meant that Jewish dentists' patient base would be limited to those
few patients willing and able to pay privately for dental services.[60] Few
dentists, Jewish or non-Jewish, even if they were willing to work with
a young Jewish female dentist, could afford to have someone in a practice who could not accept patients' insurance. Needless to say, this
made it impossible for Lotti to pursue her dream of opening her own
practice in Germany.

In addition to Lotti's difficulties in establishing herself professionally, her love life was also in turmoil in the early years of the
Third Reich. After her father's death Lotti's search for a life partner
reflects an almost desperate yearning for stability and security. Lotti's
complex love life, entering into one relationship before extricating
herself completely from another, greatly concerned her younger sister.
Even though the two sisters did not live in the same town – not even
in the same country – at the time, Lotti and Marianne shared in their

Figure 4.1 Portrait of Lotti, 1932

letters many intimate details regarding their love lives, relying on each other for advice in matters of the heart. Since not many of the letters from the early to mid 1930s are extant, most of what we know about Lotti's relationships stem from Marianne's Diary, which is naturally colored by her own interpretations and views as a younger sister. (See Figure 4.1.)

While Lotti was working as a substitute dentist in Erlangen in early 1933, one of her colleagues was smitten with her and asked his friend, Heiner Frohmann, to meet her and give him his opinion of her. Lotti likened her colleague's idea to "setting the fox to guard the henhouse,"[61] because she and Heiner immediately fell in love with each other.[62] In a November 1933 Diary entry Marianne expressly hoped "from the bottom of my heart and with my entire soul that Lotti will be happy in this relationship."[63] Soon after meeting Lotti, Heiner had to give up his university studies in order to take over the hops business of his recently deceased father. However, shortly thereafter Jews were excluded from the hops trade. Heiner, as the only son in his family, felt he should take care of his mother and two sisters. Once the family business was gone, he was unable to think beyond his family responsibilities and thus could not commit to a future with Lotti. Lotti described what she thought was going on in his mind: "My future lies ahead of me in complete darkness. I feel chains around my feet dragging me down. I have to be conscientious and cannot take you along into this dark, uncertain future."[64] Heiner's letters to Lotti prior to her departure for Palestine were full of "romantic *Weltangst*."[65] With a heavy heart Lotti ultimately interpreted Heiner's reluctance to commit to her to mean that he did not love her as much as she loved him.[66] Their relationship lasted less than a year. It ended when Lotti moved to work in Cologne and Heiner tried to start up a new business with which he could support his family. When this business then quickly failed, he focused on preparing himself for his own emigration and that of his family.[67]

Disappointed and heart-broken, Lotti tried to move on. She entered into a series of serious but short-lived relationships. As complex as matters of the heart are under normal circumstances, finding a life partner was further complicated for 26-year-old Lotti by the fact that was also trying to find a way out of Germany. Her sister, Marianne, was optimistic, given Lotti's many "love affairs," that she would find the right partner.[68] Yet Marianne was quite worried that Lotti's constant search for a steady relationship would deprive her of inner peace. In early 1934, quite soon after the break-up with Heiner, Lotti briefly considered marriage to a Karl Levetz of Essen. He was planning to accept a director's position at a large company in France, not far from the Swiss border. Lotti confided in Marianne that Karl wanted to pay for Lotti's French lessons. Lotti adamantly declined Karl's offer to pay and, independent and proud, began learning French on her own since "he [Karl] mentioned that he might need me there [in France] soon." While hoping that Karl might be "the one," Lotti was also torn and tried to protect herself:

> *If everything works out, he [Karl] will leave Germany*
> *already in fourteen days. I am very sorry about that*
> *because I wish we had had more time to get to know each*
> *other. You know, after all I have been through I have*
> *become terribly pessimistic. I am always afraid he might*

*disappoint me. I also know that there is much I would
need to get used to and to which I would need to adapt.
But I also know that he is essentially a wonderful and
honest person.*[69]

Lotti's fantasy of emigrating to France with Karl remained just that. Marianne expressed her relief in March 1934 that Lotti's relationship with Karl had "thankfully" ended.[70]

A few months after Lotti and Karl went their separate ways and quite soon after the relationship with Heiner had ended, Lotti became engaged to the dentist Albert Sulke, for whom she worked in Hanover.[71] Lotti became taken with Albert while she assisted him and saw him work for and tend to his patients. She valued in particular Albert's "incredible sincerity, care and love for his patients and for his profession."[72] Even though Lotti hoped very much that this relationship with a highly respected fellow dentist would succeed, she was also afraid of yet another disappointment. Lotti, ever the romantic, dreamed about a potential double wedding, with her sister marrying Edgar Meyer, whom their mother let it be known she would embrace as a potential son-in-law.[73] As Lotti wrote to Nanna: "Wouldn't it be incredibly wonderful if our mother had both her daughters marrying at the same time?" Lotti's relationship with Albert, however, also ended abruptly. Albert was, in contrast to Lotti, a "deeply religious person." Lotti suspected Albert was distraught over the possibility that he might have caused Lotti and Heiner's breakup, after realizing she and Heiner had still been involved when Lotti arrived to work with Albert in autumn 1933. She wrote: "Albert reproached himself for having destroyed our relationship. Given his feelings of guilt, he could not believe that he would ever be able to live happily with me."[74]

Marianne reflected in the summer of 1934 on Lotti's dilemma: "I am very worried about her and her relationship with Albert Sulke. It would not be a great misfortune if she did not marry him. I was quite surprised when I met him to learn that he was the man of her choice. Things are very complicated for her right now – her former relationship with Heiner Frohmann, and her present one with Sulke. If I only knew what I could do for her!"[75]

Meanwhile Marianne herself was thrilled to be a student again, despite having to adjust to living in Nazi Germany. An ecstatic Marianne described her joy over learning medicine while working in a pediatric clinic and living in student quarters again: "Dear God, the things I dreamed about in my darkest hours in England are now reality. In peace I can learn about medicine. I can sit with friends undisturbed in my room – work, sit and feel good. I thank you, dear God." Yet she realized the comfort that she found while sheltered as a student again, "undisturbed in [her] room" and away from the reality of the outside world, had very real limits:

> *Naturally the restrictions on happiness are apparent.*
> *Suddenly out in public I am hit with the feeling: Here you*
> *are considered a Jew, but it doesn't humiliate me, because*
> *I hold my head high. Why am I doing all this? I want to*
> *try to complete my state and doctoral exams. Seriously*
> *I don't want to have to think any further than that.*[76]

Yet she had been forced to think beyond that when, not long after her return from England, Marianne and a group of Gentile friends on their way back from Berlin were stopped by police and asked if there were any Jews in the car. Although Marianne's Jewishness was kept secret, the experience of denying her identity and recognizing her friends' worry apparently scarred her.[77]

Marianne was never able to focus just on the present. She did not want to leave her family, but she knew she could not stay in Germany and had no ideal destination in mind where she might feel at home and be fulfilled professionally. At this point she once again revived the possibility of returning to Britain to study, having now received a promise of a scholarship for two years from the International Student Service. In addition she prepared for her trip to Tours to see Edgar, the first time in close to a year. She knew that this visit would determine how she "would respond to his serious intentions."[78]

Marianne's visit with Edgar in France provoked her into analyzing her emotions and instincts about what would really be best for her.[79] Once back in Düsseldorf she turned to her Notebook "to find some clarity about [her] feelings." She not only debated whether this was *the* relationship for her, but also recounted all she had absorbed in France about Zionism and xenophobia and anti-Semitism. While she was in Tours, Edgar's director, who was also a German Jew and a resident alien, had been fired and expelled from France. As Marianne expressed it: "For Edgar that was a slap in the face. The veil was lifted and the fate of immigrants – perhaps his own fate – was revealed." Edgar saw the rug being pulled out from under this man whom he so "admired and whose position he dreamed of having." Experiencing Edgar's distress over the fate of his boss, and impressed by their visit to a *kibbutz* in France, Marianne contemplated whether Eretz Israel was the way to avoid such a fate for young Jews like themselves. She ruminated:

> *Edgar said to himself this can happen to you at a moment's notice ... and the only possibility for a homeland, the homeland, he sees – and so do I – in Palestine. The thoughts about Palestine have been intensified by our visit to a* kibbutz *8 km away from Tours ... In the sun and fresh air boys and girls are preparing themselves for "Eretz."*[80]

Edgar's sister Ruth, whom Marianne met in 1932 when both she and Edgar lived in Würzburg, worked in the *kibbutz* they had visited outside Tours and had been transformed by the experience.[81] No longer a "silly, immature girl," Ruth was now someone "diligent and helpful and full of idealism and very intent on learning, even more so than Edgar." Marianne described her own epiphany in the midst of seeing Ruth in the setting of the *kibbutz*: "There are sanitation and dirt problems in the *kibbutz*, overcrowding... At first I was repelled by it all, but then I saw my task as a woman and a physician. O God, my mission is now clear. I want to finish my studies and then ... join a *kibbutz*, go to Eretz and there work as a woman and doctor." Noting that she had imagined something like this before, Marianne revealed how the experience of caring for young patients she had seen in the *kibbutz* had brought out her "maternal feelings." She expressed her doubts about traditional ideals of domestic tranquility and materialism and was convinced that "happiness is not collecting silver spoons in the sideboard ... [but rather] living joyfully with the awareness of creating something, an idea, with and for people one loves ... I see this with my own eyes and know that it is my true mission."[82] Prior to 1936, by which year entrance requirements to the British mandate of Palestine had been tightened, more German-Jewish physicians fled Germany to go to Palestine than to any other country, so in 1934 it was not unrealistic for Marianne to imagine working there as a physician on a *kibbutz*.[83]

Knowing that Edgar was waiting on her decision about joining him in France, Marianne admitted to herself that she had recognized in Edgar a visceral intolerance and "blind fanatic hatred" which repelled her. "He is so immature and foolish ... This hatred is directed not only against people who have acted against him but rather more or less against everything." Marianne criticized Edgar's self-centeredness and "his lack of idealism ... [noting] that he could never sacrifice his own will for the will of the community." Drawn to the communal and anti-materialistic Zionist ideals she encountered during her brief visit to the *kibbutz* in France, Marianne contrasted Edgar with her beloved brother Kurt.[84] Kurt was serving the Jewish community in Germany, at apparently some considerable risk; he was detained and interrogated by the police for several days in 1934.[85] Marianne, upon reflection on their reunion and their incompatibility, decided to end the relationship with Edgar.[86]

After her visit to France Marianne was confronted with the reality that her mother and Tante Henny almost had to shut down their store, the Geschwister Kaufmann, when their lack of sales forced them to suspend their payments to their creditors.[87] Marianne helped out in the store during her semester break and, along with her brother Kurt, helped get the business, at least temporarily, back on its feet. In the midst of these worries Marianne briefly lost interest in her studies, not knowing how, without the prospect of help from home, she would be able to finance her studies the next semester, and troubled by stories of increasing violence against Jews, physicians in particular.[88]

A financially strapped Marianne was able to move in with a couple, the Calmsohns, and in return help care for their two young children, in Düsseldorf. She gave Frau Assy Calmsohn credit for pulling her "out of [her] resigned state" and giving her "the impetus to do something." Marianne applied for financial aid to the Reich Representation of German Jews (Reichsvertretung), an organization representing all German Jews that had just been formed in the fall of 1933. To her surprise she received in February 1935 a subsidy of 75 RM per semester from a total of 150 RM – as she put it, "not a lot, but something."[89] This subsidy and the free room and board at the Calmsohns kept her afloat for yet another semester.

Marianne's determination to become a physician was complicated by her desire to remain close to her family: her "parents," her beloved brother and Lotti, whom she considered her "best friend."

Figure 4.2 Lotti, Henny, Selma, Hans on family property across the street from store, Altenessen, summer 1935

Yet when Lotti decided to marry Hans Kaiser-Blüth, a Zionist from a prosperous Jewish family in Cologne, Marianne realized the separation of her family, however temporary, was inevitable. (See Figure 4.2.) Marianne wrote: "I am relieved and happy that these two good people are away from here – and especially that they are in Palestine." Although she had not mentioned Palestine in her Notebook for over a year, she now declared that she wanted to do everything possible to avoid any long-term fragmentation of her family and "to achieve that all of us are eventually there."[90] Yet Marianne felt that "things are so complicated now" and wondered about her own future: "if I just knew what I could do."[91]

After her sister's March 1935 wedding and mid-summer emigration, Marianne became acutely aware of her lack of a soulmate. In August 1935 she confessed in her Notebook that she was still "in search of him even more strongly and intensely the older I get." Yet she consoled herself: "I have my work and my God whom I love, and I feel my work makes me a better person and my future husband will therefore have a better spouse."[92]

Increasingly Marianne's social circle was limited to a small group of Jewish friends and her family, with the exception of Lotti's former classmate, a friend of the entire family, Herta Poth.[93] This is easily understood in the context of the progression of Nazi disenfranchisement of Jews and the increasing social ostracism practiced by more and more Gentile Germans. Especially in the wake of the September 1935 announcement of the Nuremberg Laws Jews were bound to draw together into a more closely knit Jewish world within an increasingly hostile Nazi Germany. Marianne reacted to the Nuremberg Laws with this challenge in her Notebook: "The new laws (differentiating between Aryans as Reich citizens and Jews as only state nationals, ban on mixed marriages, the domestic servant law) should make the path we need to take much clearer: to be proud Jews."[94]

Her study of medicine was what brought Marianne inner peace. She wrote in the summer of 1935 that she was completely "satisfied with the tranquil work of studying medicine." Together with Ursula Zade, a colleague from her exam study group of four, all of whom were Jewish, Marianne studied in her room in the safe space of the Calmsohns' house in Düsseldorf from 9am to 7pm daily during the week in preparation for their upcoming state exams (*Staatsexamen*). This sheltered, "tranquil" existence allowed Marianne to avoid public situations where she might experience shunning or discrimination.[95] (See Figure 4.3.)

Marianne was not oblivious to the politics in the world around her. On 4 October 1935 she reported in her Notebook that "war between Italy and Abyssinia [Ethiopia] had actually broken out despite England's efforts and Abyssinia's willingness to compromise." Referring to Mussolini's efforts to incite Italians to war with a call to avenge the late nineteenth-century defeat of Italy by Abyssinia, Marianne issued a plea: "Poor world, you aren't going to be able to have peace despite the League of Nations, despite culture, despite your humans becoming older [but not wiser]." She continued: "And yet we want to hope, believe and behave as if we could [have peace]. And there is [a] God and eternal justice; of this belief no one can rob me." On this page of her Notebook she attached a copy of a Yom Kippur prayer, a plea for keeping up one's strength through faith and learning how to achieve peace.[96]

In early October Marianne's study group added a new German-Jewish member by the name of Mühlfelder, who had just returned from completing his doctorate in Basel. Like other Jewish medical students at the time, Mühlfelder was not allowed to get a doctorate

Figure 4.3 Marianne and Ursula Zade studying for anatomy exams, Düsseldorf, summer 1935

in Germany, so he had gone to Switzerland and now was returning to Germany to take his German state exams, which Jews could still do. He then planned to go to India to practice medicine.[97] Marianne's decision soon thereafter to go to Switzerland to complete her own doctoral studies stemmed perhaps from meeting Mühlfelder in the fall of 1935 in Düsseldorf. Within a few months she received a stipend to pursue her doctoral studies in Bern from the same International Student Service that had offered her a scholarship to study in Britain.[98]

On 15 December 1935, five days after passing her German state exams, Marianne left for Bern to get her doctorate. As an avid skier, Marianne was thrilled to be in Bern in the winter, yet she also missed being with her family.[99] On New Year's Eve she found letters from her family waiting for her in her hotel: "I cried tears of happiness over the unending love that my mother spoke of in her letters, this wonderful, smart and self-sacrificing woman." Marianne was pleased that in Palestine her brother-in-law Hans had concluded his first big business deal and that Lotti too was optimistic. She was relieved to learn the Christmas season had been very good for the family business: "If only we can manage to make it happen that our Mother, who has always worked so hard, can have an easy, happy sunset to her life! Good God, this I beg of you from my whole heart, with my whole soul and with all my means. My Mother, you still have to work so hard!"[100] Marianne was worried about her Tante Henny, who had been diagnosed with uterine cancer, and about the physical and psychological burdens her mother was now shouldering at home and in the store.[101] In the spring of 1936, after attending a lecture on the meaning of free will, Marianne questioned whether "the will is stronger than the intellect" or whether "one's character is stronger than the intellect," ultimately concluding that "ethics are the most valuable ... and see us best through life."[102] This belief in ethics would help see her through many difficulties yet to come.

Although Marianne enjoyed her time in Switzerland, she never felt at home. Besides an especially close friendship with a Swiss non-Jewish woman, Urs von Greyerz, she socialized with a number of German Jews, transients like herself, who were also pursuing their doctorates in Bern. Marianne officially spent two semesters at the university, passing her oral medical exams in early 1936, which qualified her, on paper at least, to practice medicine. She then chose to write her dissertation in psychiatry on suicide in Bern from 1929 to 1935, a topic apparently suggested to her by her doctoral advisor.[103]

In early 1936 she received news from the International Student Service that as soon as she began to earn an income she would need to repay its scholarship. The International Student Service staff in London only realized once Marianne was in Bern that her doctoral work was ineligible for its scholarship, which had been earmarked for undergraduate studies. Marianne explained to the staff in London that, after finishing in Bern, the next stage of her medical training would be a year-long unpaid internship at the Jewish hospital in Cologne. As it turned out, the Relief Work Office of the International Student Service had its own financial difficulties, and after aiding so many German student refugees like Marianne it had to shut down in mid 1937, long before Marianne earned a regular income and thus before she had to repay the funds.[104]

Marianne returned home in late March 1936 to visit Tante Henny in hospital. Just as this youngest Steinberg child had prayed that she might be able to help her mother to have an easier old age, Marianne now prayed not only for the return of Tante Henny's health but also that her siblings and she might be able to repay her in some way for all her devotion to and sacrifices for them: "Our Tante Henny! Our beloved, good, capable, courageous aunt! Dear God, it can't be and it can't be, allowed to be, that we are not able to return a portion of that to her that she has given to us."[105]

In the spring of 1936 Marianne entered into a relationship with a German Jew by the name of Fritz Beildeck, with whom she got involved while back in Essen to visit her sick Tante Henny. As wonderful as their time together that spring was, Marianne accepted that they were limited by Fritz's impending emigration to South America. She was not fazed by the fleeting nature of this relationship, perhaps bowing on some level to her increasing powerlessness over the fate of those she loved. Once Marianne had returned to Bern in the late spring and Fritz had left for Brazil, she seemed to draw strength from focusing on the good memories she had of their times together. Fritz wrote her several times as he packed up to leave Germany, sharing with her his trepidations about what lay before him and wishing he could simply be just a vagabond and traverse continents at will.[106] She told herself: "We'll never see each other again, I suspect … Maybe you'll come to me in a dream."[107] Fritz wrote her a year after his arrival in Brazil, but the tone and contents of the letter betrayed that this first year in a foreign culture had not been an easy one. He warned Marianne, who he presumed would one day face something similar, that the first year was filled with learning the language and becoming acquainted and accustomed to life. As he put it: "perhaps in the second year one would be able to become human again."[108]

It was apparently at this point that Marianne once again considered emigrating to Palestine. After waiting more than two years, she followed up on Goodman's WIZO offer of 1 March 1934 to help Marianne if she needed it in the future. In her June 1936 letter Goodman regretted that they could do nothing for Marianne at the moment: "We are overfilled with desire for certificates [of immigration to Palestine] – from our [Zionist] Federations in Central and Eastern Europe, which we cannot meet. Two years have made this whole question more poignant than before." Goodman did encourage Marianne to contact Dr. Lauterbach, her former employer, who now was living in Palestine.[109] Unfortunately, on 1 December 1935 a new law dampened Marianne's enthusiasm for Palestine: it made Palestinian citizenship a precondition for trained physicians to practice medicine there.[110]

Marianne soon found herself once again preoccupied with her family's financial situation in Germany, their "Going out of Business Sale" and a move out of their flat. In late December 1936 Marianne nostalgically described her mother and Tante Henny's move from the Altenessen flat, the place one floor up from the family store where her siblings and she had all been born. After assisting her "parents" with their move, Marianne herself relocated to Cologne to wait, several months, to work full time as an intern at the Jewish hospital in Cologne, the Israelitisches Asyl. Because the only place Jews could work as interns in Germany was in Jewish hospitals, there were many other young Jews waiting to work as interns and, relative to their numbers, few Jewish hospitals. In the interim Marianne worked on her dissertation and lived with Lotti's in-laws, Julius and Flora Kaiser-Blüth, in Cologne. Flora and Julius Kaiser-Blüth by then had become very much part of the Kaufmann–Steinbergs' extended family. Marianne was convinced that Flora, whom she called Tante Flora, truly liked her, and in many ways the Kaiser-Blüths regarded her as the daughter they never had.[111] Julius's half-brother and business partner, Karl Kaiser-Blüth, was a long-term member of the Jewish hospital's board of directors.[112] This family connection may have shortened Marianne's wait to work as an intern in the Asyl.

Already in February 1937 Marianne was able to work half-days in the Asyl, which allowed her to continue writing her dissertation. She was very pleased to have Ursula Zade, her old study group colleague from her days in Düsseldorf, there at the Asyl with her.[113] "Reliable, responsible" Ursula, who had already been at the Asyl apparently ever since passing her state exams, and whose physician father was on the staff there, reassured and supported Marianne through the transition.[114]

Her February 1937 Notebook entry, the first after Marianne started part-time training in the Asyl, included the earliest mention of "my 'Arnöldle' or the 'Oe' as I call him in my thoughts." Arnold Oesterreicher, a German-Jewish civil engineer she met in Cologne, who had completed his studies in Berlin the previous year, would from then on play a very significant role in Marianne's life. Meeting Arnold, however, was eclipsed in significance by her training to become an intern "in a real hospital." Marianne was ecstatic: "Dear God, thank you that I can finally earn my own living. Two big things have come to fruition: 1 – I work in medicine. 2 – I can provide financially for my own necessities." Starting full time on 1 April 1937 she was given responsibility for overseeing patients in wards and private rooms during the late shift while the staff internist was off duty. This made Marianne feel both powerful and yet humbled by the responsibility.[115] Throughout most of the following year Marianne's Notebook focused either on details of the actual medical cases and patients she was treating, including the great joy she experienced when she first saved a patient's life, or on her relationship with Arnold.[116] The combination of these two developments in her life, putting into practice the medicine she had studied and falling in love with Arnold, colored not only this last year she would spend in Germany but also her decision-making about her future.

As evidenced by Arnold's daily phone calls and regular visits in the spring of 1937 and their Easter break holidays together in Belgium, their relationship developed quickly. (See Figure 4.4.) Marianne quipped in mid May: "Love is good and makes for happiness."[117] Entering into a serious relationship in 1937, when both the medical and engineering professions already were closed in Germany to Jews, carried with it real emotional risks for young people determined to work in their professions. Few doors were open to German Jews for immigration. The odds were against an unmarried professional couple working out their relationship while each tried to find a place to emigrate to where career prospects were advantageous.

Marianne and Arnold's relationship was far too young in the summer of 1937 for either of them to consider a firm commitment to the other, especially in the context of Nazi Germany. Yet when Arnold spoke of his plans to resign from his job in Cologne on 1 October so that he could leave for the United States soon thereafter, Marianne was devastated. She did not want to imagine that "his departure would really mean a permanent separation." She suspected that he probably loved her and then confessed to herself: "I love him very much, I now know that."[118] Three weeks later Marianne was busily trying to convince herself, as she had done with her relationship with Fritz the previous spring, that the outside world could be closed out and that it was possible to have "no past with its regrets or future with its expectations."[119] This time she was much less successful in living simply for the moment.

On the first evening of Rosh Hashanah 1937, after Marianne had dined with her Asyl colleague Trude Löwenstein and was alone

Figure 4.4 Marianne and Arnold in Ghent, Belgium, spring 1937

in her room in the Asyl, she thought back to her family and previous Rosh Hashanah celebrations in the flat in Altenessen.[120] Marianne dreaded the prospect of being separated on future high holidays from her family, but she also thought about Arnold and confessed that:

> ... *with my thoughts of Arnold I immediately think about the future. Where will I be Rosh Hashana next year? Still here? In Essen? In America? In Palestine? Arnold will be*

*in America. I will certainly not be with him. Would I wish
to be? I certainly wish it, if he wishes it. But I am just too
proud to say that to him. Aren't I?*[121]

In late September 1937 Marianne spent five days at home visiting
with her sister Lotti, who had accompanied their mother back from
Palestine. In Essen all three siblings and their "parents" were reunited
for a short visit. Arnold also dropped by and met the family. Lotti soon
thereafter returned to Palestine.[122] By the time Marianne returned to
Cologne Arnold had just received his visa to the United States.[123] She
found herself "yearning for good, loving words from him, which would
connect his departure with his previous life." But instead Arnold was
now focused on the next stage of his life, and disengaged from and
noncommittal toward her. She speculated that Arnold's womanizing
Onkel Rudi, with whom he had lived in Berlin and whom he visited
often in London and Amsterdam in the months prior to his departure,
had corrupted him. But she admitted she was less disappointed "with
Arnold the individual than with life. I pray to God for work so that I
can find my way back to myself." She committed herself to finishing
her dissertation, "in order to go away in April, at the end of my medical internship – either to Palestine or to America in order to be able
to [financially] support Mother. That is indeed a task!"[124] As upset as
she was by Arnold's upcoming departure and his unwillingness to even
mention a possible future for their relationship, his now concrete plans
for emigration from Germany and immigration to the United States
reminded her that she had to take the initiative in order to move on
with her personal and professional life and secure a land of immigration, wherever this might be possible.

Heartbroken, Marianne could not fathom that Arnold,
whether he did so consciously or not, needed to draw a line between
his past and future. With a US visa in hand, he prepared himself emotionally to leave Germany behind and to strike out on his own in a
new land. He was unsure of what he would do there, how he would
support himself, or how he would manage with the English language.
Having lost his mother to tuberculosis as a pre-schooler and his father
to renal cancer in his late teens, Arnold's only family was a younger
brother, Hellmuth, who was married to a Swiss Gentile woman, and
his mother's younger brother Rudi, who had emigrated to England.[125]
Arnold, whose family had owned a furniture store in Leipzig,[126] had

many more financial resources at his disposal than did Marianne and in 1937 had sufficient transferable wealth to vouch for his own financial security in the United States.[127] Marianne promised herself not to betray the depth of her emotions to Arnold before he left, if just for the sake of her pride and sense of self.[128] This she managed, even when he left Cologne by airplane on 20 December 1937, some two weeks prior to his final departure by ship from England. Afterwards Marianne replayed the events at the airport: from Arnold's firm but business-like grasp of her hand to his cool, almost passing remark "Maybe I'll see you again sometime," and her own response "I don't know." Overwrought after his departure, she turned to God: "Dear God, I don't know what to pray for. Do look out for and protect him and let your countenance illuminate his path! Amen!"[129]

Arnold contacted Marianne again while he was still in Europe, prior to his departure for "Amerika," convincing her to meet him for a special tryst in Belgium. Their brief rendezvous in Lüttich was quite lovely for both of them and became a frequent reference point in their letters during the following months.[130] Just before boarding his ship at Southampton Arnold wrote Marianne that those two days in Lüttich were among his best, "because you were there."[131] Arnold's brother Hellmuth surprised her with a visit only days later, and in her view Hellmuth had treated her almost "like his sister-in-law and seemed to take it for granted that I would be going to America."[132] At this juncture Marianne and Arnold began a frequent correspondence, of which both sides are extant. Her letters to him were friendly and warm, but guarded. In January and February 1938 entries in her Notebook Marianne frequently expressed not only her doubts and confusion about Arnold but also her personal deliberations about where to emigrate to.

Marianne now truly was undecided about whether she should try to go to Palestine or "Amerika."[133] Arnold's unclear intentions and his lack of commitment made it easier for her to consider a future in a country without him. As long as Marianne was undecided and did not state directly that she planned on coming to the United States, Arnold's numerous letters to her in January 1938 were quite affectionate. He even overtly encouraged her to come to the United States, giving her all sorts of unsolicited advice about how to travel there, which ships were best, what to pack, what to bring clothing-wise, what was fashionable, and how to deal with customs officials, all, in her view, as if he were awaiting her arrival.[134] He even went out of his way on his third day in New York to visit relatives, a husband and wife, who were both physicians. In great detail he reported to Marianne what he had learned about immigrants practicing medicine in the United States, namely that Marianne would probably only be able to get an unpaid position in a hospital, because to work as a physician she would first need to take the medical board exams and a language test.[135]

Marianne had heard it was very difficult, especially for a woman, to find a position as a doctor in a hospital in New York.[136] This was actually true across the country. But New York State was more hospitable in some ways. For example, unlike the majority of the other states in the country, New York State did not require US citizenship prior to physicians' even being allowed to take state licensing exams.[137] For admission to the medical licensing exam New York only required foreign physicians to have received their first citizenship application papers, namely proof of an initial Declaration of Intent to become a citizen. Some states required that internships be completed in the state prior to licensing, but not New York. For these reasons, along with the fact that so many refugees settled in New York City, more refugee physicians were licensed there than anywhere else in the United States.[138] Yet even in New York refugee physicians aroused more animosity from their American counterparts than any other professional group.[139] As a result, they often faced discrimination when applying for hospital positions. Private practice became more attractive to refugee physicians, but the training that European, especially German, medical schools provided stressed research and specialization rather than the broad clinical experience expected of most general practitioners in private practice.[140] Fortunately, Marianne's training during her internship at the Asyl in Cologne had been rather broad. Nevertheless, a 1946 survey of refugees found that female physicians had a more difficult time resuming their medical practices than men in the United States, but that more women went into private practice than any other medical position, such as hospitals or clinics.[141] Given that female physicians faced gender discrimination in US hospitals, it is not surprising they turned to private practice.[142] But Marianne had not yet decided that the United States was the best place for her and concluded her 23 January 1938 response to Arnold's report on practicing medicine there with: "If I were to actually go to America ..."[143]

Six days later Marianne shared with Arnold that she had finally decided to go to "Amerika." She had even visited the Jewish self-help agency, the Hilfsverein, which advised German Jews on immigration everywhere except Palestine, to learn how best to go about it.[144] She knew it would not be easy "but was willing to face the difficulties." But three days after reaching this decision Lotti had thrown a monkey wrench into Marianne's decisiveness. Lotti wrote her, as she had done before about other possible positions in Palestine, but now very urgently, about a nursing job at Mt. Carmel. Marianne described to Arnold the pressure she felt now from the type of arguments Lotti used to convince her to move to Palestine: "That we sisters should not be separated and that one especially these days has to be willing to make sacrifices to maintain such priceless attachments – whether for the poorer financial circumstances, whether for the worse chances for a position as a physician in Palestine." Conflicted over how best to help her family, Marianne was convinced there was more potential to earn and save money in the United States than in Palestine.[145]

Marianne spelled out to Arnold, and to herself, in this 29 January 1938 letter the pros and cons of a move to Palestine, even a temporary one so that "later one could see what else develops." She then shared with Arnold her turmoil and entrusted him with her innermost thoughts in a way that she had typically up until then reserved for the private thoughts she committed to her Notebook.[146] She told him how "very depressed" she had been since reading Lotti's letter:

> *I know that everything Lotti says is right and in principle I think the same way. That doesn't change the fact that the economic chances are better for me in America, especially for my future as a physician. What should I do? ...*
>
> *I'm so confused. I'm being pulled every which way. Arnold, how would you advise me? I know that one has to make such decisions oneself, someone else can't really help the other person much. But you are now in America and have gained a certain perspective on the country. And you know me. Lotti tells me I am right for Palestine. Do you believe that I am "right" for America? I would so like to hear your advice. Please write soon.[147]*

Arnold in the meantime had found his situation in the United States less rosy than he had imagined. He wrote Marianne two days before she sought his advice, and more than a week before he actually received her 29 January letter, that he had sadly come to the conclusion that he would not be able to work in his field. In the job market of a still Depression-era United States Arnold saw no other choice than going back to school for two years in State College, Pennsylvania. This, however, Arnold did not consider so bad, because in State College he had a very close non-Jewish friend from Berlin, Hendrik Andresen, with whom he could live and share expenses.[148] In these January 1938 letters Marianne thought Arnold had been encouraging her to come to the United States, even possibly to State College. In her Notebook she recounted the telegram, letter and present he had sent for her twenty-seventh birthday on 2 February 1938. As Marianne remarked in her Notebook, "anyone would think we were getting married; his own brother takes this for granted."[149] Yet as soon as Marianne directly asked Arnold his advice about whether he thought the United States was best for her or whether she should go to Palestine, as her sister advocated, Arnold became once again very businesslike and distant. He told her directly that she should not be looking to him for any advice about America, "because I don't know how I could in any way be helpful to you [there] in the coming years." Addressing and closing this 10 February letter with simply "Dear Marianne" and "very cordially" was in direct contrast to the much more romantic and intimate variety of kisses and terms of affection delineated in his letters of the previous six weeks since their tryst in Lüttich.[150] Marianne was livid and very hurt, describing his letter in her Notebook as "a real cold shower." She wrote:

> I knew he didn't want to marry me. But then all the things I listed before [presents, money, Lüttich, telegram, flurry of letters]. I convinced myself, when I'm honest, that he'll notice when we're separated and with the distance the significance of his relationship with me. This letter gives the message more strongly than everything else – it is final.
>
> Dear God, give me the strength to give up Arnold once and for all to forget him. Well, I could forget him more quickly if I lived differently …[151]

Marianne and Arnold were not destined to forget each other. But indeed Marianne's life in Germany in early 1938 was tentative at best. Although she was living and working in the relatively sheltered environment of the Cologne Jewish hospital, the Israelitisches Asyl, she was constantly aware of the steady flow of medical personnel emigrating while other, especially older, unemployed Jewish physicians, medical students and nurses anxious to find some place they could work replaced them.[152] Her free time was spent, now that Arnold was not there to distract her, writing her dissertation and figuring out where she should best emigrate to and how to arrange it. Her one-year position with the Asyl would end on 1 April 1938, so she really had very little time before she would need a place to live and to earn some income. Even though she did not yet have specific departure plans, it was clear to her and her family that her leaving was imminent. The sense of this impending loss of family must have weighed on her greatly and have contributed to Marianne's desire for a close and secure relationship with Arnold.

Arnold's message to her of 10 February 1938 not to count on him for help in the United States came when she had already, with the strong urging of her family in Essen, made up her mind that going there was the best choice for her and for the future of her family. On 29 January 1938, just over a week after receiving Lotti's plea that she immigrate to Palestine, Marianne received an affidavit of support for immigration to the United States from Flora's cousin, Arthur Stern. The brother-in-law of Siegfried Schweizer, Moritz's brother, offered her a back-up affidavit as well.[153] Still conflicted and not sure what was best for her family as a whole, Marianne had waited to submit Mr. Stern's affidavit to the US consulate in Stuttgart. But then her discussion in Essen on 5 February 1938 with her mother, Tante Henny and Kurt became decisive: "My family is unanimously for America and against Palestine," she wrote Arnold.[154] She felt relieved to have decided on a goal, the United States, and explained to Arnold her decision: "I feel so much better since my family told me that America means the best and right decision for me and for the rest of them. Especially Kurt expects a lot out of my going to America. I fancy he thinks that I'll get him over one day."[155] Being able to share the responsibility for this decision-making with her family in Essen clearly helped Marianne in terms of weighing out both what was best for her and best for them.

Marianne admitted to Arnold that "with tears of sadness and tears of joy with regard to Palestine and Lotti," she would be submitting in the coming week Stern's affidavit to support her application for a US visa.[156] Her "love of Palestine did not suffice to make up for the probable downward social mobility" and the concerns she had about being able financially to create a nice life for her mother and aunt.[157] Selma offered to break the news to Lotti about Marianne's decision, probably to reinforce the idea that this was the family's choice and to ease the pressure on Marianne to have to be the one to tell her. Selma wrote Lotti and Hans "how difficult it was for [Selma] to have to tell them that on the basis of many different considerations they had come to the conclusion to stay with A. [America], for purely practical, material reasons." Selma explained that "there was too large a surplus of people in Marianne's profession there" in Palestine and that it would take years before Marianne could make a living as a doctor and "that she simply could not afford that any more."[158] Indeed, by 1935 Palestine had a ratio of 1 doctor per 174 residents, among the densest in the world at the time. The law that required Palestinian citizenship as of 1 December 1935 as a precondition for practicing medicine in Palestine was a serious roadblock to the immigration of more physicians and would have postponed even further Marianne's ability to practice medicine there.[159]

Five days after Marianne confidently sent her affidavit from her sponsor, Arthur Stern, off to the US consulate in Stuttgart, she was notified that the affidavit did not suffice. Now all was up in the air until some indefinite date when a revised affidavit with more financial details would hopefully be accepted and she would receive a date to appear in Stuttgart.[160] Marianne was dejected.

Then, on 20 February 1938, she received Arnold's "cold shower" letter, which he had written on 10 February. Waiting an unusually long ten days to respond, Marianne let Arnold know, in a reserved and businesslike tone, that she certainly had not expected his help with money matters. She did note that as a friend she thought he might have been otherwise willing to help her.[161] Perhaps Arnold feared her request implied financial help, despite her assurances to the contrary, or perhaps he suspected there was a subtext involving some sort of commitment he was not willing to give. In any event, the relationship did survive: Marianne and Arnold continued to correspond, and eventually the tone warmed back up.

Mr. Stern sent the revised affidavit, and, five weeks after her initial rejection, Marianne received notice of her 20 April 1938 visa interview in Stuttgart. She was thrilled. Following her last day at work in the Asyl, she moved into Kurt's vacated room in Essen to have more space to pack than in the small flat belonging to her "parents."[162] Kurt had just started a new job as general counsel for the Hessian Centralverein in Frankfurt am Main. Marianne had speculated two weeks earlier that their "old folks" might be moving to Frankfurt with him.[163] There is no other evidence that they were considering a move to Frankfurt, but perhaps the prospect of it allowed Marianne more peace of mind as she prepared to leave her "parents" behind.

Marianne mentioned to Arnold all the people she knew in Essen and Cologne who were now getting interviews in Stuttgart and preparing as a result to leave soon for the United States. After enjoying a wonderful farewell celebration with wine, liqueurs, cake and cookies at the Asyl, Marianne scrambled during the following few months to prepare for her departure.[164] She had to complete and formally submit by mail her dissertation to the University of Bern, shop for clothing and surgical instruments to take to the United States, make her farewell visits to relatives and friends, and complete all the bureaucratic and financial processes involved in legally emigrating from Germany, especially as a Jew.[165]

In early April 1938 she wrote Arnold about this "politically very active time," noting the March 1938 German *Anschluss* of Austria with the Reich and the referendum in Austria that followed. She relayed the news that Jewish communities across the Reich, which as of 28 March 1938 no longer had legal status as public institutions, were losing their financing through local taxes as well as their special tax exemption: "For the Jewish communities this is a harsh blow."[166]

She also described to Arnold an Indian merchant, a Mr. H. C. Bhatia, whom she had just met in Ohligs, where she had traveled to buy medical instruments.[167] Mr. Bhatia had strongly encouraged her "instead of America to go to Bombay," because of the shortage of "lady doctors" in Bombay and Indian women's cultural reticence to visit male doctors. He assured Marianne that she would have a good practice in Bombay. He even offered to take her in as his guest until she found her own place to live. Hesitating initially to take Bhatia very seriously, Marianne decided she should investigate this opportunity in India as a fall-back plan in case "things don't go well in the U.S."[168]

Between April and June 1938, from his various business locations across Western Europe, Bhatia wrote Marianne a dozen letters to try to convince her to come to India. Marianne did inquire about the prospects for a medical practice in Bombay, contacting two German physicians who lived and practiced there, asking them their impressions of Mr. Bhatia's offer.[169] She also had her friend from Essen, Herta Poth, who, unlike Marianne, still had her German citizenship, contact the German embassy in Bombay to get the embassy's impressions as well. Ever since the Nuremberg Laws of 1935 Marianne was no longer a German citizen but merely a national. Whether she would have gotten a response from the German consulate had she herself inquired is unclear. Herta indicated that she was asking the advice of the embassy officials on behalf of an unnamed friend.[170] All the responses made clear that Mr. Bhatia's motives were unclear at best and unseemly at worst.[171] A small number of German-Jewish physicians did flee the Third Reich to settle in India and practice medicine there, although it is doubtful that many women, especially single women, did.[172]

Marianne joked to Arnold about whether Mr. Bhatia "was a fairytale come true or a sex slave trader."[173] In any event she did not go to India, but the time and effort she spent investigating this option confirm that she was trying to cover all bases in case she did not get to the United States or the situation there did not work out for her to practice medicine as she hoped.

Less than a week before her interview in Stuttgart Marianne panicked over not having all the necessary police reports about her behavior and finances from all the places she had lived in Germany.[174] She could not book her passage until she knew for sure that she would receive her visa. On 19 April Marianne took the train to Stuttgart and managed to arrange to stay overnight in a hotel right by the station.[175] Marianne wrote Arnold on 20 April that she "loved what [she] had seen of Stuttgart the previous afternoon, yet regretted the reason that brought [her] to the city for the first and indeed also the last time." The day of her interview, ironically enough Hitler's birthday, and complete with cold weather and hail, Marianne received her visa and triumphantly wrote Arnold of her success as she waited for the return train.[176]

Her sister Lotti wanted her to travel first to Palestine and then on to New York. But Marianne soon realized she would not be able to pay for the two ship passages in Reichsmarks.[177] Given the tight currency controls in Nazi Germany, she could not take out or send the Reichsmarks she would need to pay for an additional fare from Palestine, even if she had the financial resources. Ultimately she paid a German travel agency for her fare in Reichsmarks for the departure on 23 June from Rotterdam to New York. She thus avoided currency restrictions, but was unable to arrange a visit to see Lotti. Marianne also had to pay various emigration fees and, with the help of Onkel Hermann, the interest on the half of the scholarship that she had received from the Deutsche Studienstiftung, as a precondition to emigrate from Germany.[178]

As Marianne psychologically prepared herself for her immigration, she remarked on the frequent contacts in State College that Arnold had with Germans, a term they used to refer to both German Jews and non-Jews alike. His Onkel Rudi had even visited him twice already from England. Marianne commented to Arnold on 1 May 1938: "It appears that one doesn't really emigrate any more to the 'new world,' at least not today. One sees and speaks with so many people from 'the old homeland' and thus has a piece of the familiar and customary over there." Marianne proceeded to report on upcoming marriages of friends prior to their planned departures to the United States and the arrival of affidavits of friends of theirs and colleagues of hers from the Asyl.[179] All of these pending departures by acquaintances of her generation to the United States, together with the sense that there one easily could meet other Germans, and might even have family members come to visit, helped Marianne to orient herself toward her prospective life on the other side of the Atlantic.

Marianne found little time during her last six weeks in Germany to write letters. When she did, she expressed a certain nostalgia mixed with trepidation for Germany. She remarked that the beauty of spring in mid-May Cologne "was not infrequently destroyed for us by the steadily worsening situation." Her handwriting, normally exceptionally neat, now was uncharacteristically filled with numerous words scratched through, perhaps reflective of her growing anxiety about conditions in the Germany in which she would be leaving loved ones behind. The brevity of her remarks and her striking-out of some words suggest she was indeed wary of writing anything that might provoke censors and endanger her departure. She struggled through the process of getting permissions from currency control offices to have some money while on board ship and perhaps even have some left over to help her upon her arrival. She also tried to arrange visiting her friend Doris Meakin or even Arnold's Onkel Rudi in England, but due to difficulties surrounding her passport she could not leave Germany soon enough to fit in such visits prior to her 23 June ship departure.[180] At Marianne's request, Arnold wrote Lotti in order to arrange to have Marianne's money, which Lotti had in safekeeping, sent to the United States. Those refugees who left Germany after 1937, including Marianne, were legally allowed to take only 10 RM ($4) out of the country with them and therefore arrived in the United States virtually destitute.[181] Arnold told Lotti that although he realized that the situation in Palestine was not easy, it was not rosy the United States either: he had no job, had had to resort to being a student again and had taken a graduate assistantship.[182] Lotti probably did not find this news particularly reassuring, especially since her younger sister was emigrating to the United States rather than Palestine for financial reasons, and for the sake of her own future and that of her family left behind in Germany. Lotti sent the money, $250, not to Arnold but directly to a bank in New York, so that it was waiting for Marianne upon her arrival.[183]

Marianne busily tied up the last loose ends in her life in Germany in June as she embarked on this, the most dramatic journey of her life. She made her final farewell rounds to relatives, first to her aunt and cousin in Kassel, then to other relatives in Hanover and finally back to Essen before her final departure to Rotterdam. (See Figure 4.5.) Just as she was embarking on this last trip within Germany she got word from her mentors in Bern that she was now officially a Dr. med. She also received her first job offer, from a gynecologist in Bombay to join his practice. This news must have buoyed her sense of professional identity and worth as she set out for the uncertainties of life in the United States. She closed her last letter to Arnold from Germany excitedly with "Until I write again from America."[184]

After not having written in her Notebook for four months, Marianne wrote one last entry from Germany. In between the pages she placed a leaf which she identified as "from the grave of my dear Father." After a remark about this being her last day in Essen she wrote a prayer: "Dear God, watch over and protect my [loved ones] and let your countenance show them the way! And along with them the whole society! Amen."[185] She did not mention that as she was about to close up her last suitcases under the watchful eye of the Essen police officer

Figure 4.5 Marianne's farewell in Essen (from left): Marianne, Selma, Kurt, June 1938

assigned to ascertain that she did not pack any contraband valuables, the officer politely excused himself to have coffee in the other room with her mother, Frau Steinberg, intentionally allowing Marianne time to slip into her suitcase whatever she could.[186]

Moritz Schweizer, Marianne's older second cousin, accompanied her to Rotterdam. As the general counsel for the Essen synagogue community he was allowed to travel freely across the German border and was happy to escort Marianne. Marianne found letters from her mother, Tante Henny, her brother and her sister all waiting for her on the ship when it departed on 23 June. Her mother, perhaps understanding Nanna better than anyone else, wished her "a wonderful, free life with fulfilling work in your profession."[187] She arrived in New York safely and was greeted by Moritz's brother Siegfried, with whom she initially stayed. Yet despite this welcome and Arnold's surprising her with a visit on her first weekend in the country, Marianne found herself constantly worrying, mostly about money and about getting the rest of her family out of Germany.[188] (See Figure 4.6.) The $250 her sister sent was waiting for her in New York.[189] These funds had to tide her over and pay for multiple expenses until she could begin to earn an income. She needed to pay for her day-to-day living expenses, but also

Figure 4.6 Marianne's first weekend in the United States (from right): Marianne, Arnold, unidentified person, Poconos, July 1938

for the exams she was required to take to get licensed as a physician in the United States. In addition she had unexpected customs fees. She had apparently written on the customs form that the family linens she was bringing were not new, but she had also told the officials that they had not been used. Both answers were correct, but appeared contradictory to the US customs officials. The linens had been folded neatly for years, in some cases as gifts handed down from her grandparents many decades before, as part of an intended dowry. The customs officials charged her an import fee of $124 for her presumed attempt to smuggle in new linens without paying any import tax. Initially she was fined $350 for providing false information, which she appealed. But in the interim all the trunks she had shipped were confiscated, and half the money she had counted on lasting until she took her exams in January was committed to an import tax on her not new, but not yet used, dowry linens.[190]

Marianne was quite taken with the expanse of the city and state of New York that she experienced during her first summer in the United States. Yet she was distressed by all the initial difficulties she encountered in "this land of opportunities and wonders."[191] Within her first three weeks in New York she moved five times, staying with distant relatives and then acquaintances for a few days each at a time, and then finally renting a room of her own for $3 a week.[192] Due to the customs fiasco she calculated she had only enough money to live on until September. Panicked, she started work within two weeks of her arrival as a companion to a German woman from Kassel for 10 hours a day with only a 15-minute lunch break. Yet she so disliked this woman that she quit after less than a week. Her German-Jewish exam tutor suggested she first focus on getting licensed as a physician by trying to take the exams in September and, if she failed, take them again in January. In the midst of all this financial and professional anxiety Marianne worried about what she could do for her family in Germany.[193]

Marianne's first news from home, which came in a letter her mother wrote her on 30 June 1938, made her worry even more about her loved ones remaining in Germany. Less than a week after her departure, Onkel Hermann had been dismissed from the job he had held for over forty years.[194] Adding to her concerns, Kurt wrote her a few weeks later about numerous other dismissals of family acquaintances from Jewish businesses that were being "Aryanized." Kurt then asked her about what his professional options might be in the United States.[195] Lotti also encouraged Marianne once again to think about settling in Palestine, along with Kurt and their mother, and asked Marianne her advice about how best to help Kurt, in particular, get out of Germany.[196] These developments kept Marianne from celebrating her arrival or appreciating the excitement of a new start in America. Instead, she felt compelled to focus on helping her loved ones, which to her meant trying to save money to facilitate their immigration.

As the ground continued to shift under her family back in Germany and Marianne's own future in the United States continued to be uncertain, she sought clarification of Arnold's intentions.[197] Following her sister's early July advice either to get a commitment from Arnold or to break with him completely,[198] Marianne asked Arnold to come up from State College to New York City to discuss their relationship in mid August.[199] His visit reassured Marianne, although they could not even plan future visits, given her need to work and never knowing how long a job might last. Marianne also felt a little better about the status of her family once she learned in late July that her mother had been able to sell the family property in Altenessen.[200] Marianne knew its sale would make her mother and aunt less dependent on Kurt's salary, which in turn would mean that Kurt could feel freed up to focus on himself and, she hoped, "immediately leave Germany."[201]

Marianne spent August and the first half of September studying for her exams and adjusting to the unaccustomed summer heat of New York City, missing Arnold and wishing she could either be with him or put him out of her head so that she could concentrate.[202] She took her exams on 19 September but felt less than confident that they had gone well; in fact, she would have to repeat only a few of them in January and one in internal medicine in June 1939. The day after her exams she was distraught to learn that the result of her customs appeal was that she would have to pay a total of $254 customs duty and fine in order to get back her belongings. She took a job that same day as a 12-hour-a-day nurse with a salary of $23.50 a week plus food.[203] She had borrowed money from her exam tutor as well as from another acquaintance but felt compelled to repay them as soon as possible.[204]

In the autumn her own immediate debts weighed on her not only because of the restrictions they meant for her day-to-day life-style but also because they meant she was not earning money for her much larger goal, that of helping her family. Marianne recognized the seriousness of the situation for her family and all German Jews in October 1938 after the Munich Conference.[205] She lamented to Arnold: "Mr. Hitler's success. Of course, everybody is happy that there will be no war. But the 'monstrous betrayal' of Chamberlain and Hitler's big triumph are a fact. And there will be no peace in the world, especially for the Jews unless Mr. Hitler is scattered [sic] and smashed by a war. Amen!"[206]

Both Marianne and Arnold became particularly concerned in the early fall of 1938 that their remaining family members get out of Germany. Arnold's brother Hellmuth had just spent the Jewish holidays of Rosh Hashanah with him in State College, and apparently the two brothers were convinced that Hellmuth was now all set to secure an affidavit for himself. Marianne congratulated Arnold on his brother's affidavit, while puzzling over the fact that Hellmuth was now, of all times, returning to Germany. Marianne wrote Arnold in English: "Funny boy, your brother! Going back to Germany at a time like this! But after all, I quite understand him. And finally, he himself must know what he's got to do." She apparently assumed he needed to make arrangements for his Gentile Swiss wife and to wrap up finances in Germany prior to his final emigration. She then announced triumphantly that Mr. Stern, her own sponsor, had offered her "without my asking him! – to make out an affidavit for my brother Kurt."[207]

It was not easy to navigate the contradictory information that one received from different sources about waiting lists and when to send affidavits, etc. In mid October 1938 Marianne visited the New York section of the National Council of Jewish Women. She checked on what she might do to help her brother and was told his registration number should come up to be considered for a visa in six to eight months. In response to her inquiries she was instructed that affidavits were valid for one year and that therefore the one for Kurt could already be submitted. She shared this news with Arnold so that he would make sure his brother's affidavit would also be submitted. Recalling that her own and Arnold's affidavits had been valid for only four months, she was a bit concerned about the accuracy of the information she had been given.[208] When her brother wrote her shortly thereafter that there was a sign in Stuttgart indicating that all registration numbers over 14,000 had a wait of at least two years, she wrote Arnold that they should wait to send the affidavits for their brothers.[209] Yet already at the beginning of November Arnold's brother learned that he would have an interview in February 1939 at the US consulate. Marianne was quite impressed at how quickly this was happening, although it is not clear what special circumstances might have allowed Hellmuth to be eligible for non-quota immigration and thus skip ahead of the long waiting list of quota registrants.[210] When at this juncture Arnold also sought Marianne's advice about how he might help his 45-year-old cousin, Marianne told Arnold she feared it could be years before someone of his cousin's age would get a visa, an impression she might well have also had with regard to her own "old folks" – her mother, Tante Henny and Onkel Hermann.[211]

On 10 November 1938 Marianne got an inkling from the news in New York of what was occurring to Jews in Germany in what became known as Kristallnacht, or the November Pogrom.[212] Responding three days later to the news she had just received from Arnold about his brother Hellmuth's arrest, Marianne wrote: "Your letter [regarding your brother's arrest] did not surprise me. It seems that almost every Jewish man in Germany shares the fate of your brother and mine. Wherever I go, the people received telegrams with similar requests as you and I received ..."[213] Arnold and Marianne now both knew that their brothers had been arrested. They did not know their brothers' fates but feared the worst and tried to think of anything they might do to help.

For Marianne this was especially difficult, as her current job was coming to an end prematurely. She had given up her $3-a-week room to save money while she worked as a live-in nurse and now did not even know where she might be living two days later. Her sense of helplessness about Kurt was compounded by her own day-to-day uncertainty and the recognition that she could not rely on the mail, her only lifeline to Germany, to get news to her in a timely manner. She did not yet even have a forwarding address, and needed urgently to find work and a place to live.[214] Even more desperately she wanted to help her brother. The professional security for herself and safety for her family that Marianne sought in deciding to emigrate to the United States seemed all too elusive in mid November 1938, and would remain so for many years.

5 THE NOVEMBER POGROM (1938) AND ITS CONSEQUENCES FOR KURT AND HIS FAMILY

The events in Germany are so terrible that one is baffled and helpless. I do not think that private individuals like your brother and my "old folks" will get harmed. But I do not know if my brother is still sitting safely in his room.[1]

Marianne's worry about Kurt expressed in this letter of 10 November 1938 was not unfounded. On the night of 9 November and over the following two days about 26,000 Jewish men were arrested all over Germany and detained in concentration camps (KZ). The violence of the November Pogrom (Kristallnacht) foreshadowed what was yet to come: the arrest, deportation, expulsion and subsequent murder of Jews in Europe. Kurt was particularly vulnerable due to his precarious position as an official of the Centralverein and because he had been arrested once before in 1934.

Kurt had passed his second set of state law exams (*Assessorexamen*) in Berlin with honors and returned home to Altenessen in November 1933 to write his doctoral thesis.[2] However, he was, as a Jew, not allowed to work within the judicial system. Anti-Jewish legislation had closed the door on Kurt's being able to enter either private or public practice as an attorney in Nazi Germany. Having worked with the Reich Youth Association of the Centralverein for several years, Kurt did, on 1 March 1934, get a job as deputy legal counsel at the Essen office of the Rhineland-Westphalia State Branch of the Centralverein.[3] His primary responsibilities there included providing counsel in legal and financial matters, as well as taking care of the

Figure 5.1 From right: Kurt, Doris Meakin, Hanna and friends, September 1933

Essen office's correspondence.[4] Kurt earned his doctorate in jurisprudence from the University of Bonn in August 1934, which nevertheless did not make it any easier for him to practice law in Nazi Germany. (See Figure 5.1.)

Only three months after he began work with the Essen Centralverein he and two of his superiors were arrested and placed in "protective custody" for allegedly spreading "atrocity propaganda." The Gestapo suspected that the Centralverein and other Jewish groups in Germany were reporting negatively on the treatment of Jews to the international press and other contacts abroad and encouraging a boycott of German goods.[5] As a result, Centralverein officials all over the country faced intimidation and interrogation.[6] During one of the raids, the Gestapo had gotten hold of a circular sent by the Rhineland-Westphalia Centralverein office in Essen to its local groups on 27 April 1934. The branch chair of the Essen office, Ernst Plaut, responded to members' complaints about hearing more and more anti-Jewish songs, which were sung in an aggressive and provocative manner.[7] The Gestapo alleged that the Centralverein used this circular to discredit the Nazi regime abroad. However, Essen's police president had to admit in a secret report to the Gestapa police bureau in Berlin that the investigation found no evidence of any wrongdoing on the part of the leading members of the Centralverein office in Essen. Therefore, the charge of "atrocity propaganda and pro-boycott campaign" had to be dropped.[8] Kurt and his two superiors, David Krombach and Ernst Plaut, were released after one week from "protective custody" on 13 June 1934.[9] While the Centralverein and its leading members who remained in Germany were under constant surveillance by the Gestapo, they were mostly able to concentrate on their responsibilities as a Jewish self-help organization, that is, until the fateful events of the November Pogrom.

Kurt worked in the Essen office until his promotion to general counsel to the Hesse-Nassau and Hesse State Branch of the Centralverein in Frankfurt am Main on 1 April 1938. His predecessor, Wolfgang Matzdorff, had emigrated with his wife to New Zealand in March 1938, and others around him were also emigrating. Marianne's departure early that summer to the United States must have been very difficult for Kurt. Both his sisters now had left Germany. While on a business trip to Fulda Kurt wrote a brief message to Marianne that he hoped would reach her on the ship in Rotterdam. He himself admitted in his parting words, which included a hopeful "until we meet again," that Marianne's future looked "better than that of us here."[10]

After his transition to the Frankfurt office and having worked for fourteen months without a break, Kurt was able to go on vacation in August.[11] He visited family and friends and made the important decision to register himself for immigration at the US consulate, which he did on 1 September. At that point he was not yet ready to discuss his plans with his family in Essen or his colleagues in Frankfurt and asked his sister Marianne in the United States for utter discretion and silence: "My intentions [to emigrate] are to be kept secret. By no means is anyone here to find out about them."[12] He told his loved ones in Essen some time in September about his registration with the US consulate in Stuttgart. (See Figure 5.2.) Anticipating a long waiting period, he had registered himself just in case he decided to leave, although he could not yet truly envision emigrating from Germany.[13] To leave the older family members behind would have caused him too much emotional anguish and, he feared, would have left those family members too vulnerable.[14] Kurt had financially helped support his mother and aunt from 1934 to 1938, as he put it, "considerably."[15] While waiting for his anticipated US immigration papers, Kurt planned to improve his English and learn shorthand. Kurt imagined that he might need these skills for a position in the private sector.[16]

Figure 5.2 Kurt with Selma and Henny, Essen, June 1938

When Kurt returned to his professional obligations at the
Centralverein in Frankfurt am Main in September 1938[17] he was
surprised to discover that the name of his street had changed from
Mendelssohnstrasse to Joseph-Haydn-Strasse: The Reich Ministry
of the Interior had decreed the replacement of all "Jewish street
names."[18] He also noticed that several colleagues and acquaintances

had managed to find a way to escape an increasingly hostile environment for Jews in Germany: "Many people in my circle who have been 'untouched' until now will soon be gone."[19]

Kurt resumed his responsibilities at the Centralverein while political tensions in Germany increased throughout the fall. On 11 November 1938 Selma learned that he had been arrested that morning in Frankfurt. Not knowing any more details, Selma's first impulse was of course to find ways to get him released. She had found out that prisoners could get released from concentration camps if they demonstrated their willingness to emigrate and their ability to immigrate. In Kurt's case it seemed prudent to pursue his emigration to the United States, since he had already registered himself for immigration at the US consulate.[20] Selma immediately sent a telegram to Marianne begging her for help in accelerating Kurt's immigration. In that telegram Selma tersely pleaded: "Send Kurt's papers [affidavit] immediately."[21] Concerns about censorship prevented her from mentioning Kurt's arrest that very morning. In response to her mother's telegram Marianne drafted a letter without delay to the "Honorable American Consul" in Stuttgart, requesting a visa for Kurt and assuring the US authorities "I would be only too glad to help him [Kurt] in this country in any way and as much as I shall ever be able to."[22] Marianne wrote anxiously to Arnold in State College on 11 November:

> I received a telegram from my mother today requesting
> that I immediately send the papers for Kurt. That probably
> means that he is either in prison or in a concentration
> camp. My sponsor will send his affidavit [for Kurt] on
> Monday. I am hoping with all my heart that it will help
> my brother. In the meantime I do not even know what
> happened to him, if he is still alive.[23]

Several days later Selma sent another telegram in response to Marianne's, which read: "Received telegram. Registration number 19590. Ask for urgent preferential treatment at consulate. Kurt not reachable. Send Stern's address. Mother."[24] Sending a telegram from Germany was expensive and usually limited to important messages and emergencies, of which this was clearly one. Selma's nervousness, confusion and fear are evident between the lines of her letter of 12 November; some of her sentences are unfinished, written hastily with commas instead of periods. The letter reads like a breathless cry for help:

> *I am urging you to see to it, I do not know what is written*
> *in the affidavit, to write [to the US authorities] that*
> *this matter is very urgent and that the sponsor asks for*
> *preferential treatment. The registration number is very*
> *high, but maybe something can be done. Maybe you could*
> *ask at the consulate, no that's probably wrong, at some*
> *other authority if we could take some steps from here in*
> *Stuttgart. But there is probably nothing that can be done.*
> *I do not know what to say about the affidavit, do not*
> *know the sponsor's address. It is probably better if the*
> *sponsor makes the next steps from over there.*[25]

Over the following days Marianne in the United States and Selma in Germany tried everything to accelerate Kurt's emigration while not even knowing his whereabouts. Marianne, worried about her brother's fate, had sought advice from different Jewish organizations and individuals in New York. Within a few days she realized just how many families were affected by the sweeping arrests in Nazi Germany. Marianne passed on the advice that she had received concerning her brother's case to Arnold, in hopes of helping his brother, who also had been arrested.[26]

Lotti in Palestine had long been anxious about Kurt's apparent blind optimism regarding the worsening conditions in Germany. Analyzing gender differences in emigration decision-making, historian Marion Kaplan concluded that German Jewish men were more closely connected to German politics, culture and commerce than women, and therefore often hesitated to uproot themselves and their families.[27]

Flora Kaiser-Blüth's cousin, Arthur Stern, had provided an affidavit for Marianne and in October 1938 was willing to do the same for Kurt.[28] But it made no sense for Stern to send the affidavit just yet, because it had to accurately reflect the sponsor's financial status at the time the applicant's registration number came up. Kurt wrote Marianne that his registration number was "between 19,000 and 20,000! Considering the present pace this would mean a waiting period of two to three years ... There is no rush for the affidavit. On the contrary, it would not make sense to secure one now."[29]

The pressure on Jewish communities in Germany intensified noticeably in the fall of 1938. When the Polish government issued new passport regulations for Polish citizens living abroad in October 1938, the Nazi government understood this measure to mean that the increasingly anti-Semitic Polish government intended to strip Polish Jews of their citizenship to prevent them from returning to Poland. The German government then used this as a pretext for the deportation of Polish Jews from Germany. Even while the German and Polish governments appeared to try to resolve their differences over the deportations and alleged "misunderstandings" of the situation by means of diplomacy, the German government continued the deportation of about 20,000 Polish Jews. Among them was the family of 17-year old Herschel Grynszpan, who had been born in Hanover, where his family had lived for more than twenty-five years. He was living at the time in Paris and took revenge for his family's deportation and detention under terrible conditions at the German–Polish border. On the morning of 7 November Grynszpan shot a minor German embassy official, Legation Secretary Ernst vom Rath, at the German embassy in Paris, mistaking him for the ambassador. Once this desperate act of a desperate young man became known, and even before vom Rath died of his wounds at 5:30pm on 9 November, the German Minister of Propaganda and Enlightenment Joseph Goebbels encouraged the media to propagandize and embellish this latest attack by "World Jewry."[30]

The November Pogrom (Kristallnacht) was organized by the highest echelons of the Nazi Party and executed primarily by Nazi SA storm-troopers, the elite Nazi guard unit (SS) and the Hitler Youth (HJ), albeit mostly in civilian clothes to disguise their official connections. Their actions were received with generally passive acceptance and occasionally active participation on the part of the public.[31] The relatively quick orchestration of the pogrom was aided by the fact that on the evening of 9 November many local Nazi Party groups and SA units were celebrating the fifteenth anniversary of Hitler's Beer Hall Putsch, in most cases with considerable alcohol consumption.[32] Even though the pogrom was obviously staged, the Nazi government maintained that it was popular outrage that led to "spontaneous" acts of violence, to the demolition of Jewish stores and to the burning of synagogues.[33]

On the evening of 9 November Goebbels and Hitler in Munich learned about vom Rath's death during their own commemorative dinner for the Beer Hall Putsch. After Hitler abruptly left the restaurant where they were celebrating, Goebbels announced at 10:30pm that "[r]iots against Jews and their synagogues are not to be disrupted."[34] Chief of the Security Service (Sicherheitsdienst or SD) Reinhard Heydrich decreed at 1:20 a.m. on 10 November that "[t]he only measures permitted are those that do not endanger German life and property, e.g. arson in synagogues only in cases that do not pose danger to the surrounding areas."[35] While these orders were strictly followed in most parts of Germany, the Essen fire department was not only a passive observer of the raging fires but also an active participant in setting them. Historian Ulrich Herbert has pointed out that special skills were required to set fire successfully to a synagogue, in particular the large synagogue at the Steeler Tor, the Steinberg family's synagogue.[36] An eyewitness shared his own observations of the November Pogrom in Essen: "The SA and SS people in plain clothes, following a precise plan, went from door to door with axes and crowbars, gasoline and matches." He further recalled his shock at the destruction of Jewish businesses in Essen: "On my walk I noticed that all Jewish businesses were destroyed and plundered. The synagogue and the Jewish Youth Center were in flames. The firemen only protected the buildings nearby, but did nothing to actually extinguish the fire."[37] According to the logbook of the main fire station, the Jewish Youth Center was ablaze on 10 November at 5:55 a.m. The building, which had been designed in a modernist style by the famous Jewish architect Erich Mendelsohn, burnt to the ground.[38]

Hanna Levy, Kurt Steinberg's girlfriend, lived in the Jewish Youth Center, which was managed by their friends, Hanna and Walter Sternberg. She worked in the kitchen of the restaurant there. The news of the assassination attempt at the German embassy in Paris had quickly spread throughout Germany. Jewish communities were also aware of the fact that vom Rath was dying and feared that the Nazi regime would exploit his death. In her 1988 written testimony about the events of that night Hanna noted that the level of anxiety was already extremely high among those in the Jewish Youth Center restaurant early on the evening of 9 November, hours before the November Pogrom began:

After the restaurant was empty, my friends asked their
employees to leave (their 2-year old daughter had already

*been sent away to friends). The only ones left in this huge
house were the Sternbergs, the librarian and I ... Suddenly
we heard the horrible sounds of pickaxes smashing against
doors, breaking glass, and yelling. In the darkness, I
grabbed a coat, wore it over my nightgown and ran with
all the others to the basement. All of a sudden, I found
myself alone because I was not familiar with the exit to
the street through the bowling alley. There and then I
experienced the fear of death... I finally fled through the
light shaft, determined to escape the furious mob. I ran
through the vegetable garden and "flew" over the fence.
To this day I am convinced that I was so panic-stricken
that I indeed "flew" over the fence, which was of regular
height but had barbed wire on top... Having landed on
the other side of the fence, I walked dazed and aimlessly
around – barefoot and dressed in my nightgown, with
an ill-fitting coat thrown over it that I had found in the
darkness.*[39]

Fearing for her life and in utter despair, Hanna encountered, in the
early hours of the morning, several helpful and sympathetic passers-by,
who gave her some coins to telephone the police headquarters. After
hearing her describe her plight and how she still feared for her life,
the police officer on the other end of the telephone recommended that
Hanna seek help in a nearby house. When Hanna countered that she
did not "see a single window without a Nazi flag and was convinced
that hundreds of eyes had seen the narrow escape over the fence and
that none of the residents came to help," the police officer repeated that
he was only following his orders and claimed "Our hands are tied."[40]

Hanna's account juxtaposes, perhaps unintentionally, uncar-
ing if not hostile neighbors near the Youth Center, who stood by
passively and perhaps even sympathized with the Nazis, with helpful strangers who reached out to her and brought her to the Catholic
Johanniter hospital, and helped her regain her composure. The hospital
watchman tended her wounds, gave her slippers to keep and made the
necessary phone calls for Hanna to reconnect with her friends.[41] On
her way to find Walter and Hanna Sternberg later that morning, she
passed the burning Youth Center, which only hours before had been
not only her place of work but also her residence. Selma, Henny and

Onkel Hermann, fearful of the violent rampages in Essen, sought refuge with Herta Poth, their non-Jewish family friend. Herta, nicknamed Pötte, and her parents selflessly took the three older people into their apartment at a time when it was unclear how long the pogrom would last.[42] Lotti informed Marianne about their loved ones' fate during the pogrom: "By the way, Pötte has proven herself once again. Our three "old folks" stayed there one day and one night when the synagogues and houses were plundered. It must have been horrible in Essen."[43] Kurt later found out that Nazi thugs actually had looked for him at his family's home in Essen, but he apparently did not learn about his family's experiences during the November Pogrom until much later, when he was in relative safety.[44] Kurt then also relayed the sad news regarding the destruction of the Youth Center and all the synagogues in Essen to Marianne, mentioning that "the services are now held in Mr. Silber's former store in the Hindenburg-Strasse."[45]

While Kurt's immediate family members in Essen were relatively safe with Herta and her parents, Selma and Henny's older sister Bertha Kaufmann Lachs, a 68-year-old widow in Hochkirchen, about 50 miles south of Essen in the district of Düren, experienced the violence of the pogrom first-hand. As a local chronicler recorded:

> On 10 November 1938, the day after the infamous
> Kristallnacht a pack of Nazi thugs arrived also in
> Hochkirchen. A group of men attacked the home of the
> Jewish Lachs/Haase family, broke the windows, smashed
> the furniture and destroyed the goods in the store. A
> crowd of Hochkirchen residents stood horrified in the
> street and watched without taking action. As in all of
> Germany, nobody dared intervene.[46]

The news from Plettenberg, a town in the Sauerland region about 40 miles southwest of Essen, where Alex Steinberg's cousin Julius Bachrach and his wife Olga lived, was also not good. Selma's message to Marianne on 14 November about an invitation to Plettenberg sounds like a regular family visit: "Tante Olga has invited us. She has much more space now."[47] But, taking into consideration the next message from 13 December, the reader realizes that Selma had conveyed the distressing news about a relative's arrest, albeit in carefully coded language: "Tante Olga was here yesterday and was very, very depressed.

Her husband has been absent for a while."[48] Selma even disguised the fact that Julius Bachrach had been released from a concentration camp in this seemingly innocuous sentence in her letter to Marianne of 8 January 1939: "We had a lot of guests this afternoon, including Onkel Julius from Plettenberg."[49] After Julius Bachrach's return from KZ Sachsenhausen on 16 December 1938 his wife Olga begged the US consul, unsuccessfully, to issue a visa for her husband.[50] From then on Julius carried with him cyanide capsules, "determined not to have such a fate as he had experienced in the concentration camp befall him again."[51] (See Figure 5.3.) The intimidation, violence and traumatic experiences of the November Pogrom and detention in concentration camps often led to broken psyches among the former inmates.[52]

Kurt's letter to Marianne briefly described his experiences during the November Pogrom:

> *After I had been unanimously elected to the Frankfurt Representation [of the Israelite Community], the synagogues burned down a few hours later and Jews were arrested en masse on 10 November, I met the same fate at 6:30 a.m. on 11 November. I did not want to leave my post the day before because even though we anticipated numerous arrests, we at first expected them to be on an individual basis. I heard about mass arrests late on the night of 10 November, and decided to spend the night in a garage.*[53]

The Frankfurt Israelite Community (Israelitische Gemeinde) held a regularly scheduled meeting on the night of 9 November, at which Kurt was elected one of its delegates. (See Figure 5.4.) Another lawyer and a member of Frankfurt's Israelite Community, Julius Meyer, attended the same meeting. He recalled from the vantage point of 1940 that the police had long before drawn up lists of names of Jews, indicating, in his view, that the arrests that occurred on 10 November were planned, but he also pointed out that the lists had not been recently updated.[54] This would explain why the Nazi thugs first looked for Kurt in Essen, and why he was not arrested already on 10 November in Frankfurt, but one day later.

After having spent the night of 10 to 11 November together in a garage, Kurt and one of his colleagues mistakenly thought that they were safe. Kurt recalled: "In the morning we heard from a reliable

Figure 5.3 From left: Selma, Julius and Olga Bachrach, Henny, winter 1939–40

source that the arrests had been halted. I let myself be talked into going home for a short time, and that is where they caught me, with my friend and colleague."[55] The "reliable source" might well have listened to the radio and heard Goebbels' order of 10 November to halt the "operation" and taken it at face value.[56] In fact, as historian and archivist Wolf-Arno Kropat points out, while Goebbels' call to end the pogrom was broadcast propagandistically on the radio, he did not

Figure 5.4 Portrait of Kurt, 1938

give an order via the official channels.[57] Therefore, the pogrom continued in many locales. In addition, Goebbels' radio announcement merely addressed the end of violence and plundering, not the end of anti-Jewish measures per se. On the contrary, at the end of his radio announcement he threatened: "The Jews will receive the final answer to the Jewish assassination in Paris by laws and decrees."[58] After Müller and Heydrich's secret orders from the previous night primarily to target "wealthy Jews who are not too old," the arrests of Jews from their homes, businesses and off the streets not only continued but were intensified.[59]

Although Selma knew of Kurt's arrest in Frankfurt, she did not know where he had been taken until a week later. Plagued by uncertainty, she wrote in her letter to Marianne on 18 November: "Somebody from Kurt's office wrote to me today that due to Kurt's high registration number, we should request preferential treatment in Washington. I am not sure it will help."[60] Since 10 November 1938 all Centralverein offices had been shut down, but those of Kurt's colleagues who had managed to avoid arrest were trying to comfort and advise their arrested colleagues' very distressed family members.

While the details of Kurt's arrest are unknown, we can glean some information from other eyewitness accounts of Jewish men in comparable, high-profile positions in Jewish organizations, such as that of Julius Meyer from the Frankfurt Israelite Community:

> *Then we were loaded onto buses and were taken to the exhibition hall [Festhalle]... We were led into the hall, and we immediately knew what was happening. SS men were chasing inmates, and ordered them around... We had to empty our briefcases and pockets. Money and valuables were put in a sealed envelope.*
>
> *Then we were put in groups, each with an SS man who was in charge of drilling us. The official reason given was that in order for us not to get cold in this big, cold hall we had to move around.*[61]

Julius Meyer described the initial hours after his arrival at the exhibition hall in Frankfurt in great detail. The inmates had to yell "We are Jews" while performing the most rigorous military drill exercises. They had to run, crawl, get up and get down, with their luggage, and for hours without a break. Meyer recalled one particularly horrifying moment: "Finally we were ordered to sit down, but had to turn to the wall. The reason was whispered through the rows: Somebody had died. He did not survive the mistreatment and collapsed ... He was covered with a cloth, and we had to march, crawl and run around him. The corpse remained there until late in the afternoon." Just as horrible as the strenuous physical activities were the taunts and the humiliation the inmates had to endure. When the detainees arrived at night at the train station in the southern part of Frankfurt, the Südbahnhof, an astonishing number of onlookers had gathered.[62]

Kurt was arrested one day before Julius Meyer, and most likely was also detained at the exhibition hall.[63] Meyer's dehumanizing experiences were presumably similar to those of Kurt. Both prominent members of the Jewish community, they fell victim to abuse by the SS, who particularly targeted Jews in leadership positions. But, as Meyer reported, the detained Jewish men were also confronted with the virulent anti-Semitism of "ordinary people" who gathered at the Südbahnhof in Frankfurt:

> *There were masses of people who came to watch the*
> *spectacle, screaming at us. We left the bus quickly and ran*
> *through the underpass, up to the platform. We were the*
> *lucky ones. The inmates behind us were not only yelled*
> *at. Several girls, women and also men beat the defenseless*
> *Jews with sticks, umbrellas and heavy objects. But that*
> *torment also passed, and we were herded onto the train*
> *that took us to the northeast... We knew then that we*
> *would probably end up at the camp close to Weimar.*[64]

The harassment continued during the trip and upon arrival in Weimar. Kropat summarizes several eyewitness accounts: "The Jews destined for the concentration camp Buchenwald were chased to the underpass under the Weimar train station. They were beaten and abused. Many of the Jews suffered serious eye and head injuries. In the morning, they were taken by truck to the concentration camp."[65] The detainees were forced to run down steps coated with soap to the underpass. Anyone who fell down was beaten with a rifle butt. After a night of sleep deprivation, violence and abuse, the inmates arrived at the camp gate with its infamous inscription "To Each His Own" and were beaten again by double rows of SS men. Buchenwald Memorial Museum archivist Harry Stein cites the report of one of those Jews arriving at the Buchenwald concentration camp (KZ Buchenwald): "Inmates who had been at Buchenwald for a longer time greeted us at the gate and calmed us down. Then they took us in groups to the roll call area [*Appellplatz*] where we had to line up and stand until late into the night, since the barracks for the Jews were not yet ready."[66]

In addition to 32-year-old Kurt, two of his cousins from the Rhineland region, 18-year-old Ernst Kaufmann of Drove[67] and 41-year-old Eugen Roer of Kreuzau, were arrested and interned at KZ Buchenwald. Years later, from the safety of his new American homeland, and after serving in the US army during World War II, Ernst recalled his own experiences of November 1938:

> *I found mechanic's work with Christian family friends*
> *in towns where no one else knew that I was Jewish, until*

*the morning of 10 November 1938 [near his hometown
of Drove]. I got a phone call from my sister [Lotte
Kaufmann], telling me to go home immediately, because,
as she said to me in English, "All the synagogues are
burning." I got on my bike and headed for home, some 15
miles away, passing our burned [down] synagogue on the
way. No sooner had I arrived at home than [sic] our local
policeman, a neighbor and longtime customer of ours
until my father [Leo Kaufmann] was forced to close his
[butcher's] shop, came and apologetically said that they
had orders to arrest every Jewish male between the ages
of 16 and 65 "for their own protection from the enraged
German populace," because a young Polish Jew had killed
a German Consular Official in Paris. The policeman
knew my father was not yet 65, said that he would
disregard his orders, but I would have to come along. It
was the only time I ever heard my father raise his voice,
when he asked what ever for [sic] he [had] spent four
years in the trenches fighting for Germany, and for what
his wife's – my mother's – two brothers gave their lives
fighting for the Fatherland. Our good neighbor of course
had no answer for him, and off I went with him, to jail, a
converted room in the local firehouse.*[68]

Ernst's arrest might have been typical for a rural area: The families
were allowed to bring meals to the few detainees. After spending two
nights there, the detainees were brought by car to a collection point
in the nearest big town, Düren. Once under the control of the SS,
Ernst and his cousin Eugen came to the realization that the SS would
take every opportunity to further humiliate and beat any detainee.
Ernest Kaufman's recollections in his 2005 interview give an idea of
the routine at the camp:

*Lined up for roll call, our heads were shorn and then we
were marched off to barracks that had bunks arranged in
several layers, like shelving, each one about 3 feet above
the next. It was 13 November, and having arrived with
just the clothes on our backs that we lived in as long as
we were in camp, lying close together on the bare boards*

kept us from freezing. Fed once daily, we were lined up
in columns, and the first rows of us were handed mess
kits and spoons by so-called "other" camp prisoners
who wore striped clothes, given a ladle full of some
unidentifiable slop and ordered to finish eating while
standing in place.

The primitive and crowded conditions in KZ Buchenwald, reportedly much worse than those in the concentration camps at Sachsenhausen or Dachau, became even more horrific with every new transport. Thousands of detainees captured in the aftermath of the November Pogrom were initially crammed into two barracks and a former laundry room while three more barracks were still being built. These so-called *Novemberjuden*, Jewish men arrested and detained in the midst of the November Pogrom, did not receive prison uniforms and wore their own clothes during their entire stay.[69] They had no scheduled activities or work assignments and were housed in provisional "emergency" barracks, without heat, windows, floor coverings or toilets in the special "pogrom camp" called the Sonderlager (or Sonderzone), described by the Buchenwald archivist Harry Stein as follows:

The Sonderlager, which the SS opened following the
November Pogrom next to the roll call area [Appellplatz],
remained provisional in every aspect: It was not only
that the accommodation, food supply and hygiene for the
10,000 Jews that arrived between 10 and 14 November
were catastrophic but also that the administration of the
concentration camp failed entirely. In the beginning, the
personal data of the detainees were often incompletely
listed. As a result, and for the first time in the history of the
camp, the names of the deceased were often unknown.[70]

The Sonderlager inmates were separated from the rest of the camp prison population, which included some of the 10,000 generally non-Jewish inmates of KZ Buchenwald who were incarcerated there for being members of the political resistance, prominent communists and social democrats and other anti-Nazis, those previously convicted as criminals, Jehovah's Witnesses, "asocials," and homosexuals.

Even though more than 1,000 Jews had already been detained in KZ Buchenwald as a result of the June Action (Juni Aktion) against so-called "asocials," the mass deportations of Jewish men after the November Pogrom reached an unprecedented scale.[71] The inmates of the special camp or Sonderlager endured dehumanizing treatment, including physical violence and psychological terror, especially in the days of 10–14 November, commemorated as the *Mordwoche* or "Week of Murder."[72] Ernest Kaufman (formerly Ernst Kaufmann) remembered these horrific events:

> *It was horrible to watch the SS hang people, or see them*
> *tie a man to a pole and flog him until he was unconscious,*
> *or tie a man's hands behind his back and then hang him on*
> *what looked like meat hooks on a wall, cut down only after*
> *he had fainted, or worst of all, stick a man into a spiked*
> *barrel, roll him down a hill and let dogs finish him off.*[73]

Magnus Heimann of Meiningen, the 68-year-old father-in-law of Eugen Roer, was deported to KZ Buchenwald, despite being over 65.[74] He died there of so-called natural causes on 21 November 1938. Ernest recalled that Herr Heimann succumbed to the horrendous conditions, degradation and lack of sanitation, but conjectured that he probably had died of a heart attack due to the stress.[75]

Following the November Pogrom about 400 Jewish men from all over Germany died in three concentration camps, 227 of them in the Sonderlager Buchenwald alone.[76] All the corpses were cremated in the main cemetery of the nearby town of Weimar. In most cases the families were notified of their loved ones' deaths after cremation and were then forced to engage in a bureaucratic battle with the city government to retrieve the ashes.[77]

The arrests, deportations, terrible conditions and the bestiality of the SS in the concentration camps served one primary goal: to frighten and intimidate the 26,000 Jewish detainees and their families so that they would see no alternative but to emigrate.[78] According to Ernest Kaufman: "Our families were told where we were and that we could be released if we found our way out of Germany. That got our families going of course."[79]

Immediately after Selma found out about Kurt's incarceration at KZ Buchenwald she began pursuing any and every possible option for Kurt's emigration or interim refuge. While trying to accelerate his immigration to the United States with Marianne's help, she also contacted several personal relations in England, Holland and Palestine, where Kurt might be able to wait safely for his US immigration number to come up. After briefly considering having Kurt stay with his cousin Moritz in Holland, Moritz found himself unable to obtain a visa for Kurt.[80] Then the prospect of an interim stay in England also became less and less likely.

In addition to trying to find a safe haven for Kurt, if only a temporary one, Selma and Kurt's girlfriend Hanna were primarily concerned with securing his release from KZ Buchenwald. Both appeared together at the police headquarters in Frankfurt on 26 November, where Hanna, who had known Kurt for several years and whose relationship with him had become quite close in the fall of 1938, declared herself Kurt's de facto fiancée, although Kurt was not yet privy to his engagement. This allowed her to legitimate her advocacy for Kurt. Selma provided Hanna with a power of attorney authorizing her as his fiancée to take care of Kurt's "passport matters."[81] When describing what led up to his release to Nanna in late November Kurt noted: "Mother and Henny had been extremely busy with my matters, and still are. It was a great help that Hanna was there, otherwise it might have been too much for the 'old folks,' especially since everything had to go through Frankfurt."[82]

During Kurt's incarceration his former superior at the Centralverein Essen, Ernst Plaut, tried to arrange for Kurt to emigrate to Argentina with a "transport of about twenty-five people."[83] Plaut had apparently been in contact with one of the so-called Riegner groups, which had developed a project to help German-Jewish youths to do just that. Kurt Riegner's initiative, which indeed had ties to the Centralverein, managed to organize and implement the emigration to Argentina of three German-Jewish youth groups over the course of three years.[84] Ernst Plaut, who had not been detained during the November Pogrom, also contacted the Jewish Rural Labor Service (Jüdische Landarbeit or JLA), which trained Jews for agricultural work abroad. The JLA issued a letter on Kurt's behalf, assuring him of his imminent emigration/immigration, a prerequisite for Jewish Sonderlager inmates' release from KZ Buchenwald.[85]

Kurt, unable to communicate with his family and colleagues while in KZ Buchenwald except to send a single postcard with prescribed text, was caught by surprise when he was "suddenly released, without any explanation."[86] When he called his mother from Weimar on 28 November he learned that Hanna was in Frankfurt waiting for him. What Kurt did not know at the time was that Hanna had presented her own written request for Kurt's release from KZ Buchenwald on the basis of the JLA letter to the State Police in Frankfurt that had been signed by Fritz Schwarzschild, secretary of the JLA.[87] The fact that the JLA letter specified such details as the exact departure date of 10 December 1938, cabin number 265 on the steamship *Ozeania* leaving from Trieste, points to the strong possibility that the letter was written on behalf of another detainee whose name was illicitly replaced with Kurt's. But nevertheless the State Police did not notice the forgery and sent a telegram to KZ Buchenwald requesting Kurt's immediate release.[88]

Hanna's next obstacle to getting Kurt released and his papers in order was the Gestapo. While the regular police usually handled passport matters, passport applications from Jews had also to be approved by the Gestapo.[89] Since the Gestapo was, at the end of 1938, primarily interested in an accelerated emigration of Jews, they granted passports to Jews wishing to emigrate in almost all cases. But Kurt's case was somewhat complicated. The precondition for the Argentinian visa was a valid German passport issued prior to 19 July, since that was the date of the original addressee's visa application, and in order to have an application one had to already possess a valid German passport. The forged JLA letter stated that the Argentinian government had authorized its consul in Germany to issue the visa. Kurt now needed to prove that his passport had been issued before 19 July. Therefore, Hanna had to convince the Gestapo officials to pre-date Kurt's passport.[90] She suppressed her discomfort, went to the intimidating Gestapo offices and heard the iron door shut behind her. She went to see a Gestapo official by the name of Müller, who was notorious for harassing and tormenting the desperate Jews who were forced to leave Germany. Müller often prolonged their misery by making them wait longer than necessary for their passports.[91] Waiting to see Müller in his office, Hanna had witnessed his intimidation of another visitor, a scene that left her trembling. But she was very lucky and Müller hesitantly obliged, disarmed by Hanna's argument that because she was Kurt's fiancée, he "could get rid of two Jews at once."[92] Kurt and Hanna's son retold this episode in almost the exact same words: "My mother said to the official: 'You want to get rid of a Jew, and I want to take him with me.'"[93] Müller ordered his subordinate to pre-date Kurt's passport back to 15 July. Another Gestapo official advised Hanna to send 100 RM to the headquarters of KZ Buchenwald in order to pay for Kurt's "room and board," which Hanna did the same day, 28 November 1938.[94]

Thanks to the JLA letter confirming Kurt's emigration to Argentina, Kurt was released from KZ Buchenwald on 28 November, after almost three weeks of detention.

He described this event to Marianne:

> I called home from Weimar and heard that Hanna was already in Frankfurt (where I was required to return). Once there I would find out more. You can imagine how happy we were to see each other. She had managed to get me released with documents guaranteeing my emigration to Argentina, which was supposed to happen ten days later. I was to be part of an artisan group of the JLA – founded by the Centralverein – that had accepted me due to my special situation.[95]

The Sonderlager inmates who were fortunate enough to be released returned to their home towns by train, either individually or in small groups, but without Gestapo guards, departing from the Weimar train station, the town closest to KZ Buchenwald. Jewish women from the towns of Weimar, Erfurt and Apolda, who, unlike the men, had not been targeted for mass arrests during the pogrom, assisted the released inmates and helped get them on the trains. The men had to pay for their tickets home. If they did not have enough money with them at the time of their arrest, either nearby Jewish communities or fellow Jewish inmates helped out.[96] Although Hanna had encountered recently released detainees at the Gestapo office, whom she described as "horrible looking creatures with shaven heads and smelling terrible,"[97] nothing prepared her for facing Kurt in the same condition. But despite his poor physical state and mental anguish following his release from KZ Buchenwald, Kurt could not afford to take time to convalesce.

After weeks of suffering and intimidation, Kurt, like all the other surviving Jewish detainees, was warned at the time of his release never to talk about his experiences at KZ Buchenwald. The rupture in their personal and professional lives, the loss of human dignity and the deprivation of basic needs deeply affected former inmates for the rest of their lives. Apparently Kurt could never bring himself to describe his time at KZ Buchenwald to his family, presumably because it was too painful to relive the horror and fear he experienced there, but also probably because he did not wish to traumatize them. He only hinted at the "almost three weeks of the most horrifying experiences in the worst concentration camp by far" to his sister Marianne some six weeks after his release.[98] Kurt's suffering in KZ Buchenwald eventually resulted in permanent hair loss and severe health problems, including a heart condition and high blood pressure.[99]

As was the case for others arrested in the aftermath of the November Pogrom, a precondition of Kurt's release from KZ Buchenwald was that he had to sign a statement that he would leave Germany by 31 December 1938. The German authorities, well aware of the fact that it was extremely difficult, if not impossible, for those arrested during the pogrom to get all the formalities in order in such a short time, used methods of intimidation and harassment to increase the pressure for emigration. Time constraints and long lines at every office notwithstanding, the released prisoners also had to report regularly to the Gestapo or police.

Because the letter that got him out of KZ Buchenwald was fabricated, Kurt was not actually part of the group scheduled to leave for Argentina on 10 December, as the letter had stated. His hope remained, though, to leave Germany for Argentina by the end of the year as part of one of the Riegner groups.[100] With the help of the American Jewish Joint Distribution Committee, also known as the "Joint," three Riegner youth groups had been able to leave Germany for Argentina between 1937 and April 1939, under ever-increasing difficulties. The third group, most likely the one that Kurt was supposed to join, encountered almost insurmountable problems. Selma's allusion at the end of November to "major difficulties in Frankfurt" that would need to be overcome before Kurt could emigrate was most likely tied to the group's delayed departure, which finally occurred in April 1939.[101] Several Jewish organizations in Germany, such as the Centralverein, had long-standing connections with the Jewish Colonization Association (JCA), which maintained major settlements in Argentina and Brazil. Hanna's immediate family had already emigrated to Argentina and become financially quite secure there.[102]

Hanna did not even consider emigration to Argentina before November 1938, and by then Argentina had introduced more immigration restrictions.[103] In the aftermath of the Evian Conference, the Argentinian government further restricted immigration. Claiming economic reasons, but probably in response to domestic political and international pressures, the Argentinian government effectively curbed immigration to the country.[104] From then on its immigration policy was centralized in Buenos Aires, which meant less leeway for consuls abroad, including those in Germany.

The so-called *llamaden*, namely requests for family members to join those who had already emigrated to Argentina, were now further complicated by a new requirement for a "permission for disembarkation" (*permiso de libre desembarco*).[105] Under these new, stricter regulations, immigrants in Argentina could submit requests only for parents, spouses and children. The immigrants also had to prove that they had already lived in Argentina for at least two years. They were no longer allowed to pursue immigration proceedings for siblings, and therefore Hanna's only hope was her mother, Sofie Levy. In dire need, Hanna had asked her mother to submit a *llamada* (request) for herself and her soon-to-be husband Kurt. But Sofie had not yet established the required two-year residency and thus could not help.[106] The search for a safe haven continued.

After weeks of alternating between hope and despair, and ceaseless efforts to pursue their emigration to whichever country would take them, Kurt and Hanna learned in early December that they would not be able to emigrate to Argentina. Kurt later wrote: "When this matter [emigration to Argentina] did not go through despite our hopes and expectations, we chased after any possible visa for the next six weeks. My deadline had already passed, and our energy lessened. There was literally no border open, otherwise we would have left even without an immigration visa, perhaps to Holland or Belgium."[107]

Hoping that the United States might expedite immigration proceedings for incarcerated German Jews after the November Pogrom, Marianne had prompted her US sponsor, Arthur Stern, to act quickly and send the affidavit for Kurt to the US consulate in Stuttgart. Apparently Stern's affidavit, which Selma reported as having arrived in Stuttgart on 22 November 1938, got lost thereafter at the US consulate.[108] The affidavit and the letter of support that Marianne had managed to get from New York Congressman Bruce Barton allegedly could not be found in the consulate for months. In February 1939 the consulate in Stuttgart informed Barton, who had apparently inquired about the status of Kurt's immigration proceedings, that they had just discovered Stern's affidavit.[109]

Kurt was understandably very nervous regarding his departure and the details of his immigration status to the United States in particular. Two weeks before the deadline he had been given to leave Germany, he wrote Marianne:

> I thank you and Mr. Stern once again for all your help. Unfortunately, it has been of no use so far. I can only ask you most urgently not to send any affidavits to the consulate or the shipping company. It is absolutely useless to do so if the e/immigrant has not yet been asked to submit his documents [to the consulate]. To send the affidavit to the consulate does not make sense at this point, especially if you over there forget to indicate the registration number, as I am to assume in my case. The affidavits are piled up high in Stuttgart and no consular official knows which ones are there. You absolutely have to send all affidavits directly to the emigrant/immigrant himself. That is the only way he would be able to get the "preliminary examination" in Stuttgart for the transit visa [Zwischenvisum] for England. I have to ask you therefore to send a second affidavit to my Essen address as soon as I request it by telegram.[110]

The US consulate in Stuttgart was entirely incapable of processing the flood of telegrams, affidavits, requests for appointments and visitors showing up without any appointments. When US State Department Visa Division Chief Avra Warren inspected several US consulates in Europe in late 1938 and early 1939, he realized that most consulates were inadequately staffed to accommodate the 300,000 people seeking refuge under the German quota. He also became aware of some irregularities, such as the unlawful sale of visas at the Stuttgart consulate.[111] To ameliorate an untenable situation, Warren assigned ten more staff members to the Stuttgart consulate. This might have been the background to the "major revision" at the consulate in Stuttgart that Kurt mentioned in his letter to Marianne: "Some things were not in order there, but details are not yet known."[112]

Desperate to find a way out of Germany, Kurt followed up all the leads that his mother and fiancée had already pursued. With the help of his former colleagues from the Centralverein, and from the Hilfsverein and elsewhere, Kurt tried to gain entry into different countries in order to escape the hostile environment in Germany and to wait for his immigration papers to the United States. In his 1998 memoir Hans Reichmann, Kurt's colleague from the Centralverein in Berlin, retold a bitter joke that circulated in early 1939 among the Jews under orders to leave their *Heimat*:

> *A German Jew who was released from the KZ and had to leave Germany asked at the Hilfsverein to name a country to which he could emigrate. The counselor points to the globe. The man in need turns the globe, looks it over from the North Pole to the South Pole, from east to west, and asks: "That's all you got?"*[113]

In December 1938 Kurt urgently needed to find a country where he might wait for his visa to the United States. Given his relatively high registration number with the US consulate and an estimated wait of more than two years, his only chance of finding refuge in Britain in the meantime was a guarantee from a British resident who could vouch for him and promise to take care of his material needs. But that too had become more complicated and now involved more than a simple invitation. Selma reported the new regulations to Marianne: "If Kurt wants to spend the waiting period for the U.S. in England, which will hopefully not take as long as it seems now, one needs to show the [British] Home Office a bank account, in addition to an invitation. An invitation with the assurance to support the immigrant is not enough any more."[114]

Following up on an offer from Marianne's British friend, Doris Meakin, that she and her husband would welcome any member of the Steinberg family in England, Selma had asked Doris for help in securing a temporary permit for Kurt, but new restrictions in England became a significant obstacle to Kurt's immigration.[115] As he reported later to Marianne: "England did not work out for me because Doris was unwilling to sign the new guarantee papers."[116] It was quite likely that Doris either did not have the necessary funds or did not feel financially able to set aside that much money in a bank account for Kurt.

Another acquaintance of Marianne and Kurt's in England, Nora Kaufmann (no relation), also tried her luck on Kurt's behalf, first "at Woburn House and then at the Home Office."[117] By late 1938 the Home Office and the Aliens Department in Britain were flooded with requests by relatives and friends to help rescue their loved ones from Germany and allow them to escape to Britain.[118] This made it very unlikely that Kurt would be able to get to Britain.

In his book *The Abandonment of the Jews* historian David Wyman criticizes the immigration policies of the United States and Great Britain. He argues that both powers tried to avoid floods of refugees, and "[c]onsequently their policies aimed at obstructing rescue possibilities and dampening public pressures for government action."[119] When the US government did not increase the German quota in the immediate aftermath of the November Pogrom, British Home Secretary Samuel Hoare on 14 November suggested a quota transfer from the underused British quota to German Jews. This idea was rejected by Prime Minister Neville Chamberlain because he did not want to further strain Britain's relationship with Germany.[120] With little public pressure and only moderate media attention in Great Britain and the United States, the humanitarian aspect of the refugee crisis was often overshadowed by foreign policy considerations between Britain, the United States and Germany.

In its *Annual Report for the Year 1938* the official German organization of Jews, the Reich Representation (Reichsvertretung) of Jews in Germany, stressed the severity of the situation by the end of the year:[121]

> In the view of the long waiting list within the American
> quota, an extremely great need has developed to spend
> this waiting period in a transit country. For this, however,
> considerable sums are necessary, which cannot be raised
> by the relief organizations. Nevertheless, at least in those
> cases in which a guarantee existed for cost-of-living
> expenses by relatives, as well as of further migration within
> a short period, the possibility of a stopover was created in
> a number of European countries, above all in England.[122]

Great Britain played indeed the most crucial role among European countries in accepting refugees from Germany. The British authorities provided temporary haven for thousands of transmigrants on their way to a more permanent refuge elsewhere, primarily during the time between the November Pogrom and 1 September 1939, the beginning of the war.[123] Disagreements among British Cabinet members notwithstanding, the British government decided on 16 November 1938 to increase the quotas granted to temporary refugees.[124] This positive change was partially due to the efforts of the Council for German Jewry in Britain, which negotiated several agreements with the British government, including the allocation of more staff and funds for government agencies dealing with refugee questions, as well as the assurance to accept more transmigrants from Nazi Germany and Nazi-occupied territories.[125]

Back in Germany, the first priority of the British embassy and consulates in the time following the November Pogrom was to get Jewish prisoners released from the concentration camps.[126] Many British officials realized that time was of the essence and in many cases tried to speed up the visa process. Several British officials, including Consul General Robert Smallbones in Frankfurt am Main, took it upon themselves to negotiate with the Gestapo for the release of detainees from concentration camps by promising to the German authorities an immigration visa for the person in question.[127] Whether Smallbones would have been able to help with Kurt's release from KZ Buchenwald is questionable. Since Kurt gained his release with fabricated papers for immigration to Argentina, he could not be placed concurrently on any prospective immigration list of detainees kept by British refugee organizations. They were so overwhelmed with demands from those who had no other options that they could not offer help to those who already appeared to have other possibilities. Kurt faced a panoply of obstacles in his attempt to emigrate to England, but in his quest for a visa he eventually would meet with the British consul in Cologne, a meeting that would prove most consequential for the future.

Kurt had never seriously considered emigration to Palestine because he was concerned that there would be no appropriate work opportunities there for him.[128] However, under the extremely difficult conditions he found himself in after his release from KZ Buchenwald, he was anxious to obtain a visa anywhere, including Palestine. The

British consuls in Germany had in the past granted tourist visas to Palestine for up to six months, with the option of renewal if the trans-migrants could prove that they had the necessary financial security for the limited period they intended to stay in Palestine. They also had to demonstrate that they were only in transit in Palestine and would emigrate to another country. After Selma returned to Essen from the British consulate in Frankfurt am Main she sent detailed instructions to Lotti on the day after Kurt's release from KZ Buchenwald:

> In order to obtain a tourist visa to Palestine one needs
> a notarized invitation with the guarantee to take care
> of the applicant's living expenses. You have to send this
> letter here. Kurt has to fill out a form with his registration
> number [at the US consulate] and send it together with
> your letter to the British consulate. The officials there
> initiate the examination of the affidavit [at the US
> consulate], and if everything is in order, one could have
> a [limited] visa within a week.[129]

Lotti's first concern of course was to help her brother get out of Germany. She was also very much looking forward to having a family member living close to her and wanted to change Kurt's preconceived notions about Palestine. In the minds of Lotti and Hans, Palestine was the best new homeland for Jews: "I am hoping that Kurt will come here. I wish for him to get to know Palestine. I am convinced that no other country of the world will ever become a homeland [*Heimat*] for us again."[130]

This plan did not work, however. Due to Kurt's high registra-tion number at the US consulate (the United States being his ultimate emigration goal), the British consul in Frankfurt did not grant him a tourist visa to Palestine, despite the fact that Lotti and Hans had pro-vided LP 200 (Palestine pounds) as a deposit for Kurt's tourist visa. The British consul argued that the projected waiting period for Kurt's emigration to the United States would go far beyond the term of a tourist visa. At this point Kurt and Hanna were not even sure if they could emigrate to the same country. They had plans to marry eventu-ally, but they were uncertain about an interim solution. Hanna now pursued her own emigration options to Argentina, and because Kurt had to get out of Germany he tried to go anywhere.[131]

Kurt's situation had grown increasingly desperate: he had now been forced to promise the Nazi authorities he would leave Germany by 31 December 1938. Already several days overdue and fearful of being arrested again, Kurt received crucial help from Hans Jacobi, the director of the Emigration Counseling Office of the Hilfsverein, in Cologne.[132] In this position Jacobi was accustomed to negotiating with the Gestapo and police authorities, as well as foreign consular officials, regarding the release of Jewish prisoners from concentration camps, providing exit visas for them and trying to ensure their safe emigration. Jacobi recalled:

> *The released prisoners who had to report to my office*
> *often told me in confidence what they had to endure*
> *in Dachau, Sachsenhausen and other camps. I had*
> *to gather all my courage again and again in order to*
> *remain composed in my position. I often had to testify at*
> *doctors' offices and to foreign consuls that the illnesses*
> *and disfigurations of the recently released prisoners are*
> *entirely due to the abuse they just had experienced in the*
> *concentration camps and are not from any other source.*[133]

After Kurt had already twice tried in vain to receive a tourist visa for Palestine, Jacobi intervened on his behalf and pleaded with the British consul to meet personally with Kurt.[134] The fact that the British consul in Cologne, J. E. Bell, had witnessed the November Pogrom in Cologne and reported his outrage to the British authorities might well have contributed to his understanding of how critical the situation was for Kurt.[135] Only when Kurt realized that giving the consul a detailed account might possibly get him out of Germany did he venture to take Bell into his confidence and share with him the horrors of KZ Buchenwald.[136] This was perhaps the only time he did so to anyone.

When Kurt told Bell of his treatment in KZ Buchenwald and his precarious situation after his release, Bell first promised Kurt a tourist visa for Palestine for himself but then also included Kurt's fiancée Hanna, provided they got married right away.[137] In a postwar interview Marianne described her understanding of Kurt's desperate plea to the British consul, of course through her own lens:

*My brother was released from the concentration camp
under the condition that he leave Germany, I don't
know, in a matter of days. But he was not killed. After
he left the concentration camp he went to Cologne to the
British consul to apply for a visa for Palestine. This he
received, and one even got to hear his story, although the
Nazis told him at the time that he would be finished off
if he ever talked about what he had seen and heard in the
concentration camp. They would always know where to
find him. But he spent hours with the British consul and
told him everything.*[138]

The British consul was supposed to halt issuing tourist visas to Palestine
at this time. But Bell nevertheless granted Kurt and Hanna a tourist
visa. As a consequence of his disobedience Bell lost his job in Germany
and was transferred to Switzerland.[139] (Despite the intended punish-
ment, this may well have been a more comfortable post to hold in the
Europe of 1939.) It was not until Kurt found himself in dire straits trying to find a safe haven that he even considered obtaining a tourist visa
to Palestine. He did not envision himself as part of what was widely
regarded as a "Zionist experiment" and was also very concerned about
his work prospects in Palestine as a lawyer trained in Germany, with
few other skills. When it came to what appeared to be a matter of life
and death, however, Kurt seized what seemed to be his last chance to
escape an increasingly hostile environment in Nazi Germany. Within
a matter of days, Kurt and Hanna had to get married, take care of
passport and financial matters, pay all sorts of fees and taxes, pack up
their belongings, and say their difficult good-byes to friends and family – some of whom they would never see again. With great relief Kurt
wrote Marianne from his safe haven in Palestine:

*After I had to report to the authorities once again about
the status of my emigration, I then tried once more to get
a visa for Palestine [at the British consulate] in Cologne.
You know the rest. Everybody envied us. Here [in
Palestine] everybody wanted to know how we managed
to get out so that they could tell their relatives. But we
received about the last tourist visa in the entire Reich.*[140]

While the German authorities enforced the Jews' speedy emigration, they also made emigration an extremely profitable business for the German economy. According to historian Avraham Barkai, the German state gained revenue of over 2 billion RM in the months between the November Pogrom and the outbreak of World War II by collecting an "atonement fee" (*Sühneleistung*), for the material damages caused by the pogrom, and the Reich Flight Tax, in addition to having insurance companies pay their claims to the state, not the Jewish owners, for damages incurred during the November Pogrom.[141]

Kurt summarized his and Hanna's material situation at the time of their emigration from Germany in his letter to Marianne:

> *I received a very decent settlement from the Centralverein, which paid for our emigration, including new purchases. Of course all my savings are now gone. Hanna also had about 800 RM. Considering the hurry with which we had to leave, we still managed to pack many useful things, such as clothes, including some new suits and dresses, bed linens, tablecloths, undergarments, some household items, dishes, wedding gifts, a serving table, a fan and several of mother's things, including silverware.*[142]

At the time of its dissolution in November 1938 the Centralverein had considerable assets, at least its operating budget for an entire year.[143] Kurt's settlement from the Centralverein, in addition to his savings, paid for his and Hanna's emigration/immigration. In calculating Hanna's assets for the purpose of the "atonement fee," the fact that she had lost most of her personal property during the November Pogrom was taken into consideration. Kurt, on the other hand, had to pay 320 RM to the German Gold Discount Bank.[144] This was the Disagio fee Kurt had to pay for his assets and the property for personal use that he took with him or shipped out of Germany.

Kurt and Hanna packed a total of seven suitcases and made arrangements to ship a container with furniture, clothing and household items, which they counted on arriving in Palestine a few months later.[145] The Nazis confiscated the container carrying their belongings in Antwerp after they had invaded Belgium. Kurt and Hanna lost all their possessions, except those in the suitcases with which they traveled on the ship. With only days to prepare, the couple celebrated their wedding on

15 January 1939, with their Essen Rabbi Hugo Hahn officiating, and about forty-five guests at the home of Selma, Henny and Onkel Hermann in Essen. For this momentous occasion the doctors granted Henny one day's leave from the hospital, where she was recovering from a renal tumor operation. Concerned for her sister's health and her son's future, Selma tried nevertheless to appear upbeat in her letters to Marianne. She hinted at how "hectic" life had been and at the "upheaval" since Kurt's release from KZ Buchenwald. At the same time Selma also assured Marianne of the sense of relief she felt regarding the preliminary solution for Kurt and Hanna, their emigration to Palestine.[146]

After their joyous wedding Kurt and Hanna left Essen with heavy hearts, yet they were optimistic they would soon be followed by and reunited with Selma, Henny and Onkel Hermann. In Cologne, several family members and friends came to the train station to see off the newly-weds. Kurt's letter to several family members written during their stopover at the home of Hanna's cousin, Lore Ross-Landau, and her family in Milan overflowed with his excitement over finally having left Germany. However, the Landaus' situation as Jews with German passports had become quite tenuous after Mussolini tightened anti-Jewish legislation in Italy on 1 September 1938.[147] The Landaus had been ordered to leave Italy by March 1939 and had no idea where they would go. Nevertheless, they welcomed Kurt and Hanna when they arrived in January of that year.

In his letter from Milan Kurt reported his anxiety regarding all the formalities involved in emigration. Trying to follow all the rules, and even anticipating possible bureaucratic snares, Kurt had brought along written documentation from his local finance office and the municipal tax office to prove he had made his final tax payments which he had to produce at the Swiss border.[148] To Kurt and Hanna's great relief, their four big suitcases had been cleared for customs and sealed in Germany so that they did not have to worry about their luggage during the trip.[149]

While the general tenor of Kurt's letter from Milan to all the family members was upbeat and optimistic, the enclosed addendum to Marianne was more nuanced and reflected Kurt's worries for the family members left behind:

> *You cannot imagine how happy we are that we made it out. Despite the difficult parting from her, mother*

was greatly relieved. We have no idea about our future, not even as much as "normal" immigrants in the last few years would have known. [What is] important is that we are "out" [of Germany]. This seems even more desirable considering the great worries that our relatives experience here [in Italy] after they no longer thought of themselves as immigrants. The three of us [siblings] have to try everything to get our "old folks" out of Germany as soon as possible.[150]

6 NEW BEGINNINGS IN PALESTINE, 1935–1939: LOTTI AND KURT

A few months after their March 1935 wedding, Lotti had emigrated to Palestine with her husband Hans, one of the two sons of Flora and Julius Kaiser-Blüth. Julius and his half-brother Karl owned Mannsbach & Lebach Company on the Lindenstrasse in Cologne, a textile factory that manufactured occupational clothing, until it was "Aryanized" in December 1938.[1] Hans had been an active member of the Zionist youth organization, Blue and White (Blau-Weiss).[2] Studying in Munich and Berlin, he was trained as a mechanical and electrical engineer.[3] Although he had gotten an apprenticeship with the prestigious Deutz Company in Cologne, he could not find work in his profession once the Nazis came to power. Hans did manage to get hired as a commission-only sales representative for Palestine by the MAN (Machine Factory Augsburg–Nuremberg) Company in March 1935, but only after it was clear that he would be emigrating to Palestine.[4]

Lotti met Hans Kaiser-Blüth in a Hebrew class organized by the Zionist movement in Cologne.[5] Hans, unable to find work as an engineer in Germany and, as a committed Zionist, anxious to pursue the ideal of settling in Palestine as a Jewish homeland, had already made immigration plans when he first met Lotti. Within a matter of months Lotti and Hans married and planned their move to Palestine.

Lotti's former boyfriend, Heiner Frohmann, who remained in touch with her for several months after their break-up, was not ready to have all contact cease. He sent a wedding present from Erlangen: a coffee machine.[6] Heiner wrote Lotti:

The present turned out to be more sizeable than intended, possibly because I wanted to include all my best wishes for both of you ... I decided on something practical. I do not think a personal present would be appropriate since I wanted something that both you and your fiancé could equally enjoy. I would be very happy if your fiancé would understand the sincere friendship that connects the two of us.[7]

In the same letter Heiner alluded to his great respect for people who were willing to make sacrifices for their convictions, "whatever they might be." While he told of his own initial youthful attraction to Zionism and his ongoing support for a Jewish homeland in Palestine, he also wrote of how he had grown skeptical of what he perceived to be opportunism in the Zionist movement. Heiner chose to be faithful to his principles, sometimes to a fault: "But nobody except you, Lotti, knows that I gave up *everything* for my convictions, my sense of obligation. I am left to pray that I will continue to have the strength to make sacrifices."[8] Heiner attempted to convey to Lotti the pain he experienced as a consequence of not having been able to pursue a future with her. Instead of following his heart, he felt obliged to sacrifice his love and a possible future with Lotti in order to provide for his mother and sisters.

After multiple relationships and near or broken engagements, which all represented disappointments for her, Lotti was anxious to marry when she met Hans Kaiser-Blüth. As Hans' father recalled to the young couple in his 1938 Hanukkah letter: "Enjoy the wonderful mood when on Sunday the Menorah will shine over Tel Aviv, just as much as I did when I returned home on a Saturday night four years ago. That was when you, my dear Lotti, were at our house for dinner for the first time. A few days later I learned that you would be my daughter-in-law."[9] After a whirlwind engagement Lotti and Hans married on 28 March 1935. Lotti's second cousin, Marianne Bachrach, Julius and Olga's daughter from Plettenberg, remembered the wedding reception as an "elaborate affair with many courses that went on for hours."[10]

Lotti's decision to emigrate to Palestine was definitely influenced by feeling excluded and trapped in Germany without a professional future, yet she clearly retained a strong sense of German identity.

We know of only a few instances in which Lotti felt she needed to stand up for herself as a Jew in Nazi Germany. One such incident highlights the ludicrous claims of anti-Semitic propaganda and the stereotypical assumptions about Jews, as well as Lotti's self-confidence. It occurred on a trip she took after her grand wedding, when she visited her "very dear relatives," the Bachrachs in Plettenberg, to say good-bye before leaving for Palestine. A man wearing Nazi Party insignia entered her train compartment, sat across from her and proceeded to flirt with her. When she pointed out to him that she was both married and Jewish, he expressed his disbelief, remarking on her "lack of racial characteristics." She told him off, stressing to him that he was giving a Jew this "compliment."[11] Examples of such "mistaken identity" were fairly widespread. Once the Nazi propaganda effectively portrayed Jews as "the other," ordinary Germans often had no compunction about pointing out who "looked Jewish."

Lotti's marriage into the wealthy Kaiser-Blüth family presented her with a more promising personal and professional future, as well as access to a new homeland. In addition to providing the necessary funds for them to emigrate to Palestine, Lotti's in-laws also purchased state-of-the-art Siemens equipment for her new dental practice. In 1922 the British mandate government of Palestine established immigration applicant categories according to the personal assets, profession or age of the applicant or his or her familial relationship to a resident of Palestine. The Kaiser-Blüths provided the necessary funds so that Lotti and Hans were eligible for a Capitalist Certificate, also known as category A1, which was limited to prospective immigrants with significant personal assets. Immigrants applying under this category had to prove that they had liquid assets of at least LP (Palestine pounds) 1,000, equal to 1,000 British pounds, with 50 percent or more in cash.[12] At the time of Lotti and Hans' immigration LP 1,000 were worth about 15,000 RM.[13] This was more than the annual income of a lawyer or doctor.[14] A couple, or parents and one or two children under the age of 18, were allowed to immigrate on one certificate.

Immigration to Palestine had become financially more attractive to German Jews after the summer of 1933 due to the Ha'avarah [Transfer] Agreement.[15] In short, this controversial agreement between Zionist leaders and the Nazi government was geared to stimulate German-Jewish immigration to Palestine by means of favorable financial conditions and selling German goods to Palestine.[16] It also helped the dire foreign currency situation in Nazi Germany, as reflected in the reasoning behind the Reich Flight Tax. In the first years of the Nazi regime the exchange of Reichsmarks for other currencies was strictly limited, but then in 1936 it was forbidden altogether.[17]

Under the Ha'avarah Agreement, however, prospective immigrants from Germany to Palestine could bypass these currency exchange restrictions by depositing their Reichsmark funds into blocked accounts in one or other of those banks approved by the Palestine Trust Society for Advice to German Jews Inc. (known as the Paltreu).[18] They would then receive a Ha'avarah certificate, which entitled them to the equivalent of their blocked funds in Palestine pounds in the form of imported German goods or property in Palestine.[19] Importers of German goods in Palestine deposited the funds for the purchase of these goods with the Anglo-Palestine Bank. This was where Lotti and Hans, and, after their arrival in Palestine, Kurt and Hanna, did all their banking.[20]

The Ha'avarah Agreement drew international criticism from many corners and was hotly debated when it was made public. Some opponents pointed out that this agreement only facilitated the immigration of wealthy Jews into Palestine, while the poorer majority would remain in Germany. Jewish opposition came mostly from groups outside Germany that advocated an economic boycott and rejected any deals with the Nazi regime. However, the Ha'avarah Agreement enabled a major resettlement of German Jews to Palestine. Most of the 60,000 German Jews who emigrated to Palestine between 1933 and the outbreak of World War II were direct or indirect beneficiaries of the Ha'avarah.[21] During this same period some 100 million RM were transferred to Palestine.[22]

The chances for Jewish engineers to work in their profession in Palestine were significantly lower than in many other countries of immigration.[23] Even though engineers who came as active Zionists received some support in finding jobs, they were often unemployed for a long time and had to work in unrelated fields. Palestine, which in the 1930s was only at the beginning of its industrialization, had a limited need for engineers or for many other professionals. Hans Kaiser-Blüth's connection to the German Zionist Federation (ZVfD) and his contract with the MAN Company as one of their sales representatives for Palestine allowed him to make some business deals through the

Ha'avarah Agreement. Hans' son Michael later recalled that it was his father's representation of the MAN Company that helped get him a work permit in Palestine.[24] For Hans and many others in his situation the Ha'avarah Agreement provided a financial foundation on which to build, but, as it turned out, not a solid or lasting one.[25]

One of the reasons for Hans' fluctuating business success was the precarious political and economic nature of the Ha'avarah Agreement. By the end of 1935 he had managed to complete his first successful business deal, as Lotti proudly reported to Marianne.[26] This coincided with increased Jewish emigration from Germany after the Nuremberg Laws of September 1935.[27] In order to facilitate the flight of Jews from Germany to Palestine, but perhaps also to encourage it under the Ha'avarah Agreement, German imports to Palestine had to be competitively priced. The Ha'avarah therefore introduced measures in 1935 that effectively lowered the price of imported German goods and made them more competitive on the Palestinian market.[28] Hans' brief success in concluding a business deal at that time might have occurred owing to this 1935 economic stimulus.

More Jews immigrated to Palestine in 1935 than in any other year (61,900). The same year, however, saw the lowest annual number of *German* Jews immigrate to Palestine (14 percent of total Jewish immigration) than in any other year from 1933 to 1941.[29] The total of German-Jewish immigration during these eight or more years amounted to 24 percent of all Jewish immigration to Palestine. Of all German Jews, only about 10 percent (about 60,000) immigrated to Palestine during the Nazi regime.[30] Of these 60,000 German Jews, 80 percent settled in cities,[31] almost half of them in Tel Aviv.[32] In other words, Hans and Lotti belonged to that minority of *German* Jews who immigrated to Palestine but once there, were part of an overall Jewish immigrant majority who decided on urban living.[33] Lotti and Hans settled in Tel Aviv, which was founded by Jews in 1909, not far from the ancient Arab harbor town of Jaffa. By 1936 the Jewish population in Palestine was about 28 percent of the total, the Arab population constituting almost 72 percent.[34]

Although there are few extant descriptions of Lotti and Hans' first months in Palestine, it is quite certain that, like most German-Jewish immigrants in the mid 1930s, they experienced a difficult period of adjustment. Arriving in the extreme summer heat, they had to get used to an entirely foreign environment, climate and lifestyle. They were lucky to have landed at the modern harbor of Haifa rather than Jaffa, where many immigrants had to jump from their ship into little boats, in which Arab workers rowed them to the beach.[35] Even though life was not easy for Lotti in those first months, and many amenities and the infrastructure that she had taken for granted in Germany were no longer part of everyday life, she reminisced fondly even decades later about the pioneer spirit, "the sense of belonging together, the mutual help" in Palestine.[36]

Lotti recalled their wonderful reception in Palestine from some of Hans' Zionist connections: "From the very beginning we had a very nice circle of people around us. We felt very welcome."[37] In Palestine the Association of German Immigrants (HOG),[38] part of the Jewish Agency for Palestine,[39] was very active in providing initial help, although with limited resources. It often distributed information fliers and organized Hebrew-language courses for new immigrants from Germany.[40]

While Lotti and Hans were reportedly "in good spirits, having rented a room in Tel Aviv" for a few weeks from one of Lotti's cousins, their loved ones in Germany were worried about them.[41] Marianne remarked in her Notebook on 4 October 1935: "I am afraid they will have a hard time over there because of the war that broke out between Italy and Abyssinia [Ethiopia]."[42] Fascist Italy's invasion of Ethiopia threatened to destabilize the Middle East. In the years to come worries about unrest within Palestine preoccupied Lotti's family members outside the country. Fortunately, life in Tel Aviv was fairly safe. Almost to the day that Marianne wrote of her worries regarding Lotti and Hans' safety in Palestine, Lotti was optimistically planning for her relatives, including Marianne, to join them in their new environment:

> In any case, we are awaiting your [Nanna's] arrival soon. And it would be great if the others could come, too. I would like to propose that Onkel Hermann apply for a category A1 visa very soon. It might take years until he gets it. If he then did not want it, he could just decline. It would be no problem for us to get mother and Tante Henny here by request, especially if you are here, too. In any case, I think that we won't have problems proving that Tante Henny is like our second mother. The category A1 visa should be no problem. About three months before

the number came up, everything would need to be sold. The money would need to be deposited only about four weeks before the transfer. One does not need to set aside any extra funds. The profit from the sale of all properties would probably exceed the necessary LP 1000. I even believe that we could apply for a second A1 visa for Kurt if Onkel Hermann liquidated all his savings, which I would expect him to do. I would hope that, before all that, you and we would be settled and established so that we all can help out our "old folks" financially. About LP 150 per year would be more than enough. The "old folks" could also partially live off their savings. So, I strongly advise you to apply for a visa in any case, even if nobody in our family intends to immigrate at the moment. So much for the economic side.

As far as living conditions go: after having experienced part of the hottest time of the year here, I am certain that the climate would be bearable. You just stay inside at the hottest time of day, if you do not have to go out. And why would our "old folks" have to go out then? There is a home delivery for all kinds of food. They could easily manage their own apartment with the help of a maid who would work 2 hours a week. They would only need a two-room apartment with kitchen and bathroom. Although one has to sweep and dust more, it is quite easy for people who are used to it. The kitchens and bathrooms are tiled. Many houses have built-in closets and also hot and cold running water.[43]

After having lived in Tel Aviv for about three months, Lotti had conjured up this detailed plan for the settlement of her family in Palestine. Marianne indicated to Lotti that both she and Kurt doubted that they could easily uproot their mother, but they also felt great relief that Lotti and Hans might take in their older family members if the need arose.[44]

Lotti did not seem to doubt at that point that her sister would immigrate to Palestine and then help to resettle their mother, Tante Henny, Onkel Hermann and brother Kurt there. While Lotti was convinced that her family's future lay in Palestine, in the mid 1930s neither Marianne nor Kurt, primarily for professional reasons, seriously considered settling there.

When describing their lifestyle in Palestine to her family Lotti made sure to sound very upbeat and to emphasize what they would be used to, especially the availability of familiar food items, and the desirable, such as frequent visits to the beach, which was walking distance from their apartment. In the hot October days of 1935 Lotti bragged about serving her husband a three-course meal for lunch – "soup, potatoes, cucumber salad and steak on one day; bouillon, chicken thighs with cream sauce, beans and pudding for dessert on the next."[45] Like many German-Jewish immigrants in Palestine, Lotti maintained the cooking style she had learned in Germany. Many German Jews disliked unfamiliar food like hummus and techina,[46] but often enjoyed the abundance of local vegetables.[47] Even though Lotti claimed optimistically that the climate would be manageable for everybody, she admitted a few days later in the same letter to her sister that Hans had initially suffered terribly owing to the unfamiliar heat. He had been lethargic, irritable and unable to work.[48]

Lotti and Hans, similar to other bourgeois Jews from Germany, furnished and decorated their apartment with European flair. In a family photo from 1936 Lotti and Hans sit around their tastefully set table for *Kaffee und Kuchen*, complete with white table linen, a bouquet of flowers and delicate china cups and saucers. The elegant old-world glass cabinet, displaying valuable china and glass items, the comfortable sofa and the print of Vermeer's *Girl with a Pearl Earring* further contributed to this picture of bourgeois taste and comfort. The traditional dark and heavy interior design favored by this *Bildungsbürger* couple from Germany, including bookcases with classical literature, seems to clash with the intensely bright outdoors. (See Figure 6.1.) A 1936 photograph from Lotti and Hans' balcony reveals newly built rows of three- and four-storied white houses in the Bauhaus or International style. The street looks bare, with very little vegetation and only the occasional young tree.[49] (See Figure 6.2.)

Lotti hoped to set up her dental practice immediately upon arrival in Palestine. But the dental instruments and equipment that her in-laws shipped were held up for a year in the port of Jaffa because of unrest in Palestine at the time.[50] After arriving in Palestine she did manage to begin treating patients, using space at the office of other dentists she knew. One such office, she bragged, "was located in one of

Figure 6.1 Lotti and Hans in their living room, Tel Aviv, 1936

the most modern buildings that one of the best architects had built for himself."[51] Once she was able to set up her own office, she managed to establish a successful and well-regarded dental practice. Lotti treated a younger family friend in Tel Aviv, who was originally from Plettenberg. He recalled sixty-five years later: "Lotti was one of the best dental surgeons, and also certainly one of the most attractive ones." With very few of Hans' business deals actually coming to fruition and his parents unable to continue their initial financial support due to unfavorable German regulations, the majority of the family income was generated through Lotti's dental practice.[52]

After Hans and Lotti got themselves settled in Palestine, Hans' parents and Lotti's mother, Selma, visited them there, albeit on separate occasions. Yet neither considered staying or immigrating at the time. The Kaiser-Blüths visited Lotti and Hans in the summer of 1936 for about three or four weeks. This timing is remarkable, since tensions in Palestine had worsened just before. Presumably the trip was planned long in advance, and the passage had already been paid. In April 1936 the Arab Higher Committee (AHC), led by the controversial Grand

Figure 6.2 Lotti on her balcony, Tel Aviv

Mufti of Jerusalem, Haj Amin El-Husseini, demanded an end to all Jewish immigration to Palestine and the prohibition of land transfer to Jews.[53] The AHC declared a general strike, which was followed by riots, protesting the surge of Jewish immigration to Palestine.[54] One major center of the strike and riots was Jaffa, the ancient harbor not far from Tel Aviv where Lotti's dental equipment was held up. Between April and June 1936 almost every issue of the weekly *Jüdische Rundschau*, a publication of the German Zionist Federation in Berlin, featured front-page articles on the violent unrest in Palestine. Articles entitled "Bloody Riots in Jaffa"[55] and "Continued Arab Terror"[56] reported on the outbreak of violence at several locales. Nevertheless, the elder Kaiser-Blüths followed through with their planned visit to Palestine.

Lotti and Hans were delighted to welcome Selma and Hans' parents in Tel Aviv. Very few details are known about the Kaiser-Blüths' trip to Palestine in 1936. One family photo shows Lotti and her mother-in-law Flora smiling on the beach in Tel Aviv, happy to be together, even for a short time. Julius, not at all tempted to move

Figure 6.3 Selma visiting Lotti and Hans in Tel Aviv, 1937

himself or his assets to Palestine, still believed that the Nazi regime would pass quickly and that he and his profitable business in Cologne would ride out the hard times.[57] Even as late as the end of 1938, following the November Pogrom, Julius would still not waver from his determination to stay in Germany. Selma commented to Marianne on Lotti and Hans' frustration regarding Julius' delusions: "Lotti and Hans are furious that Hans' parents have not taken any steps towards emigration. Onkel Julius' fantasies have become obsolete. He must have lost touch with what is going on."[58]

Selma visited Lotti and Hans in the spring and summer of 1937. (See Figure 6.3.) One family photograph of Selma's visit pictures her in a long-sleeved dress on Lotti's balcony seeking refuge in the shade from the intense sunlight reflected off the white Bauhaus-style houses. Another photograph depicts a pensive Selma in Lotti's living room, with potted plants, porcelain candleholders and delicately draped white, sheer curtains in the background. Selma had to stay much longer in Palestine than she had intended owing to an emergency operation (an appendectomy) and the subsequent recuperation. Lotti accompanied her mother back home to Essen in September 1937, with a stopover in Italy.[59] In retrospect Lotti very much regretted not having tried to convince her mother to stay with them in Palestine.[60] But both during and for months after her visit in Palestine, Selma did not even consider emigration/immigration.

In the interim, the AHC increasingly contested further Jewish immigration to Palestine. The British government sought a territorial solution to the ethnic conflicts in Palestine and proposed two states, a Jewish one and an Arab one. When the plan was made public in July 1937, a new spate of violence erupted in Palestine. The leadership of both Jewish and Arab constituencies rejected the idea of this Partition Plan.[61] Still trying to honor the 1917 promise of the Balfour Declaration to establish a "national home" for the Jews, the British government did not achieve a workable solution for all involved.[62]

In July 1938, when world leaders were meeting at the Evian Conference to discuss the refugee crisis of German Jews, the situation in Palestine remained tense. The front-page news in the Zionist *Jüdische Rundschau* in Germany caused great worries among Lotti's friends and relatives: "In recent days a large number of terror acts, attacks and battles were reported from Palestine. The total number of Jewish deaths was seventeen. In Tel Aviv and Haifa several bombings cost the lives of many victims."[63] The newspaper even commented on "conditions that resemble a civil war."[64] Lotti's friends Lucie and Chaim, who had visited Tel Aviv at about the same time Selma did, recalled to Lotti: "We now only have our memories [of our visit last year], because the situation has so drastically changed. I have followed the present horrible events with interest and compassion. Unfortunately, the outcome is still unclear ... Do you have any plans for the future, or are you holding out and waiting for better times?"[65] Lotti's 81-year-old Tante Johanna, her father's sister, was also very worried about Lotti: "We all wish and hope that the government [in Palestine] will succeed in re-establishing law and order for everybody in the country so that the economy will flourish again."[66]

Interestingly, in her letters to Marianne Lotti expressed much more concern about the unsettling events in Germany but did not comment on the violence in Palestine.[67] In turn, Lotti's friends and relatives in Germany voiced their fears about Palestine but did not reflect on their own situation in letters. Of course, they were always conscious of censors and might not have wanted to risk having their letters intercepted or being punished for writing about the dangers for Jews in Germany. Both sides perceived the other to be in greater danger than the situation in which they found themselves. Lotti might have wanted to spare her friends and relatives such bad news, but she may have also not thought to mention it since such events did not directly affect her daily life. At that time Lotti also had many private concerns: In addition to being overworked, suffering from migraines, feeling ill for several weeks herself and running her busy practice, she also had taken care of a sick friend.[68] Furthermore, she was still hoping that her loved ones would leave Germany for Palestine and likely wanted to avoid giving them any unfavorable impression. Lotti remained positive that Palestine would become the future home for her siblings and her older family members.[69]

Lotti's dental practice was flourishing by early 1938,[70] as evident in descriptions about her "good clientele"[71] and the fact that she "could afford shopping sprees."[72] The fact that Lotti was able to open her own successful dental practice after a relatively short time in Palestine was mainly possible due to the high-end dental equipment that her in-laws had purchased for her. Many other professionals often had to accept menial work and a severe drop in social status.[73]

While Lotti had become a successful dentist, Hans' business was suffering terribly. The details of the development of the Ha'avarah Agreeement show that by 1938 the funds had been reduced by more than half compared with the previous year.[74] Hans was unaware in 1938 of the conflicts in Germany between the Reich Economics Ministry, the Foreign Office and the Interior Ministry regarding continuing support of the Ha'avarah Agreement and their economic impact on his business chances.[75] Moreover, when the 1936 Nazi rearmament program, the Four Year Plan, swallowed up more and more foreign currency, the Reich Economics Ministry drastically reduced the volume of German goods allowed for exports under the Ha'avarah Agreement. The Ministry created a list of German products that could or could not be exported to Palestine.[76] The MAN machinery that Hans was trying to bring into Palestine might well no longer have been allowed for import. This would offer one further explanation for his declining business deals. Despite the political controversies, the reduced number of German goods cleared under the Ha'avarah Agreement, rising transfer costs and the drastically

declining exchange value of the money needed for a "capitalist certificate," the volume of goods involved in the Ha'avarah Agreement
peaked in 1937.[77] However, just one year later the amount of goods
transferred had sunk drastically to an all-time low.[78] A very disappointed Hans reported to Marianne that his business had suffered
because of the political situation in Palestine and Europe in the summer of 1938. He received another blow when the transfer of certain
machinery was discontinued in the fall. Nevertheless, he was already
pursuing the sale of alternative products and was hoping for other,
larger projects.[79]

Although Hans' income fluctuated and remained below his
own and Lotti's expectations, their standard of living was rather
high compared with that of many other *olim*, the Hebrew term for
legal immigrants. While many memories of immigrants who settled
in Palestine in the 1930s stressed the unifying pioneer spirit and the
sense of community and belonging in Eretz Israel, the realities at the
time were often more complicated. The frictions within the Yishuv
(Jewish community), primarily between Eastern European and
Western European Jewish immigrants and refugees, many of whom
had fled Nazi Germany, often arose from different cultural practices
and customs, as well as from the perceived social-class differences
related to Jewish identity and religiosity. The "language battle" of the
1930s between Yiddish and Hebrew was decided in favor of the latter.[80] Lotti and Hans, however, as well as Kurt and Hanna, like many
other immigrants from Germany, continued to speak German at home
and in their social circles. As was the case with most immigrants, however, they used more and more Hebrew words in their correspondence.
Many of these words, such as *ima* (mother) and *osereth* (household
helper), *assutah* (maternity ward), *b'rith milah* (circumcision celebration), indicate the intersection of this German-speaking family with
the Hebrew-speaking "outside world."

The Jewish immigrants from Germany, dubbed *yekkes* (*Jeckes*),
often recalled their difficulties in learning Hebrew.[81] Even though the
Association of German Immigrants (HOG) offered language courses,
the combination of obsolete teaching methods, the perceived lack of
encouragement to practice everyday Hebrew, and German Jews' deep
attachment to German language and culture often hindered a speedy
acculturation process.[82] While no statistics on Hebrew-language acquisition by German-Jewish immigrants to Palestine are available, anecdotal

evidence suggests that many more men than women enrolled in intensive language courses so that they could improve their chances of finding work.[83] Of course there was a stronger presumption that men rather than women would need to join the workforce. In the case of Lotti and Hans, however, it was Lotti who, as a service professional in a field in demand, had to learn Hebrew in order to communicate with her patients, and as a result she spoke Hebrew better than Hans. Their son recalled: "She was more involved in the East European milieu where Hebrew was much more common. She had a mixed group of patients."[84]

Lotti and Hans maintained strong ties to their families and friends in Germany. While the situation in Palestine was also unsettling, the danger of war became imminent in Central Europe due to Hitler's aggressive demands for the Sudetenland in late summer 1938. Since the majority of Jewish and non-Jewish Germans could not have imagined the extent of the horror and destruction that Nazi Germany would wreak in Europe just a short time later, they favored avoiding war at all costs. Hence, they celebrated the fragile peace brought about by the appeasing Munich Agreement rather than hoping for the Western powers to defeat Hitler via aggressive intervention. Lotti and Hans expressed their relief in letters to Marianne. Summarizing Lotti's and his own response to what he considered the end of the "serious situation in Palestine" and "the European crisis," Hans optimistically proclaimed: "But now peace is guaranteed in any case. I am convinced that there will be no war any time soon."[85] Lotti and Hans wished they could expedite their loved ones' immigration to Palestine. Lotti, who had been worried about Kurt's fate in Germany for some time, assured Marianne that it would not be difficult to obtain an immigration certificate for Kurt, but doubted at the same time whether he would find work in Palestine.[86]

The political tensions in Palestine and Germany coincided with difficulties in Lotti and Hans' relationship. Even though they did not openly discuss them in their correspondence with family members, the careful reader cannot help but notice the underlying conflicts. Letters from both Lotti and Hans may have been sent to Marianne in the same envelope, but they convey very different perspectives and priorities. Lotti complained about Hans' and her incompatibility in terms of their preferred leisure-time activities. While she enjoyed going dancing, Hans rarely went dancing with her or to the movies or a café. More serious than their differing recreational choices was Lotti's fear of having to become the primary breadwinner. Little did Hans know that Lotti clearly understood the seriousness of their financial situation when he urged Marianne not to let Lotti know that he had confided to his sister-in-law a much bleaker picture of their financial situation than he had let on to Lotti.[87] Lotti shared with Marianne how truly burdened she felt:

> *My dental practice provides a certain stability. But now since our income depends on this practice I have begun to resent it. I have always known that I do not belong to the "strong women" who wish to compete with men in terms of work and income. Even though my work and income provide great joy for me, it would be much easier if it were less of a necessity and more of a choice. Given our dependence on my income and the costs associated with a baby we cannot even think of having children at the moment. This decision is very bitter for me at my age and contributes to my state of mind.*[88]

Lotti was not yet ready to articulate it directly, but she suspected that she might be pregnant and was worried about the financial implications if she were.

While on vacation with Hans on Mt. Carmel, Lotti enjoyed her days of relaxation, not yet certain of the changes that life had in store for her: "I am looking at green Mt. Carmel and am seeing the wide expanse of the blue sea. There are hardly any views on this earth that are as beautiful … Just so you have an impression of our meals here: For lunch we had soup, pâté, roast goose with mashed potatoes, peas, coleslaw and a dessert."[89]

After returning from vacation to Tel Aviv, Lotti learned that she was indeed pregnant. Within a week her priorities changed. While both she and Hans agreed that the timing was "less than perfect," they were looking forward to having a baby. Lotti even decided to inform the future grandparents in Germany of her pregnancy earlier than she otherwise would have done so that they could begin sending her baby clothes, diapers and accessories "bit by bit." She also wondered: "Who knows how long this will be possible?"[90] Selma happily reported that the greatest birthday present she had received was Lotti's announcement of her pregnancy.[91]

Only three days after Selma wrote this letter the terrible events of the November Pogrom in Germany dramatically changed the situation for Jews in Germany. Living in relative safety abroad, Lotti, Hans and Marianne were very worried and immediately jumped into action, trying to rescue Kurt and planning the immigration of their "old folks." Desperate and more determined than ever, Lotti and Hans thought of ways for the older generation to make it to Palestine. Lotti wrote her sister Marianne on 5 December 1938, a few days after Kurt's release from KZ Buchenwald:

> *I am convinced that no other country but Palestine can become a new homeland for us. I am still hoping that we all will be united here in the future. Therefore your proposal is quite absurd to have our "old folks" immigrate first to Palestine and then relocate to the United States. This is the* only *country in which our old folks could feel well and be at home. They could speak German everywhere, the people are familiar to them and not that much would change for them. One does not feel foreign here at all, not for one moment. I also believe that mother would want to be here sooner rather than later. I will do everything I can to get an immigration certificate for her.*[92]

Hans also had not yet given up hope of his and Lotti's "old folks" being reunited in Palestine, and presented Marianne with what he considered a plausible scenario and the necessity of Marianne's financial contribution toward it:

> *If my parents could still transfer LP 1,500 to 2,000 they could live here off the interest… Just so you have an idea about the expenses here: The accommodation for all five of our older relatives would cost LP 24, food about LP 3 per person. That does not include trips, entertainment and illnesses. I assume that we would all eat together for lunch and separately for the other meals. The cost of living is much lower here than in America, but the salaries are higher there. So you would not notice your contributions that much. Lotti has already explained to you that our old folks' permanent residence ought to be Palestine.*[93]

Indicative of how unfamiliar their lives were to each other, Hans had no idea of the degree to which Marianne was financially strapped. In order to make ends meet and in hopes of eventually saving enough to help her mother and aunt, she had accepted a six-month 24-hour-a-day nursing position with an elderly couple in Florida, a thousand miles away from her boyfriend Arnold and the few people she knew in the United States. Hans' wishful thinking also included an unintentionally humorous solution to the question of how Lotti and Marianne's loved ones could acquire immigration certificates to Palestine: If Onkel Hermann married Selma, he conjectured, they could immigrate on one certificate.[94]

But even more pressing than getting their older family members out of Germany was the urgent need to help Kurt. His arrest and incarceration in the aftermath of the November Pogrom set into motion his sisters' intense rescue attempts in the United States and in Palestine. While Marianne was frantically trying to accelerate Kurt's immigration to the United States, Lotti and Hans deposited LP 200 with the British consulate in Frankfurt for what Kurt described as an "interim stay" in Palestine.[95] Lotti and Hans also submitted the necessary paperwork to the consulate to secure a tourist visa for Kurt. Lotti had offered to obtain for Kurt a certificate or residence permit for him until he could emigrate to the United States.[96] She wanted to be sure that he would agree and waited to get word from him once he was released from the concentration camp. Kurt's telegram reached a very worried Lotti in Palestine on 2 December: "I am back. Send deposit slip and notarized invitation immediately."[97] Thanks to what Lotti called her "connections," she managed to send Kurt the required papers the same morning, including a notarized invitation and a receipt for funds wired to Germany.[98] Yet for some reason these efforts to get him to Palestine were unsuccessful. Fortunately, however, a few weeks later the sympathetic British consul in Cologne, J.E. Bell, granted a desperate Kurt and his soon-to-be wife Hanna one of the last tourist visas to Palestine.[99]

Kurt and Hanna were lucky to have received visas for Palestine and, despite the difficult circumstances, enjoyed their trip to Palestine via Italy. Kurt vividly described in a letter to Marianne and his loved ones in Germany the train ride from Milan to Trieste, the beauty of the Adriatic coast, the exotic vegetation and the Mediterranean architecture. Since Kurt and Hanna had to wait in long lines to have passports and luggage

Figure 6.4 Hanna and Kurt on ship en route to Palestine, February 1939

checked at the harbor in Trieste, they did not have time to enjoy the delicacies of the Caffè degli Specchi as Selma had hoped they would.[100] (She
might well have visited this famous café with Lotti on their stopover in
Italy in 1937 on her return trip from Palestine to Germany.) After a night
on the train from Milan to Trieste, they were very excited when they
were finally allowed to board the *Gerusaleme* and had a relaxing
passage to Cyprus and from there to Palestine. (See Figure 6.4.)

Kurt and Hanna landed at Jaffa harbor near Tel Aviv in early
February 1939. In a letter to his loved ones in Germany Kurt described
his awe at what he considered exotic surroundings and strange cultural codes when Hanna and he first landed there:

> *On the next morning, earlier than expected, I discovered*
> *several anchored ships when I looked out of our cabin*
> *window. Then I saw land and a city. It was Jaffa!*
> *Soon our ship came to a halt and all of a sudden it was*
> *swarming with all kinds of people – Arabs, baggage-*
> *handlers and salespeople. One of them [Arabs] waited*
> *in front of our cabin door and followed me everywhere,*
> *even to the restroom. In the end my suspicions were eased*
> *when it turned out that he only wanted* mayim *[water].*
> *Of course I helped him and had made a friend.*[101]

Kurt's letter reveals his lack of familiarity with cultures different from his own and his preconceived notions about and fears of Arabs. He looked in astonishment at what he considered an exotic place with interesting looking people, realizing that it would take him a while to understand new cultural codes and behaviors. His expectations were challenged more than once. Kurt and Hanna's son, Gideon, captured his father's first encounter ever with olives in a symbolic anecdote: "When my father saw his first olive he expected it to be as sweet as a cherry. When he tried it, he could not stand it and spat it out. After that, he would not even try to eat olives for years."[102]

Kurt and Hanna were welcomed upon their arrival by Kurt's thrilled sister Lotti and her husband Hans. The reunion must have been so moving that Kurt, barely finding words to express his utter delight and joy, left it up to the recipient of his letter to imagine his emotions. He commented in an understated manner: "Well, and then … What shall I say? We talked and we all were happy." Kurt expressed how very much he was looking forward to the next night when the two couples were planning to celebrate his and Hanna's wedding with a festive meal, a roast goose.[103] (See Figure 6.5.)

The euphoria surrounding Kurt and Hanna's arrival, however, soon gave way to everyday concerns about employment, housing and setting up lives in a completely alien culture. Not choice, but dire circumstances and luck led Kurt and Hanna to Palestine. For the first few months they shared a crowded household together with Lotti and Hans, who were expecting their first child in June. This was a taxing time for all. A shortage of apartments in Tel Aviv made it very difficult for new refugees to find a place to rent. Luckily, Lotti discovered that the family of one of her patients was about to move out of their one-room apartment. She arranged for Kurt and Hanna to get this apartment, even at a reasonable rent. To live in their own one-room apartment greatly helped Kurt and Hanna's process of adjustment. Kurt raved about their new place. Even though their furniture had not arrived, they were very happy with their modest but independent living conditions.[104] As newly-weds Kurt and Hanna had not yet lived together anywhere on their own and were now quite happy to do so.

Almost immediately after Kurt and Hanna moved out, however, Hans' brother Ernst, who had just immigrated from Germany, moved in with Lotti and Hans.[105] Again, the initial joy of having another family member join them in Palestine soon collided head-on

Figure 6.5 From left: Hans, Lotti, Hanna, Kurt, Tel Aviv, spring 1939

with the challenges of everyday life. This was a particular burden for the pregnant Lotti. It would be more than seven months before she and Hans would have their small apartment to themselves again. Similar to Kurt, Hans' brother Ernst Kaiser-Blüth considered Palestine only a stepping-stone on his way to the United States. But, unlike the initial reaction of Kurt, who was thrilled to be out of Germany, where he suffered internment and maltreatment at KZ Buchenwald, Ernst's first observations and critical attitude toward Palestine did not bode well for even a short stay there. Ernst was among the lucky few young or middle-aged Jewish men who had not been interned in a concentration camp following the November Pogrom. He presumably felt less concerned about survival than about finding an acceptable new homeland, and wrote Marianne: "You are lucky that you went directly to America. There is nothing to gain here. The smart ones here are the ones who live off their savings. That way they lose less than if they worked."[106] Ernst expected to stay in Palestine for only a few months, as his relatively low registration number for the US quota seemed to guarantee his immigration to the States by the end of 1939.[107]

At the beginning of their new lives in Palestine, Kurt worked for several weeks on a *moshav*, or cooperative farm, that raised chickens in Ramoth Hashavim and where Günter, one of his university friends, also worked.[108] Kurt and Hanna's son, Gideon, explained:

> *Well, there are* kibbutzim *and* moshavim. *The* kibbutzim *had no private property, and everything was according to communist principles. Everything belonged to everybody: To each according to his needs, from each according to his abilities.* Moshavim *were something different. They also exist today. Everybody has a piece of land: one grows bananas; the other has chickens, and so on. But they have a communal system of distribution. That is the main difference: In the* kibbutz, *there is a food store where everybody takes what they need… And then my father, the state's attorney* (Oberlandesgerichtsrat), *worked in a chicken coop.*[109]

Lotti recalled in a 1988 interview that in Palestine "Kurt and Hanna had a very, very difficult time at the beginning."[110] Trained in Germany as a lawyer in Roman rather than Anglo-American common law, Kurt could not work in his profession. Yet he was eagerly looking for jobs and needed to make a living quickly.[111] Kurt lived on the *moshav* for a few weeks but then left because he made hardly any money there. Back in Tel Aviv, Kurt decided to enroll in a Hebrew-language course and take private lessons in English conversation.[112] He was still intent on emigration to the United States and in the meantime hoped to increase his job opportunities with British employers. Hanna, without any special education or training in Germany or Palestine, did find a job as a waitress but lost it after a short time, presumably because she could not speak Hebrew.[113]

Another worry for Kurt was Hanna's and his temporary legal status. As a German lawyer and bureaucrat Kurt was still psychologically tied to following the rules and felt the urgent need to have all their papers in order. Given his plans to stay in Palestine only temporarily, he hesitated to take any steps to set up even semi-permanent residency in Palestine and agonized over the decision to apply for a renewal of their tourist visas. He had heard a rumor that it would be better not to alert the immigration officials to the upcoming deadline. But not having the correct legal papers would have, as Kurt put it, "gone against my convictions."[114] To Kurt's great relief Marianne and Arthur Stern's affidavits for his immigration to the United States had arrived at the US consulate in Stuttgart.[115] Kurt and Hanna's tourist visas were renewed for another three months at the beginning of May 1939, apparently because Kurt was able to produce the proof of sufficient funds. Whether the affidavits for immigration to the United States helped them to get their tourist visas for Palestine renewed is not clear. However, Kurt seemed to think it did and was glad to have them. With regard to how the British officials in Palestine treated immigrants, especially tentative ones, Kurt wrote: "They are very petty toward all groups of immigrants here right now."[116] Kurt did not know at the time that the British Parliament was developing drastic changes in immigration policies, which were published two weeks later in a White Paper. The White Paper effectively and drastically limited Jewish immigration to Palestine to a total of 75,000 people over a five-year period, beginning in 1939.[117]

Lotti, who had adjusted rather quickly and quite well to life in Palestine, became a little impatient with what she perceived as Kurt's reluctance to pursue new opportunities and what she considered his "passivity" in looking for jobs. Lotti saw Kurt as a "typical German academic," who lacked pragmatism and made mountains out of molehills instead of vigorously embracing new challenges.[118] Yet Lotti might have underestimated the effects of Kurt's traumatic experiences and the stress of his last months in Nazi Germany, as well as his initial culture shock. Kurt and Hanna did adjust to their new realities, but that, of course, took some time.

Kurt's search for work eventually met with some success. He waited for weeks to receive approval by the British for a job with a "very important [British] distributor of books, newspapers and journals" at the end of May.[119] He was first hired as a salesman on a probationary basis, with minimal income. After two months he and Hanna were supposed to be able to open a combination newspaper stand/bookstore in the main British military camp on the outskirts of Sarafand, where a new shopping center was planned.[120] Kurt was very much looking forward to receiving the British authorities' final approval and prepared himself for his new job by reading a lot of British and American publications. Kurt's delight at being able to recommend English-language journals and books to Marianne was offset by the difficulties he experienced a few weeks later:[121]

> *This matter takes its normal course, which means here*
> *a particularly slow one. I like the job and think that we*
> *will have a decent income. However, the construction in*
> *Sarafand has not even started. This is not my company's*
> *fault, which is very interested in a faster pace. The military*
> *government is to blame for the slow progress. And before*
> *the opening I cannot demand any income. But I have*
> *to admit that I am not being exploited, but trained. If it*
> *should take much longer, I will get another advance. But*
> *no matter how long it will take, I consider it better to*
> *just follow this lead, which seems to be a solid company,*
> *instead of looking for some kind of inferior job. This would*
> *always limit me, and even this I would need to find first.*[122]

Kurt and Hanna's financial situation was now very serious. All that Hanna earned was LP 4 a month as a part-time waitress.[123] At that time Hans calculated that the monthly subsistence income needed for a couple was LP 10.[124] This was indeed subsistence level, considering that in the mid 1930s the General Federation of Laborers in Eretz Israel (Histadrut) calculated that a bachelor needed to earn a minimum of LP 8 plus LP 3 for any additional person per household.[125] Kurt and Hanna's difficult material situation was exacerbated by the fact that their entire container with furniture, clothing and household items had been held up in the harbor of Antwerp already for eight months when war broke out.[126] As it turned out, Kurt and Hanna never saw their belongings again.

Family members wanted to help, but that was not easy. Much to Selma's disappointment, she was not allowed to send money from Germany to Palestine.[127] Marianne, who, although overqualified, was working as a nurse in a summer camp infirmary in 1939, was the only hope. She managed to get some money to Kurt and Hanna, most likely by selling part of Kurt's treasured stamp collection.[128] Kurt, a passionate stamp collector, had asked Marianne to take part of his valuable collection with her to the United States for safekeeping. When it had become obvious that Kurt might not be allowed to emigrate there in the immediate future, he asked Marianne to either send him or sell some of his stamps so that he could receive the urgently needed proceeds. In July 1939 Kurt suggested his sister send him the selected stamps she held in safekeeping:

> *You want to know how much the stamps are worth?*
> *These seven stamps would be worth about 320 RM in*
> *Germany, abroad of course less. So, please send them to*
> *me if it does not look like war. At the moment I would*
> *suggest you send them. They are supposed to be in their*
> *appropriate place in the album. I am contemplating*
> *sending several complete albums of the collection to you.*
> *In the meantime, I have gotten several more valuable*
> *stamps here than you have there [from my collection].*[129]

In the spring of 1939 news from Palestine was not good. In an effort to curb Arab revolts and discontent over the growing number of Jewish immigrants, the British government released its White Paper. After that, further Jewish immigration would be contingent on the agreement of the Palestinian Arabs. The White Paper also severely restricted Jewish land acquisition and aimed at a bi-national state with a Jewish minority of about one-third of the total population.[130] After the White Paper was publicized enormous Jewish demonstrations erupted in Tel Aviv. Kurt and Hans were among those protesting. Kurt, for one, deeply resented:

> *this recent British policy, if one could call it that. The way*
> *the British now treat the promises they once made [the*
> *Balfour Declaration] and their "solution" to the future*
> *of Palestine is unbelievable… You might have heard or*
> *read about the demonstrations here in the news. Hans*
> *and I were among the 50,000 protesters, a quarter of*
> *the population of 200,000. We all marched in wonderful*
> *order and discipline – and unlike Nazi Germany without*
> *any pressure – to the stadium, where we listened to*
> *speeches in Hebrew and sang the Hatikvah.*[131]

The White Paper represented a significant setback for the Jewish population in Palestine and those remaining in Europe who had hoped to immigrate. Just as the number of European Jews seeking refuge in Palestine rose dramatically, the British government all but closed its doors to Jewish immigration. While almost all Jews in Palestine rejected the White Paper, the varying responses revealed underlying internal political conflicts between the Labor Party (Ma'pai) under David Ben-Gurion and the opposition Revisionist Party, also known as the Union of Zionist Revisionists (Ha-Zohar), led by Zeev Jabotinsky. Both groups agreed on the necessity of a "national home" in Palestine for the Jewish people but differed on how to achieve this goal. They also disagreed on such issues as immigration, religious identity and sovereignty, among others.[132] The main goal of the militant Revisionist Party was the imminent establishment of a sovereign Jewish state that they were prepared to achieve by means of violence.[133] The Revisionists also rejected Ma'pai's official policy of compromise toward the British as lacking purpose and called for private investments as the fastest way to bring larger numbers of Jews to Palestine, including to the land on both sides of the River Jordan.[134] Kurt and Hanna, and presumably Lotti and Hans, opposed the Revisionists' divisive and provocative politics. Within a few months of their arrival Kurt and Hanna were directly affected by the precarious political situation in Palestine. Hanna wrote Marianne that the "stupid Revisionists had murdered an Arab. That's why we have a curfew here and are not allowed in the streets after 9:30 p.m."[135]

Since the disappointing outcome of the Evian Conference and the increasingly restrictive British immigration policy in Palestine, the refugee problem in Central Europe had reached tragic dimensions, even before the outbreak of World War II. By 1938 the Committee for Illegal Immigration (Mossad le Aliyah Bet) had become one of the main forces behind the clandestine immigration of German and Eastern European Jews into Palestine. The illegal immigrants (*ma'apilim*) risked their lives trying to reach Palestine, mostly on boats and ships, not even knowing if they would be able to disembark after their dangerous passage. While thousands died in their attempts to land on the shores of Palestine, more than 40 percent of those who arrived there between 1939 and 1941 were *ma'apilim*.[136] Clandestine immigration was of course a controversial undertaking. Nazi authorities such as the Security Service (Sicherheitsdienst or SD) and the Gestapo were not only aware of these operations but actively supported them in order to reduce the number of Jews in Germany.[137] The human tragedies experienced during these immigration attempts caused great concern among Jews in Palestine and in countries from which Jews were trying to escape.

Hans alluded in a letter of late April 1939 to a "ship with illegal immigrants that was recently sent back. The fate of these poor people must be terrible. They are usually on board an old freight ship for about five weeks, with barely a place to sleep, insufficient food and horrible sanitary conditions."[138] Hans might have been referring to one of two boats that sailed in March and April from Romania, the *Sandu* and the *Assimi*. Both ships were listed as "captured and returned." They had 270 and 470 people on board respectively, none of whom were allowed to disembark.[139]

In these dramatic times the birth of Lotti and Hans' son, Michael Alexander, on 9 June 1939 took center stage for the Kaiser-Blüth family in Palestine. The proud father sent telegrams and letters with detailed accounts of the birth to the overjoyed grandparents in Essen and Cologne: "After the nurse handed the baby over to Lotti, he rested his little head on his hands like a philosopher and pensively looked at his *ima* [mother]."[140] Lotti's genuine elation as a new mother shone through every one of her sentences about her lovely baby boy. Even on the day after giving birth she admitted "the joy was worth the pain."[141] After Lotti's release from the hospital, a nurse, Hedwig Schwarz, who had worked as a nurse for fourteen years in the women's ward at the Israelitisches Asyl in Cologne, helped Lotti for the following two weeks at home.[142]

Hans marveled at his newborn son, describing his physical features in great detail, proudly mentioning a resemblance to himself, which Lotti had gleefully detected the day after Michael's birth. After some deliberation, Lotti and Hans decided on the name Michael Alexander. Hans explained that the name Michael means "he who is like God" and that the middle name Alexander honored Lotti's late father.[143] Just before Lotti and Michael were allowed to go home from the maternity ward, the *bris* (*b'rith milah*) or ritual circumcision was performed there.[144] Hanna was Michael's godmother, and Hans' brother Ernst the godfather, as Hans put it, "standing in for grandfather Julius." Following the *bris* the joyous celebration at home with about forty guests was clearly tempered by the absence of grandparents and Marianne, a stark reminder of the sad reality of the family's separation. Yet hopes for a family reunion kept up everybody's spirits. Hans made sure to take pictures of Lotti and Michael on their first day home to send to their loved ones in Germany. In order to give the grandparents a lively impression, he even recorded Michael's coos.[145]

Kurt was also very proud of his nephew and noted with surprise Michael's ability to smile with his entire face: "He already looks quite human and grows tremendously. I cannot confirm his similarity to Hans that Lotti initially reported. The question is still open after whom Michael will take."[146] While still in Germany at the beginning of 1939 Kurt had purchased a baby carriage that Julius shipped to Palestine.[147] To the proud parents' delight, it arrived shortly after Michael's birth.

From the very beginning, Lotti fully embraced motherhood, joyfully reporting on Michael's growth and physical development. She kept her own and Hans' families entertained with loving stories of his progress and sunny disposition, considering motherhood a fulfillment of her "womanly life."[148] Even though the grandparents in Germany, especially Hans' parents, helped out generously with furniture, clothing and all sorts of other material needs for the baby and the young parents, Lotti and Hans' savings had shrunk precipitously. Lotti wanted to stay home with the baby for a while but was afraid that her lack of income would put even more pressure on their economic situation. Lotti sounded very disappointed when she reported in late May 1939 to Marianne: "We have to save every piaster."[149] Then their big hope that one of Hans' important business deals would come through seemed finally to materialize:

> *Last Friday we received the good news. The MAN*
> *Company succeeded after one and a half years in getting*
> *the approval for Hans to transfer machinery valued at*
> *around 14,000 RM plus 45 percent in foreign currency.*
> *That means that Hans would need to find buyers [in*
> *Palestine] who would be willing to pay the equivalent of*
> *25,000 RM. They would need to transfer the 45 percent*
> *in foreign currency to Germany and pay him the rest here.*
> *Hans would pay for this transaction from his RM account*
> *here. All this will not be easy, but at least there still seems*
> *to be the chance of a favorable transfer.*[150]

Hans was delighted not only because this significant project promised urgently needed income but also because it involved travel to

Germany. The final negotiations on this very important business deal, which apparently involved the outfitting of a cement plant,[151] were to take place in Augsburg.[152] From today's perspective it is hardly fathomable that a German-Jewish man in exile would voluntarily return to Germany on a business trip, especially after the November Pogrom, in which 26,000 Jewish men had been interned in concentration camps and mistreated. But in the summer of 1939 it felt like the right thing to do. Hans worked for MAN and had been involved in Ha'avarah deals with Germany for quite some time, and he had been waiting for years for this chance. Even though rumors about an impending war were in the air, the hope remained that it could be averted, like it had with the Munich Agreement less than a year before.[153] Hans' project was further delayed, but he had decided not to pass up this enormous chance "despite the critical situation."[154]

Apparently, MAN's management had asked Hans by telegram to come to its Augsburg headquarters. Because he now held a British mandate passport, the German company had to convince the Gestapo in Berlin to have the German consul in Jaffa issue Hans a visa for three weeks.[155] At the end of July Hans bade farewell to Lotti and their six-week-old son Michael, optimistic that he would finally make a good profit from this deal.[156] While he was sad to leave his family in Palestine, he was also very much looking forward to escaping the oppressive mid-summer heat there and to seeing his parents in Cologne and visiting with Selma and Henny.

Hans' business trip, which had looked so promising just a few weeks before, was cut shorter than he expected once he arrived in Augsburg. Hans asked for a slightly longer extension of his visa, possibly in order to visit his mother Flora once again, this time for her fifty-ninth birthday at the end of August. By the time he asked about renewing his visa his manager at MAN, Herr Carstanjen, had an inkling of the impending war and decided it was best not to petition the German authorities for a renewal of the visa.[157] Hans and Lotti's son, Michael, retold the events as he remembered them from his father's stories of years before: "The manager's name at MAN was Carstanjen. He came out of a certain meeting and told him: 'Look, Mr. Kaiser-Blüth, I cannot tell you much, but if you want my advice, forget about any business, pack up your things and leave Germany as fast as possible.'"[158]

After months of planning and high hopes it became painfully clear to Hans that the major precondition for his promising business deal, namely no war, was no longer guaranteed.[159] Fortunately, Hans followed Herr Carstanjen's advice and left Germany just in time. He admitted that he too "believed up to the last day that it would only be a war of nerves. The opinion about Hitler and Nazism in Germany was: You must regard them like the movement of waves. Within two months the time of Hitler will be over. This was the opinion of world-renown[ed] industrialists. I am not so optimistic."[160]

Michael relayed the story of his father's narrow escape:

> My father still went to Cologne to bid farewell to his parents, then he had to wait for the next Italian ship sailing from Trieste to Haifa. He decided to stop in Bled in Slovenia, at a lake. The next morning, he was sitting down for breakfast and reading in the Times from London about the Molotov–Ribbentrop agreement... Then he went to Trieste, boarded the vessel and sailed down the Italian coast. The ship got instructions to turn back to Trieste, as the war had started, and wait for Italy's decision... What did il Duce say? Italy is not joining the war. So they all sailed to Haifa, and my father came back.[161]

Lotti was beside herself with worry regarding Hans' safe return. While anxiously waiting for him she could not bring herself to write letters and left it up to Kurt to relate the most important news to a concerned Marianne:

> Hans has not yet come back from Europe. He was on board of the Galilea when she was called back to Italy from Rhodes. We had bad days. There were [sic] no news, neither from him nor from the shipping company. Some days ago we received a telegram from Hans... They have started yesterday from Trieste again and will be here on Saturday. In the meantime the situation has become better as far [sic] as Italy has remained neutral.[162]

After traveling for more than two weeks on the eve of and during the outbreak of the war, with his loved ones praying for his safe return, he finally arrived back in Tel Aviv on 9 September 1939. Lotti was greatly relieved when Hans finally returned; as a young mother she felt

particularly vulnerable and exhausted. While both considered themselves very lucky that Hans had made it back to Palestine, they also
were very distressed to see their hopes for prosperity evaporate. Upon
his return to Palestine, Hans realized that, after having waited for this
deal for four years, he had in the end lost orders that would have been
worth about LP 250–300,000, in addition to his travel expenses. Hans
likened his misfortune to a "mountain climber who is almost at the
summit when an avalanche takes him down into the abyss before he
reaches his goal."[163] According to his contract as a sales representative
working on commission with MAN, Hans was eligible for the reim-
bursement of his travel costs and other expenses only if he successfully
concluded a business deal.[164]

Of course, at the outbreak of the war the family members
spread over three continents hoped that it would not last long. Kurt
described the double-bind that many German-Jewish refugees with
loved ones still in Germany painfully experienced at the outbreak of
the war. In order to distance himself consciously from any association
with Nazi Germany Kurt wrote this letter in English to Marianne:

> *Hitler has begun war! As to the general viewpoint, there
> has [sic] nothing to be said. All is perfectly clear, the
> causes and the aims. The Jewish Agency and especially
> Dr. Weizmann are right: The [sic] Jewry has to stand and
> stands by Great Britain. But as to the personal side, you
> will understand that I think every hour of our mother and
> the other ones concerned. We only can hope that we shall
> see them again afterwards.*[165]

With the outbreak of World War II Palestine, as a British mandate
territory, and Germany had become "enemy countries." While Kurt
was fully ready to support the war against Hitler, he was of course
also very concerned about what war would mean for his loved ones
in Germany. By 1 October 1939 about 135,000 Jews, which was 85
percent of all Jewish men in Palestine, had registered themselves for
voluntary service.[166] Kurt informed Marianne about the severity of the
situation and his further plans:

> *Beginning next week Jews can enroll themselves at
> the Jewish Agency's initiative in its special offices for*

*voluntary service in Palestine, that means maintaining
the economy, protecting order and safety, and being at
the disposal of the British forces in the country. Although
there is no immediate danger of attack, Italy being
neutral, the situation can change from one day to another.
And therefore this measure is most important both for the
National Home and Great Britain. I think I shall enroll
myself too.*[167]

Apparently, Kurt and Hans, both 33 years old at the time, registered
to serve in September 1939, but, according to Kurt, only younger men
were called upon to serve.[168] In addition, by and large the British army
only allowed German Jews from Palestine to serve in combat units
during the last phases of the war.[169] Nevertheless, German-Jewish
immigrants helped the British war effort in many other ways, such
as manufacturing and delivering supplies, building anti-tank trenches
and fortifying borders.[170]

   Kurt was very worried about the widening of the war in May
1940 when Nazi Germany invaded France and the Low Countries.[171]
He feared that his and Hanna's modest business prospects would
greatly suffer if the war spread further to the Mediterranean.
Fortunately, after having lived in Palestine for about eighteen months,
Kurt and Hanna could finally realize their project of managing a
bookstore in the main British military camp in Sarafand. Kurt was
very proud of their store, which included a lending library. They also
sold newspapers, magazines, typewriters, gifts and, in Kurt's words,
"high-grade stationery."[172] An undated family photograph, presumably taken in 1940, shows a happily smiling, suntanned Hanna
selling newspapers to two customers from the British military base.
Among the Hebrew- and English-language newspapers on display the
Palestine Post appeared to be the most prominently featured publication. (See Figure 6.6.)

   In June 1940 Kurt and Hanna moved into an airy apartment
in the nearby village of Rishon le-Zion. The one drawback seemed to
be that they had to work shifts and rarely saw each other outside the
store. As Kurt described it in a letter to Marianne: "The only problem
is the long working days. We begin selling newspapers at 5:30 a.m. and
work all day long without a break, until 7 or 8 p.m. Because the store
has to be open every day, Hanna and I are never off on the same day,

7 RESCUING LOVED ONES TRAPPED IN NAZI GERMANY, 1939–1942

Having to bid farewell to her only son and his new wife, Selma felt torn between sadness and relief. She wrote Nanna, who had been in the United States for six months: "Our children are now getting ready to leave. When you receive this letter they will soon arrive in Palestine, God willing. I am so relieved that they found an interim solution. It had been a very stressful time with lots of upheaval and a hectic pace. We hardly managed to sit together for an hour."[1] With her last child leaving Germany Selma's lugubrious sigh, "Now all I have left of you are your letters,"[2] echoed a frequently used expression among German Jews at the time.[3] The sense of having to replace, at least temporarily, the immediate personal contact with postal exchanges was often accompanied by the hope that this painful separation would pass quickly.

Of the more than 170,000 Jews in Germany at the outbreak of the war, 32 percent were over 60.[4] By 1941 about two-thirds of Jews in Germany were past middle age, with a disproportionately high number of women remaining. Historian Marion Kaplan concludes that for older women "age, even more than being female, worked against a timely flight; together they were lethal."[5] In 1939 the members of the extended family remaining in Germany were almost exclusively elderly, and mostly female, although there were also a few couples and two 69-year-old men, the bachelor Onkel Hermann and Karl Kaufmann, the widower of Selma and Henny's younger sister, Paula.[6]

In early 1939 Henny had to have a renal tumor operation, and although she fully recovered in the spring of 1939, many significant

challenges were in store for Selma and her. Their Gentile landlady terminated their lease, even though a new anti-Jewish law that severely
restricted the rights of Jewish tenants had not required her to do so.[7]
Selma's appeal to the landlady, who claimed her property had been
damaged during the November Pogrom on account of her Jewish
tenants and that she needed to protect her property, was unsuccessful.[8] Forced out of their apartment in Essen, the two sisters decided
with heavy hearts to move to Cologne and to move Onkel Hermann
along with his sister Johanna to an old people's home there. Onkel
Hermann's physician diagnosed him with progressive arteriosclerosis,
with no prospects of recovery, and vehemently advised against his emigration.[9] The realization that Onkel Hermann would need to remain
in Germany was indeed distressing. However, securing a long-term
assisted-living arrangement for him in Cologne would also free up
the sisters to pursue their own emigration plans. Selma mentioned her
relief in her letter to Marianne:

> *I always had to think about what would be best for Onkel*
> *Hermann. Now I am much less worried. I could not bear*
> *the thought of leaving him behind without adequate care.*
> *I hope that we made the right decision. It has become*
> *entirely impossible to even consider his emigration in his*
> *current condition… I am hoping that he will soon get used*
> *to his new surroundings.*[10]

Meanwhile, in Palestine, once Kurt and his wife Hanna began to settle in, they tried "very hard to get Mother and Aunt to Palestine."[11]
This was not an easy undertaking, especially since neither Kurt nor
Hanna had a regular income and were still adjusting to the climate,
language and culture. Nevertheless, having had his own terrible experiences in Nazi Germany Kurt was determined to get his loved ones to
Palestine. Lotti and Hans were in total agreement. Expecting her first
baby in June 1939, Lotti yearned for her mother and aunt to join her
in Palestine. Once they had found out about Lotti's pregnancy, the
grandparents in Germany began shopping for the baby's layette set to
send to Palestine. Selma reported how thrilled she and Flora were at
the prospect of becoming grandmothers.[12] Julius insisted they buy only
the best and the most beautiful things.[13] But their joy also gave way to
pain because of the separation from their children and now from their

first grandchild. Selma's only solace was the comforting hope that she and Henny would eventually live with Lotti, Hans and their baby in Palestine.[14]

Shortly after Onkel Hermann was admitted to the Jewish old people's home section of the Israelitisches Asyl in Cologne, where Marianne had completed her residency, Selma and Henny were caught up in commotion and upheaval, preparing for their move to Cologne. Yet they tried to remain positive. Before leaving Essen, where they had lived for thirty-seven years, "in good times and bad,"[15] Selma and Henny, as Jews, were required by law to turn over their modest assets in gold and silver.[16] The municipal pawnshop weighed and registered Selma's eleven silver spoons and ninety-three silver coins, one golden ring and one golden necklace. In line with the Nazi practice of shamelessly profiteering from Jewish property, Jews received a paltry amount for their valuables. The municipal pawnshop in Essen paid Selma the absurdly low sum of 41.14 RM, about 12 percent of the actual value.[17]

At the end of June 1939 Selma, Henny and their sister Emma moved in with Hans' parents, the Kaiser-Blüths, in Cologne. Six months after their textile factory had been "Aryanized," Flora and Julius chose to rent their second floor to Selma and her sisters. The board of their synagogue had encouraged the members of its congregation on several occasions that spring to take in Jewish tenants "voluntarily" before the city's lord mayor forced them to do so.[18]

Even though they lived in a roomy, beautiful house in a suburb of Cologne called Braunsfeld, space for the three additional occupants on the second floor was limited to two rooms and a closet.[19] Selma and Henny had to sell their non-essential household items, including their beds. Trying to make the best of the situation, Selma was holding out hope that the move to Cologne would be a very short-term solution: "We will sleep in Ernst and Hans' beds, with our own bedding. We kept our own horsehair mattresses and will have them turned into couches once the immigration to Palestine is getting closer."[20] Since the upstairs rooms in the Kaiser-Blüth house were heated by coal stove the sisters, now well into their 60s, needed to carry coal briquettes sixty-five steps upstairs from the basement.[21] Selma was a little apprehensive about having to live there through the winter: "Hopefully we will not have to heat our new place and would be at Lotti's by then."[22]

Lotti had applied in April for her mother and aunt to immigrate to Palestine. But the following month the British government released its White Paper, dramatically restricting Jewish immigration to Palestine. Lotti reported to Marianne in late May: "The authorities did not yet accept my immigration application for our old folks. They had just issued certificates under the present schedule, but these are only for people who are already here."[23] The British government set a schedule, or quota, every few months for a certain number of persons eligible to receive an immigration certificate. According to the *Jüdisches Nachrichtenblatt*, however, a large portion of the certificates were reserved for young people.[24] Unfortunately, Lotti erroneously sent the immigration materials to the authorities in Palestine rather than to the British consulate in Cologne. The British consulate finally returned Lotti's application for Selma and Henny's immigration in August, informing Lotti only then that no applications would be considered "until further notice."[25] Given the emphasis on granting priority on this schedule to young people and those on either tourist visas or settled illegally in Palestine, it is very unlikely that Selma and Henny would have been included in this June–September 1939 quota, even if Lotti's mistake had not occurred. This turned out to be the last pre-war schedule. Legal immigration to Palestine from Germany, only 52 percent of the total Jewish immigration to Palestine in 1939, dropped to 20 percent in 1940, which amounted to 900 people.[26] These were the last legal immigrants into Palestine from Germany.

Lotti and Kurt's dream of getting their mother and aunt to Palestine was rekindled by Hans' summer 1939 trip to Germany. Once there he hoped to convince his parents in person of the absolute urgency of leaving Germany and emigrating to Palestine. He also planned to accompany his mother-in-law Selma to the British consulate in Cologne in order to request a review of her application there. But because he had to cut his trip short owing to the imminent outbreak of war, he was unable to accomplish anything regarding his or Lotti's "parents'" emigration.

The outbreak of war was a shock for the Kaufmann–Steinberg family, albeit not entirely unexpected. It was, of course, terrible news for the family spread out across three continents. Hans' mother Flora wrote: "I seem to have been too optimistic. I was convinced of a peaceful solution. Poor humankind!"[27] His father Julius added: "We are now sitting in the second war, but I still hope that the conflict can be resolved. I am trying to lift the spirits of the ... ladies here."[28] Selma, Henny and Emma sent several reassuring but nonetheless worried letters and postcards to their children. Selma's touching letter captured her feeling of being torn between great sadness and hope:

> *This letter is to let you know that we are all healthy. We longingly wait for any news from you. I am hoping with all my heart that this war will soon be over for the well-being of all humankind. I am also hoping that there will be a time when wartime exists only as a sad memory and will not happen yet again. Hopefully we will be able to remain in touch with each other. This is the only thing we old people have left of you.*[29]

The outbreak of war immediately resulted in delays and interruptions to the postal service between Germany, Palestine and the United States. The postal connections between Germany and the United States were interrupted for at least the first month of the war.[30] The direct official mail service between Germany and Palestine as a British mandate and thus a territory at war with Germany was discontinued entirely for the duration of the war. Therefore Marianne in the United States took on the role of sending correspondence back and forth between her relatives in Germany and Palestine. Initially, Selma's nephew in the neutral Netherlands, Moritz Kaufmann, and his wife Bertl, also sent family mail to and from Palestine and Germany.[31] Moritz made sure to note on the envelopes "written in German" so that the letters would get through the censors more quickly. The German invasion of the Netherlands on 10 May 1940 was very disconcerting for the extended family. The spread of war meant that the family correspondence could not be sent via Moritz any more, but it also signaled an uncertain future for Moritz Kaufmann and his family, who had deemed themselves safe in a neutral country. To secure another line of communication, and to stay in touch with relatives, Selma also reached out to Hanna's mother, Sofie Levy, who had emigrated to Argentina in 1937. Selma and Sofie corresponded for a couple of years, but because letters took up to sixteen months to arrive this was hardly a regular exchange.[32]

During the 1939 High Holy Days of Rosh Hashanah and Yom Kippur the family prayed for peace and an uninterrupted postal service. Selma wrote Marianne:

> Our most heartfelt wish is of course for peace among all people so that we all might be freed from the nightmare of war. We hope to be able to live as we did before and that the memory of this time might only be just that, a memory. May the almighty Lord help us! The best present for the holidays would be peace. May all weapons rest and all people of all nations live in peace and harmony together.[33]

In consideration of stricter censorship rules during wartime, Selma even changed her handwriting. She explained to Marianne: "I am writing in Latin script that might be more legible for the censors at the border. I am hoping that this way my letters will reach you faster."[34] To avoid provoking the censors, Selma did not report to her children new restrictions on Jews. On Yom Kippur, 23 September 1939, Jews were forced to turn their radios in to local police stations.[35] This measure further degraded Jews who observed this Day of Atonement in solemn prayer and fasting. Radios were not only sources for news but also entertainment. Flora had written of the family sitting together to listen to radio dramas, concerts or operas.[36]

While praying for a quick return of "peace and normal conditions," Selma and Henny were distressed that so many older family members were left behind in Germany. Selma described their visit to her younger sister in a letter to Marianne: "We went to visit Tante Thekla for a few days. There are lonely parents everywhere ... We will have almost no young people left in our family [in Germany] ... The old people are getting more and more lonesome."[37] In between their trips to see their youngest sister Thekla, brother Leo and other relatives, Selma and Henny lived, as they described it, "quietly and secluded." Typical of women of their generation in Germany, they were busy in the fall preserving vegetables and fruit. Selma reported to her children in early September: "We also preserved some fruit and are now ready for the winter. Tante Flora's plum trees produced generously. But who knows who will eat them with us."[38] Selma and Henny might have also sensed that storing provisions at a time of war could be a necessary precaution against shortages. The Nazi government began food rationing after the outbreak of war and explicitly limited more and more items available to Jews from the list. First, the amount of butter and meat was limited for Jews. Then they were prohibited from buying cocoa and rice. By January 1940 Jews were not allowed to purchase most legumes, fruit and meat.[39] In addition to limited food items that Jews were allowed to buy, they could shop only at severely restricted and inconvenient times.[40]

Even though Selma and Henny tried to appear upbeat in their letters to their children, Marianne commented to her siblings on their "depressed mental condition," which she noticed when reading between the lines of their letters.[41] Along with many other "lonely parents" Selma hoped to be reunited with at least one or two of her children soon.[42] Yet the signs were not very optimistic. Before the war Selma had briefly considered emigration to Palestine, but hesitated. She thought that the economic strain on Lotti and Hans would be too much, especially since they needed to help Kurt and Hanna get settled in Palestine. Three weeks into the war Lotti described herself as "trembling at the thought of our loved ones in Germany. It is too terrible that we did not succeed in getting a certificate for our beloved mother and aunt in time."[43]

Although the outbreak of war dashed any hopes for Selma and Henny's emigration to Palestine, Kurt did not give up trying to get them out of Germany. Despite the fact that Kurt and Hanna had settled themselves in Palestine, Kurt continued to keep active his registration number for immigration to the United States; both he and Hanna still considered emigrating there and held out hope of getting Selma there as well. Selma calculated that it might take up to six years before her registration number for immigration to the United States would come up. She wrote in the fall of 1939 to Marianne: "If we could only be together! I would love to help you make your nice apartment even cozier. Let's hope that we will be reunited in the future … But until then we have to be patient."[44]

In November 1939 Kurt contacted the US consulate in Jerusalem and asked to:

[t]ransfer the application of my mother Selma Steinberg (registration number 31691) under my own above mentioned. My mother, as a widow, has always lived in

*my household and we were intending to emigrate together
to the U.S. ... Before we got our visas I was forced to
leave suddenly on order of the Gestapo... I was not able
to take my mother with me, because I did not succeed in
getting a visa for Palestine for her... We are anxious to
[be] join[ed] again in my household in the U.S.*[45]

It is likely that he and Hanna would have emigrated to the
United States if Kurt could have obtained a visa for Selma to emigrate there. In mid April 1940 he was disappointed by the answer from
the US consulate in Jerusalem: "The Consulate General cannot place
on its immigration waiting lists names of persons not residing in this
country ... Should your mother come to this country I shall take pleasure in according her on the waiting list the same priority which she had
by virtue of her registration."[46] If Selma somehow miraculously did find
her way to Palestine in wartime, the US consulate in Jerusalem would
honor her individual registration as part of the German quota, but it
would not place her under her son's registration or move her up any
faster on the quota list. Kurt's hope, illusory at best, was shattered.

Kurt updated Marianne on Selma's potential immigration
to the United States and asked Marianne to intervene at the State
Department in Washington, DC on Selma's behalf:

*We tried again to get a certificate for mother [to Palestine],
but in vain. I did not succeed in getting Mother included
in my immigration application [to the United States] at the
consulate here. Maybe you could try it in the U.S. Please ask
for Mother to be included under my "priority" registration
number [at the US consulate] in Stuttgart. This should be
possible since Mother and I always shared a household. We
were separated "due to circumstances beyond our control."
I was forced to leave, and Mother could not get a visa for
Palestine. We would like to resume living together as soon as
possible... As you know my registration number has already
come up. The US consulate here would issue a visa [for Kurt
and Hanna, but not Selma] right away. I already requested,
before I left Germany, at the US consulate in St[uttgart] that
Hanna and Mother be included in my visa application. This
was possible for Hanna, but not for Mother.*[47]

US immigration policy – and practice – was more complex than Kurt realized. Just having one's registration number come up did not guarantee a visa, only a review of one's application to be considered for a visa. Other requirements also had to be met for a visa to be granted, such as proof of income and assets, including affidavits from close relatives or friends, to ensure that the applicant would not be "Likely to become a Public Charge," the so-called LPC clause in US immigration law.[48]

The National Origins Immigration Act of 1924, which was in effect until 1965, aimed to "limit the immigration of aliens into the United States" and provided for the issuance of visas against national quotas based on 2 percent of each national origin group in the population in the United States at the base year of 1890. By the time of the *Anschluss* of Austria in March 1938 the US immigration quota for Greater Germany, Germany and all the Austrian territory now annexed to Germany was for fewer than 27,000 immigrants.[49] Yet during the entire Third Reich it was only in the single federal budget year from 1 July 1938 to 30 June 1939 that the quota was filled, even surpassed. This was because of a combination of intentionally restrictive instructions from the State Department to its consuls abroad and the practice on the part of many consular officials to issue visas selectively to a much smaller number of applicants than the quota.[50]

US immigration law, which was implemented by the State Department, did not make any special provisions for refugees. The State Department frequently instructed its consular officials abroad, who had exclusive authority to grant visas, to be wary of refugees.[51] The consuls' individual, and often subjective, views determined each individual immigration case. There was considerable variation not only between the four different consulates in Germany but also among individual officials in the same consulate, especially with regard to the evaluation of whether an affidavit or combination of affidavits sufficed to convince the official that the applicant was not "likely to become a public charge."[52] Because affidavits were not legally binding, many consular officials were reluctant to accept any but the most probable guarantees that a new immigrant would not become a public charge.[53] Consuls were not obliged to explain their decisions, and there was no right of appeal.[54]

Once the war broke out in Europe US consuls imposed stricter affidavit standards, including often requiring sponsors to place cash deposits for refugees in American banks. This stricter practice and the fact that refugees leaving Germany could take no German currency with them had a devastating impact on direct immigration from Germany. After September 1939 consuls judged only about 10 percent of the applicants for immigration to the United States to be qualified for visas when their quota numbers came up.[55]

In 1940 State Department officials curtailed the entry of refugees into the United States because of fears of Nazi agents, even among German Jews.[56] This anti-refugee "public safety" policy, combined with anti-Semitic views within the various echelons of the State Department that were also prevalent in US public opinion at the time, worked directly to the detriment of German-Jewish visa applicants.[57] The State Department considered those Jewish visa applicants with close relatives they would leave behind in Germany and German-occupied territory to be especially vulnerable to serving the Nazis due to their worries about the welfare of their loved ones. Already in June 1940 it instructed its US consuls in Europe to deny visas to such persons.[58]

Unfortunately for Selma, consular officials in Stuttgart were known to be especially strict toward Jewish applicants.[59] Examples abound of apparently arbitrary decisions, like the one in the fall of 1938 when a German Jew's visa application was accompanied by an affidavit from an acquaintance with an annual income in excess of $15,000 and an average bank account balance of $5,000. Even this wealth failed to persuade the consular official in Stuttgart that the applicant was not likely to become a public charge because he deemed the affiant, at age 67, too old to guarantee anyone financial support.[60] The likelihood of Selma's ever earning a living was negligible, and thus the probability that Selma would be judged likely to become a public charge loomed large unless she had a very strong affidavit.[61] Neither Marianne nor Kurt realized in 1940 the extent to which the cards were stacked against the possibility of bringing their mother to the United States.

Not having received any mail from her children for several months Selma's July 1940 letter to her children showed signs of strain and depression. Her reports of mundane daily activities were laced with a sense of melancholy and sadness, and concluded: "And so the days are passing by."[62] She felt even further isolated because Jews could no longer have telephones.[63] (See Figure 7.1.)

Figure 7.1 Portrait of Selma, Cologne, April 1940

The combination of Selma's unsuccessful steps toward emigration/immigration just before the war broke out, the new and longer delays between letters and the increased anti-Jewish measures in Germany once the war began intensified the family members' stress levels. Kurt, clearly frustrated by the lack of progress in Selma's immigration, unburdened himself in his August 1940 letter to Marianne. Reacting to Italy's recent entrance into the war and the encroaching danger of war nearer to Palestine, Kurt remarked that despite the danger of the war's spreading into Palestine he believed that his mother "would prefer to be here with us than alone." Kurt asked Marianne pleadingly if she still could not get their mother to the United States since, in his view, her registration number would be coming up soon.[64]

Kurt seemed to recognize the urgency perhaps because he had suffered Nazi violence against his own person. In his letter of 18 August 1940, Kurt began to dwell on what he thought his sister Lotti could and should have done the previous year to get his mother to

safety in Palestine. Venting his own frustration over feeling so powerless to secure his mother and aunt's immigration, he wrote:

> I cannot spare Lotti the serious criticism of not having
> applied for Mother's immigration much earlier. She tried it
> after Hanna and I arrived and then it was too late. Hans
> and Lotti always criticized Julius [Kaiser-Blüth] for being
> so unbelievably short-sighted and not wanting to get out of
> Germany. And then they did not even get Mother here, who
> so ardently wanted to come. Now of course Lotti claims
> that Mother would have not wanted to leave "before all her
> children were out." I am not aware of that, and actually it
> was exactly the opposite: It was not I who was an obstacle to
> Mother's emigration, on the contrary, the fact that our "old
> folks" were still in Germany was one of the main reasons
> that I could not previously have conceived of separation
> from them, neither emotionally nor financially. Well, there
> is nothing that can be changed now. I am sure that Lotti and
> Hans did not act in bad faith. It is just Lotti's well-known
> sluggishness that got in the way. She always just let things
> happen. I thought it was very strange when Lotti asked
> Mother in her letters last year to buy all kinds of things for
> their household and have all kinds of furniture alterations
> done. Finally I forbade her her to prevail upon Mother
> to spend any more before she acquired her [immigration]
> certificate, even if it means that not everything is ideally
> furnished. Instead Mother should have some money there [in
> Germany] for the things she more urgently needs. She even
> asked Mother to buy a refrigerator![65]

Kurt then expressed his hope that Marianne might be able to get their
mother to the United States, but in 1940 Marianne was in no situation to vouch for anyone else's financial security. Shortly before she
received Kurt's August 1940 plea to "take in" their mother, she had
confided to her Notebook her many worries – about finances, the war
and her loved ones:

> I am in mental and economical [sic] distress as never
> before. The world situation is terrible and as such involves

our personal lives. There is the disastrous European
situation affecting my dear ones in Cologne and Palestine.
There are all terrible threats to this country as ... to what
is happening in Europe now threatening everybody here,
including both of us particularly you [Arnold] as a man.

By the end of this year I shall be without a position,
my few savings that were never much to speak of will be
used up by then. Some months later there will arise the
problem of getting my mother and probably my aunt,
too, over here.

That's the way the future seems to look like.[66]

Marianne had struggled to make ends meet from the time of her arrival
in the United States in July 1938. She worked sometimes as a private
companion but mostly as a private nurse, for many months on call 24
hours a day while concurrently preparing for her New York State medical licensing exams. Earning $250 a year in 1938, an amount less than
what she owed that year in customs fines, she doubled this amount in
1939, plus a further $125 from working at a girls' summer camp. She
passed her exams and managed to get her medical license that year
but still needed to complete an internship in the United States in order
to practice medicine. In 1940 she worked as an unpaid intern at the
Tewksbury State Hospital in Massachusetts. The only income she had
that year was the $150 she earned by working once again at the girls'
summer camp.[67] Marianne would not have been able to provide a convincing affidavit with either her income history or her paltry savings.

In the late summer of 1940 Marianne worried about her relationship with Arnold, whom that year she saw only rarely between
her various jobs and her internship in Massachusetts. Marianne's
Notebook entries from early summer 1940 indicate she was hopeful
that Arnold was about ready to marry her.[68] Yet Arnold, as a German
immigrant, found it difficult to get hired in the mostly defense-oriented
engineering jobs for which he was qualified and instead worked as
a draftsman – and worried about keeping even this job.[69] Whether
Marianne asked him at this juncture for his help in providing support
for her loved ones is unclear, but Arnold, in Marianne's view, suddenly
withdrew from her: "And now what happens? The moment when I
need you most, when you realize that there is not only joy and cheer-
fulness awaiting us, that moment you want to leave me. You prefer a

comparatively easy life without me if this, our mutual life, might ask some sacrifice of you."[70]

A heartbroken Marianne, aware that she was in no position to provide an affidavit for her mother and aunt's immigration to the United States, hoped to finish her internship by the end of 1940. She thought that once she could practice medicine she would soon be capable of supporting Selma and Henny. Marianne debated taking an offer to remain at Tewksbury Hospital after Arnold wrote her on 7 January 1941 from New York City: "I cannot help to feel [sic] that I am not yet in a position to be married and that each of us can better carry along by himself."[71] Instead, she responded to Arnold's backtracking by moving to New York City. Finally, living in the same city seemed to make a difference, because within two and a half months they were married, and by a rabbi. In order to save money both to open her own practice and to provide a reasonable affidavit for her mother, Marianne worked again as a private nurse from 8am to 8pm seven days a week, earning $70 per month. Not long thereafter Arnold's professional situation also improved; he found work designing power plants in New York.[72] Marianne was delighted to be able to sleep under the same roof, however cramped in their one-room studio apartment, with her new husband.[73]

Within a week of her wedding Marianne received important news from Selma and Henny: a new announcement from the US consulate in Stuttgart had raised their hopes. Apparently, all visa applicants with a registration number below 54,000 were allowed to hand in their papers. That would mean that she and Henny would soon be eligible to submit the papers for their visa application. Selma, concerned and yet hopeful, wrote her youngest:

> If everything goes well, our number might be up soon. I am convinced that many numbers will not be used, first because of the transportation problems during wartime and second because of the high costs for the ship passage that have to be paid in dollars. I heard that a passage including minimal luggage costs $300 to 350. I understand that due to this steep price one can only take the most essential things in luggage. How could we get the affidavit and the money? Tante Flora assured me that her other relatives might be able to help, but I am not sure about

that. I am always thinking about all that, but I just can't
find a way. There are endless difficulties.

Selma's worries about an affidavit were quite justified. After Flora's
cousin, Marianne's US sponsor, Arthur Stern, died in December 1940,
Selma did not know of any wealthy US citizen who might have been be
able and willing to provide an affidavit.[74]

Marianne wrote her siblings on 27 March about her wedding
the week before and relayed the news from the consulate in Stuttgart,
enclosing her mother and Tante Henny's letter of 18 February 1941.
Marianne told Kurt and Lotti about the results of her inquiries: the
cost of a ship passage, $850 for both, living expenses, a minimum of
$60 per person per month. She wrote Kurt and Lotti via airmail with
a sense of urgency and anxiety about the task at hand and her worry
that neither she nor Arnold could afford the passage or the monthly
support. She asked them about contributing and how she might get
their funds, pleading for their advice:

> *I don't know what to write them [Selma and Henny]. It's*
> *terrible. But I don't know where to [get] the $850 and I*
> *don't know how to support them either, both of them, if*
> *they are here. If it would be only one of them, but of course*
> *it's impossible to separate mother and Tante Henni [sic]*
> *now. So what shall we do? Please answer immediately.*[75]

Marianne quickly responded to Selma and Henny's letter of 18
February 1941, explaining the costs of the passage. She confessed that
her current savings were $215, adding:

> *You will understand that under these circumstances I*
> *have to check with them [Kurt and Lotti] before I am*
> *capable of undertaking anything definitive ... Besides our*
> *affidavit, which because of its monetary value can only*
> *be a supplemental affidavit, I also have an affidavit from*
> *Trude's husband. Then we will still need an additional*
> *affidavit for you two, and my next task is to find one.*

She asked her mother and aunt to telegraph her if anything changed
before they heard back from her and "to remain brave."[76]

Marianne's letter of late March with the news that her loved ones were now ready to emigrate did not reach Palestine until 11 May. Although Kurt responded to Marianne within two days of receiving her March letter,[77] and Lotti did so two weeks later, their responses did not reach Marianne until early July.[78] These long delays in the midst of such an urgent family issue complicated matters, especially because Marianne felt she should wait on her siblings' reply about how to pay for the passage, while realizing she needed to move quickly on getting affidavits.

In the meantime Selma and Henny continued sending letters to Marianne, while trying to strike a balance between a sense of urgency and their consideration for Marianne's difficult financial and professional situation. Marianne wrote them on an almost weekly basis, but her letters took four to eight weeks to reach them. However, Marianne's wedding telegram reached her loved ones the same day. Selma immediately responded:

> I was so happy and sad at the same time. I was sad
> because I could not be with you and share your joy. I was
> with you in my thoughts, thinking back to our little but
> festive celebration we organized for Kurt's wedding.
>   Your mother's blessing will always be with you.
> I wish you all the happiness for your life together...
> Unfortunately I cannot send you my congratulations in
> a faster way. We can now send telegrams only when they
> concern emigration matters and have to do so through
> an agency... I have to ask you once more to do whatever
> you can to make our immigration possible. We can only
> hope that you will find ways and means. Please do not
> get upset that I am asking you again to inquire about all
> possibilities for us.[79]

Now that Selma and Henny's registration numbers at the US consulate apparently would come up soon, proof of a paid ship passage became a high priority. Ship passages could only be paid for by persons in neutral countries.[80] Selma reported to Marianne that she had also tried to do her part by getting advice from the Hilfsverein.[81] Worrying about whether Marianne could raise these funds, Selma promised her daughter that, once in the United States, she and Henny would take care of household chores while Marianne could build up her own practice as a physician, her long-time dream.[82]

The older generation felt the grip of the Nazi regime tightening. Many in 1941 described feeling torn between fear and hope. Selma mentioned all the efforts her relatives were pursuing to emigrate to the United States: Leo and Else Kaufmann in Drove, Leopold and Thekla Heumann in Linnich, and Karl Kaufmann in Lüxheim. They, as well as the Kaiser-Blüths in Cologne, were all full of hope while exploring every possible venue. Julius optimistically wrote Marianne in March 1941:

> I hope and wish that we will be able to witness your
> happiness firsthand this fall. We have reasons to believe
> that this is not too far-fetched. Our papers [at the US
> consulate] in Stuttgart are being processed. I hope that my
> cousin Langsdorf can help us with the funds for the ship
> passage. Then we will have an appointment in Stuttgart.[83]

Once the US consulate processed immigration papers and decided in favor of granting a visa, it sent the successful applicant a clearance notification. Then, after the applicant proved that the ship passage was paid, the consulate would summon him or her for the issuance of the visa.[84] Flora had a less optimistic outlook than her husband Julius and related the realities more directly to Marianne in her letter, written on 24 March 1941: "Our chances of being able to come to you are getting slimmer every day, despite the AC [American consulate] notification. It just does not make sense to plan anything, because the situation changes from day to day. Your mother and aunt are courageous and are not giving up."[85]

Selma and Henny had even begun to learn English in anticipation of their immigration. However, they had made little progress, due to what Selma described as "not so very pleasant distractions."[86] This was very likely an allusion to her sister Thekla and her husband's forced move to a "Jew house" [Judenhaus] in Kirchberg. The district administrator in Jülich ordered all remaining Jews in the district to vacate their residences and move into Villa Buth, a "Jew house," in Kirchberg by 24 March 1941 at noon. Following this order, a total of ninety-six Jews moved there, including Thekla and Leopold Heumann.[87] Out of censorship concerns Selma did not reveal any more information, but her heart-wrenching conclusion sums up best their state of mind: "We are very much burdened with so many worries and troubles, but we have to overcome them. There is no other way."[88]

Back in the United States, Marianne had not received any response from her brother or sister about the news she had sent them regarding their "parents" ' registration numbers and her request for financial help for the passage. Then their cable arrived on 25 May 1941, stating: "Any delay unbearable. Immigration Palestine wartime impossible. We applied half ticket costs. Don't wait. Wire."[89] By then Marianne had already gotten the first promise of affidavits from friends. When her mother and Tante Henny's letter dated 23 March 1941 arrived, congratulating her on her marriage and reporting that they had begun to learn English, Marianne realized she could no longer wait. In this letter Selma and Henny minced no words and urged all the children to do everything in their power to facilitate their immigration to the U.S. Selma pleaded: "See to it that you do whatever you can to make our immigration possible, and hopefully means and ways can be found."[90] Marianne focused on securing the affidavits, making inquiries with the New York section of the National Council of Jewish Women about how best to submit an affidavit of support and how to find out what type of details needed to be included in order to make it more likely that the affidavit might be accepted. This group did give her a printed sheet with rather intimidating guidelines about what would constitute a convincing affidavit but provided no help on where she might secure more funds for either the passage or to enhance the assets she could list to guarantee the support of her loved ones. Marianne, feeling pressured and bereft over not having heard from her siblings, wrote Lotti on 1 May 1941. She expressed her concerns in a manner that, much later in July when they read it, provoked both Lotti and Kurt:

> Ever since 6 weeks ago mother is bombarding me with the most urgent desire to come here. I explained the financial difficulties in my last letter to you. Nevertheless I am trying my best to make their coming here possible. What expects [sic] them over there – heaven knows. I got affidavits for them this week, that means, the promise; they are not made out as yet. It was so much harder to get them than I thought. We mustn't forget that they

are 2 old people unable to make a living here – and the
people whom I asked for the affis [affidavits] are afraid
of the responsibility. The other difficulty is Arnold. He
says – and to tell the truth, he is right – that we cannot
support them, not as yet at least. Besides, these terrible
$850 for the passage – I don't know how to get them. You
know I have been working and saving like crazy these
past months to be able to get started with my practice in
July or September. And yet, I have only $360 now. And I
do need this money for the practice, otherwise I'll never
get started. Anyway, I want to send the affis out next
week and also to make a down payment (Anzahlung) *on*
the passages. Since I have the feeling we have to try to
do everything possible to get them out of there. But God
knows how we can manage later.[91]

It did take time for Marianne to secure other affidavits, but she submitted her own on 17 May 1941 for her mother and Tante Henny,
accompanied by a request to the US consul in Stuttgart:

I should appreciate it highly if you would be kind
enough to issue an immigration visa to my mother Selma
Steinberg, and my aunt, Henriette Kaufmann, both 17
Raschdorffstrasse, Cologne-Braunsfeld, Germany.
  I am most anxious to have both living with me, my
mother as well as my aunt; the latter having always lived
in my mother's household and she being as dear to me as a
second mother.
  May I emphasize that I have no other dependents and
therefore shall be well able to support my mother and aunt
so that they will not at any time become a public burden.[92]

On her affidavit form Marianne, as a non-citizen, was required to
state when she had submitted her Declaration of Intent to become a
citizen once she was eligible. She listed her "regular occupation" as
both a physician and nurse with average earnings of "$35.00 a week
plus board," and a "bank account of $420.00." The vice president
of her New York City bank, where she had had an account since 2
May 1939, attested to the balance in her account "as of that day." Her

current employer provided a letter certifying her pay of $35 plus board a week and employment since 27 February 1941, describing her as "sincere, honest and always ready to meet her obligations."⁹³

Marianne submitted the affidavit under her maiden name, although she had been married over two months. In an airmail letter Marianne clarified to her mother and aunt that she had used her maiden name on the affidavit because it was her professional name under which her bank account and license, etc. were listed, mentioning that nowhere in the paperwork did she have to declare her marital status. Marianne explained the fact that Arnold was not sending an affidavit on account of "certain circumstances that prevent him from doing so, which take too much time to explain here." It is not clear what circumstances prevented Arnold from providing an affidavit. Perhaps she used her maiden name so as not to raise questions with the US consul about why her husband was not providing an affidavit.⁹⁴

Marianne had been advised by the National Council of Jewish Women to go ahead and send her own affidavit but to wait to hear the reaction of the consul before sending additional affidavits, which she did not yet have in hand anyway. Besides the supplemental affidavit for Tante Henny from her friend Trude and her husband, she also had secured a promise from other friends to guarantee Selma's support by depositing money into a special escrow account. Marianne promised her mother and aunt she would send the other affidavits as soon as she heard from the consul. She also explained that rushing was pointless because she was still trying to get the money together for the passage. She asked that they understand that Lotti and Kurt at this point were unable to help.⁹⁵

Marianne was dubious whether Lotti and Kurt would be able to send money. She responded to her siblings' 25 May 1941 cable: "I understand that you are trying to get a permit to pay half the costs of the passages. Of course, I don't know, but I am doubtful that you will succeed." She briefly described the affidavit she had sent and the ones she had in reserve, simply stating: "Arnold did not make out an affidavit for them." She then warned: "The whole thing will take a long time until they'll really be here – the passage, the money for the passage, the problem of their being supported here, etc. But the sooner it's getting started the better. And it will give them some new hope when they see that something is being done."⁹⁶ This airmail letter of 4 June 1941, in which Marianne reported to her siblings in Palestine on having sent affidavits to Selma and Henny, took two months to arrive, a delay that exacerbated the tensions and misunderstandings between the siblings.

Once Kurt and Lotti received Marianne's letter of 27 March 1941 they had no way of knowing what had happened in the six weeks since she had written them. In her response, on 23 May 1941, Lotti was quite agitated that Marianne had not sent them a telegram about their loved ones' news from Stuttgart and worried it might already be too late. She feared that Marianne's financial concerns about supporting their mother and aunt after they arrived had prevented her from immediately moving forward with preparing their immigration. Lotti did not realize her sister's concerns were directly related to whether the affidavits would suffice for a visa. Just as Kurt had vented to Marianne a year before his feeling that Lotti had not acted early enough, Lotti now reproached Marianne for not having acted sooner and in what she considered a more decisive way:

I am sorry, but I just don't get how your thoughts of a time "afterwards" [after their relatives' arrival in the United States] could prevent you from immediately trying everything to prepare the immigration from your end. I do understand the financial problems regarding the ship passage. I also don't get why you didn't send us a telegram. If the possibility exists to pull our mother and aunt, whom we owe everything, out of this hell, then we have to do everything we can to help, no matter however rash. Who knows how much longer we can do anything for them, given their old age and the horrendous situation in which they find themselves... I pray to God that in the meantime you've taken all necessary steps. Three months have passed since Mother's letter! I cannot imagine the situation if Julius and Flora were to leave, and Mother and Tante Henny had to stay behind! And America can enter into the war any week now and then the door for our Mother and Tante Henny will be slammed shut. It is absolutely impossible for them to come to Palestine at the moment. Residents of enemy countries or enemy-occupied countries are not permitted to immigrate. That's why their only chance is immigration to the United States.[97]

Lotti, in a calmer tone, then explained that their making a financial contribution depended on getting a permit from the controller of foreign currency in Palestine, but, provided they could get this, they would be able to put together the money for the passage and contribute toward their monthly support. Hans added that he had learned that they could wire money to the American Jewish Joint Distribution Committee in New York toward the ship passage, but it would only be available after Selma and Henny's departure from Germany or German-occupied countries. Thus Marianne would need to find a way to pay for the ship passage up front and only thereafter could she expect help from her siblings.[98] Kurt responded quickly to Marianne in his letter of 13 May once he received her March letter:

> For now I can only say this: Both of them should get out, if it is in any way humanly possible. You [and Arnold] can rely on us on 100 percent, now and later. But I see for the moment no possibility of bringing them over here. And that is a crying shame, because we could easily support them and would not need a contribution from you. It will naturally be more difficult to send you money, first because of the strict currency laws here (I will check into the exact regulations for such cases) and secondly because the sum that we could send would probably have significantly less buying power in the United States.[99]

Kurt went on to suggest that Nanna and Arnold try borrowing the money privately or from a Jewish organization, assuring them there was nothing shameful about this, since they would want to repay the money and, if humanly possible, would be able to do so. He even suggested Nanna turn to the couple she had worked for in Miami Beach, or their former rabbi, Dr. Hahn, who now was leading a Jewish congregation in New York. He concluded: "I fear that for the moment we have to leave this matter in your hands, but we will check into what is possible from here and stand by you financially to the utmost. My heart aches that from here we are condemned to inaction, but nevertheless I feel this matter should not fail because of financial difficulties."[100]

The older family members in Germany worried about how German expansion into Yugoslavia and Greece and even North Africa in the spring of 1941 might affect their emigration/immigration chances. Selma, who usually tried to strike an optimistic and hopeful tone in letters to her children, poured out her worries in mid May 1941 to Hanna's mother, Sofie Levy, in Argentina:

> *Sometimes I get totally discouraged. One grows older and the chances for emigration become more and more difficult. We are now trying to learn English. It must be too horrible to be in a foreign country whose language one does not speak. One would be so helpless. But we are not yet in America. It will take quite a while. Sometimes we lose all hope. There is so much distraction, usually nothing good. We will soon have another address, as we have to move.*[101]

The seemingly innocuous reference to a change of address represented, however, a major rupture for the five members of the Cologne household, who often shared meals, worries, memories and their children's letters with each other. After having lived together for about two years they were all forced out of the Kaiser-Blüths' beautiful house. The police in Cologne issued an order that the Jewish population had to vacate their apartments and houses in the suburbs.[102] Marianne reported the disconcerting news to her siblings in Palestine:

> *They had to move out of Raschdorff Street, and they live now, the three of them, in one room, Linden Street 19. Aunt Flora and Uncle Julius moved a week later into the same house, they occupy one room on the second floor. They seem very depressed, everything must be very narrow, in addition to the disappointment as to immigration – it is so terribly sad.*[103]

Apparently the living quarters at this new location in the Lindenstrasse had belonged to the Kaiser-Blüths. The building had been attached to the factory of their company, Mannsbach & Lebach, until it was "Aryanized" in late 1938. These living quarters were used as a "Jew house" (*Judenhaus*) as of May 1941. The Kaiser-Blüths moved upstairs, while Selma and her sisters lived downstairs.[104] The process of the expulsion of Jews from their homes and their concentration in overcrowded living spaces in "Jew houses," sometimes referred to as "ghettoization," was a further degradation. The Nazis did not establish ghettos in Germany proper, as they did in the occupied territories in Eastern Europe, but the "Jew houses" served a comparable purpose.[105]

The Kaiser-Blüths, Selma and her sisters had to leave the neighborhood close to their beloved Stadtwald, Cologne's vast city park, and relocate from the tree-lined suburb of Braunsfeld closer to the more urban Cologne-Neustadt Süd. The forced move not only meant less space but also a less hospitable neighborhood for Jews. Flora had remarked on overt anti-Semitism there while shopping already in January 1939: "I feel more comfortable in Braunsfeld than here. I feel totally isolated here; a very unpleasant feeling."[106]

With two and three people in one room the living situation for the Kaiser-Blüths and the three Kaufmann sisters became increasingly tight and difficult, especially after the Kaiser-Blüths were forced to take in even more tenants. Marianne became concerned when she heard that her Onkel Leo and Tante Else had to accommodate all the Jews of their town. The twenty-six Jews of Drove all had to live in their house for several months. As Marianne described the situation: "The meaning of all this is only too obvious: ghetto."[107] In his article, "The Jews of Drove," West German author Heinrich Böll commemorated those who were "herded together in Leo Kaufmann's house waiting to be dragged to their death, a death which they believed to the last moment [w]ould not happen."[108]

In the summer of 1941 the war reached the Rhineland. Cologne, as one of the largest industrial cities in the area, became a prime target. British air raids destroyed part of the local industry, but also residential areas, such as Cologne-Braunsfeld.[109] As before, but now under much worse conditions in the cramped Lindenstrasse quarters, the Kaiser-Blüths took in acquaintances in need. When Hanna's Tante Paula did not have any place to stay, she moved in for ten days. Despite the utterly crowded and challenging living situation, the Kaiser-Blüths and Kaufmann sisters tried to maintain a sense of normalcy. They sometimes had Hanna's aunts over for meals. Selma and Henny continued to visit Onkel Hermann and his sister Johanna in the Israelitisches Asyl.[110]

In early July Marianne learned that the US consulates in Germany and German-occupied countries had all closed as of 1 July and that all visa-related requests now had to be made to the State

Department in Washington, DC.[111] After wiring the State Department to get the new visa application forms, she learned they were not available for people in Germany or German-occupied countries. In addition to the requirement for the customary affidavits of support, now prospective immigrants had to submit a "biographical statement" in order to prevent the immigration of "unwanted elements (fifth column)."[112] Critics at the time suspected that this measure, allegedly aimed at Nazi spies, was just a welcome excuse for the United States to curb immigration.[113] After all, many of the applicants were older Jews like Selma and Henny. Their immigration chances became slimmer by the day.

With the July 1941 closing of the US consulates in Germany, the only hope for Selma and Henny was to find a transit country in which they could stay until their immigration to the United States was granted. Marianne inquired about transit visas to Cuba, initially for both her mother and Henny. In the fall of 1941 both the German-Jewish newspaper *Aufbau* in the United States and the highly censored *Jüdisches Nachrichtenblatt* in Germany encouraged potential emigrants to pursue "transmigration" via third countries, recommending Cuba, Mexico, Ecuador and the Dominican Republic. The only problem was getting the authorities in those transit countries to agree.[114]

In the late summer and fall of 1941 Marianne explored the possibilities of both Cuba and Switzerland as transit countries. When Marianne calculated the price for a passage and visa to Cuba and the associated costs of having to wait in Cuba for an immigration visa for the United States, it became clear that the funds she had available would suffice for at most one person. She therefore had to ask her mother with a heavy heart to consider emigrating alone, without her beloved sister Henny. Marianne instructed her mother to immediately send her a telegram once she had made this decision.[115] Not realizing the extreme time pressure, Selma did not respond with a telegram as Marianne had urged her to do, but several weeks later sent a letter agreeing to her interim stay in Cuba without her sister. However, by the time Marianne received Selma's response in early October the situation had changed completely. Following Cuba's expulsion of the German consul in mid August, Cuba issued no visas for a time.[116] After this interruption not only did the charge for a Cuban visa rise considerably but the process became more difficult. Marianne wrote her mother and Henny: "You are right, the Cuban matter has become quite unreliable and somewhat fraudulent. That's why everything has become more complicated and expensive."[117] However, at this point Kurt's former colleague from the Centralverein, Fritz Schwarzschild, took care of Selma's "Cuban matter."[118] Three years earlier Fritz Schwarzschild had provided the fabricated letter for Kurt to get released from Buchenwald concentration camp. He then emigrated to the United States and worked for a travel agency. Schwarzschild's involvement alleviated some of Selma's fears regarding Cuba as a safe and sound option, given the catastrophic journey of the *St. Louis* just two years before.[119] This transatlantic liner was transporting more than 900 Jewish refugees, mostly from Germany, who were not allowed to disembark in Cuba and had to return to Nazi-occupied Europe. Among the passengers were two family acquaintances.[120] Selma worried that her children might lose their hard-earned money if the ship passage turned out to be a shady undertaking.[121] In early October Selma put all her doubts aside and sent an urgent telegram to Marianne: "Same address. Rush Cuban visa."[122]

It is not difficult to reconstruct the reasons for Selma's new sense of urgency. The conditions for Jews in Germany had become unbearable, and preparations to deport German Jews to Poland were under way.[123] Several of Selma's siblings and their families had already been interned in collection points (*Sammellager*). In fact, Selma's allusion on 3 October 1941 to the fact that "Tante Bertha is now in the same situation as Tante Thekla – she does not yet know her new address"[124] was a coded message that Bertha would soon be interned in one of the many German collection points.[125] Selma was very distressed by this news and was now even more eager to get out of Germany. In October 1941, in the aftermath of her siblings' and their families' "departure" and at the beginning of the first mass deportations, but while she still had hopes of getting to Cuba, Selma confided her despair to their Gentile family friend, Herta Poth, who had sheltered Selma, her sister Henny and Onkel Hermann during the November Pogrom:

> But now I would like to give you Marianne's address in case something unforeseen or terrible happens to us. The times are so ominous. One never knows what will happen the next day. I am hoping it never comes to that, but just in case please let Marianne know…I am very tired and exhausted, not only physically.[126]

Herta had continued to visit Selma and Henny in Cologne even after her own move from Essen to Berlin. Even a decree threatening "Aryans" with protective custody or incarceration for up to three months in a concentration camp for "public display of friendship with Jews" did not stop her.[127] She recalled her visit in the fall on 1941 to Lindenstrasse in a letter to Marianne after the war:

> I met your mother, Tante Henny and their Cologne sister
> [Emma] in a house where the Kaiser-Blüths also lived.
> Your mother and her sisters lived in a spacious, cozy room
> with a kitchen and a bathroom. The outer circumstances
> were still bearable. But there was a lot of commotion.
> People came and went and all brought unpleasant news.
> But to have old friends around was also a great comfort.
> Your Tante Emma's health was quite fragile, as was Tante
> Henny's emotional disposition. Your mother, however,
> had maintained her calm kindness and even a glimmer of
> humor, if her smiling detachment from the daily hardships
> could be called that. The knowledge that all three of her
> children had become successful was more important than
> anything else to her.[128]

Selma and Henny learned on 1 September 1941 that within a few weeks Jews would need official permission to leave their residential community and would have to wear a yellow star.[129] They planned a trip to their sister Bertha's seventy-first birthday celebration in Hochkirchen, fortunately before these new restrictions took effect. But unlike a few years before, they could not stay there overnight any more because "she now ha[d] many people living in her house."[130] Like their brother Leo's home in Drove, Bertha's house in Hochkirchen had also become a so-called "Jew house."

How could one maintain a sense of normalcy after being stripped of so many basic rights? Selma wrote her children: "I am telling myself again and again that we need to hold our heads up high. We have to try to stay healthy and keep the hope alive that we will see each other again."[131] The same day that Selma wrote these reassuring lines all Jews in Germany were required to wear a Star of David badge.[132] Historian Marion Kaplan argues that this requirement indicated a new level of persecution because it was more visible within the public sphere than previous measures.[133] Jews in Germany had been vilified and tormented and stripped of their rights for many years already, but to be publicly branded as a Jew, a second-class citizen, was for many an unbearable humiliation. They could now be easily targeted for harassment and violence. Once they had to wear the Star of David badge many Jews opted for staying in their tight living quarters rather than endure the feeling of being publicly shamed. In addition, since the outbreak of war Jews in Germany had been placed under an 8 p.m. curfew in winter and a 9 p.m. curfew in summer.[134] The widely circulated Cologne newspaper, the *Kölnische Zeitung*, echoed the typical anti-Jewish propagandistic justification given for the branding at that time: "The German soldier has seen the Jew in his utter repulsiveness and inhumanity on the Eastern Front ... These experiences have led the German soldier and the German people as a whole to demand that the Jew cannot be allowed to hide in his homeland any longer."[135] In her letter of early October 1941 Flora discreetly revealed the effects of this new indignity: "I can't tell you any news. We rarely go out."[136]

Meanwhile Kurt and Lotti in Palestine had felt increasingly frustrated and helpless during the summer, imagining all sorts of things. They did not receive their sister's letter of 4 June 1941 with the news that Selma had received her affidavit until August. Marianne's already months-old letter was full of her own frustrations and a truncated version of what she had done for their loved ones' immigration, as opposed to the good news that had developed in the interim that their loved ones would soon be leaving Germany. Kurt and Lotti were beside themselves with reproaches and frustration over what they imagined might or could have been. Marianne's siblings were not fully aware of her situation in the United States or the advice she had received about which affidavits to send when, US visa procedures, etc.

Kurt, full of frustration over his perception of the lack of progress, had already written to Marianne and Arnold on 9 July 1941:

> *We did everything we could from our end immediately, but unfortunately that was not much. We were planning to have considerable funds available by selling some of Lotti's valuables and by contributing Hanna's and my modest savings, for which of course we would have needed a foreign exchange permit. And we waited for your telegram ... It looked like you were waiting for our answer*

before you somehow organized the money and paid
[the ship passage] right away. Lotti and I just could not
understand you any more, since we were convinced that
you would not wait after sending your letter but instead
act. The sum might seem high for both of you under the
present circumstances, but considering the "object" and
American conditions it does not seem that bad. We still
cannot grasp that you could not have been able to get
a loan either from a Jewish aid organization or from a
private lender. After all, both of your professions should
guarantee a solid chance of paying back this loan. It is
even less comprehensible to us that both of you emphasize
the difficulties that would occur after the arrival of our
loved ones. We have all said: "Once they are there [in
the United States] everything will work out." ... It would
be very painful for me to imagine that we children failed
at the very first opportunity we had to give something
back to our mother in gratitude for all her sacrifices and
concerns for us. You, dear Nanna, will have to admit
that this opportunity should have happened years ago. I
became teary-eyed when I read that Mother at her age is
learning English now.[137]

Marianne responded to Kurt and Lotti on 22 August 1941: "Both
your last letters sound very disgusted and reproachful as to the stand
of matters in mother and our aunt's immigration. It seems that you do
not understand at all that I did what I could – they had the affidavits
in hand when a week later the news about the closing of the consulates
became official." She informed them dryly of the situation with the
closing of the consulates, adding: "As you see – the problem has largely
[sic] increased. The passage is no more the only one but first of all
the possibility of getting the visa."[138] Marianne made sure her siblings
were now aware that she was being proactive and that indeed she was
capable of taking, and had taken, matters into her own hands.

Marianne then explained the possibility of getting Selma and
Henny to Cuba in order to wait there to have American visas issued,
but that there were enormous costs involved: $1,200 to $1,400 per
person.[139] In a restrained tone, Marianne described to her siblings
what she had written her mother about this option: "Unfortunately,

on account of the high costs we could not have her [Mother's] sister come at the same time but we would do for her later whatever possible. She should, please, wire back immediately that she is willing to come by herself and we would start the necessary steps right away."[140]

Marianne then returned to their criticisms:

> *Your remarks as to the value of money here – it appears that it does not matter to you whether one has $900 or not – surprise me. For one thing, I myself do not own so much money. [By the time] mother will be here all my savings will be used up and I cannot [then] think of opening a practice. First, I won't have any money left to do it with, and second, I have to make more money immediately since I won't be able then to sit and wait for patients … There was a time, as you all know, that they could have come [sic] to Palestine with less trouble and expense and to an – apparently – at that time – more secure household than ours is at the present time.*
>
> *Though there is no comfort, everybody is in the same boat. Marianne Bachrach's parents [Alex's cousin and her husband from Plettenberg] and a great many others of [sic] people we know – they just can't get visas. Hans, you asked me how your parents are. As Ernst told us … they [have] had their passage paid for since February at the JDC [American Jewish Joint Distribution Committee], but no date is set as yet. The passage does not help them either now, since they don't have the visa. Marianne Bachrach told me yesterday on the phone that she wanted to try to get their parents to Switzerland for the issuance of the visas. But she was told at the Swiss consulate that there is no transportation from Germany to any foreign country at the present time. In brief, you can be assured that I will try anything I can do. But don't forget that the situation is extremely difficult, in fact, beyond what one can do. I keep informed about the chances there are and as soon as something can be done you can be sure we'll do it.*[141]

Because of the backlog caused by postal delays these emotionally charged letters would arrive and be responded to into the early fall, months after they had been written and long after the context, and developments, had changed. The recriminations reached a climax with Kurt's letter of 12 August 1941, his response to Marianne's letters of 1 May and 4 June. Unable to suppress the disappointment and resentment he felt, Kurt was infuriated that Marianne had felt "bombarded" by Selma's letters about her desire to emigrate. He also could not fathom that his new brother-in-law had not been prepared to provide an affidavit. Kurt criticized what he considered Marianne's haphazard way of having sent off the affidavits. He could not comprehend the priority she was placing on starting up her practice as opposed to, as he saw it, putting their mother and aunt's immigration first. He exclaimed that he and Lotti did not feel they even recognized her any more, reminding Marianne:

> You have always, especially in all the years since 1933, but especially after 1933, worked exclusively on your own medical training. You know how terribly worried I always was when I still had my post that we wouldn't have a refuge set up for mother and Tante Henny so that they could emigrate, so that the migration of our family could go forward in an orderly manner. I always feared ... I would not be able to hold out until you and Lotti had managed to have Mother and Tante Henny join you. And now it has really come to that. And when later, at this point not to be expected, a chance arises for you to turn everything to this good cause, then all other interests and concerns, and without exception, have to be put on the back burner.

Kurt concluded this theme with a sense of foreboding: "Is it clear to you that over there by now they must also be having financial problems? According to my estimation all the means available to them must be used up by now, and only heaven knows how our old folks are managing to live or will manage to live in the all-too-near future."[142]

The reproachful words and the emotions behind the siblings' overwhelming fear that they might not get their loved ones out in time were bound to take a lasting toll on their relationship with each other. Lotti and Hans did not write Marianne and Arnold again for close to six months. Correspondence between Kurt and Hanna and Marianne and Arnold focused primarily on explanations that Marianne and Arnold provided about their arrangements for their loved ones' passage to Cuba and what they had or had not heard from Germany. Lotti finally did write on 6 December 1941, expressing a certain emotional exhaustion and resignation, despite the mention of hope: "There is rather nearly nothing to be said: one can only hope – and wait. I pray that you now already know more than we do, and that the news is favorable." Then she struck a touching tone of reconciliation: "But, whatever may be – take my heartfelt thanks for what you have done in this case and may your intentions succeed with God's help!"[143]

When it appeared that Cuban doors would shut on immigration in August 1941 Marianne wrote a German acquaintance in Switzerland in hopes of finding a way for her loved ones to get a transit visa there and from there a visa to the United States.[144] When she finally got a response, written on 5 November 1941, the news about transit visas was not good; her friend was still trying to rescue her own parents.[145] Fortunately, in the fall of 1941 Cuban visas appeared once again to be available, but rumors abounded that bribes might be needed. Marianne and Arnold set to work planning Selma's immigration and getting the funds together. It had been very difficult for Marianne to confess to her loved ones that they could only afford to bring one of them over for the moment, knowing how hard it would be for Selma to face this decision of leaving, however temporarily, her beloved sister Henny behind. But now Marianne thoughtfully planned Selma's interim stay in Cuba, advising her what to pack for Cuba's warm climate and New York's cold winters, and explaining to her that a representative of the Overseas Travel Service would meet her in Havana upon her arrival. Everything looked so promising. Selma was supposed to board the *Nyassa*, a Portuguese ship, in either late December 1941 or early January 1942.[146]

Selma was overwhelmed by the intricacies of the emigration/immigration process. She was trying to get all her papers together, have her passport photo taken and get immunized while taking care of her sister Emma, who had become ill, all the while living in terrible conditions. When speedy communication between Selma and Marianne would have been most essential, letters took several weeks to arrive and as of November 1941 telegrams could no longer be sent from Germany to the United States, as Selma informed her children.[147] Nevertheless, Selma tried to remain optimistic and composed in her letters to Marianne and Arnold, who had managed in October 1941 to arrange for Selma's visa to be issued by the Cuban legation in Berlin and to book the ship passage.[148] Selma's departure for Cuba looked almost certain in November 1941: She had her passport with a valid visa in hand for Cuba[149] and a passage on the *Nyassa*.[150] Apparently, Flora and Julius also had their transit visas for Cuba in hand by the end of the year.[151] Everything seemed finally to be working out for Selma and the Kaiser-Blüths.

While Selma calculated that she would need to depart from Cologne around 25–7 December in order to reach her passage from Lisbon to Cuba on 4 January, she became increasingly worried that the German authorities would not issue her the required exit visa (*Sichtvermerk*) in time for her departure. The delay in getting her exit visa, which Selma assumed to be a temporary or momentary delay, turned out to have had much more serious causes and far-reaching implications.[152]

For many prospective refugees the visa for Cuba seemed to be the light at the end of the tunnel. The *Aufbau*, however, on 5 December 1941 warned its readers in the United States not to consider the Cuban visa as anything more than a "narrow emergency exit out of the brown cauldron. But many will not be able to squeeze through it." The article criticized the Nazi government for providing so little information regarding the future of Jewish emigration from Germany and appealed for the "rescinding of the present halt in transports [to safety]."[153] Of course two days later the Japanese bombed Pearl Harbor and Germany declared war on the United States, seemingly closing off any possibility that Cuba would accept transmigrant refugees from Germany, whose chances of getting a visa to the United States had all but disappeared overnight. Kurt, in a letter dated 18 January 1942, expressed his gratitude to Marianne and Arnold for getting Selma the visa to Cuba, but had no way of knowing whether in fact Selma had ever been able to get out of Germany. Writing in a conciliatory tone toward his sister and brother-in-law, he nevertheless was not optimistic about his mother: "I am so thankful to and even proud of both of you that you still managed to get the Cuban visa. Your letter of 30 October relieved me so much ... But I dare not hope that they really got off [*sic*]. In mid December the USA were [*sic*] already in the war."[154]

As became known much later, in October 1941 Heinrich Himmler had secretly ordered a halt on further Jewish emigration from Germany for the duration of the war.[155] This order was issued two months before the United States entered the war in early December 1941. Following the 1 July closing of the US consulates and the probability of the widening of the war, the Nazi government, especially the Reich Security Main Office, was alarmed that German Jews might not be able to continue to immigrate to the United States in wartime.[156] In October 1941 Nazi planning for what has become known as the "Final Solution of the Jewish Question" was underway. The Nazi government was no longer willing to dally with Jewish emigration once it geared up to begin mass deportations. Anti-Jewish policy had changed from persecution, expulsion and concentration to brutal incarceration and annihilation, as the protocol of a special meeting of Nazi Party and German government officials at the Wannsee Conference on 20 January 1942 documented.[157]

Since the Nazis kept their emigration ban a secret, Selma thought the only reason for her failed emigration was Germany's declaration of war on the United States in December 1941. Months later Selma summarized the tragic turn of events when she could no longer receive the exit visa required to leave Germany: "I had everything together for my trip to Cuba, except for the exit visa. The ship's passage was already paid for. Then came the war and that was it. The children [Marianne and Arnold] had already rented a new apartment with one room for me."[158] Any refugees from Germany who were on board when the *Nyassa* finally departed from Lisbon either had left Germany prior to the emigration ban or had found a clandestine way to Portugal.[159]

Once Germany declared war on the United States on 11 December 1941 direct communication between the two countries was no longer possible. The only recourse was twenty-five-word messages transmitted via the International Red Cross. The message recipient could write a reply on the back, although countries at war generally limited communications to one form per household per month.[160] Selma and Henny sent several messages in the winter of 1941–2 and the spring of 1942 to Kurt and Lotti in Palestine as well as to Marianne in the United States, which they received out of sequence between March and November 1942.[161] Kurt repeated the news of the birth on 19 April 1942 of his daughter Miryam to his mother and aunts in several messages, not knowing when or whether they were getting the news.[162] Marianne had waited to send a message until she heard from her loved ones: "We can answer Mother's Red Cross letter but we can write on our own account to her only once a year." Therefore she did not send a message to Selma and Henny until she could send a reply, and this was not until July 1942.[163] Trying to determine who had heard what and when and the basis of information for references in letters was not an easy task for the siblings. Their own correspondence to each other often took months to arrive, and Red Cross letters to and from Germany were even more unpredictable.

After receiving Selma's Red Cross messages dated February and March 1942 with the unsettling news that Selma and her sisters Henny and Emma had to move to what was euphemistically called a "communal camp" (*Gemeinschaftslager*) in Cologne-Müngersdorf, a clearly worried Marianne wrote her siblings in Palestine on 24 July 1942: "So they had to leave the Lindenstrasse, too. All I hope is [*sic*], that they are still there and [have] not [been] deported. Ernest Kaufman (formerly Drove), who is now in the Army, wrote us that his parents and Aunt Thekla and husband were deported in March." Marianne feared that Müngersdorf was just "a stepping-stone for deportation" and was relieved to learn from Kurt that he and Lotti were receiving more regular messages from Selma and Henny.[164] They had received the most recent one, written 13 April, two months later, in June. According to Kurt's rendering of their April letter (see Figure 7.2):

> The three sisters are still together and report good
> health. Their address is now: Köln-Müngersdorf,
> Wohngemeinschaft, Baracke 17, Zimmer 4. They are
> separated from Julius and Flora, who had to move to
> Rubensstrasse. Uncle Leo and the other relatives of ours
> are reported to have been deported [sic]. All this is too
> terrible to imagine, and my deepest wish is to be able to
> prepare mother still a long good time later and to see us
> all rejoined [sic], preferably in this country.[165]

The last Red Cross message any of the siblings received from their mother was written on 27 May 1942 from Müngersdorf, and in it Selma once again reassured the children that she and her sisters were healthy but were distressed over not hearing from their children.[166] Selma and Henny had received at least some of the replies, which the

Figure 7.2 The Cologne-Müngersdorf collection point (reproduced with permission of NS-Dokumentationszentrum Köln)

children had quickly written in response on the back of the original messages.[167]

Unable to contact her children, Selma maintained her correspondence with the only two people with whom she had exchanged letters before: Sofie Levy in neutral Argentina and Herta Poth in Berlin. Selma wrote Herta that she had received "a very sad farewell letter from dear relatives" before they were deported.[168] Selma's only solace was the thought of her children, her one grandson, and Kurt and Hanna's baby, who she had learned was expected to be born in April.[169] Yet the situation for Selma and her sisters worsened in early 1942.[170] Selma's atypical punctuation and run-on sentences read like a breathless cry of desperation in her February 1942 letter to Herta:

> *Now our fate has also been decided. We will have to move into the barracks on 18 February. I am hoping for a little reprieve (Galgenfrist), but all living quarters have to be vacated by the end of the month. You can imagine our mood, I don't want to say more about that, but hope that now one won't lose the nerve to survive this time. Only the hope that it will get better for us at some*

point and that we will see our children again keeps us alive.[171]

Henny, also trying to be strong, encouraged Herta to visit them again and added: "We won't think about it now and will need all our courage to survive. This is our obligation towards ourselves and our loved ones."[172]

Despite the risk that Herta ran when visiting Jewish friends, she dared to visit Selma and her sisters one more time, in late February 1942, before they were forced to move again. In gratitude, Selma sent her a small package. Selma, even under extreme duress, remained her generous, considerate self:

> *I am sending you some of Kurt's beautiful postcards ... I cannot afford the luxury of keeping them in our more and more restricted space, as hard as it is for me to part from these remembrances of culture... Please enjoy the few enclosed sweets. After your visit I was mad at myself for neglecting to send you off without anything to eat on your trip back.*[173]

As of March 1942 Selma and her sisters had been living with 2,000 other Jews in Cologne-Müngersdorf.[174] Since the end of 1941 Jews in Cologne had been housed there before their transport "east." Even though they probably had heard rumors about Müngersdorf, they were not prepared for the cruel reality: "It was a huge adjustment for us to live in one room with seven people."[175] Selma might have used this understatement in order to divert the censors' attention. The winter of 1941–2 was an extremely harsh one, and the conditions in Müngersdorf were atrocious: "no sewage system, water from a hydrant and other 'comforts'."[176] In extremely cramped living quarters, water dripped from the walls. A few people had managed to smuggle in a personal item like a picture or a doily, which made the sad conditions look even more distressing.[177] Another eyewitness reported: "Each barrack had about four rooms with about eight people each. Each room was about 6 × 8 meters."[178]

Feeling desolate in the barracks of Müngersdorf, 70-old Selma received the terrible news that her siblings Leo, Thekla and Bertha and their family members "had departed for the east at the end of March."

Selma was devastated and remarked in her letter to Sofie Levy: "You might understand how very painful this separation is for all of us since we were very close to our siblings." Selma informed Sofie that Sofie's sisters-in-law had also been taken to Lodz (Litzmannstadt): "But there is no postal connection to and from there. The only appropriate thing one can send there is money transfers."[179]

It is difficult to ascertain what Jews, and non-Jews for that matter, understood under official obfuscating terminology like "departure" (*Abwanderung*), "resettlement" (*Umsiedlung*) or "evacuation" (*Evakuierung*). These euphemisms were part of the Nazis' strategy of deception. Most people initially assumed that the "transports to the east" were headed to work camps. This belief was soon dispelled by the disproportionate number of elderly detainees and the lack of news from those deported. To alleviate any further suspicions the Nazi government circulated the rumor that Theresienstadt, a garrison town north of Prague in the German-occupied Czech protectorate, would serve as the "Reich Ghetto for the Aged," a quiet place where elderly Jews could peacefully retire.[180]

Although the question of the German population's knowledge of the deportations to the east is still debated among historians,[181] it is fairly certain that a large section of the German public, Jewish and non-Jewish, had an inkling, if not reliable information, that deportation could mean death.[182] Yet even though one might have heard rumors about the mass gassing of Jews in the east by the end of 1942, it seemed too unbelievable to be true.[183] Some information about ghettos, camps and mobile killing units trickled into Germany from soldiers on home leave from the eastern front, German employees of railroad and postal services, and from young women who served in the Compulsory Work Service. All had seen first-hand detained and deported Jews, and although they were forbidden to talk about it, some naturally did.[184]

Even though few details of the "transports to the east" might have been known at the time, most Jews knew it meant forced relocation, loss of personal freedom and inadequate living conditions in ghettos or camps. Powerless to stop the deportations of loved ones and faced with the sad prospect of one's own deportation, the most widespread responses were resignation and suicide. Feeling trapped and hopeless, thousands of Jews committed suicide, especially as rumors of imminent deportations spread. During the deportation years 1941–3 there was a dramatic jump in the suicide rate among German Jews. At its peak it reached 2 percent.[185] Historian Konrad Kwiet characterized the suicides among German Jews as a "mass phenomenon." Just as the Jewish population still in Germany was often older, the average age of those who committed suicide was between 60 and 70.[186]

As the family found out after the war, Flora Kaiser-Blüth, the vivacious social center of the extended family, was so desperate that she had also attempted suicide with sleeping pills. She was found in time and revived.[187] A testament to Flora's distraught disposition is a note that she wrote on the back of a photograph of her father's tombstone:

> *Even though your body has turned to dust, your spirit*
> *lives in me. My dear mother has lain next to you since*
> *March 1918. It was my wish to join you both, but my dear*
> *Julius keeps me from it. Our children are dispersed in the*
> *big wide world. Your spirit and ours keeps living in them.*
> *Our grandson, Hans' son, will carry on the good of the*
> *world, with God's help.*[188]

Selma and Henny must have been deeply affected by these tragedies surrounding them.

Under the emotional strain of having lost so many family members and friends of her generation to an unspecified but doubtless horrible fate, and living under the inhumane conditions in the Müngersdorf barracks, Selma found her despair turning to resignation and doom. She had not received any mail from her children for many months and wrote in her June 1942 letter to Herta Poth: "It had not been easy for us, but we have now nothing left that connects us to our previous lives. There is no other way but to accept the facts, as hard as it might be… One loses all will to live."[189] She had given up the thought of escaping deportation, being reunited with her children and getting to know her grandchildren. At this low point Selma might have had an inkling that the worst was yet to come, especially since rumors about deportations were always circulating and some of her siblings had already been "transported to the east." Herta, upon receipt of this letter, planned another visit to Selma and her sisters. But due to emergency oral surgery in Essen she was unable to travel to Cologne as planned.[190]

Many more people were brought to Müngersdorf, especially following RAF air raids on Cologne the night of 30–1 May 1942 which caused great damage. This resulted in even more overcrowding.[191] A young Jewish girl, who was detained in Müngersdorf at the same time as Selma and her sisters, recalled the air raids after the war:

> *Müngersdorf was an old fortress. It was set up as a collection point. We were restricted to this camp. The air raids had a terrible emotional and physical effect on me. I had horrible stomach cramps. Sirens are a terrifying thing... We wanted Germany to be bombed, but on the other hand we were on the receiving end.*[192]

In response to the air raids the German authorities ordered the Jewish hospital and old-age home, the Israelitisches Asyl, to be vacated for non-Jewish Germans and for the Jewish elderly and sick patients to be taken to Müngersdorf. Onkel Hermann and his sister Johanna did not have to endure this ordeal: they both had died of natural causes at the end of 1941.[193] Many of the elderly and sick patients were brought to Müngersdorf, Selma's 71-year-old widowed brother-in-law Karl Kaufmann among them.[194] The sisters wrote a letter to Karl's son Moritz in Holland the next day, assuring him that they were all healthy. This would be the last letter from Müngersdorf to any Kaufmann family member. Karl's almost illegible script, shaky handwriting and his confusion of his previous location of Ehrenfeld with Müngersdorf convey better than his literal words his disorientation and utter despair: "What else could happen? Everything is just horrible."[195] Henny tried to appear strong and optimistic: "We have to hold our heads high in hopes of seeing our loved ones again." Selma, who usually tried to sound optimistic, added these despairing lines:

> *One needs strong nerves to bear the burden of these times. If we could only see a glimmer of light and receive a message from our children! My grandson [Michael] will turn 3 in a few days, God willing. Will I ever see him? I do not have any hope. I also do not know about Kurt's baby. It was supposed to arrive in April. A few days ago Red Cross messages from America arrived here, unfortunately not for us.*[196]

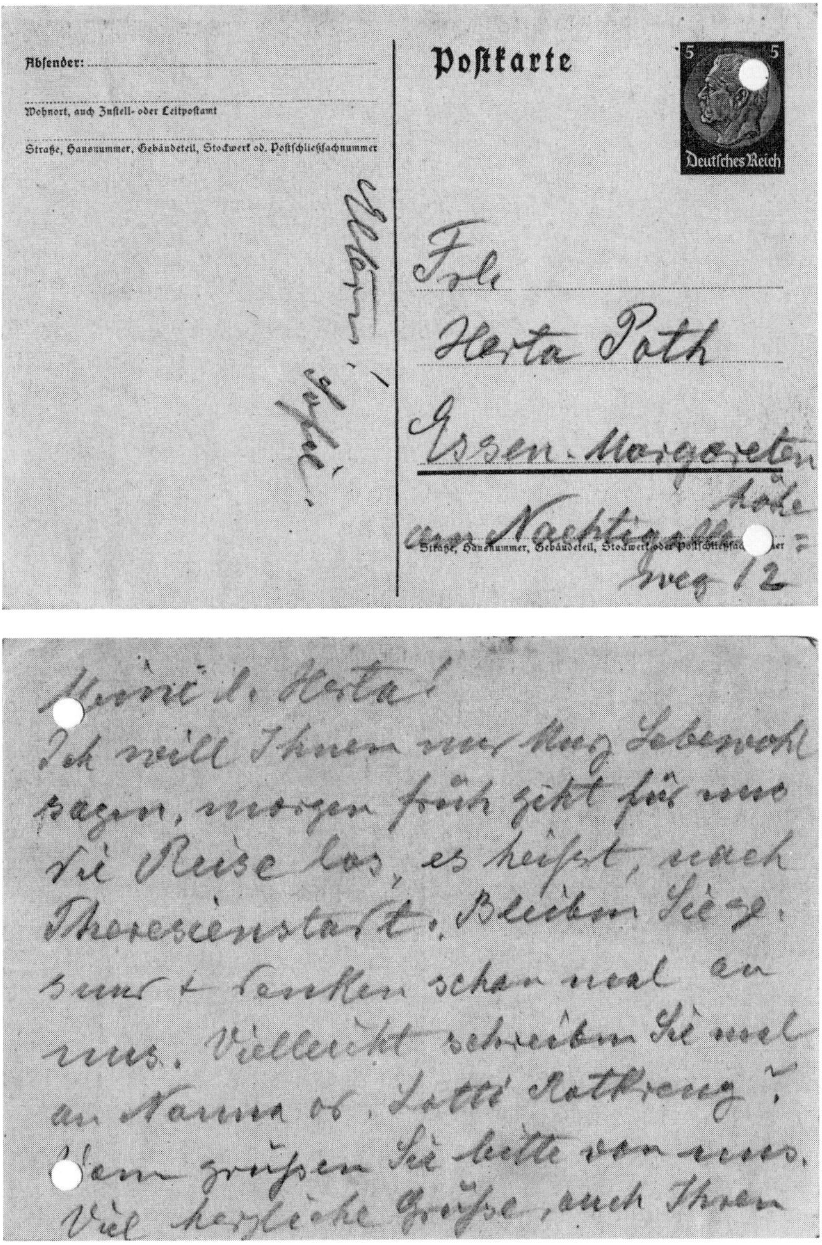

Absender:

Wohnort, auch Zustell- oder Leitpostamt

Straße, Hausnummer, Gebäudeteil, Stockwerk od. Postschließfachnummer

Postkarte

5 Deutsches Reich 5

Frl.
Herta Poth
Essen-Margarethenhöhe
am Nachtigallenweg 12

Straße, Hausnummer, Gebäudeteil, Stockwerk oder Postschließfachnummer

Meine l. Herta!
Ich will Ihnen noch Lebewohl
sagen, morgen früh geht für uns
die Reise los, es heißt, nach
Theresienstadt. Bleiben Sie ge-
sund & denken schon mal an
uns. Vielleicht schreiben Sie mal
an Nanna od. Lotti Rothkranz?
Denen grüßen Sie bitte von uns.
Viel herzliche Grüße, auch Ihren

Figure 7.3 a and b Selma's postcard to Herta Poth, Cologne-Müngersdorf, June 1942

While living conditions worsened the three sisters and their brother-in-law stayed in Müngersdorf two more weeks. In mid June 1942 Selma wrote a sad farewell postcard to Herta Poth at her parents' Essen address (see Figures 7.3a and 7.3b):

> *Dear Herta,*
> *I just quickly want to bid you farewell. Our trip will begin tomorrow morning, apparently to Theresienstadt. Stay healthy and think of us. If you write Nanna or Lotti via the Red Cross, please give them our heartfelt greetings. Our warmest wishes to you and your parents, too.*[197]

8 WARTIME RUMORS AND POSTWAR REVELATIONS

Strewn across continents themselves, Marianne, Kurt and Lotti received in early November 1942 their mother and their aunt's last Red Cross message, dated 27 May 1942. In late November Kurt relayed a "sad message" to Marianne from the brother-in-law of their cousin Ernst Roer:

> *Richard Rothschild at Tel Aviv got a Red Cross message*
> *from [his wife's brother] Ernst Roer, then in Essen ...*
> *that they were leaving for the "Reich Aged Ghetto"*
> *at Theresienstadt "where the Cologne aunts had gone*
> *already beforehand." That is all we know. Of course*
> *among the "Cologne aunts" we certainly must count our*
> *dear mother... I think you spare me [sic] to tell you my*
> *thoughts and feelings, particularly in connection with the*
> *awful general news about the European Jewry which are*
> *[sic] in the papers just now.*[1]

Kurt and Lotti sent inquiries about their mother's fate to the office of the Prague Jewish Community (Jüdische Kultusgemeinde) at the end of 1942 and encouraged Marianne to do the same.[2] Even if the Prague Jewish Community had had information about their loved ones' internment in the former garrison town of Theresienstadt (Terezín), their office would not have been able to readily send news to countries at war with Germany, given the ongoing internment and deportations of its community members. Nevertheless, Hans and Lotti inquired in

Red Cross messages there and even at the Vatican about their loved ones' fate. Hans did find out through his contacts with his former business associates at the MAN Company in Germany that his parents, Julius and Flora Kaiser-Blüth, had also been deported from Cologne to Theresienstadt.[3]

Family members with relatives interned in Theresienstadt struggled to keep each other abreast of any news. Walter Sternberg, who had worked with Hanna at the Essen Jewish Youth Center, and his sister Liesel found themselves in a situation similar to that of the Steinberg siblings. Torn between hope and apprehension, the Sternbergs, who separately had escaped Nazi Germany following the November Pogrom to different corners of the world, tried to get in touch with their father, who had been deported to Theresienstadt. Walter wrote from Chile in September 1942 to his sister Liesel in England:

> Today is Father's seventy-fourth birthday. How and where will he spend this day? How will he have survived the trip to Theresienstadt? We are desperately trying to find out how we can get in touch with him, perhaps via the Red Cross... We heard that one is allowed to send money. We will just try that, and send some small amounts, even if they do not get there... Two days before his deportation he received your Red Cross message and was overjoyed.[4]

Unbeknown to his children, Leopold Sternberg had been deported to Treblinka six days before.[5]

We now know that when detainees, such as the Kaufmann sisters and the Kaiser-Blüths, were eventually informed that their names had been placed on a deportation list, they received detailed guidelines from the Reich Association of Jews in Germany: They were allowed to take one suitcase or backpack weighing no more than 50 pounds, one bedroll, 50 RM and food for three days per person. If they had not yet done so, they were required to fill out a sixteen-page Declaration of Assets.[6] It is not hard to imagine how disconcerting this bureaucratic act of having to declare one's assets must have been. Told they were being sent to a "retirement retreat," the deportees must have wondered why they had to sign away their assets.

Selma's bonds were transferred from her bank in Essen to "special bank account W" of the Commerzbank Cologne on 16 July

1942.[7] The Nazi government's Reich Security Main Office (RSHA) had ordered the Reich Association of Jews in Germany to open a "special bank account W." This account was designated for what was euphemistically called "voluntary contributions." The Gestapo "encouraged" deportees to transfer any assets they had left to the Reich Association.[8] Although this "special bank account W" officially belonged to the Reich Association, in reality the Nazi RSHA had control over it. Many Jews hoped that their "donations" would support Jewish communities, but instead most of these funds directly or indirectly benefitted the Nazis. By September 1942 the Jews in the Rhineland alone had deposited 1,089,676.27 RM into this account of the Cologne Commerzbank. Historian Michael Zimmermann argues that the funds the Gestapo had to pay the Reich Railways for the deportations were covered by "special bank account W": In other words, the deportees had paid for their own transport.[9]

The personal recollections of Theresienstadt survivors help to reconstruct the Theresienstadt experiences of Selma, Henny, Emma and the Kaiser-Blüths. Whether the Jews were rounded up from the collection point in Cologne-Müngersdorf, like Selma and her sisters, or from the synagogue on Roonstrasse, like Cologne Rabbi Isidor Caro and his wife Klara, or from the Jewish community center building on Rubensstrasse, like the Kaiser-Blüths, they were all herded together in the exhibition halls in Cologne-Deutz.[10] There they were fenced in with barbed wire and guarded by police and SS troops. Reports speak of the brutal conditions and treatment of the detainees.[11] One Jewish eyewitness, who was forced by the Gestapo to help with six transports from Cologne-Deutz, recalled the sad scenes in his postwar testimony:

The first transport of elderly Jews [from Cologne] to Theresienstadt saw the most heartbreaking scenes. It was so inhumane to deport all those old people, most of them over 70, and those war-disabled. Many people were unable to carry their luggage and were psychologically broken... One thousand old and desperate people were waiting on Platform 5, knowing that they would never have their final rest in their hometown.[12]

The deportees, all wearing Star of David badges sewn onto their clothes and with personalized identification tags around their necks, were forced to wait until the SS had rummaged through everybody's luggage for forbidden items.[13] Selma and her two sisters were on the first mass transport of about 1,000 Jews from Cologne to Theresienstadt on 15 June 1942, Transport III-1. Also on that same transport were the four Kaiser-Blüths: Julius and his half-brother Karl, along with their wives, Flora and Else, respectively, who were sisters, as well as Cologne's Orthodox Rabbi Isidor Caro and his wife Klara. Apparently, many members of the Jewish community felt comforted by the fact that some of their most prominent leaders were among them.[14] While most trains leaving from Cologne-Deutz station at that time were passenger trains,[15] Klara Caro recalled in her memoirs that on 15 June 1942 they were transported in boxcars to Theresienstadt, in an apparent exception to the rule.[16]

Jews from Germany were misled into believing they were going to a "privileged ghetto" for the elderly, complete with decent accommodation, entertainment and medical care.[17] The miserable train ride lasted three days and three nights. The deportees arrived at the train station of Bauschowitz (Bohušovice) sleep deprived, disoriented and desperate.[18] This railroad station, the closest to Theresienstadt, was about 1.6 miles from the garrison town. The inmates were forced to walk this distance in the summer heat carrying their hand luggage, often rushed and pushed by the guards.[19] A walk that would usually take thirty to forty minutes for healthy, younger people took a largely older, exhausted group, burdened with luggage, about two hours.

After having been subjected to a long wait to get to the "sluice" (Schleuse), the area where their hand luggage was processed or simply pillaged, the deportees from Cologne were housed in the attic of a barrack for four weeks.[20] Exhausted from arduous traveling and walking, weakened by sun and thirst, humiliated by guards and the desolate conditions, several Jews from Cologne died during their first days in Theresienstadt.[21] After the Nazis had forcefully "resettled" the Gentile Czech residents of the town of Theresienstadt in order to enlarge the space for the ghetto, the deportees of Cologne Transport III-1 were moved into their living quarters (Ubikationen).[22] Men and women were separated, and fifty or more people were housed together in small rooms, often being forced to sleep on the bare floor. Each inmate was "entitled" to 1.6 square meters of living space.[23]

The diary of 67-year-old Philip Manes from Berlin provides detailed accounts of his first days in Theresienstadt. He captures the disorientation and the need to adjust to unexpected challenges with a dark sense of humor, sometimes pierced with existential questions such as when, if and how he and his fellow inmates would ever find a way back to civil society and civilized lives.[24] The inmates received "ghetto numbers," which were a combination of their general transport number and their individual number.[25] Many inmates spent their first days in disbelief and shock, trying to adjust to the harsh conditions and the interminable wait for soup or ersatz (substitute) coffee, for their luggage and, most of all, for an event that would end this nightmare. But the soup was too watery, the bread moldy and the so-called coffee brackish brown water, and thus the nightmare dragged on. After days of futile waiting to receive one's suitcases and with it items that would have brought back a remembrance of home and a sense of normalcy, it became clear that many personal items, such as clothing and toiletries, seemed to have been arbitrarily confiscated.[26]

The first days were particularly difficult for the elderly, who often became petrified and emotionally numb.[27] Selma and her sisters Henny and Emma arrived in Theresienstadt on 18 June 1942, the peak month for deportations from Germany. Within a month the number of inmates not only doubled,[28] but the demographic composition also drastically changed: Over the summer months the percentage of inmates older than 65 rose from 36 percent in July to 57 percent in September,[29] and female inmates outnumbered males in August 1942 by 10,000.[30] Up until May 1942 only Czech Jews had been interned in Theresienstadt, but now with the mass transports there from Germany and Austria national, cultural and class differences led to animosities between the respective groups. The SS naturally used conflicts between any groups of inmates to their advantage. They encouraged the national strife between German Jews and Czech Jews so that they would irritate each other and not unite against their tormentors.[31]

Overpopulation, unsanitary conditions and inadequate food caused epidemics and diseases, which, in addition to suicides, contributed to an enormous surge in the mortality rate.[32] It must have been a challenge for 71-year-old Selma and her slightly younger but less healthy sisters[33] to stay alive under the atrocious conditions during the hot summer of 1942, which Theresienstadt historians Miroslav Kárný and H.G. Adler call "the cruelest chapter in Theresienstadt history."[34] We can only speculate that their being together, supporting each other and drawing comfort from the dream of seeing their families again provided the Kaufmann sisters, the Kaiser-Blüths and many others with spiritual sustenance. Or, as Theresienstadt historian Anita Tarsi puts it: "The older women helped each other voluntarily ... The [continued] existence of one woman also meant the hope of survival of another."[35]

Although Selma and Henny had lived in Cologne for only a relatively short time, they had developed a very close relationship with the Kaiser-Blüths since the mid 1930s when Lotti and Hans married. In Theresienstadt Selma and her sisters benefitted from the Kaiser-Blüths' connections with the Jewish community in Cologne; many of its members arrived in the same transport. Friendships, mutual help and support were crucial factors in making life there bearable, as eyewitnesses recall. In her study of behavior in Theresienstadt, historian Anna Hájková argues that social relations were the main focus of the recollections of former female inmates. These women stressed again and again how important it was to have been deported together with loved ones, or to have met them again in Theresienstadt.[36]

It is impossible to determine which barracks housed which individual inmates, especially for the early period of summer 1942. We do not know the exact living arrangements in the barracks but can assume that Selma and her sisters were housed together. Klara Caro reported after the war that she and Flora were assigned to the same quarters, but separate from Selma and her sisters.[37] The inmates were free to visit each other even if they did not live in the same barracks, at least for a few hours in the evening.[38] Most of these older inmates had no work assignments, but some tried to make themselves "useful," whether at the post office or by helping other elderly or sick inmates. Yet other women were in charge of cleaning and improving the barracks.[39] However, taking care of their own basic needs and those of their more vulnerable loved ones took most of their time and energy. The demanding daily routine of standing in line for food, coping with dirt, vermin and substandard hygiene conditions required inner strength, patience and the willingness to adjust. This was particularly difficult for older women whose value system now became severely challenged. Their sense of self was deeply violated under the stark reality of Theresienstadt. In addition, rumors in Theresienstadt of "transports to the east" instilled fear.[40] Many were frightened of the unknown, fearful of leaving loved ones behind. Even though the inmates did not know exactly what these transports meant, they

guessed that in any case their conditions could only worsen dramatically. The inmates' daily struggle was not to succumb to lethargy and
depression despite the inhumane conditions, hunger, lack of personal
space and humiliation. Almost all personal accounts of survivors credit
their survival to the hope they maintained of seeing their loved ones
again and resuming a regular life.

After the war Klara Caro described her memories of seeing
Selma quite frequently in Theresienstadt. According to Caro, Selma
was never sick and always looked well. Selma and Henny, like many
other inmates, including Caro herself, never stopped hoping they would
get out of Theresienstadt.[41] The lack of communication between Selma
and her children must have been very painful. Shortly before Selma
and her sisters arrived in June 1942, the Nazi camp administration
had just issued a prohibition on postal services in response to "recent
infractions to postal regulations." Apparently, some of the inmates had
smuggled in letters and were found out. Subsequently, this sole means
of communication with recipients in Greater Germany, maximum
thirty-word postcards, was halted. In the "Daily Order" (Tagesbefehl)
of 14 May 1942 the Jewish Council of Elders at Theresienstadt publicized the Nazi camp administration's latest punitive measure.[42] This
measure was not revoked until 16 September 1942, which meant that
Selma, her sisters and the Kaiser-Blüths were not allowed to send
any mail for three months after their arrival. The Council of Elders
announced:

> [E]ach ghetto inmate is allowed to write thirty words to a
> recipient in the Greater German Reich once a month. The
> correspondence has to be in German. It is not allowed to
> comment on political affairs, to degrade the reputation
> of the German Reich and its representatives, and to
> misrepresent life in the ghetto. The senders must write
> their names and accurate address, including the name of
> their transport and transport number, building and room
> number.[43]

This was good news, under the circumstances, especially since Cologne
Transport III-1 was the first group scheduled to receive blank postcards,
provided to them by the camp administration on 20 September 1942.[44]
This meant that Selma, her sisters and the Kaiser-Blüths were on track

to receive their first opportunity since their arrival in Theresienstadt to send a message to their children.

Thanks to Richard Rothschild the children knew as of November 1942 that their loved ones had been deported to "a ghetto for the aging" called Theresienstadt, but they had very little sense of what this really meant. In late 1942 Kurt and Lotti excitedly reported to Marianne that they had talked to a released internee from Germany who had just arrived in Palestine with a group of about sixty-nine Jewish people. The German and the British governments had agreed on an exchange of Jews from Palestine trapped in wartime Europe in return for German (Gentile) residents of Palestine.[45] The exchanged Jewish men, women and children were residents of Palestine who had become trapped while visiting Europe at the outbreak of war. Unlike the more fortunate Hans, they had received no advance warning. As part of the exchange agreement they were allowed to return to Palestine. A small group of exchanged Jews arrived in Palestine on 18–19 November 1942 and relayed alarming news about the situation for Jews in Europe.[46] However, the released detainee, with whom Lotti and Hans met, alleviated their worst fears when, on the basis of rumors he had heard in Germany about Theresienstadt, he told them: "Evacuation to Theresienstadt is almost desirable under the circumstances. Only people older than 65 are taken there. Everybody who is able to work is getting paid according to a point system. The pay is usually sufficient to purchase necessary food items. The treatment is supposedly humane and they even have a cultural life of sorts there."[47] The siblings felt somewhat reassured and hoped against hope that Selma and Henny would receive their Red Cross messages in Theresienstadt, even if they could not or were not allowed to reply.[48]

War between Germany and the United States had created a serious rupture in the siblings' communication with their loved ones in Germany and also restricted their access to news about Germany. The combination of lack of information and the news of deportations of their family members from Germany complicated further the Steinberg siblings' association with their German past. Kurt, a new father, became almost nostalgic about family roots and described to Marianne his and Hanna's sheer pleasure with their baby Miryam. He explained that "the name of Miryam is by no means an accident, but is meant to follow the Steinberg tradition including yourself, Nanna, and at the same time being a beautiful Hebrew name, the only one known to me out of our [*sic*] family."[49] Bringing a new generation into this new culture while trying to honor family and religious traditions brought Kurt joy but also sadness. Both he and Hanna and Lotti and Hans spoke German with each other and with their children, yet by living in Palestine they found that the Hebrew language and Jewish identity had become a more overt part of their consciousness. Kurt, who often reminisced with fellow German-Jewish refugees, missed old friends from Germany and asked Marianne if she ever saw any of their acquaintances who had emigrated to the United States.[50]

Marianne, however, had little interest in such connections, which conjured up memories of Nazi Germany for her. She replied to her brother that she hardly had any social contact with such acquaintances and then made it clear this was by choice:

> *Though Rabbi Hahn lives only 2 blocks from here and we*
> *were there and meet him on and off in the street there is*
> *no real connection between us. He probably expects us,*
> *or expected us, to join his community but we don't want*
> *that. The service is held in German and on the whole I*
> *do not like the mood and atmosphere of a circle like that.*
> *You may consider me intolerant and chauvinistic but this*
> *is the truth: I do not like to even speak German. It makes*
> *me think of the Nazis and I don't want to even have their*
> *language in common with them. Let's hope that soon*
> *and completely that what the German language stands*
> *for to me at this moment will be over; so that to think*
> *of Germany and its language does not make me think of*
> *terror and horror but of good things. I am sure that then*
> *I'll speak German again and shall enjoy speaking it.*[51]

The correspondence between the siblings became increasingly less frequent in 1943. They were discouraged by the postal delays and lack of any news from their loved ones. They were also very busy with their own lives. Marianne had finally opened her own medical practice in part of their flat in the Washington Heights neighborhood of New York in December 1941 but needed to supplement her income by working as a school physician and, intermittently, in a pediatric dispensary in a hospital.[52] She did not have an easy time making the practice profitable. Arnold finally found a good job in September 1943 as an engineer in Port Jervis, New York, some 100 miles from their flat in Washington Heights. They continued to commute until September 1944, when Arnold was hired by the Otis Elevator Company in New York.[53] Marianne finally became very busy in her practice in 1946, but it was partly because she was willing to see patients late in the evenings either in extended office hours or during house calls.[54] Marianne and Arnold had their first child, Thomas, in March 1944, and, interestingly enough, their old Essen Rabbi Dr. Hugo Hahn conducted the *bris*, although they never joined his congregation.

Beginning in mid 1943 Kurt and Lotti were also caught up in their own personal problems and did not write Marianne for months. Kurt and Hanna struggled with health issues and trying to make ends meet at the bookstore they managed while raising Miryam and learning in 1944 that they were expecting a second child. Lotti and Hans, on the other hand, experienced marital problems.[55] In fact, after more than two years of what Kurt called a "permanent crisis" Lotti had finally decided in the summer of 1944 to divorce Hans.[56] By the end of the year the divorce was final and she moved to a new apartment with their 5-year-old son Michael.[57]

The years and the miles of separation added to the scars left from the siblings' mutual recriminations over not having been able to get their loved ones out of Germany. Despite these scars and their preoccupation with their own lives, the siblings did make special efforts to contact each other on the occasion of family birthdays and religious holidays. They always contacted each other whenever they heard even rumors about Theresienstadt or anything related to family members who had been left behind in Germany. In late 1943 both Marianne in New York and Kurt in Palestine discovered familiar names on the lists of Theresienstadt inmates that the World Jewish Congress compiled, and they worked together to process and interpret the information. Marianne discovered that not all the information they had learned from the World Jewish Congress was accurate. An "Emmy Kaufmann" was listed as deported from Cologne-Müngersdorf 17/4, the last address before deportation to Theresienstadt of Selma and her sisters, Henny and Emma. However, Emmy was not their aunt's correct first name and the birthdate did not match either. Given the lack of reliability of the information Marianne was hopeful once again: "I have to say I have again a little hope that the three of them are in Theresienstadt and that we may see them again."[58] However, Marianne had not forgotten the worries she had expressed to her siblings in early 1943 about the possibility of "further transport" of detainees from Theresienstadt, worries which were of course well founded.[59]

In late December 1943 Kurt reported to Marianne:

> *Of our beloved ones in Europe we have no news. All our Red Cross messages remained unanswered and without any commentary from the Red Cross. But in a list of Theresienstadt inmates we found: Tante Bert[h]a, Tante Emma, cousin Martha [Lachs] with husband. Nothing of mother, T[ante] Henny or Hans' parents. But this is not disquieting. The list is absolutely incomplete, revealing nothing in the negative, only for some fortunate people a lot in the affirmative.[60]*

The siblings clung to any sign of hope. It is not hard to imagine their excitement when they found out about another exchange, this time a "prisoner exchange," as it was called at the time. One of their acquaintances from Cologne, Paula Schwarzschild, arrived in Palestine in June 1944 along with her daughter Eva among a group of 222 exchanged former inmates from Bergen-Belsen.[61] A very excited Lotti informed her sister Marianne:

> *You probably also read about the recent prisoner exchange. Among them was Paula Schwarzschild, Else Klipstein's sister, with her oldest daughter Eva. Her husband Leo unfortunately died of a heart embolism last year. Paula and Eva have arrived in relatively good condition. The last eighteen months they have lived in Holland. Since they already had a valid certificate [for Palestine] they were brought to a special camp in Germany. The miracle has really happened and they were exchanged. They left Germany eleven days before they arrived here. It sounds like a miracle. The biggest deal for them was to be able to eat enough and to not be surrounded by barbed wire any longer.[62]*

The two Schwarzschild women's "relatively good condition" was due to the fact that they were part of a group of Jews that the SS intended to exchange for German nationals who had been captured in British territory. In April 1943 the SS opened the "temporary residence camp" (*Aufenthaltslager*) at the Bergen-Belsen complex for about 4,000 Jewish prisoners under the pretext of their imminent exchange. The prisoners, mostly Jews from the Netherlands, but also from North Africa, France, Yugoslavia and Albania, came primarily from the Westerbork transit camp in the Netherlands. These prisoners did not have to wear uniforms, only the Star of David badge sewn onto their clothing. Therefore the part of the camp in which they were housed was known as the "star camp." One of the former "star camp" prisoners wrote a series of articles in *Aufbau* about the "exchange transport" after his arrival in Palestine. He painstakingly detailed the harsh camp conditions and the difficult time between April, when the transport was announced for holders of "Palestine papers," and 5 June 1944, when the prisoners finally left the camp.[63] Encouraged by the exchange transport from Bergen-Belsen, Kurt and Lotti joined an initiative:

> [t]o get relatives of Palestinian residents out of Theresienstadt to Palestine. There are many obstacles and doubts of course, besides the big question if the persons ... are still there, but at least the authorities seem to do everything possible ... We wanted to apply for Aunt Emma as well, who is definitely on the list of Theresienstadt internees, but this application ... for an aunt "only" was not accepted yet.[64]

While Paula Schwarzschild's arrival in Palestine provoked great hopes for further prisoner releases, she also brought devastating news for the Steinberg siblings. According to Schwarzschild, their beloved Tante Henny had died two years before in Cologne, prior to deportation, as Lotti sadly reported to Marianne.[65] Kurt conjectured that Henny and her sisters had survived the late May 1942 "big thousand-bomber raid on Cologne unharmed. Then Tante Henny died afterwards, about July 1942." The siblings mourned Henny's death, which they attributed to her "old illness," and vowed anew to do everything to locate their mother and make possible her emigration to the United States or Palestine.[66]

Kurt and Lotti's attempts to secure an immigration certificate to Palestine for their mother in the summer of 1944 seemed like they would be successful. The caveat, however, was that Selma's release was contingent on at least one of three things: another prisoner exchange via a neutral country; the liberation of Theresienstadt; or the defeat of the German army. Kurt, encouraged by the recent "exchange transports" from Theresienstadt to Palestine, resumed sending Red Cross messages to Theresienstadt, his mother's last known address. Kurt and Lotti anxiously searched for their mother's name in every published list of Theresienstadt inmates while awaiting the reply to their application for her immigration to Palestine.[67] They rejoiced in December 1944 that they had just received confirmation they would obtain the immigration certificate for their mother.[68] Although he actually had not yet received the immigration certificates to Palestine, Kurt reported to Marianne and Arnold that he "managed to get Immigration Certificates for Mother and Aunt Emma at Theresienstadt." Then, with a tinge of irony, he added: "We never succeeded before the war when it would have been very easy to get her [Mother] out."[69]

In November 1944 the US government informed Marianne that it had granted her mother "preferential status" for her immigration application.[70] Marianne had acquired US citizenship after five years of residency, on 23 November 1943. That meant that her mother Selma could now immigrate to the United States as the parent of a citizen. Once again, Marianne prepared and sent off an affidavit. This time Arnold did as well.

In either case, whether to Palestine or the United States, Selma could finally join her children after years of separation. If only they could find her! Selma's children needed to locate her and figure out how to get her out of Europe. Their hopes of contacting their mother were again rekindled when Klara Caro, whose husband Rabbi Isidor Caro had died in Theresienstadt in August 1943, arrived from Theresienstadt in Palestine as part of another prisoner exchange, in this case for money. In late 1944 the Nazi leadership's interest in negotiations with the Western Powers led to a deal with a Swiss intermediary, Jean-Marie Musy.[71] In "exchange" for 5 million Swiss francs that international Jewish organizations deposited in a Swiss escrow account, the Nazis agreed to release 1,200 Theresienstadt prisoners.[72] These former inmates arrived in Palestine via Switzerland in March 1945.[73] Before the German guards put released prisoners on comfortable trains they also gave them food and vitamins and had them remove their Star of David badges.[74] On 16 February 1945 *Aufbau* published the names of the "liberated" Jews from Theresienstadt, Klara Caro among them.⁷⁵ The article reported on this "mysterious transport" and concluded: "This story sounds strange, but no stranger than what happened in the last four years."⁷⁶ *Aufbau* also gave its readers detailed instructions on how to submit visa applications for the refugees on this transport.⁷⁷

Lotti, Kurt and Marianne were very excited to hear about the "refugee transports" leaving Theresienstadt for Switzerland. Marianne checked the lists and reported to her siblings in Palestine:

> *The name lists are available, there was not Mother's name*
> *amongst them nor anybody else's that I knew. I was*
> *told, however, by the organization of Orthodox Rabbis*
> *that is responsible for this rescue work that according to*
> *promises such a transport of 1,200 people will arrive from*
> *Theresienstadt every week from now [on]. The organization*
> *has no choice in picking the people. They just have to take*
> *those that are being let out by the Nazis. So we'll keep on*
> *hoping and checking the name lists. It was interesting for*
> *us to hear that you, Kurt, got Palestine visas for Mother*
> *and Aunt Emma. We were advised here by the organization*
> *that helped us with our visa application that it seems that a*
> *Palestine visa is at times helpful to get people out.*⁷⁸

In March 1945 Kurt asked Marianne for help:

> *There seems to be more difficulties than anticipated. I*
> *want to urge you once more to do everything possible*
> *for your part. You cannot rely at all on the more vague*
> *chances for our succeeding. Act as though your endeavors*
> *were the only ones. Also, please, make use of the food*
> *parcel arrangements of the "Joint" [American Jewish Joint*
> *Distribution Committee]. We learned that the people in*
> *Theresienstadt are dependent on food sent from outside.*
> *The time may not be far away when we shall know finally*
> *about Mother and the others.*⁷⁹

Even though Selma's name was not on any of the lists, promises of further transports to Switzerland galvanized Kurt, Lotti and Marianne into action.[80] Hoping for the best, fearing the worst, they inquired about Selma's whereabouts at the International Tracing Service of the Red Cross, the World Jewish Congress and other aid organizations. Marianne called the American Jewish Joint Distribution Committee or "Joint" in Washington, DC to verify the rumors that "the Nazis had evacuated Jews from Theresienstadt."[81] The "Joint" did not have an answer, but told her that they were sending food packages regularly via the Red Cross to Theresienstadt. Marianne interpreted this information to mean that the "Joint" assumed that the addressees would actually receive the packages.[82]

Family members in the United States and Palestine were elated when Germany's impending defeat seemed apparent in the fall of 1944. Marianne felt some relief about what she considered justice:

*[I]t gives me a great feeling of satisfaction to know that
Dueren and neighborhood [sic] towns are being shelled. It
had to be [for] once that the Germans have war in their own
country so that they do feel what it means to have war in
their cities, in their land [sic]. Maybe they now understand
what they did to Russia, Belgium and all the many other
lands they violated. Arnold felt that the Allied bombings
had done some justice in leaving German cities in ruins.*[83]

In April 1945 Kurt captured his own contradictory feelings of joy and sadness in a letter to Marianne: "[With] all this overflowing joy at the [A]llied victory march into Germany and the satisfaction about what, at last, the *Herrenrasse* [master race] has to experience is much damp[en]ed. Why cannot Mother be with us?"[84]

Three days after Germany surrendered (on 7 May 1945) Arnold relayed his thoughts to Kurt and Hanna:

*We were fortunate enough never to have been as close
to the war as you, certainly not in the physical respect,
so we are just relieved that it is over. The horrible facts
of concentration camps taken by the Allied troups [sic]
in Germany during the past weeks were described amply
in newspapers and shown in magazines and moving
pictures and finally proved that all that was so though we
had known it for twelve years. Through very complete*

reporting in newspapers we have a fairly clear picture
of how it looks in Germany now. We saw quite a few
pictures of Cologne, of the remainders I mean; and I hope
that other German cities are in the same condition now.[85]

Kurt, however, was worried about the "depressing news that the Nazis have evacuated all Jews from Theresienstadt and that nothing is known about there [*sic*] fate."[86] At the beginning of May 1945 Kurt asked his former superior from the Centralverein in Essen, Ernst Plaut, who had fled to England, for help in finding out more information about Selma, Henny and Emma. Kurt hoped that Plaut might be able to have more direct access to information about the three sisters through Jewish organizations in London. Kurt wrote:

> *In the list of 1,200 refugees [who] arrived in Switzerland*
> *some time ago from Theresienstadt we have not found*
> *any one of our relatives... My mother and her sister*
> *[were] carried away from Theresienstadt, with unknown*
> *destination. You will [sic] imagine my feelings. I*
> *retained, though, a very tiny spark of hope reading that*
> *Theresienstadt was cleared from Jews altogether and that*
> *they were supposed to have been transferred to Bergen-*
> *Belsen. Then came the horrifying reports about this place,*
> *when it was overrun by the British.*[87]

The three siblings felt understandably burdened by the uncertainty about their loved ones' fates. Lotti relayed Klara Caro's distressing words to Marianne: "Sorry to say parents, Uncle Charles, Aunt Else dead. Steinbergs with transport away." Lotti added: "I am assuming that 'Steinbergs' means Mother and Tante Emma."[88] Apparently Flora Kaiser-Blüth died in December 1942 owing to an infection she caught when helping to take sick people to the hospital. Her sister Else died two months after their arrival at Theresienstadt from sepsis, and Julius had died several months before from enteritis.[89] Saddened by the deaths of the Kaiser-Blüths, Lotti held out a flicker of hope of finding, still alive, her mother and Tante Emma whom Caro had apparently last seen in Theresienstadt.[90] She did not know the true meaning of "with transport away," and even Klara Caro did not know their destinations.[91] Bit by bit the siblings found out more about the terrible conditions in Theresienstadt and were aghast at eyewitness accounts. Marianne lamented:

> *All these horrible reports appeared in the papers about the real situation in Theresienstadt. This together with the answer you received from Caro points to the saddest explanation. Apparently the Kaiser-Blüths died in Theresienstadt and that might not have been the worst. After the latest news here there are about 1,000–3,000 of the original inmates of the town left and the lists of these are not available yet on account of quarantine and typhus... Dear Lotti, I have little hope left.*[92]

Lotti, Kurt and Marianne tried to come to terms with the incomprehensible answer to their questions about their loved ones' fates but were still holding out hope for a miracle. They had heard rumors about "what it means to be transported away from Theresienstadt," but they could not entirely fathom it.[93] Kurt had heard that the US army kept current lists of former concentration camp inmates and therefore believed that Marianne would be the first of the siblings to have access to updated lists. In the unlikely event that she might find Selma's name on any of the lists, Kurt asked Marianne to immediately arrange for food packages and proceed with making their mother's immigration to the United States a reality.

In the months after the war more and more details about Theresienstadt and the ominous transports from there to the east became known, but the full truth that it was not simply a benign camp for the privileged and elderly was revealed only much later. On 6 October 1945 Kurt confessed to Marianne: "What we here, even the official organization, did *not* know [about] are these awful transports from Theresienstadt to 'unknown destinations' (no more unknown by now). We thought always that our beloved ones in Theresienstadt would either survive there or not, but were unaware of this third alternative. It is too terrific [*sic*] to think about it."[94]

From newspaper reports and eyewitness accounts that were publicized in the aftermath of the war the three siblings tried to piece together what had happened to their relatives. Their cousin, Moritz Schweizer from Essen, who had accompanied Marianne to her ship in Rotterdam in June 1938, had endured the horrors of a concentration camp and miraculously survived Bergen-Belsen. In his postwar letter to Marianne Moritz tried to shed some light on unanswered questions:

> *I am not sure whether Tante Henny died in Cologne and assume that she was deported with your mother and Tante Emma. Some of my acquaintances who saw your Onkel Karl from Lüxheim in Theresienstadt did not know what happened to your relatives... In any case, I do not see any chance that the three would have survived. All in all, we can only hope that their suffering did not last long. Death is not the most difficult part ... it is the terrible suffering that is hard. Judging from a general practice we can assume that the three elderly ladies perished right after their arrival.*[95]

Having to give up hope of finding their loved ones alive and come to terms with the sad reality was a very difficult process. Within one year the siblings placed two announcements in *Aufbau*: first, a search notice for their mother Selma and Tante Emma, assuming Henny had died in Cologne,[96] and then, after having received Moritz's interpretation of events, the siblings honored their mother and aunts, Henny and Emma, with an obituary notice in *Aufbau*.[97] It was Kurt's suggestion that they include in the obituary Auschwitz as their loved ones' final destination.[98] The siblings assumed that their loved ones were deported to Auschwitz because they had heard that most transports from Theresienstadt ended up there.

With Marianne's encouragement Kurt pursued further steps to seek out more information about their relatives' fates and to secure compensation for their material losses. In September 1946 Marianne reported news to Kurt about their cousin Ernst Kaufmann, who had changed his name to Ernest Kaufman and had fought in the US army against Germany during the war:

> *[He] wants to rejoin the army and is about to get ready to return for a while to Germany with his wife. He intends to attend to their claims of property and real estate. How is that with us, Kurt? Did mother still have real estate (Gronau) or was she obliged to do a forced selling? I am*

*sure one could claim such property… If something could
be done about it, it should be now.*[99]

However, Kurt was in no position in the early postwar years to initiate any steps toward restitution. The unstable political situation in Palestine, his dissatisfaction with his bookstore job and related financial problems made him contemplate, once again, emigration to the United States.[100] Once the State of Israel was founded (in May 1948), however, Kurt sounded much more content. In 1950 he began filing restitution claims with the United Restitution Office (URO). The Western Allies founded the URO as a legal aid organization in 1948, with offices in several countries. Its main goal was to secure restitution for material losses and compensation for personal damages during the Nazi period for Jewish claimants living outside of Germany. But along the way it also came across information about the fate of Holocaust victims.

The URO had worked together with the Prague office of the Jewish Religious Communities in Bohemia and Moravia[101] and sent Kurt this reply: "In answer to your inquiry from 5 November 1950 we inform you that your mother Selma Steinberg … had been deported [on 16 June 1942] from Cologne to Terezín, transportation number III–1–652, and from there to an unknown location in the east on 19 September 1942, transportation number Bo-1509. We do not have any further information." The URO also mentioned that it was not at liberty to issue death certificates because the "cause of death" had first to be declared in accordance with German law.[102]

In the early 1950s Kurt discovered and informed Marianne that their Tante Henny "did not die of natural causes in Cologne, but was also deported."[103] While in Germany on a work assignment for the Israeli government in 1955, Kurt conducted his own research into the fate of his loved ones. He acquired Tante Johanna's and Onkel Hermann's death certificates in Cologne and confirmed that all three sisters had been deported together to Theresienstadt and then further "east."[104]

As we now know, the frequency of deportations from Theresienstadt to the "east," mostly to extermination camps, intensified in the fall of 1942. From 14 July to 29 September 1942 13 transports left Theresienstadt with a total of 18,004 inmates, of whom only 55 survived.[105] But the transports from 19 to 29 September 1942 differed from all the others. With a peak inmate population in Theresienstadt of 58,491 on 18 September, the so-called "transports of the elderly" (*Alterstransporte*), with 2,000 people each, were supposed to leave to make more room for new arrivals.[106] The elderly inmates were told that they would be transported to another "privileged ghetto."[107] They had to stand for many hours in long lines to be "registered" before they were herded in cattle cars or passenger trains, with fifteen to twenty people per compartment. The inhumane treatment was exacerbated by the fact that nobody was allowed to help these poor elderly inmates.[108]

The exact destinations of these transports of the elderly have been difficult to reconstruct. Scholars assumed for many years, from the late 1950s until the late 1980s, that the transport designated Bo (train number Da 83) on 19 September 1942,[109] which early editions of the *Theresienstadt Memorial Book* (*Theresienstädter Gedenkbuch*) lists as having Selma and her sisters on board, was destined for Maly Trostinec.[110] Maly Trostinec was a smaller, lesser-known camp located alongside an extermination site in the forest near Minsk in Belorussia, where prisoners were shot to death. It was not until 1988 that Czech historian Miroslav Kárný's seminal study clarified what happened. Kárný argues that the extermination methods at Maly Trostinec could not have allowed for the annihilation of the large number of inmates from the Theresienstadt *Alterstransporte*. In order to facilitate their systematic murder the Nazis had opened another killing center in July 1942 by the name of Treblinka. Transport Bo with 2,000 victims, we now know, arrived in Treblinka on 21 September 1942. Victims number 1508 and 1509 were the sisters, Henny Kaufmann and Selma Steinberg.[111]

In 1947 Marianne asked Erna Karsen, one of her American acquaintances whose husband was stationed with the US occupation forces in Berlin, to help find Herta Poth, their old family friend from Essen.[112] Marianne assumed that Herta and her mother, Selma, would have kept in touch if at all possible and hoped that Herta might be able to shed some light on Selma and Henny's last months in Germany. Erna Karsen did manage to track down Herta's address, and Marianne contacted her. A very emotional Herta, who had carefully saved all of the letters that Selma and Henny had written in 1941 and 1942, sent them on to Marianne, who shared them with Lotti and Kurt. Herta also passed on the keepsakes that Selma and Henny had given her

for safekeeping before their deportation to Theresienstadt, in hopes
that Herta would be able eventually to get them to their children.[113]
Reading their mother's final letters, the siblings were able to recapture
their loving mother and aunt's last months in Germany. These were
the last words anyone received from Selma Steinberg and Henriette
Kaufmann.

9 EPILOGUE

Requiem for a Family

The family: on both sides deeply rooted for centuries in Germany, on Mother's side in the Rhineland and on Father's in [the kingdom of] Hanover.

Today would be the 106th [actually 105th] birthday of my father – if he were still alive. Thank God – I shudder to say that – he left this world at age 66 and was able to take his last breath in his own bed, lovingly surrounded by his family.

That was in June 1933.

My Mother was not that fortunate: the day after tomorrow she would have completed a full century. Unfortunately her health was so good – I shudder to have to say that – that she held on to become almost 70, only to be sent to Auschwitz, with a short detour in Theresienstadt. What that means I certainly don't have to explain.

That was in September 1942.

And me? I have a simple motive in mentioning myself. Once again, two days following what was Mother's birthday – and up until now I have had a remarkable constitution, despite everything – so provided all goes well I will also experience my own birthday. I don't want to say "celebrate," as that is what we used to do …

That was in the good old days … a real week of celebration in our family: That Sunday was also designated as the shared big day of celebration for all three birthdays: flowers and poems in the early morning at all three bedsides, then, echoing from the parlor, the old bronze table clock from our grandparents' house would strike the hour, and my brother Kurt would begin playing a processional on the piano, so that all three birthday children could be led ceremoniously to the gift table. Lovely surprises, touching, heartfelt hugs all around, and then we went into the living/dining room to the decorated breakfast table. That was the prelude to our annual family celebration, to which all the devoted members came together anew with genuine love and enthusiasm. What is left of this intimate, warm atmosphere? Who is left from this joyful, harmonious, loving family?

Mother and Tante Henny, that faithful soul, her unmarried sister and our second mother – they went on that last difficult road together, just as they had always been there for each other through joy and suffering. Onkel Hermann, the bachelor, the much-loved "uncle" – not only for us, but for all of our friends – could at least die in his bed in the Jewish old-age home. My brother Kurt, who was a totally healthy, highly talented young man, singled out as a "Student Scholar of the German Volk," had to meet his end as a result of an insidious heart condition, the origin of which lay in his atrocious experiences in the Third Reich, culminating in the Buchenwald concentration camp, from which he was barely able to be rescued. But the physical and psychological injuries emigrated with him. Only my younger sister Marianne is still here – she is a physician in North America and I have wound up in South America.

Three siblings – three continents. Our children don't know each other. An intimate extended family life they have never known, and they won't ever experience it, at least until the family grows to have their own children, and fate will hopefully allow them to live in *one* country. May God grant this![1]

CHARLOTTE STEINBERG FROHMANN,
November 1971

Interestingly enough, Lotti dedicated and sent this lament over the loss of family to her former classmate and still best friend, Herta Poth, in Germany. Herta, although not a family member, had remained close to the family from the age of 10 until she died in the late 1970s. The only exception to this came during the war, when contact was interrupted after Selma and Henny were deported, up until 1947 when Marianne was able to trace Herta's whereabouts in Berlin. Whenever any of the three Steinberg siblings returned to postwar (West) Germany, not an easy return on numerous levels for any of them, they had warm reunions with Herta. Just as she had saved and returned Selma and Henny's letters, Herta saved this *Requiem*, and, before she died in the late 1970s, left instructions that it be sent back to Lotti in Buenos Aires.[2]

In 1971, when Lotti wrote the *Requiem*, it had been six years since her second husband had died, and neither of her two children, Michael from her first marriage and Alicia from her second, were living close by. After beginning proceedings to divorce Hans, Lotti had asked Marianne to place a search notice in the German-Jewish newspaper *Aufbau* to try to find out the whereabouts of her long-lost love, Heiner Frohmann. Heiner, who had never married and who was contacted by a friend who saw the notice, began to correspond from his home in Buenos Aires with Lotti in 1945. Then, on the eve of the founding of Israel, in fact on the last plane to fly out of the British mandate of Palestine, Lotti and her 9-year-old son Michael, who were denied visas to Argentina, flew to Uruguay to rendezvous with Heiner.[3] After a few days of being together again for the first time in close to fourteen years they were married in Montevideo by an Orthodox rabbi and then were able to settle together in Buenos Aires.[4] (See Figure 9.1.)

Lotti's son Michael lived with them in Argentina, together with their daughter Alicia, who was born in 1951. Michael, as Lotti had promised Hans, then returned to Israel in 1953, on the eve of his bar mitzvah. Lotti did not practice dentistry ever again. She focused now on her family and adjusting to yet another country and culture, although she never became fluent in Spanish. In 1959 she visited Kurt and Hanna, and, of course, her son Michael in Israel and Marianne in the United States. Travelling to Germany on the same trip, her first time back since 1937, Lotti had an emotional reunion with her friend Herta. In Buenos Aires she and Heiner were active in a mostly German-Jewish synagogue community but were also part of a larger German community. After Heiner died in 1965 and her daughter Alicia attended university, Lotti increasingly reconnected with several old German schoolfriends, both in letters and on occasional visits to Europe and within Argentina. Lotti also began in the 1970s to teach German to opera singers who sang Wagner and Mozart, even Schubert's *Lieder*, as well as to philosophy professors who wanted to

Figure 9.1 Lotti and Heiner in Buenos Aires, 1949

read Hegel in the original language. In her daughter Alicia's view, after initially distancing herself from Germany Lotti developed, following Heiner's death, a growing desire to reconnect with her roots. Although she held, as Heiner's wife, an Argentinian passport, she never became a citizen of Argentina. Like her household with Hans and Michael in Palestine, her household with Heiner and Alicia and, for a time, Michael in Argentina was German-speaking. Lotti accepted the West German government's offer of a return of her German citizenship.[5] Besides that of British mandatory Palestine, German was the only citizenship she would ever possess. With Alicia and Alicia's daughter and Marianne and Arnold, Lotti celebrated her eightieth birthday in Essen in 1988. Lotti had convinced Marianne to attend a reunion at their high school and to be official guests of the city of Essen. Both sisters were interviewed at the archives of the Alte Synagoge, the renovated building which had once been their synagogue, about their experiences growing up in Essen before and during the Third Reich. This was the last trip either of the sisters took to Germany.[6]

In 1992 Lotti moved to Santiago, Chile to live closer to her daughter Alicia and her Chilean husband and their two children. This followed a visit to her sister in the United States, on the occasion of Marianne and Arnold's fiftieth wedding anniversary, and unfortunately a rapid decline in her health. This was the last time the sisters would see each other. Lotti brought with her to Santiago the same framed photograph of her parents with small photographs of her Tante Henny and Onkel Hermann placed in each corner of the frame, which she had taken with her from Essen and had kept next to her bed until the day she died in March 2003. Every 3 and 5 November, the birthdays of her mother and father, Lotti placed flowers next to their picture, at her own bedside, reminiscent of the first Sunday each November in Essen when they had all had flowers at their bedside to celebrate collectively their birthdays.[7]

Unlike Lotti, Marianne fully embraced the immigrant experience, albeit in a traditional land of immigration, the United States. She also felt less ambivalent about Germany. Quite soon after her arrival in the United States in mid 1938 she avoided speaking German and preferred to correspond in English with her siblings and her then boyfriend, Arnold. Once they married and finally lived together, their household was English-speaking, although bookshelves full of German classics, which Arnold had brought with him in early 1938, lined the walls of their home. Once the war ended Kurt and Lotti resumed writing their letters to Marianne in German, while Marianne did not. She wrote them on 6 April 1946:

> [Tommy] speaks English as we do in our house but knows a
> few German words like Schmeichelkatze, ringel rangle rose
> [sic] and "tut dem Kindchen nichts mehr weh." The latter
> stops most every little hurt he suffers. I am sure, though,
> he does not know what it means. When I tell him German

*words, particularly the latter little rhymes I have to think of
Mother and that she used to comfort us that way.*[8]

Since her own childhood memories of nursery rhymes and maternal comfort were in German, Marianne naturally reverted back to
these, although interestingly enough without pointing out to her
young son that this was German. As adults, Tom and his younger
sister Sue, who was born in 1948, could not remember hearing their
parents speak German unless they were with Lotti or someone who
insisted on speaking German. But certain traditions such as German
Christmas cookies prevailed in the Ostrand family, although the
children did not realize until much later in life that these were a
German or a Christmas tradition and assumed they were part of
Hanukkah.[9]

It took almost two decades for Marianne to make a living from
her own medical practice, a delay that she attributed to the professional roadblocks she faced in Nazi Germany and then all the related
difficulties she had in getting licensed to practice in New Jersey after
moving there in 1952.[10] Nazi Germany had denied Marianne her medical license, and Marianne felt this worked against her professionally
in the United States. In 1955 she returned to Germany to pursue, along
with her brother Kurt and sister Lotti, their quest for restitution for
lost property and damages. Marianne visited and made a special plea
to the North Rhine-Westphalia Ministry of the Interior in Düsseldorf.
She asked that she be granted her German medical license retroactively,
since she had been denied it solely because of her "non-Aryan lineage"
after having successfully passed her state exams in 1935 and completed
her internship in 1938. The State Interior Ministry acknowledged that
she had met all the necessary requirements and offered Marianne her
German medical degree provided she "revive" her German citizenship, inviting her to do so. In 1955, when she requested the retroactive
issuance of her German medical license, only German citizens could
hold German medical licenses. When she was offered the receipt of the
medical credentials along with the return of her German citizenship,
she insisted that she did not want to become a German citizen, just
receive her medical license. Ultimately, after special exceptions were
deliberated and agreed upon, she was granted the German medical
license without having to accept German citizenship.[11] This accomplishment represented an integral part of what Marianne considered

her own personal restitution for all the damages and financial losses she had suffered by being driven out of Germany.

Before arriving in Germany in 1955 Marianne had first spent several weeks with Kurt and Hanna in Israel, her first visit with either of her siblings since she had left Germany in 1938. Landing in Düsseldorf, Marianne was greeted by a tearful Herta, with whom she stayed for several days. (See Figure 9.2.) Kurt had arrived in Germany a few days earlier, to get settled before beginning his new Israeli government liaison position with the International Tracing Service (ITS) in Arolsen. Kurt and Marianne united to visit and survey the condition of their relatives' graves in Essen: those of their father, their father's sister Fanny and their Steinberg grandmother. In Cologne they arranged for tombstones to be made for Onkel Hermann and his sister Tante Johanna. They sought to determine which gravestones had either been vandalized or destroyed by wartime bombing and would need to be restored or repaired.[12] They also needed to decide what to do about a memorial marker for their mother and Tante Henny. Ultimately they opted to have a new stone made for their father's grave and to add two insets into it to memorialize the deaths of their mother and aunt. Based on their understanding of their ultimate deportation, they listed Auschwitz on the insets.[13] Years later they realized their loved ones had not been deported to Auschwitz. The new family gravestone reflects the uncertainty of the place of their death but the certainty of the date: On 19 September 1942 Selma Steinberg and Henriette Kaufmann were "sent to their deaths from Theresienstadt." (See Figure 9.3.)

Upon her return from her trip first to Israel and then to Germany Marianne wrote her cousin Marianne Bachrach (Luedeking), now living with her husband in Nicaragua, about her impressions:

> … but my general feelings for Germany have in no way changed … I never lost this certain feeling of antagonism, this feeling of not being in the right place, this feeling of contempt for the land where the Nazis had been able to rule. Here at this spot, I must now add to my impression of Israel: In Israel I felt at home.[14]

After completing two more internships in New Jersey in the late 1950s, in surgery and obstetrics, Marianne developed a quite

Figure 9.2 Marianne and Herta Poth at Düsseldorf airport, 1955

successful practice.[15] She had her first reunion with her sister in 1959, when Lotti visited her in the United States before going on to Israel and finally Germany. Marianne returned to Israel several times. She visited Lotti in Argentina once, and Lotti visited her in the United States on multiple occasions.[16] (See Figure 9.4.)

In 1986, after retiring, Marianne donated to the German-Jewish history archives at the Leo Baeck Institute in New York copies

Figure 9.3 Gravestone for Alex and Selma Steinberg and Henny Kaufmann, Essen-Segeroth

of the letters her mother Selma had sent to Herta in 1941 and 1942. Some of these letters were among those she saved for herself, but some of the most painful letters she apparently did not keep for herself. She also donated copies of a number of photographs and documents related to having to repay her German scholarship once the Nazis had come to power, as well as those related to the restoration of her German medical license, apparently all documents she considered

Figure 9.4 Marianne and Lotti in Tenafly, New Jersey, 1959

of historical interest.[17] In the 1980s and early 1990s Marianne gave a number of talks to various Jewish community groups about both her own and her family's experiences in the Third Reich, as well as about her impressions when she returned to Germany as a guest of the city of Essen in 1988. After moving to Columbia, Maryland in 1993 to be close to her daughter and her family, Marianne eventually developed Alzheimer's disease. She had not told anyone that she had saved most of the correspondence between herself and her siblings and her loved ones left behind in Germany, as well as her own diaries from the 1930s and 1940s. Marianne and Arnold's daughter Sue discovered them as she was preparing to put her parents' house in Columbia, Maryland up for sale. The sale was necessitated by Marianne's Alzheimer's symptoms requiring her to have long-term medical care and Arnold moving into a retirement home. Marianne, who died in 2002, was no longer sufficiently lucid to answer the many questions her daughter had about the letters.

Kurt, the beloved older brother of Marianne and Lotti, died while only in his early 60s, in 1969. Up until 1951 Kurt continued managing the bookstore, feeling increasingly frustrated by the dead-end nature of this job and his unrealized potential. As the family bread-winner after he and Hanna had children, Kurt moonlighted first as a financial auditor and then as an English tutor to help make ends meet. Unfortunately he began showing signs of a heart condition already in 1950.[18] Many, including his physician sister, thought his heart problems stemmed from the hardships he endured in Buchenwald concentration camp in 1938.[19]

Kurt was able in summer 1951 to get a civil service position with the Israeli defense ministry but still needed to moonlight.[20] He began in the early 1950s working on compiling information about the restitution case involving his family's sold property in Essen and Gronau. Kurt contacted the wife and children of Herr Krell, who had bought the Altenessen property across the street from the family flat and the Geschwister Kaufmann store, and Herr Reising, the former tenant, who had bought his grandparents' Gronau house and woods. Both he found to be quite forthcoming and willing to pay restitution to compensate for the below-market-value price each had paid to Selma and her in-laws back in 1938–9, at a time when such "good deals" with Jewish property-owners were preferable, for Jews anyway, to outright "Aryanization." Kurt remarked to Marianne on the good relations he had with both families, in the late 1930s and again now. Kurt did take up the offer of his old attorney friend, Erich Leeser, who was back in Germany working on restitution cases involving the United Restitution Office (URO), to represent Kurt and his siblings in their restitution cases.[21] In 1954 Kurt had his first heart attack. Fortunately, he had recently gotten the good news that as part of his own personal restitution he was being recognized retroactively as a district attorney (*Landesgerichtsrat*) and would be receiving the German pension that was due him in that position. He and Hanna were relieved that their money worries now seemed to be behind them.[22]

After he recovered from his heart attack the opportunity arose for Kurt to work, with diplomatic status, with the ITS. Established by the Allies at the end of World War II to help reunite survivors with relatives and friends, the ITS gathered documentation that included first-hand evidence of the fate of Jewish victims of Nazism. In the early 1950s the Israeli government requested and received permission to

microfilm sections of the ITS collection relating to Jewish life and suffering during World War II. From June 1955 to November 1957 some
20 million pages of documents were photographed and then placed for
permanent storage in the Yad Vashem archives in Jerusalem.[23] Kurt
oversaw the Yad Vashem team's microfilm project in Arolsen from mid
1955 until late 1957, helping, in this particular way, Holocaust survivors trace the fate of their loved ones. As a representative of the Israeli
government Kurt was required to maintain a certain distance from
German society, such as sending his two children to school outside of
Germany. But Kurt could not help but enjoy living there again, resuming a few friendships, such as that with Herta Poth, and making new
friendships with the mostly international, non-German staff associated
with the ITS. At the same time Kurt was able to take advantage of both
his legal skills and his physical location in Germany to help advocate
his siblings' interests in their deceased mother's restitution case.

Living in West Germany for over two years with their two
children, Kurt and Hanna welcomed the opportunity to take their
children to the places their ancestors had lived and to acquaint them
with Europe.[24] Kurt found himself surprisingly impressed with postwar West Germany:

> *Generally, if Germany was not connected with such*
> *horrendous memories and associations for us, one can live*
> *quite well here. It is simply Europe through and through,*
> *with everything that that means for us. And one has to*
> *admit that the German government does everything it*
> *can to make up for the past, materially and intellectually.*
> *The atmosphere is absolutely western freedom-oriented*
> *and democratic. But naturally one can't bring back*
> *to life those who were murdered or erase the years in*
> *concentration camps.*[25]

Kurt made it clear, however, that with the exception of Herta and
another old friend from Altenessen, Fritz Werner, that "my other
'friends' I have no interest in seeing again."[26] In visiting Altenessen once
more he was surprised to see how ugly it appeared to him, and although
he recognized it had experienced considerable bombing, he wrote Lotti
that he "couldn't imagine we'd spent such a happy youth there and was
glad not to have seen anyone they [he and his family] knew."[27]

Kurt briefly visited Marianne, Arnold and their children in the United States before leaving Arolsen for Tel Aviv. Since the 1930s Kurt had regarded the United States as the "land of opportunities," and it remained, until at least the late 1950s, his dream that it would become his ultimate immigration destination.[28] He even asked Marianne in 1957 to make inquiries in New York about whether the URO branch there might be hiring, but nothing ever came of this.[29]

Certainly the least inclined of the three siblings toward Zionism as a young man in Germany, Kurt was the only one of the Steinberg children to become an Israeli citizen. Because he worked for the Israeli government he was required to Hebraicize his name to Sella. Kurt, like his sister Lotti, did become fluent in Hebrew, but his wife, Hanna, never did, and their household remained German-speaking. Between his sisters taking their husbands' names and Kurt changing his name from Steinberg to Sella, none of the children remained "Steinbergs." Kurt returned to Israel at the end of 1957, with somewhat of a heavy heart and an uncomfortable amount of uncertainty about his professional future. Apparently he was offered in 1958 the opportunity to work in the German judicial system as a state attorney (*Oberlandesgerichtsrat*), a position above that for which he was receiving his pension. But after just having left Germany a few months before, Kurt did not pursue this. He was appointed chief librarian at one of the branches of the Israeli ministry of defense and was still working there part-time when, in 1969, he died prematurely at the age of 63 as a result of his heart condition.[30] (See Figure 9.5.)

The war and the Holocaust and the Steinberg children's attempts to start new lives and to cope with the losses of beloved family members divided the children both geographically and, to some extent, emotionally. Their sense of national and cultural identity diverged more and more over time as their differences overwhelmed their similarities. Their shared upbringing and national and cultural origins were inevitably overshadowed by their new identities and the painful legacy of the Holocaust. Each dealt with what philosopher Theodor Adorno has called *Aufarbeitung der Vergangenheit*, working through and coming to terms with the past, in his or her own way. Their shared experiences faded more and more in day-to-day significance as their lives in new countries set them on different paths. It was not easy to overcome the seventeen years of not seeing each other, in Kurt and Marianne's case, and twenty-two years of separation from Lotti for

Figure 9.5 Hanna, Kurt and Marianne touring the grounds of the Knesset, Jerusalem, 1968

Kurt and Marianne, especially when so many of those years held such painful memories. Each of the three siblings would see each other on several occasions after their initial long separations, beginning in the mid to late 1950s. They often wrote each other in the 1960s about how important it would be for them to all get together, but they would never again be reunited as a family.

NOTES

1 Introduction

1 Deborah Gayle, "A German-Jewish Family's Odyssey through the Holocaust." Paper in fulfillment of the requirements for History 751, November 2002, UMBC, Baltimore, Maryland.

2 The translation of any correspondence and secondary or published primary literature from German to English has also been our own.

3 A plea not to pigeonhole German-Jewish families into categories of insider/outsider or within the conventional narrative of German-Jewish assimilation, but rather to let the family's experiences speak for themselves can be found in a 2008 review of W. Paul Strassmann's story of the assimilation of his own German-Jewish family. See Gregory P. Shealy, Review of W. Paul Strassmann, *The Strassmanns: Science, Politics, and Migration in Turbulent Times, 1793–1993* (New York: Berghahn Books, 2008). H-German, H-Net Reviews. May 2009. www.h-net.org/reviews/showrev.php?id=23651

4 Recognizing the need to warn young German scholars writing biographies about some of the pitfalls of writing biography, the Ruhr University in Bochum held a workshop in December 2009 on "Identität und Lebenswelt. Praxis der historischen Biographieforschung." See www.hsozkult.geschichte.hu-berlin.de/termine/id=11820

5 Alexandra Garbarini, *Numbered Days: Diaries and the Holocaust* (New Haven: Yale University Press, 2006).

6 Marion Kaplan, *Between Dignity and Despair: Jewish Life in Nazi Germany* (New York: Oxford University Press, 1998).

7 Jürgen Matthäus and Mark Roseman (eds.), *Jewish Responses to Persecution, 1933–38* (Lanham, Md.: Alta Mira Press in association with the United States Holocaust Memorial Museum, 2010). It was published

in the series, "Documenting Life and Destruction: Holocaust Sources in Context."

8 Mark Roseman, *The Past in Hiding* (London: Penguin, 2000).

9 David Clay Large, *And the World Closed Its Doors: The Story of One Family Abandoned to the Holocaust* (New York: Basic Books, 2003).

10 Armin and Renate Schmid, *Lost in a Labyrinth of Red Tape: The Story of an Immigration that Failed*, trans. Margot Bettauer Dembo (Evanston, Ill.: Northwestern University Press, 1996). The original German Fischer Taschenbuch Verlag edition appeared in 1993.

11 Martin Doerry, *My Wounded Heart: The Life of Lilli Jahn 1900–1944*, trans. John Brownjohn (New York: Bloomsbury, 2004). The original German edition appeared in 2002.

12 The quantitative and qualitative approach to Holocaust letters by Oliver Doetzer in his *"Aus Menschen werden Briefe": Die Korrespondenz einer jüdischen Familie zwischen Verfolgung und Emigration* (Cologne: Böhlau Verlag, 2002) has never been translated into English. It, and other works in German, have helped us develop our own approach.

13 Christopher S. Browning, Richard S. Hollander and Nechama Tec (eds.), *Every Day Lasts a Year: A Jewish Family's Correspondence from Poland* (New York: Cambridge University Press, 2007). An anthology of German-Jewish family letters juxtaposed with newspaper articles is also worthy of note here, although its less scholarly approach made it less useful for our particular purposes. See Chaim Rockman, *None of Them Were Heroes: Letters between the Lines 1938–1942* (Englewood, N.J.: Devora, 2003).

2 German-Jewish lives from emancipation through the Weimar Republic

1 See David Sorkin, "Emancipation and Assimilation: Two Concepts and Their Application to the Study of German Jewish History," *Leo Baeck Institute Yearbook*, 35 (1990), 17–33. See also Jonathan C. Friedman, *The Lion and the Star: Gentile–Jewish Relations in Three Hessian Communities, 1919–1945* (Lexington, Ky.: University Press of Kentucky, 1998), 17ff. Cf. Peter Pulzer, "Rechtliche Gleichstellung und öffentliches Leben," trans. Holger Fliessbach, in Steven M. Lowenstein, *et al.* (eds.), *Deutschjüdische Geschichte in der Neuzeit*, vol. III: *Umstrittene Integration, 1871–1918* (Munich: C.H. Beck, 1997), 191.

2 Marion Kaplan, *The Making of the Jewish Middle Class: Women, Family and Identity in Imperial Germany* (New York and Oxford: Oxford University Press, 1991), 8. Kaplan defines *Bildung* as "a belief in the primacy of culture and the potential of humanity."

3 Friedman, *Lion and the Star*, 17f.

4 Ibid., 15. The so-called church tax or *Kirchensteuer* that was formalized in the 1919 constitution, but that had been the practice in many German states before then, required Germans to pay a certain percentage of their income to their religious community via a tax assessment.

5 Ibid., 18. Cf. David Harry Ellenson, *After Emancipation: Jewish Religious Responses to Modernity* (Detroit: Wayne State University Press, 2004), 269ff.

6 Ellenson, *After Emancipation*, 274ff.

7 Steven M. Lowenstein, "Das religiöse Leben," in Lowenstein *et al.* (eds.), *Deutsch-jüdische Geschichte*, vol. III, 101.

8 Friedman, *Lion and the Star*, 18f.

9 Interview with Ernest Kaufman, 11 May 2006, Lumberton, New Jersey, conducted by Uta Larkey.

10 Marion Kaplan, "As Germans and as Jews in Imperial Germany," in Marion A. Kaplan (ed.), *Jewish Daily Life in Germany, 1618–1945* (New York: Oxford University Press, 2005), 241.

11 Ibid. See also Kaufmann family tree, Ostrand Collection (henceforth OC).

12 Steven M. Lowenstein, "Jüdisches religiöses Leben in deutschen Dörfern. Regionale Unterschiede im 19. und frühen 20. Jahrhundert," in Monika Richarz and Reinhard Rürup (eds.), *Jüdisches Leben auf dem Lande* (Tübingen: Mohr Siebeck, 1997), 219ff. Such itinerant teachers were not "protected Jews" and as such were not able to reside in many communities. Protected Jews possessed capital they could loan to the local rulers, who in turn taxed them for their protection. With formal emancipation complete in 1871, Jews in Germany gained the freedom of travel and residency and more freedom to practice different occupations.

13 See Kaufmann family tree, OC, and interview with Ernest Kaufman, 11 May 2006, Lumberton, New Jersey, conducted by Uta Larkey.

14 Kaplan, *Jewish Middle Class*, 79. As late as 1906 55 percent of Jewish communities in Germany maintained a mikveh, although only about 15 percent of Jewish women practiced this Orthodox ritual by then. This number is smaller than the estimated 20 percent Orthodox Jews in Germany at the time.

15 Schiefbahn mikveh photograph, OC.

16 For the Synagogue-Internet-Archive historical listing of synagogues in Germany, go to: www.synagogen.info/en_index.php. See also www.ashkenazhouse.org/synagog/Northpercent20Rhine-Westphalia. doc. Both accessed 28 September 2009. By 1890 both parents had died and the Kaufmann children were dispersed to live among relatives, so the Kaufmanns never had their own synagogue in Schiefbahn.

17 Friedman, *Lion and the Star*, 20.

18 Peter Pulzer, *The Jews and the German State: The Political History of a Minority, 1848–1933* (Oxford: Blackwell, 1992), 78. The Rhineland's provincial assembly was the only one in Prussia to advocate equal rights for Jews before 1848.

19 Ibid., 17. See also Avraham Barkai, "Die deutschen Juden in der Zeit der Industrialisierung," in Barkai, *Hoffnung und Untergang: Studien zur deutsch-jüdischen Geschichte des 19. und 20. Jahrhunderts* (Hamburg: Hans Christians, 1998), 21.

20 Pulzer, *Jews and the German State*, 78.

21 Marion Kaplan, "Introduction," in Kaplan (ed.), *Jewish Daily Life*, 6. Kaplan presumes that assimilation included a willingness to convert and intermarry. Cf. Steven Aschheim, "German History and German Jewry: Junctions, Boundaries and Interdependencies," in *In Times of Crisis: Essays on European Culture, Germans, and Jews* (Madison: University of Wisconsin Press, 2001), 86–92. Aschheim stresses the need to consider assimilation as a two-way street, in which subcultures also shape and redefine the "majority" culture.

22 Friedman, *Lion and the Star*, 19. Cf. Michael A. Meyer, "Schlußbetrachtung," in Michael Brenner, Stefi Jersch-Wenzel and Michael A. Meyer (eds.), *Deutsch-jüdische Geschichte in der Neuzeit*, vol. II: *Emanzipation und Akkulturation 1780–1871* (Munich: C.H. Beck, 2000), 356ff.

23 Friedman, *Lion and the Star*, 17. Other scholars' figures differ slightly. Avraham Barkai maintains that over 60 percent of Jewish families were in the mid- and upper-income levels by 1871, while between 5 percent and 25 percent, with considerable regional variations, were in the lowest income level. Thus, 80 percent may be high, but may well include the lower middle class as well. See Avraham Barkai, *"Wehr Dich!" Der Centralverein deutscher Staatsbürger jüdischen Glaubens (C.V.) 1893–1938* (Munich: C.H. Beck, 2002), 13. Cf. Monika Richarz, "Introduction," in Richarz (ed.), *Jewish Life in Germany: Memoirs from Three Centuries*, trans. Stella P. and Sidney Rosenfeld (Bloomington and Indianapolis: Indiana University Press, 1991), 16. Richarz states that according to tax records in 1890 at least two-thirds of the Jewish population were middle class.

24 Friedman, *Lion and the Star*, 17.

25 Barkai, *"Wehr Dich!"*, 14.

26 David Blackbourn, *The Long Nineteenth Century: A History of Germany, 1780–1918* (New York: Oxford University Press, 1998), 308f. and 416. For an in-depth exploration of late nineteenth-century political anti-Semitism, see chapter 5 of Helmut Walser Smith, *The Continuities of German History: Nation, Religion and Race across the Long Nineteenth Century* (New York: Cambridge University Press, 2008), 167–210.

27 Blackbourn, *Long Nineteenth Century*, 425f. See also Richarz, *Jewish Life in Germany*, 25.

28 Richarz, *Jewish Life in Germany*, 25.

29 Information found in marriage license Nr. 217, Alex Steinberg and Selma Kaufmann, Altenessen Standesamt, 15 September 1905, AR 102466, "Alex Steinberg," Alte Synagoge Archives, Essen.

30 This speculation is based on the fact that Isaak Kaufmann died after being kicked in the head by a horse while at work and that many rural Jews at that time were horse or cattle traders.

31 Hans-Jürgen Schreiber, "Geschichte der Altenesser Jüdinnen und Juden," unpublished ms., Essen, 1994, 17.

32 Information derived from Kaufmann family tree, OC, and from an interview with Ernest Kaufman, 11 May 2006, Lumberton, New Jersey, conducted by Uta Larkey.

33 Interview with Marianne Steinberg Ostrand (henceforth Marianne), 2 November 1988, IN 327, recorded at the Alte Synagoge Archives, Essen.

34 See Richarz, *Jewish Life in Germany*, 12.

35 Schreiber, "Geschichte der Altenesser Jüdinnen und Juden," 17. There is no exclusively feminine plural commercial term for sisters owning a business together, unlike *Gebrüder*, when brothers collaborate in business. The term *Geschwister* is, however, derived from the feminine *Schwester* (sister) and its plural *Schwestern* and, unlike *Gebrüder*, *Geschwister* includes both sisters and brothers.

36 Richarz, *Jewish Life in Germany*, 15f.

37 These were the only two editions of the Adressbücher (address books) for the town of Altenessen following the store's founding until the town's 1915 incorporation into Essen, Stadtarchiv Essen. At the time there were only address books, as opposed to phone books, although they included telephone numbers if they existed, and commercial advertisements.

38 Schreiber, "Geschichte der Altenesser Jüdinnen und Juden," 18.

39 Michael Zimmermann, "Zur Geschichte der Essener Juden im 19. und im ersten Drittel des 20. Jahrhunderts," in Alte Synagoge (ed.), *Jüdisches Leben in Essen 1800–1933*. Studienreihe der Alten Synagoge, vol. 1 (Essen: Klartext, 1993), 22.

40 Barkai, "Zwischen Deutschtum und Judentum: Richtungskämpfe im Centralverein deutscher Staatsbürger jüdischen Glaubens, 1919–1933," in Barkai, *Hoffnung und Untergang*, 111ff. Cf. Barkai, "*Wehr Dich!*", 9.

41 Friedman, *Lion and the Star*, 21f.

42 Ibid., 22. Cf. Jehuda Reinharz, *Fatherland or Promised Land: The Dilemma of the German Jew, 1893–1914* (Ann Arbor: University of Michigan Press, 1975), 134. The entire leadership of the German Zionist organization, the Zionistische Vereinigung für Deutschland (ZVfD), before and after

World War I were German-born and university-educated and mostly quite prosperous, while the rank-and-file members were almost all Eastern European immigrants.

43 Zimmermann, "Essener Juden," 15f. Most German-Jewish men born in the second half of the nineteenth century had both Hebrew and Roman, Celtic or Germanic names.

44 Schreiber, "Geschichte der Altenesser Jüdinnen und Juden," 18f. Cf. interview with Charlotte Steinberg Frohmann (henceforth Lotti), 2 November 1988, IN 291, recorded at the Alte Synagoge Archives, Essen.

45 Schreiber, "Geschichte der Altenesser Jüdinnen und Juden," 18f.

46 See "Bochum," for the history of the Jews there: www.jewishvirtuallibrary. org/jsource/judaica/ejud_0002_0004_0_03215.html. Bochum's population was approximately three times larger than that of Duisburg at the time: 300,000 compared with 100,000.

47 Marriage license Nr. 217, Alexander Steinberg and Selma Kaufmann, Altenessen Standesamt, 15 September 1905, AR 102466, "Alex Steinberg," Alte Synagoge Archives, Essen.

48 1905 and 1908 Adressbücher for the town of Altenessen and later, after its 1915 incorporation into Essen, from Essen's Adressbücher, Stadtarchiv Essen.

49 Hans-Jürgen Schreiber, "Jüdische Bevölkerungsentwicklung in Essen und Altenessen," in Schreiber, "Geschichte der Altessener Jüdinnen und Juden," Table 1, 4. Cf. Marianne Steinberg Ostrand, "Talk about My Invitation and Visit from October 31 to November 7, 1988 to Essen in West Germany, the City of my Birth," Tenafly, New Jersey, 20 July 1989, OC. Cf. Marianne's Interview, 2 November 1988, IN 327, recorded at the Alte Synagoge Archives, Essen. Marianne stated there were only four Jewish families in Altenessen and noted that her parents' "circle of friends" was mixed, both Gentile and Jewish.

50 Marion Kaplan, Monika Richarz and other historians of German Jewry note the limits of Jewish–Gentile social interaction and stress that neighbors and business associates may have socialized publicly but rarely in each others' homes. The Kaufmann–Steinberg family apparently did, however.

51 Schreiber, "Geschichte der Altenessener Jüdinnen und Juden," 20.

52 1905 and 1908 Adressbücher for Altenessen, Stadtarchiv Essen.

53 1905 and 1908 Adressbücher for Altenessen and as of 1915 for Essen, Stadtarchiv Essen.

54 Schreiber, "Geschichte der Altenessener Jüdinnen und Juden," 20.

55 Interview with Marianne, 2 November 1988, IN 327, recorded at the Alte Synagoge Archives, Essen.

56 Zimmermann, "Essener Juden," 10ff. Only adult men who were current in their dues for at least the previous three years were included as members

on the 1910 membership list reproduced here. Although Alex's brother
Hermann was listed as a member in 1910, Alex was not. Hermann, a
traveling salesman who worked in Krefeld, some 35 miles away, overnighted
often with the Kaufmann–Steinberg family, but it is not clear why he might
have been listed as a member while Alex was not.

57 Ibid., 12. Cf. Richarz, *Jewish Life in Germany*, 23.

58 Zimmermann, "Essener Juden," 8.

59 Ibid., 15ff.

60 Ibid., 24ff.

61 Ibid., 24.

62 Information provided by Frau Martina Strehlen, archivist of the Alte
Synagoge to Rebecca Boehling, 25 May 2009, Essen. See also Zimmermann,
"Essener Juden," 8. Although Berlin represented the exception, it was typical
for the sexes to be segregated in German Liberal synagogue communities,
even into the Weimar Republic.

63 Ibid. Cf. interview with Lotti, 2 November 1988, IN 291, recorded at the
Alte Synagoge Archives, Essen. Presumably Kurt, once he got older, also sat
downstairs with the men. Both Marianne and Lotti implied that the family
attended Shabbat services regularly. Historian Michael Zimmermann notes
that, in the Essen synagogue, men's hats reflected the social caste system,
with those wearing top hats belonging to the top two of the four socio-
economic groups of men. See Zimmermann, "Essener Juden," 12.

64 Tour of the restored Alte Synagoge and explanations and photographs
provided to Rebecca Boehling by the archivist, Martina Strehlen. See also
Jüdisches Gemeindeblatt für den Synagogenbezirk Essen, AR 1179 and AR
1180, Alte Synagoge Archives, Essen.

65 Interview with Marianne, 2 November 1988, IN 327, recorded at the
Alte Synagoge Archives, Essen. See also information relating to Moritz
Schweizer's activities in the community in: Correspondence from Walter
Hoffmann, 29 October 1989, BR 241, Correspondence with Otto Grausz,
27 May 1987, BR 205, Correspondence from Gerhard Orgler, 19 May 1981,
BR 422, and Correspondence with Inge Schweizer, 19 May 1981, BR 507,
Alte Synagoge Archives, Essen. Schweizer was in charge of the Jüdische
Winterhilfe, a social welfare agency in the mid–late 1930s, and also played
a leading role in the 1930s in the publication of the synagogue's bulletin, the
Jüdisches Gemeindeblatt.

66 Interview with Marianne, 2 November 1988, IN 327, recorded at the Alte
Synagoge Archives, Essen.

67 Interview with Lotti, 2 November 1988, IN 291, recorded at the Alte
Synagoge Archives, Essen.

68 Interviews with Lotti (IN 291) and Marianne (IN 327), 2 November 1988,
recorded at the Alte Synagoge Archives, Essen.

69 Ibid.

70 Interview with Ernest Kaufman, 8 May 2009, Lumberton, New Jersey, conducted by Rebecca Boehling.

71 Ibid.

72 Interview with Marianne Bachrach Luedeking, 10 November 2006, Miami, Florida, conducted by Rebecca Boehling. Kurt and his wife would remain friends and socialize with the Neufelds even after they all emigrated to Palestine. Marianne maintained contact with Julius Bachrach and Olga Neufeld Bachrach's daughter Marianne after they both emigrated to the United States.

73 Hans-Jürgen Schreiber, "Die Familie Loewenstein," draft essay for the study of the Jews of Altenessen, Essen, 2005.

74 Interview with Marianne, 2 November 1988, IN 327, recorded at the Alte Synagoge Archives, Essen.

75 The support for the call to arms was made by the main national office of the Centralverein in Berlin and published in the *Allgemeine Zeitung des Judentums*, August 1914, 32, 7.

76 Interview with Suzanne Ostrand-Rosenberg, 3 May 2006, Baltimore, Maryland, conducted by both authors.

77 Alex and Selma Steinberg to Felix Kaufmann (Selma's cousin), 11 October 1915, OC. Gustav Kaufmann was 36 when he fell.

78 Friedman, *Lion and the Star*, 22.

79 Pulzer, *Jews and the German State*, 206. See also Rachel Heuberger, *Hinaus aus dem Ghetto: Juden in Frankfurt am Main, 1800–1950* (Frankfurt am Main: Fischer Verlag, 1988), 132.

80 Facsimile of the 2 November 1917 letter from the British Foreign Minister, Lord Balfour, to Lord Rothschild. www.mfa.gov.il/MFA/Peace+Process/ Guide+to+the+Peace+Process/The+Balfour+Declaration.html

81 Friedman, *Lion and the Star*, 22.

82 Schreiber, "Geschichte der Altenessener Jüdinnen und Juden," 20f.

83 Friedman, *Lion and the Star*, 23.

84 Interview with Suzanne Ostrand-Rosenberg, 3 May 2006, Baltimore, Maryland, conducted by both authors.

85 Correspondence of Charlotte Steinberg Frohmann (henceforth Lotti) with the Alte Synagoge Archives, 18 November 1986, BR 165, Alte Synagoge Archives, Essen.

86 Interview with Marianne, 2 November 1988, IN 327, recorded at the Alte Synagoge Archives, Essen.

87 Interview with Alicia Frohmann, 27 April 2005, Miami, Florida, conducted by Rebecca Boehling. Alicia recalled that her mother Lotti always said this was the one photograph that showed her parents as they typically were and as she chose to remember them together. Lotti kept it at her bedside through all her different moves, up until her death in March 2003.

88 Schreiber, "Geschichte der Altenessener Jüdinnen und Juden," 20f.

89 Selma to Marianne, 15 August 1923, Altenessen, OC.

90 Schreiber, "Geschichte der Altenessener Jüdinnen und Juden," 22. *Schlagball* resembles the game of baseball.

91 Selma to Marianne, 15 August 1923, Altenessen, OC.

92 Monika Richarz (ed.), *Jüdisches Leben in Deutschland: Selbstzeugnisse zur Sozialgeschichte, 1918–1945*, vol. III (Stuttgart: Deutsche Verlags-Anstalt, 1982), 13. Cf. Friedman, *Lion and the Star*, 28f. According to Friedman, from 1900 to 1930 the rate of intermarriage went from 8 percent to 22 percent; but Weimar Republic statistics were skewed by the fact that the marriage rate among Jews was down overall, so although proportionately the intermarriage rates rose for the thirty-year period as a whole, the actual number of intermarriages did not increase much. In 1930–2, in the midst of the Great Depression, the number of intermarriages declined.

93 Friedman, *Lion and the Star*, 23.

94 Ibid.

95 Ibid., 26. Cf. Richarz, *Jewish Life in Germany*, 7. Richarz attributes the increase in conversions to the rise in anti-Semitism. Individuals who seceded from the Jewish community were no longer formally counted as Jewish.

96 Friedman, *Lion and the Star*, 30.

97 Interviews with Marianne (IN 327) and Lotti (IN 291), 2 November 1988, recorded at the Alte Synagoge Archives, Essen. Until September 1933 Marianne kept a diary, which she labeled "Mein Tagebuch," cited here as her Diary. Thereafter she wrote occasional personal entries in a composition-type notebook, referred to here as her Notebook. See Marianne's Diary from the 1920s to 1933 and her Notebook from 1933 on, as well as various postcards and memorabilia, OC. Cf. Interview with Alicia Frohmann, 7 April 2010, Washington, DC, conducted by Rebecca Boehling.

98 Interviews with Marianne (IN 327) and Lotti (IN 291), 2 November 1988, recorded at the Alte Synagoge Archives, Essen.

99 Interview with Marianne, 2 November 1988, IN 327, recorded at the Alte Synagoge Archives, Essen.

100 Marianne's Notebook, which she wrote in as a diary of sorts, provides details of these 1933 developments, OC.

101 Friedman, *Lion and the Star*, 43.

102 Richarz, *Jewish Life in Germany*, 16.

103 Ibid., 24.

104 Lotti to Marianne, 31 January 1930, Munich, OC. Increasingly Marianne's family and friends addressed her as Nanna.

105 Lotti to Marianne, 31 January 1931, Berlin, OC.

106 Ibid.

107 Lotti to Marianne, 11 August 1931, Kiel, OC.

108 Kurt to Lotti and Marianne, 6 May 1931, Altenessen, OC.

109 Ibid.

110 Interview with Marianne, 2 November 1988, IN 327, recorded at the Alte Synagoge Archives, Essen.

111 Selma to Lotti and Marianne, 6 May 1931, Altenessen, OC.

112 Tante Henny to the *Mädel* (young girls), Marianne and Lotti, 6 May 1931, Altenessen, OC.

113 In fact Selma's grandchildren were surprised to learn of Tante Emma's existence, as their parents had rarely, if ever, even mentioned her. Cf. various interviews conducted by the co-authors with Selma's grandchildren, Marianne's children Sue and Tom, Lotti's children Alicia and Michael, and Kurt's son Gideon.

114 Selma to Marianne, 1 December 1931, Altenessen, OC.

115 Kurt to Lotti, 11 September 1932, Altenessen, Frohmann Collection (henceforth FC).

116 Henny to Lotti, no exact date, but early November 1932, Altenessen, FC. Marianne was not able to study in Austria once the Nazis came to power in January 1933. Instead, she matriculated closer to home, in Düsseldorf.

117 Rebecca Boehling's visit to Altenessen and her examination of a series of historical maps in the Essen Stadtarchiv in the summer of 2009 confirmed this next-door proximity.

3 Losing one's business and citizenship: the Geschwister Kaufmann, 1933–1938

Because letters from this older generation only began to be consistently saved in mid 1938 when Marianne emigrated from Germany, the reservoir of Selma and Henny's actual words is sparse for the first five years of the Third Reich. Thus, this chapter has to rely heavily on Marianne's Diary, family postcards and photographs, postwar interviews with the Steinberg children, cousins and grandchildren, eyewitness accounts and secondary literature about this period.

1 Marianne's Diary, 19 June 1933, Düsseldorf, OC.

2 *Jüdische Rundschau*, 10 March 1933, as cited in: Dirk van Laak, "Wenn einer ein Herz im Leibe hat, der läßt sich von einem deutschen Arzt behandeln: Die 'Entjudung' der Essener Wirtschaft von 1933 bis 1941" in Alte Synagoge (ed.), *Entrechtung und Selbsthilfe: Zur Geschichte der Juden in Essen unter dem Nationalsozialismus*. Studienreihe der Alten Synagoge, vol. IV (Essen: Klartext, 1994), 18. That same March the lord mayor of Essen ordered all city offices to stop making any purchases from Jews.

3 Marianne Steinberg Ostrand, "Talk about My Invitation and Visit from October 31 to November 7, 1988 to Essen in West Germany, the City of my

Birth," talk given to Hadassah in Tenafly, New Jersey, 20 July 1989, OC. Marianne recalled that only six Jewish families lived in Altenessen when the Nazis came to power. This would mean the average family size was seven, which implies she was referring to extended families.

4 Hans-Jürgen Schreiber, "Die Familie Steinberg–Kaufmann," draft essay prepared for study of the Jews of Altenessen, Essen, 2005, 1. Cf. van Laak, "Herz im Leibe," 19.

5 In fact as early as July 1933 all discriminatory actions against large Jewish-owned department stores were temporarily prohibited by the regime because of the negative foreign, domestic and international impact. See Otto Dov Kulka and Eberhard Jäckel (eds.), *Die Juden in den geheimen NS-Stimmungsberichten 1933–1945* (Düsseldorf: Droste Verlag, 2004), 591.

6 Van Laak, "Herz im Leibe," 18.

7 Doris L. Bergen, *War and Genocide: A Concise History of the Holocaust* (Lanham, Md.: Rowman and Littlefield, 2003), 61f.

8 "Aryan" clauses, or paragraphs, originated in the nineteenth century in the bylaws of various clubs, professional associations and political parties, just as Jews were becoming more assimilated into the German economy and society. In the Third Reich such overt discriminatory practices became official government policy and open public practice. See "Aryan Paragraph," in Walter Laqueur and Judith Tydor Baumel (eds.), *The Holocaust Encyclopedia* (New Haven and London: Yale University Press, 2001), 32.

9 In April 1933 the Nazis passed the "Law for the Restoration of the Professional Civil Service" to exclude opponents of the regime and so-called non-Aryans, those who had at least one non-Aryan parent or grandparent, from all sorts of public-sector jobs. These decrees in combination with other Nazi measures targeting those deemed racially undersirable prevented up to 867,00 Jews and other "non-Aryans" in Nazi Germany from entering or exercising their professions, pursuing studies at universities or completing their examinations. See Herbert Strauss, "Jewish Emigration from Germany, Part I," *Leo Baeck Institute Yearbook (LBIYB)* (1980), 326.

10 Yehuda Bauer, *A History of the Holocaust*, rev. edn. (Danbury, Conn.: Franklin Watts, 2001), 109f. See also Strauss, "Jewish Emigration," 342ff. Cf. Saul Friedländer, *Nazi Germany and the Jews: The Years of Persecution, 1933–1939*, vol. 1 (New York: HarperCollins, 1997), 24f. A good summary of the historical controversy about whether Schacht was ever protective toward Jewish enterprises and whether, if he was, that this was indicative of his relative lack of anti-Semitism can be found in Frank Bajohr, *"Aryanisation" in Hamburg: The Economic Exclusion of Jews and the Confiscation of Their Property in Nazi Germany*, trans. G. Wilke (New York and Oxford: Berghahn Books, 2002), 2f.

11 Strauss, "Jewish Emigration," 342ff.

12 Bauer, *A History of the Holocaust*, 131.

13 Avraham Barkai, *From Boycott to Annihilation: The Economic Struggle of the Jews, 1933–1943*, trans. William Templer (Hanover, N.H. and London: University Press of New England, 1989), 99f. and 173. This Disagio fee should not be confused with the emigration tax or *Auswanderungsabgabe*, which was imposed in February 1939 on all Jewish emigrants in addition to, and separate from, the Reich Flight Tax, which all emigrants had to pay. The justification for this emigration tax, the *Auswanderungsabgabe*, was to have wealthier Jews who were emigrating finance the emigration of indigent Jews. So as of February 1939 there were three different penalties that Jews had to pay when emigrating: two taxes – the emigration tax (*Auswanderungsabgabe*) and the Reich Flight Tax – and one fee, the Disagio.

14 As of 1939 emigrants could only take property for personal use out of the country; but it too was subject to this Disagio fee that had to be paid from blocked accounts in the Deutsche Golddiskontbank (German Gold Discount Bank) or Dego. In German this Disagio was often called the *Dego-Abgabe*. See Bajohr, *"Aryanisation" in Hamburg*, 121f.

15 Barkai, *From Boycott to Annihilation*, 100. Cf. Strauss, "Jewish Emigration," 342ff.

16 Barkai, *From Boycott to Annihilation*, 49f. In fact, a number of wealthy Jews did emigrate in the first few months after the Nazis came to power, before all government offices were Nazified and while it was still possible to liquidate assets without major capital losses. Despite currency controls, some emigrants were able to transfer funds abroad in the first years of the regime.

17 Strauss, "Jewish Emigration," 342ff.

18 Barkai, *From Boycott to Annihilation*, 49f.

19 Paul A. Shapiro and Martin C. Dean, "Foreword," in *Confiscation of Jewish Property in Europe, 1933–1945: New Sources and Perspectives*, Proceedings of Symposium held at the United States Holocaust Memorial Museum Center for Advanced Holocaust Studies, Washington, January 2003 (Washington, D.C.: United States Holocaust Memorial Museum, 2003), 7.

20 Interview with Lotti, 2 November 1988, IN 291, recorded at the Alte Synagoge Archives, Essen.

21 Ibid. Lotti recalled the contents of Tante Henny's letter in this interview.

22 Ibid. The Altenessen trucking company owner Adolf Holzgreve served as a witness at Selma and Alex's 15 September 1905 civil marriage ceremony. Bertie Holzgreve was described by Lotti as a young neighbor whose grandfather owned a big house in Essen. It is likely that Bertie was related to Adolf Holzgreve.

23 Ibid.

24 Ibid.

25 Marianne's Notebook, 24 February 1935, Altenessen, OC.

26 Following the Nuremberg Laws the Nazi government forced the Central Association of German Citizens of the Jewish Faith (Centralverein) to change its name to the Jewish Central Association in 1936. This required name change clearly reflected the Nazis' policy of denying Jews German citizenship.

27 Ernst Herzfeld, "Assimilation, Dissimilation, Auswanderung," *C.V. Zeitung*, XVI/8 (February 1937), 25.

28 Barkai, *"Wehr dich!"*, 345.

29 S. Adler-Rudel, *Jüdische Selbsthilfe unter dem Naziregime, 1933–1939* (Tübingen: J.C.B. Mohr, 1974), 73.

30 Mark M. Anderson (ed.), *Hitler's Exiles: Personal Stories of the Flight from Nazi Germany to America* (New York: The New Press, 1998), 4.

31 Friedländer, *Nazi Germany and the Jews*, 142f. Cf. Daniel Fraenkel, "Nuremberg Laws," in Laqueur and Tydor Baumel (eds.), *The Holocaust Encyclopedia*, 451ff.

32 Interview with Lotti, 2 November 1988, IN 291, recorded at the Alte Synagoge Archives, Essen.

33 Lotti to Marianne, 5 December 1938, Tel Aviv, OC.

34 Adler-Rudel, *Jüdische Selbsthilfe*, 73.

35 Interview with Lotti, 2 November 1988, IN 291, recorded at the Archive of the Alte Synagoge, Essen.

36 Kaplan, *Between Dignity and Despair*, 39.

37 Marianne's Notebook, 31 December 1935, Bern. See also Marianne to Lotti, 2 March 1936, Altenessen, OC.

38 Marianne to Lotti, 25 March 1936, Altenessen.

39 Fraenkel, "Nuremberg Laws," 451ff.

40 Although she would have a relapse in the late fall and winter of 1938–9. See Lotti to Marianne, 9 January 1939, Tel Aviv, OC.

41 Interview with Ernest Kaufman, 11 May 2005, Lumberton, New Jersey, conducted by Uta Larkey.

42 Interview with Ernest Kaufman, 29 March 2005, Lumberton, New Jersey, conducted by Rebecca Boehling.

43 Marianne's Notebook, 10 February 1937, Cologne-Braunsfeld, OC.

44 Sales in Germany were and are carefully regulated by law and can only be held at certain times and under certain conditions.

45 Marianne's Notebook, 10 February 1937, Cologne-Braunsfeld, OC.

46 Ibid.

47 Essen had a total population of close to half a million, with some 4,935 Jews in November 1932 and 3,915 in November 1935. Hans-Jürgen Schreiber, "Übersicht über die Geschichte der Juden in Altenessen," draft essay for

study of the Jews of Altenessen, Essen, 2005, 4. Population Table compiled by Schreiber from the *Essener Volkszeitung* and *Statistik des Landkreises Essen.*

48 Kulka and Jäckel, *Geheime NS-Stimmungsberichte*, 616. Göring was put in charge of the "Jewish question" in 1938 and later made formally responsible for the implementation of the Final Solution.

49 Ibid., 618f. The "Aryanization" process would be stepped up further on 4 January 1938, when new rules were instituted to prevent the disguising of Jewish businesses, and on 22 April strict punishments were formalized for any non-Jewish German who helped to disguise Jewish businesses.

50 Interview with Lotti, 2 November 1988, IN 291, recorded at the Alte Synagoge Archives, Essen.

51 Marianne's Notebook, 27 September 1937, Cologne, OC.

52 Raul Hilberg, *The Destruction of the European Jews* (Teaneck, New Jersey: Holmes and Meier, 1985), 118f.

53 Selma and Henny to Marianne, 21 June 1938, Essen, OC.

54 Selma to Marianne, 24 June 1938, Essen, OC.

55 Selma to Marianne, 10 July 1938, Essen, OC.

56 Selma to Marianne, 30 June 1938, Essen, OC.

57 Interview with Marianne Bachrach Luedeking, 10 November 2006, Miami, Florida, conducted by Rebecca Boehling. Olga and her husband Julius would never again see their daughter, Marianne Bachrach.

58 Selma to Marianne, 24 June 1938. Essen, OC.

59 Selma to Marianne, 30 June 1938, Essen, OC.

60 Lotti and Hans to Marianne and Arnold, 4 July 1943, Tel Aviv, OC.

61 Henny to Marianne, 12 July 1938, Essen, OC.

62 Kurt to Marianne, 22 July 1938, Frankfurt am Main, OC.

63 Selma to Marianne, 17 July 1938, Essen, OC.

64 Johanna's married name was Moses. Kurt to Marianne, 23 August 1938, Frankfurt am Main, OC.

65 Henny to Marianne, 16 July 1938, Essen, OC.

66 Bauer, *A History of the Holocaust*, 114f. Yehuda Bauer has noted that Jews operating private businesses or privately practicing law or medicine were in a better situation than those who had governmental or public posts. He does note that the conditions even for the former became increasingly difficult, thanks to unofficial boycotts, etc. He argues that the turning-point came in the spring of 1938 with various measures to identify what was Jewish-owned property.

67 Selma to Marianne, 17 July 1938, Essen, OC.

68 Eugen was presumably Eugen Roer, Selma's nephew, the son of her oldest sister, Julie. He had been apprenticed to a leather business and married the owner's daughter. He apparently had acquired considerable business acumen in the meantime.

69 Selma to Marianne, 17 July 1938, Essen, OC. The *Auflassung* refers to the time of the acceptance of the purchase offer, prior to the actual closing.
70 Marianne's restitution files, OC.
71 Adressbücher der Stadt Essen, Stadtarchiv Essen.
72 Lotti to Marianne, 16 August 1938, Tel Aviv, OC.
73 Kurt to Marianne, 22 July 1938, Frankfurt am Main, OC.
74 Kurt to Marianne, 19 February 1939, Tel Aviv, OC.
75 Herr Reising, who bought the Gronau property, had long been a commercial tenant in the building. The Reising store sign already hung over the front door of the building in the 1934 photograph.
76 Marianne's restitution files, OC.
77 Henny to Marianne, 6 November 1938, and Selma to Marianne, 22 November 1938, Essen, OC.
78 Visa-less German and Austrian Jews did sometimes manage to find refuge, namely in Shanghai. In the summer of 1938, after Germany's *Anschluss* of Austria in March, the Jewish community of Vienna discovered that no visas were required for a section of Shanghai known as the International Settlement. By June of 1939 close to 10,000 German and Austrian Jews had made passage on the Trans-Siberian railroad and arrived, often with few financial means left them, in Shanghai (Bauer, *A History of the Holocaust*, 139). None of the members of the Kaufmann–Steinberg family apparently even considered this route. Older Jews could not have easily made such a journey and were generally not yet that desperate when this avenue was still possible.
79 Selma to Marianne, 1 October 1938, Essen, OC.
80 Henny to Marianne, 6 November 1938, and Selma to Marianne, 22 November 1938, Essen, OC.
81 Leo Grünebaum, "'Jews Not Welcome' in Hotels," in Margarete Limberg and Hubert Rübsaat (eds.), *Germans No More: Accounts of Jewish Everyday Life, 1933–1938*, trans. Alan Nothnagle (New York and Oxford: Berghahn Books, 2006), 69.

4 Professional roadblocks and personal detours: Lotti and Marianne, 1933–1938

1 Interview with Marianne, 2 November 1988, IN 327, recorded at the Alte Synagoge Archives, Essen.
2 Marianne's Diary, 19 June 1933, Düsseldorf, OC.
3 Ibid.
4 Barkai, *From Boycott to Annihilation*, 29f.
5 Ibid.
6 Marianne's *Lebenslauf* (curriculum vitae), restitution file, OC.

7 Kulka and Jäckel, *Geheime NS-Stimmungsberichten*, "Zeittafel," 589. See also the *Reichsgesetzblatt* (RGBl.) 1, 225–6.

8 RGBl. 1, 969.

9 Marianne's Diary, 30 June 1933, Düsseldorf, OC.

10 Michael Kater, *Doctors under Hitler* (Chapel Hill and London: University of North Carolina Press, 1989), 183.

11 Marianne's Notebook, 6 March 1934, Altenessen, OC.

12 Marianne's Diary, 19 June 1933, Düsseldorf, OC.

13 Bruno Blau, *Das Ausnahmerecht für die Juden in Deutschland, 1933–1945*, 3rd edn. (Düsseldorf: Verlag Allgemeine Wochenzeitung der Juden in Deutschland, 1965), Nr. 45, 25. See also Kulka and Jäckel, *Geheime NS-Stimmungsberichte*, "Zeittafel," 595.

14 Lotti's statement given to Alte Synagoge Archives, Essen, 11 May 1984, BR 164.

15 Marianne's Notebook, 18 November 1933, Cardiff, OC.

16 See the following laws: RGBl. 1, 350 (2 June 1933), RGBl. 1, 983 (20 November 1933), RGBl. 1, 192 (13 February 1935), RGBl. 1, 594 (9 May 1935). After 5 February 1934 "non-Aryan" medical students and future dentists were no longer allowed to take their licensing exams. Blau, *Ausnahmerecht*, 25.

17 Marianne's Diary, 6 June 1933, Altenessen, OC.

18 Ibid., 19 June 1933, Düsseldorf, OC. See also Trudi Maurer, "From Everyday Life to a State of Emergency: Jews in Weimar and Nazi Germany," in Kaplan (ed.), *Jewish Daily Life in Germany*, 306ff.

19 Hartmut Steinecke, "Einführung 1. Deutschland," in Jenny Aloni, *"Ich muss mir diese Zeit von der Seele schreiben..."* (Paderborn: Ferdinand Schöningh, 2006), 34. See also Dvora Hacohen, "British Immigration Policy to Palestine in the 1930s: Implications for Youth Aliyah," *Middle Eastern Studies*, 37/4 (October 2001), 206–18.

20 Wealthy entrepreneurs also found it easier than most professionals to immigrate, at least as long as they were able to bring their assets with them. Among the top countries where German Jews were most likely to immigrate to during the Third Reich were the United States, Palestine, Britain and Argentina. See A. Kruse and E. Schmitt, *Wir haben uns als Deutsche gefühlt* (Darmstadt: Steinkopff, 2000), 6. Cf. Richarz (ed.), *Jewish Life in Germany*, 34f.

21 Barkai, *From Boycott to Annihilation*, 11.

22 Marianne's Diary, 19 June 1933, Düsseldorf, OC.

23 Interview with Lotti, 2 November 1988, IN 291, recorded at the Alte Synagoge Archives, Essen.

24 Interview with Marianne, 2 November 1988, IN 327, recorded at the Alte Synagoge Archives, Essen.

25 Bernd Schmalhausen, *Schicksale jüdischer Juristen aus Essen, 1933–1945* (Bottrup and Essen: Pomp, 1994), 118.

26 Interview with Marianne, 2 November 1988, IN 327, recorded at the Alte Synagoge Archives, Essen. Even in 1988 Marianne did not mention her involvement with Edgar as a factor in her being called to the local Nazi Party headquarters, but this association with him might well have been related to her having being questioned.

27 Marianne's Diary, 21 August 1932, Würzburg, OC. Marianne implied in her Diary that Edgar might well have had a few tussles with SA members prior to the Nazis coming to power. Whether Alfred shared Edgar's politics is unclear, but if he were known also as a communist or someone who wore his anti-Nazism on his sleeve, this might explain why he was murdered by the SA in the spring of 1933.

28 Interview with Marianne, 2 November 1988, IN 327, recorded at the Alte Synagoge Archives, Essen. Early on in the regime communists were the group most targeted by the Nazis. See Friedländer, *Nazi Germany and the Jews*, 17.

29 Marianne's Diary, 30 June 1933, Düsseldorf, OC.

30 Interview with Marianne, 2 November 1988, IN 327, recorded at the Alte Synagoge Archives, Essen.

31 Edgar Meyer to Marianne, 5 July 1933, Würzburg, OC. Edgar did mention that despite his satisfaction with his work in Würzburg he would not mind working abroad.

32 Interview with Marianne, 2 November 1988, IN 327, recorded at the Alte Synagoge Archives, Essen.

33 Deborah Dwork and Robert Jan van Pelt, *Flight from the Reich: Refugee Jews, 1933–1946* (New York and London: W.W. Norton, 2009), 18. But not all German refugees who crossed the border actually immigrated. France did, however, waive its visa restrictions for German refugees in 1933.

34 Interview with Marianne, 2 November 1988, IN 327, recorded at the Alte Synagoge Archives, Essen. See Deutsches Studentenwerk E.V. to Frl. Marianne Steinberg, 11 July 1933, Marianne Ostrand Collection, AR 5823, Leo Baeck Institute, New York.

35 Deutsches Studentenwerk E.V. to Frl. Marianne Steinberg, 16 March 1933, Marianne Ostrand Collection, AR 5823, Leo Baeck Institute, New York. Although Kurt never accepted a similar stipend, he was informed that he would be required to repay it before he was allowed to emigrate. See Hanna Levy Sella, "Bericht über meine Erlebnisse in der Nazi-Zeit," 1988, BR 517, Alte Synagoge Archives, Essen.

36 Deutsches Studentenwerk E.V. to Frl. Marianne Steinberg, 11 July 1933, Marianne Ostrand Collection, AR 5823, Leo Baeck Institute, New York.

37 Marianne's Diary, 21 September 1933, Altenessen, OC.

38 Interview with Marianne, 2 November 1988, IN 327, recorded at the Alte Synagoge Archives, Essen. Marianne arranged to work for Jewish families in Britain in return for room and board, but very little actual pay.

39 Ibid.

40 Marianne's Notebook, 24 October 1933, Cardiff, OC. As the historian Marion Berghahn has noted, most German-Jewish émigrés initially had similar reactions of yearning for a return to their pre-Third Reich life in Germany and a negative response to life in Britain in the early 1930s. See Marion Berghahn, *Continental Britons: German-Jewish Refugees from Nazi Germany*, rev. edn. (New York and Oxford: Berghahn Books, 2007), 77.

41 Marianne's Notebook, 18 November 1933, Cardiff, OC.

42 Ibid., 10 November 1933, Cardiff, OC.

43 Ibid., 9 December 1933, London, OC.

44 Ibid., 22 January 1934, London, OC.

45 Ibid., 2 February 1934, London, OC.

46 Ibid., 9 December 1933, London, OC. See also interview with Marianne, 2 November 1988, IN 327, recorded at the Alte Synagoge Archives, Essen. The Lauterbachs apparently introduced her to Ramona Goodman, a representative of WIZO in London, with whom she corresponded both in 1934 and 1936. WIZO was founded in 1920 as the women's section of the Zionist Federation.

47 Marianne Steinberg Ostrand, "Introductory Notes to Hadassah Talk, April 1990," OC.

48 Ramona Goodman to Marianne, 1 March 1934, Soldiers Green, OC.

49 Prof. Dr. Albert Eckstein to Marianne, 6 December 1933, Düsseldorf, OC.

50 Marianne's Notebook, 9 December 1933, London, OC. See also Marianne's *Lebenslauf* (curriculum vitae), restitution file, OC, and her interview at the Alte Synagoge Archives, Essen.

51 Marianne's Notebook, 9 December 1933, London, OC.

52 Ibid., 2 February 1934, London, OC.

53 Marianne Steinberg Ostrand, "Introductory Notes to Hadassah Talk, April 1990," OC.

54 Marianne's Notebook, 6 March 1934, Altenessen, OC.

55 Ibid.

56 Ibid., 18 November 1933, London, OC.

57 Ibid., 3 March 1934, Altenessen, OC. Marianne noted: "What a shame ... I feel sorry for my sister Lotti."

58 Adler-Rudel, *Jüdische Selbsthilfe*, 141.

59 Kulka and Jäckel, *Geheime NS-Stimmungsberichte*, "Zeittafel," 602.

60 A German medical or dental provider who was not a participant in the state insurance system either had to have a celebrity, wealthy clientele who paid

directly or via private insurance or would not be able to survive financially in the profession.

61 Interview with Lotti, 2 November 1988, IN 291, recorded at the Alte Synagoge Archives, Essen.

62 Heiner Frohmann to Lotti, Buenos Aires, 9 July 1945, FC.

63 Marianne's Notebook, 18 November 1933, London, OC.

64 Interview with Lotti, 2 November 1988, IN 291, recorded at the Alte Synagoge Archives, Essen.

65 Interview with Alicia Frohmann, 27 April 2005, Miami, Florida, conducted by Rebecca Boehling.

66 Interview with Lotti, 2 November 1988, IN 291, recorded at the Alte Synagoge Archives, Essen.

67 Heiner Frohmann to Lotti, Buenos Aires, 9 July 1945, FC. In this letter, Heiner confessed to Lotti that he took the collapse of his business as a stroke of fate that he felt he had to overcome by himself: "In hindsight, I do not understand why I thought so... And then everything turned against me."

68 Marianne's Notebook, 18 November 1933, London, OC.

69 Lotti to Marianne, 30–1 January 1934, Cologne, OC.

70 Marianne's Diary, 6 March 1934, Essen, OC.

71 Lotti's family sent her a postcard to her new, interim place of work in Albert Sulke's dental practice in Hanover already on 10 September 1933. So she must have been working there part of the time while she was seeing Heiner and then Karl.

72 Lotti to Marianne, 17 May 1934, Hanover, OC.

73 Interview with Suzanne Ostrand-Rosenberg, 3 May 2006, Baltimore, Maryland, conducted by both authors.

74 Lotti to Marianne, 17 May 1934, Hanover, OC.

75 Marianne's Notebook, 19 July 1934, Düsseldorf, OC.

76 Ibid., 14 May 1934, Düsseldorf, OC.

77 Interview with Suzanne Ostrand-Rosenberg, 9 June 2008, Baltimore, Maryland, conducted by Rebecca Boehling.

78 Marianne's Notebook, 14 May 1934, Düsseldorf, OC.

79 Ibid., 1 June 1934, Düsseldorf, OC.

80 Ibid., 5 July 1934, Düsseldorf, OC.

81 Marianne's Diary, 21 August 1932, Würzburg, OC.

82 Marianne's Notebook, 5 July 1934, Düsseldorf, OC.

83 Kater, *Doctors under Hitler*, 209f. See also Hacohen, "British Immigration Policy," 206ff.

84 Marianne's Notebook, 5 July 1934, Düsseldorf, OC.

85 Ibid. Marianne was informed of Kurt's detention (by the Gestapo) and release in a coded letter from her family referring to his having survived an "illness." See Gestapo Files, RW 58-Nr. 28854, Kurt Alfred Steinberg, HStA Düsseldorf.

86 Edgar would survive the war and Holocaust in hiding with a Christian family in France. See interview with Marianne, 2 November 1988, IN 327, recorded at the Alte Synagoge Archives, Essen. Marianne and her husband and children visited Edgar and his wife and family in France in the 1960s. Cf. Interview with Suzanne Ostrand-Rosenberg, 6 June 2008, Baltimore, Maryland, conducted by Rebecca Boehling.

87 Interview with Marianne, 2 November 1988, IN 327, recorded at the Alte Synagoge Archives, Essen. For more details about the store, see Chapter 3.

88 Marianne's Notebook, 24 February 1935, Altenessen, OC. Historian Michael Kater points out that, following the Röhm purge of June 1934, acts of violence and intimidation toward Jewish physicians increasingly occurred. See Kater, *Doctors under Hitler*, 191. The purge, also known as the "Night of the Long Knives," was directed against the SA under the leadership of Ernst Röhm. He and other Nazi leaders who were thought to pose a threat to Hitler's leadership, as well as former political allies, were murdered by the SS.

89 Marianne's Notebook, 24 February 1935, Altenessen, OC. In German the complete name of the RV is Reichsvertretung der deutschen Juden.

90 Ibid., 3 August 1935, Altenessen, OC.

91 Ibid., 19 July 1934, Düsseldorf, OC.

92 Ibid., 24 February 1935, Altenessen, OC.

93 See Marianne's Notebook entries of 1934 and 1935, as well as interview with Marianne, 2 November 1988, IN 327, recorded at the Alte Synagoge Archives, Essen.

94 Marianne's Notebook, 4 October 1935, Düsseldorf, OC. The Nuremberg Laws prohibited Jewish households from employing Gentile female domestic servants under the age of 45.

95 Marianne remained in touch with the Calmsohns for many years, even after they emigrated to England in 1936, and long after the war ended.

96 Marianne's Notebook, 4 October 1935, Düsseldorf, OC. Yom Kippur had just passed.

97 Ibid. Marianne in 1938 seriously explored the possibility of working as a physician in India. She explicitly mentioned these biographical facts about this young man, Mühlfelder, but did not note whether she was considering emigration to India or Switzerland at the time she mentioned Mühlfelder.

98 Christina Ogilvy, Secretary, Relief Work, International Student Service to Marianne, 1 May 1935, London, OC. See also interview with Marianne, 2 November 1988, IN 327, recorded at the Alte Synagoge Archives, Essen and Marianne's restitution file, OC.

99 Marianne's Notebook, 19 December 1935, Bern, OC.

100 Ibid., 31 December 1935, Bern, OC.

101 Ibid., 2 February 1936, Bern, OC.

102 Ibid., 30 May 1936, unclear location, but presumably in Germany, OC.

103 Désirée Aebersold and Sonja Stalder, "Da von dem Erwerb des Titels meine Zukunft abhängt," unpublished licensing thesis (*Lizentiatsarbeit*) at the Institut für Soziologie, Schriftenreihe Kultursoziologie, University of Bern, 2000, 131 and note 206.

104 Marianne to Miss Ogilvy, Relief Work Office, International Student Service, London, 5 March 1936, Bern, and International Student Service Announcement of April 1937 *re* the work on behalf of German refugee students, OC.

105 Marianne's Notebook, 25 March 1936, Altenessen, OC. Henny had a hysterectomy because of a malignant tumor.

106 Fritz Beildeck to Marianne, 30 May 1936 and 4 June 1936 and undated postcard, early June 1936, Essen, OC.

107 Marianne's Notebook, 11 July 1936, Bern, OC. See also 25 May, 3 June, 6 June, 13 June, 20 June entries.

108 Fritz Beildeck to Marianne, 29 August 1937, Rio de Janeiro, OC.

109 Ramona Goodman to Marianne, 23 June 1936, Soldiers Green, OC. Marianne's letter to Goodman is not extant.

110 Kater, *Doctors under Hitler*, 215f.

111 Marianne's Notebook, 10 February 1937, Cologne, OC.

112 See Barbara Becker-Jákli, *Das jüdische Krankenhaus in Köln: Die Geschichte des Israelitischen Asyls für Kranke und Altersschwache 1869 bis 1945* (Cologne: Emons Verlag, 2004), 243.

113 Later Ursula Zade would work at the Israelitisches Asyl at the same time as Marianne. Ursula Zade was the daughter of a doctor, Hugo Zade, who worked at the Asyl. Father and daughter were deported on 21 October 1941 as the leaders of a medical group accompanying a transport of 1,000 Jews from Cologne to Lodz along with Martha Zade, Ursula's mother and Hugo's wife. Their colleague, Dr. Herbert Lewin, was the only doctor from the Asyl at the time who survived this 21 October 1941 and later deportations. See Becker-Jákli, *Das jüdische Krankenhaus*, 319, 329f., 359.

114 Marianne's Notebook, 10 February 1937, Cologne, OC.

115 Ibid., 5 April 1937, Cologne, OC.

116 Ibid., 15 May 1937, Cologne, OC. After giving nitroglycerin to a patient who, just before having a heart attack, had told her, "I must be dying," and then experiencing his recovery, Marianne wrote about the sense of giving this patient hope: "It was wonderful. 'Dear God, I thank you.'"

117 Ibid., 5 April 1937, Cologne, OC.

118 Ibid., 6 July 1937, Cologne, OC.

119 Ibid., 25 July 1937, Cologne, OC.

120 Selma had written Marianne of Trude Löwenstein's engagement in Cologne after Marianne had left for the United States. Löwenstein would emigrate

to the United States in mid 1939, after marrying the photographer Herr Schiff.

121 Marianne's Notebook, 5 September 1937, Cologne, OC.

122 Interview with Alicia Frohmann, 27 April 2005, Miami, Florida, conducted by Rebecca Boehling. See also Marianne's Notebook, 27 September 1937, Cologne, OC.

123 Arnold to Marianne, 22 September 1937, Stuttgart, OC. Arnold visited the US consulate in Stuttgart on 22 September to complete the paperwork for his visa and take his physical exam. A few days later he received his visa, apparently by mail.

124 Marianne's Notebook, 11 October 1937, Cologne, OC. Information about Arnold's family from interview with Arnold Ostrand, 18 February 2004, Columbia, Maryland, conducted by both authors, and interview with Suzanne Ostrand-Rosenberg, 23 April 2008, Baltimore, Maryland, conducted by Rebecca Boehling. See also letters from Arnold to Marianne from May 1937 until January 1938, OC.

125 Interview with Suzanne Ostrand-Rosenberg, 9 June 2008, Baltimore, Maryland, conducted by Rebecca Boehling.

126 Marianne's Notebook, 27 October 1937, Cologne, OC. As an indication of his relative prosperity, Arnold traveled across Europe having suits, a tuxedo and a fur coat specially made for him prior to his emigration. In various letters from his final months in Europe he refers to his numerous flights across the continent and his stays in expensive hotels. His brother ordered furniture for Arnold to take to the United States, perhaps from whatever was left of the family's furniture store in Leipzig. See Arnold to Marianne, 24 November 1937, Berlin, OC. Cf. interview with Arnold Ostrand, 18 February 2004, Columbia, Maryland, conducted by both authors.

127 See "USA" entry in PHILO-Atlas, *Handbuch für die jüdische Auswanderung* (Mainz: Philo Verlagsgesellschaft, 1998, repr. 1938 edn.), 202f.

128 Marianne's Notebook, 21 November 1937, Cologne, OC. Arnold and Marianne told their children that they had only known each other casually in Germany and that their relationship had begun in the United States. Cf. interviews conducted by the authors with the children of Marianne and Arnold, Suzanne Ostrand-Rosenberg, 3 May 2006 (and later by Rebecca Boehling on 6 and 9 June 2008), Baltimore, Maryland, and Thomas Ostrand, 6 April 2006, Metuchen, New Jersey, conducted by both authors.

129 Marianne's Notebook, 20 December 1937, Cologne, OC.

130 Ibid., 20 February 1938, Cologne, OC.

131 Arnold to Marianne, 5 January 1938, London, OC.

132 Marianne's Notebook, 13 January 1938, Cologne, OC. Cf. Arnold to Marianne, 31 January 1938, State College, Pennsylvania, OC.

133 Marianne's Notebook, 13 January 1938, Cologne, OC.

134 Arnold to Marianne, 14 and 19 January 1938, New York and 21, 25 and 31 January 1938, State College, Pennsylvania, OC.

135 Arnold to Marianne, 14 January 1938, New York, OC.

136 Marianne to Arnold, 23 January 1938, Cologne, OC.

137 Kater, *Doctors under Hitler*, 211.

138 Maurice R. Davie, *Refugees in America: Report of the Committee for the Study of Recent Immigration from Europe* (New York: Harper & Brothers Publishers, 1947), 278.

139 Ibid., 257.

140 Ibid., 262.

141 Ibid., 277.

142 Sibylle Quack, *Between Sorrow and Strength: Women Refugees of the Nazi Period* (Washington, D.C.: German Historical Institute, 1995), 215.

143 Marianne to Arnold, 23 January 1938, Cologne, OC.

144 The Palästina-Amt handled issues of immigration to Palestine for German Jews.

145 Marianne to Arnold, 29 January 1938, Cologne, OC. Lotti's letter to Marianne is not extant.

146 Marianne's Notebook, 3 August 1935, Düsseldorf, OC. As the number of letters she wrote to Arnold increased in 1938, so she wrote less and less in her Notebook.

147 Marianne to Arnold, 29 January 1938, Cologne, OC.

148 Arnold to Marianne, 21 January 1938, from State College, Pennsylvania, OC. According to Suzanne Ostrand-Rosenberg, Arnold and Hendrik had been students together in Berlin. Interview by Rebecca Boehling, 23 April 2008, Baltimore, Maryland. On 13 November 1937 Arnold wrote Marianne about an assistant position in the architecture department at State College (today Pennsylvania State University); apparently, Andresen helped him get this assistantship as of February 1938.

149 Marianne's Notebook, 20 February 1938, Cologne, OC.

150 Arnold to Marianne, 10 February 1938, State College, Pennsylvania, OC.

151 Marianne's Notebook, 20 February 1938, Cologne, OC.

152 Michael Kater describes how those Jewish medical personnel who did remain in Jewish hospitals and clinics lost their formal status as doctors in September 1938. They were de-licensed and demoted to *Krankenbehandler*, which Kater translates as "handlers of the sick," but which is perhaps better translated as medical care-givers. In the aftermath of the November Pogrom (Kristallnacht) of 1938 Jewish medical personnel found themselves coping with more and more suicides and arrests among their own numbers;

they increasingly became spiritual as well as physical care-givers to their remaining patients. Two-thirds of the Jewish physicians who managed to leave Germany were under 45 years of age. Kater, *Doctors under Hitler*, 200ff.

153 The brothers Siegfried and Moritz Schweizer were Nanna's second cousins.

154 Marianne to Arnold, 6 February 1938, Essen, OC.

155 Marianne to Arnold, 11 February 1938, Cologne, OC.

156 Marianne to Arnold, 6 February 1938, Essen, OC.

157 Marianne to Arnold, 1 March 1938, Cologne, OC.

158 Selma to Lotti, 8 February 1938, Essen, FC.

159 Kater, *Doctors under Hitler*, 215f.

160 Marianne to Arnold, 16 February 1938, OC. She wrote also that a Jewish official had warned her just before she received the rejection that having an affidavit did not guarantee that she would get an interview for a visa.

161 Marianne to Arnold, 1 March 1938, Cologne, OC.

162 Marianne to Arnold, 22 March 1938, Cologne, OC.

163 Marianne to Arnold, 9 March 1938, Cologne, OC.

164 Marianne to Arnold, 22 March 1938, Cologne, OC.

165 Aebersold and Stalder, "Erwerb des Titels," 129. Allowing students to submit their dissertations in absentia was the university's special provision for foreign medical students like Marianne. See also Marianne to Arnold, 12 April 1938, Essen, OC.

166 Marianne to Arnold, 12 April 1938, Essen, OC.

167 Ohligs, the small town where these instruments were sold, is now incorporated into Solingen.

168 Marianne to Arnold, 12 April 1938, Essen, OC.

169 Marianne to Dr. R. J. Weingarten, 3 May 1938 and Dr. E. A. Kahn, 26 May 1938 (both in Bombay), Cologne, OC.

170 Herta Poth to the German consulate (Bombay), 3 May 1938, Essen, OC.

171 Dr. Weingarten to Marianne, 17 May 1938 and Dr. Kahn to Marianne, 7 June 1938, Bombay, OC. German Consulate Bombay to Herta Poth, 9 May 1938, OC.

172 Recent studies about the emigration of German dermatologists, a specialty with an unusually high number of Jews (some 27 percent rather than the 16 percent of German physicians overall in 1933 who were considered Jewish), show that fewer than 2 percent of German-Jewish dermatologists who managed to emigrate from Nazi Germany went to India. See A. Scholz and W. Burgdorf, "The Exodus of German Dermatologists and Their Contributions to their Adopted Countries," *Clinics in Dermatology*, 23/5 (Sept.–Oct. 2005), 520f. Cf. Wolfgang Weyers, *Death of Medicine in Nazi Germany: Dermatology and Dermatopathology under the Swastika* (Lanham, Md.: Madison Books, 1998).

173 Marianne to Arnold, 13 May 1938, Cologne, OC.

174 Marianne to Arnold, 14 April 1938, Essen, OC. See *"Unbedenklichkeitsbescheinigung,"* the special term for the document proving one had no unpaid financial obligations, in PHILO-Atlas, *Handbuch*, 199f. The special term for proof that one had no criminal record is *"polizeiliches Führungszeugnis."* See also Norbert Kampe, *Jewish Emigration from Germany 1933–1942*, in Herbert Strauss (ed.), *Jewish Immigrants of the Nazi Period in the USA*, vol. IV (New York: K.G. Saur, 1992), 276ff.

175 Signs indicating "Jews not welcome" hung in the windows of numerous Stuttgart hotels and restaurants. See Grünebaum, "'Jews Not Welcome' in Hotels," 69f.

176 Marianne to Arnold, 20 April 1938, Stuttgart, OC.

177 Ibid.

178 Interview with Marianne, 2 November 1988, IN 327, recorded at the Alte Synagoge Archives, Essen.

179 Marianne to Arnold, 1 May 1938, Essen, OC.

180 Marianne to Arnold, 4 June 1938, Essen, OC.

181 Davie, *Refugees in America*, 87.

182 Arnold to Lotti, 26 May 1938, State College, Pennsylvania, OC. Marianne could not take this money out of Germany. How it got to Palestine is unclear, but perhaps via Lotti when she returned to Palestine from Essen in 1937.

183 Lotti to Marianne, 17 June 1938, Tel Aviv, OC.

184 Marianne to Arnold, 17 June 1938, from train from Cologne to Kassel, OC.

185 Marianne's Notebook, 21 June 1938, Essen, OC.

186 Interview with Suzanne Ostrand-Rosenberg, 9 June 2008, Baltimore, Maryland, conducted by Rebecca Boehling. The officer apparently knew the family. Jews were not allowed to take any valuables with them out of the country, yet Marianne was able to slip in various silver family heirlooms, etc.

187 Selma and Henny to Marianne, 21 June 1938, Essen, OC.

188 Information derived from a photograph of Marianne and Arnold in the Berkshire Mountains labeled by Marianne "My first weekend in America," OC. See Figure 4.6.

189 Lotti to Marianne, 17 June 1938, Tel Aviv, OC.

190 Marianne to Arnold, 18 July 1938 and 24 July 1938, New York, OC.

191 Selma to Marianne, 10 July 1938, Essen, OC.

192 Marianne's Notebook, 21 July 1938, New York, OC.

193 Marianne to Arnold, 24 July 1938, New York, OC.

194 Selma to Marianne, 30 June 1938, Essen, OC. For details of Onkel Hermann's dismissal see Chapter 3.

195 Kurt to Marianne, 22 July 1938, Frankfurt am Main, OC.

196 Lotti to Marianne, 1 July 1938, Tel Aviv, OC.

197 Marianne to Arnold, 24 July 1938, New York, OC.

198 Lotti to Marianne, 1 July 1938, Tel Aviv, OC. Within her family only her sister Lotti had any idea of the intensity or the ups and downs of Marianne's relationship with Arnold.

199 Marianne to Arnold, 14 and 15 August 1938, New York, OC. See also an undated note from Marianne to Arnold placed between the early August letters.

200 Kurt to Marianne, 22 July 1938, Frankfurt am Main, OC. Cf. Selma to Marianne, 17 July 1938, Essen, OC.

201 Marianne to Arnold, 28 July 1938, New York, OC.

202 Marianne's Notebook, 8 August 1938, New York, OC.

203 Marianne to Arnold, 6 October 1938, New York, and 24 December 1938 and 6 January 1939, Miami Beach, Florida, OC.

204 Marianne to Arnold, 3 November 1938, New York, OC.

205 The Munich Conference "resolved" the Sudetenland crisis in Czechoslovakia by Britain's Prime Minister Chamberlain, France's Prime Minister Laval and Italy's Duce Mussolini agreeing to let Hitler march in and annex the Sudetenland, thus destroying Czechoslovakia's only natural defense against its aggressive neighbor, Germany.

206 Marianne to Arnold, 6 October 1938, New York, OC. Original in English. At Arnold's suggestion they both started writing consistently to each other in English.

207 Ibid.

208 Marianne to Arnold, 13 October 1938, New York, OC.

209 Marianne to Arnold, 23 October 1938, New York, OC.

210 Marianne to Arnold, 3 November 1938, New York, OC.

211 Marianne to Arnold, 10 November 1938, New York, OC.

212 The *New York Times*, which Marianne often read, had details and pictures of the pogrom on its front page on 10 November 1938 and considerable coverage in the following days as well.

213 Marianne to Arnold, 14 November 1938, New York, OC.

214 Ibid.

5 The November Pogrom (1938) and its consequences for Kurt and his family

1 Marianne to Arnold, 10 November 1938, New York, OC.

2 Schreiber, "Geschichte der Altenessener Jüdinnen und Juden," 24f. Cf. Marianne's Diary, 19 June 1933, Düsseldorf, OC.

3 Kurt's signed statement to the police following his arrest, 7 June 1934, Gestapo Files, RW 58-Nr. 28854, Kurt Alfred Steinberg, HStA Düsseldorf. Cf. Schreiber, "Geschichte der Altenessener Jüdinnen und Juden," 24f.

4 Kurt Steinberg's official correspondence as an employee of the Centralverein in Hamm, Essen and Frankfurt am Main, 1932–8, Records of the Centralverein deutscher Staatsbürger jüdischen Glaubens, Berlin (Central Association of German Citizens of Jewish Faith), Fond 721, Record Group-11.001M.31, reel 338–1547, 1550, 1556, 1573 and reel 133–2880, United States Holocaust Memorial Museum (USHMM) Archives, Washington, DC.

5 Gestapo Files, RW 58-Nr. 28854, Kurt Alfred Steinberg, HStA Düsseldorf. See also: Holger Berschel, *Bürokratie und Terror: Das Judenreferat der Gestapo Düsseldorf 1935–1945* (Essen: Klartext, 2001), 175. Cf. Daniel Fraenkel, "Jewish Self-Defense under the Constraints of National Socialism: The Final Years of the Centralverein," in David Bankier (ed.), *Probing the Depths of German Antisemitism: German Society and the Persecution of the Jews, 1933–1941* (New York and Oxford: Berghahn Books, 2000), 345.

6 The Stapo (State Police) in Düsseldorf stated in Kurt's personal police file (*Personalbericht*) that Kurt's arrest on 6 June 1934 "happened in connection with the operation against the Centralverein," Gestapo Files, RW 58-Nr. 28854, Kurt Alfred Steinberg, 28 February 1935, HStA Düsseldorf.

7 Circular, "An unsere Ortsgruppen!" 27 April 1934, Gestapo Files, RW 58-Nr. 28854, Kurt Alfred Steinberg, HStA Düsseldorf. Cf. Berschel, *Bürokratie und Terror*, 175.

8 Copy of letter from Police President in Essen to Gestapa Berlin, 18 June 1934, Aktenzeichen Nr. 285/34, Gestapo Files, RW 58-Nr. 28854 Kurt Alfred Steinberg, HStA Düsseldorf. The Gestapa was the main office of the Gestapo in Berlin.

9 Report from Police President to Stapo Düsseldorf, 13 June 1934, Gestapo Files, RW 58-Nr. 28854, Kurt Alfred Steinberg, HStA Düsseldorf.

10 Kurt to Marianne, 21 June 1938, from the train from Frankfurt am Main to Fulda, OC.

11 Kurt to Marianne, 23 August 1938, Kreuzau, OC.

12 Ibid.

13 Ibid.

14 Kurt to Marianne, 18 August 1940, Rishon le-Zion, OC.

15 Kurt to Lotti, Marianne and spouses, 28 July 1951, Rishon le-Zion, OC.

16 Ibid.

17 Ibid. Kurt stayed more than a week in August 1938 with his cousin Ernst Roer and his wife Toni in Kreuzau. They were both deported from the Holbeckshof collection point in Essen-Steele to Düsseldorf and finally to Theresienstadt on 21 July 1942.

18 Decree of the Reich Ministry of the Interior, 27 July 1938, *Ministerialblatt*, 1284. See Blau, *Ausnahmerecht*, Document 171, 49. Incidentally, even four years before this decree, the Tenants Right Association (*Mieterschutzverein*) in Frankfurt am Main had already proposed to the Lord Mayor Dr. Krebs the "gradual renaming of streets and plazas that carry names of non-Aryans." See Wolf Gruner, *Die Verfolgung und Ermordung der europäischen Juden durch das nationalsozialistische Deutschland 1933–1945*, vol. 1: *Deutsches Reich 1933–1937* (Munich: Oldenbourg Wissenschaftsverlag, 2008), Document 132.

19 Kurt to Marianne, 3 September 1938, Essen, OC.

20 Kurt to Marianne, 11 May 1940, Tel Aviv, OC.

21 Selma to Marianne, 11 November 1938, Essen, Western Union telegram, OC. This telegram arrived that same day in New York.

22 Marianne to US consul in Stuttgart, 11 November 1938, New York, OC. Original in English.

23 Marianne to Arnold, 11 November 1938, New York, OC.

24 Selma to Marianne, undated Western Union telegram, presumably 14 November 1938, Essen, OC.

25 Selma to Marianne, 12 November 1938, Essen, OC.

26 Marianne to Arnold, 14 November 1940, New York.

27 Kaplan, *Between Dignity and Despair*, 65.

28 Marianne to Arnold, 6 October 1938, New York, OC.

29 Kurt to Marianne, 18 September 1938, Frankfurt am Main, OC.

30 Wolfgang Benz, "Der Novemberpogrom 1938," in Wolfgang Benz (ed.), *Die Juden in Deutschland 1933–1945: Leben unter nationalsozialistischer Herrschaft* (Munich: C.H. Beck, 1988), 500ff.

31 For more information see: Uwe Dietrich Adam, "How Spontaneous Was the Pogrom?" in Walter H. Pehle (ed.), *November 1938: From "Kristallnacht" to Genocide* (New York and Oxford: Berg, 1991). See also Rita Thalmann and Emmanuel Feinermann, *Crystal Night 9–10 November 1938*, trans. Gilles Cremones (New York: Holocaust Library, 1972), Britta Bopf, *"Arisierung" in Köln: Die wirtschaftliche Existenzvernichtung der Juden 1933–1945* (Cologne: Emons, 2004) and Wolf-Arno Kropat, *"Reichskristallnacht," Der Judenpogrom vom 7. bis 10. November 1938 – Urheber, Täter, Hintergründe* (Wiesbaden: Kommission für die Geschichte der Juden in Hessen, 1997).

32 On 9 November 1923 Hitler and other right-wing nationalists met in a beer hall in Munich intending first to overthrow the Bavarian government and then "march on Berlin." Hitler and other leaders were tried for treason and imprisoned. While in prison, Hitler wrote his infamous memoir and political manifesto, *Mein Kampf* (*My Struggle*).

33 Wolfgang Benz, "Der Rückfall in die Barbarei," in Walter H. Pehle (ed.), *Der Judenpogrom 1938: Von der "Reichskristallnacht" zum Völkermord* (Frankfurt am Main: Fischer Verlag, 1988), 29.

34 At 11:55 p.m. Gestapo Chief Heinrich Müller sent the same order to all Gestapo district offices, 9 November 1938. As cited in Berschel, *Bürokratie und Terror*, 323. See also Friedländer, *Nazi Germany and the Jews*, 271f.

35 Telefax from Reinhard Heydrich to all Gestapo district offices, 10 November 1938. As cited in Berschel, *Bürokratie und Terror*, 322.

36 Ulrich Herbert, "Von der 'Reichskristallnacht' zum 'Holocaust': Der 9. November und das Ende des 'Radauantisemitismus,'" in Thomas Hofmann, Hanno Loewy and Harry Stein (eds.), *Pogromnacht und Holocaust* (Cologne: Böhlau, 1994), 67.

37 Harry Kaufman, "Mein Leben in Deutschland vor und nach Januar 1933," in *Life in Germany Contest* (bMS Ger 91), 1940, Houghton Library, Harvard University.

38 Michael Zimmermann, "Die 'Reichskristallnacht' 1938 in Essen," in Alte Synagoge (ed.), *Entrechtung und Selbsthilfe*, 74.

39 Hanna Levy Sella, "Bericht über meine Erlebnisse in der Nazi-Zeit," 1988, BR 517, Alte Synagoge Archives, Essen.

40 Ibid.

41 Ibid.

42 Kurt to Marianne, 19 February 1939, Tel Aviv, OC. Herta Poth, whose father was employed at the Krupp Company, lived with her parents in a company-owned housing development.

43 Lotti to Marianne, 5 December 1938, Tel Aviv, OC.

44 Kurt to Marianne, 19 February 1939, Tel Aviv, OC.

45 Ibid. Cf. Zimmermann, "Die 'Reichskristallnacht' 1938 in Essen," 81.

46 E. Dominicus (ed.), *Chronik des Amtsbezirkes Nörvenich 1932–1946*, 2nd edn. (2005), 40. As excerpted on the website, www.geschichtswerkstatt-dueren.de-juden-fundstellen

47 Selma to Marianne, 14 November 1938, Essen, OC. The Bachrachs sent their teenage daughter, Marianne, to live with non-Jewish acquaintances in the United States in February 1939.

48 Selma to Marianne, 13 December 1938, Essen, OC.

49 Selma to Marianne, 8 January 1939, Essen, OC.

50 www.plbg.de/lexikon/personen/juden/index.htm (accessed 15 December 2009). This website on "Jewish Life in Plettenberg" provides photos of Julius and his brother-in-law Hugo Neufeld's store and of the Bachrachs' and Neufelds' tombstones. In addition, the website reproduces and quotes from noteworthy historical documents, as well as a newspaper article on Wolfgang Neufeld's visit from Israel in 2001.

51 Interview with Marianne Bachrach Luedeking, 10 November 2006, Miami, Florida, conducted by Rebecca Boehling. Both Olga and Julius Bachrach

were forced to move to Cologne in 1940–1 and were then deported to the Lodz ghetto in October 1941, where they later died.

52 Benz, "Der Rückfall in die Barbarei," 41.

53 Kurt to Marianne, 19 February 1939, Tel Aviv, OC.

54 Kommission zur Erforschung der Geschichte der Frankfurter Juden (ed.), *Dokumente zur Geschichte der Frankfurter Juden 1933–1945* (Frankfurt am Main: Verlag Waldemar Kramer, 1963), 32f.

55 Kurt to Marianne, 19 February 1939, Tel Aviv, OC.

56 Rundruf des Deutschen Nachrichtenbüros in Berlin vom 10. November, 16 Uhr, as cited in Kropat, *"Reichskristallnacht,"* 233.

57 Kropat, *"Reichskristallnacht,"* 117.

58 Ibid.

59 Ibid., 92.

60 Selma to Marianne, 18 November 1938, Essen, OC.

61 Kommission zur Erforschung der Geschichte der Frankfurter Juden (ed.), *Dokumente zur Geschichte der Frankfurter Juden*, 32f. and 40.

62 Ibid., 41.

63 Archivist Frank Boblenz at the Thuringia Main State Archive in Weimar calculated that Kurt probably arrived in Buchenwald on 12 November. He commented in a letter to Uta Larkey, 6 September 2007: "We do not have the exact dates. Our estimate is based on known data of detainees' arrivals and his prisoner number [24867]."

64 Kommission zur Erforschung der Geschichte der Frankfurter Juden (ed.), *Dokumente zur Geschichte der Frankfurter Juden*, 43.

65 Kropat, *"Reichskristallnacht,"* 139.

66 As cited in Harry Stein, "Das Sonderlager im Konzentrationslager Buchenwald nach den Pogromen 1938," in Monica Kingreen (ed.), *"Nach der Kristallnacht": Jüdisches Leben und antijüdische Politik in Frankfurt am Main 1938–1945* (Frankfurt am Main: Campus Verlag, 1999), 36.

67 Ernst had lived with his Essen aunts Selma and Henny and Onkel Hermann for several months while he was apprenticed to a Jewish company in a machine repair shop, until it was "Aryanized" in early 1938 and he was let go. See Ernest Kaufman, "Holocaust-Survivor or Escapee," unpublished talk given on several occasions after 2002. Original in English. Ernst Kaufmann changed his name to Ernest Kaufman after he escaped to the United States in 1939.

68 Ibid.

69 Interview with Ernest Kaufman, 11 May 2005, Lumberton, New Jersey, conducted by Uta Larkey. See also Harry Stein to Uta Larkey, 31 March 2006, Weimar, e-mail.

70 Harry Stein to Uta Larkey, 19 August 2007, Weimar, e-mail. Cf. Stein, "Sonderlager," 32.

71 Chief of the Security Police Reinhard Heydrich was working on the planning stages of the "raid against asocials" when he became aware of Hitler's request at the end of May 1938 to "arrest asocial and criminal Jews for large-scale earth excavation work in the entire Reich." On 1 June 1938 the Headquarters of the Reich Criminal Police ordered the arrest of "asocial elements" and "male Jews ... who have been given at least a prison sentence of more than one month" in the week of June 13–18. As a result, among the 10,000 men about 1,500 Jews were rounded up and detained in three concentration camps: Buchenwald, Dachau and Sachsenhausen. This so-called Juni Aktion marked an intensification of the persecution of Jews in Germany. See Harry Stein, *Juden in Buchenwald 1937–1942* (Buchenwald: Gedenkstätte Buchenwald, 1992), 16ff.

72 Stein, "Sonderlager," 32.

73 Ernest Kaufman, "Holocaust-Survivor or Escapee," unpublished talk.

74 Eugen Roer was Ernst and Kurt's cousin.

75 Interview with Ernest Kaufman, 11 May 2005, Lumberton, New Jersey, conducted by Uta Larkey.

76 Stein, "Sonderlager," 47.

77 Ibid., 46.

78 Ibid., 47: "We can realistically assume that about 1% of the 26,000 detained Jews died immediately after their release of causes related to their incarceration, or committed suicide. It is very likely that every detainee suffered from physical or psychological short- and long-term scars."

79 Interview with Ernest Kaufman, 11 May 2005, Lumberton, New Jersey, conducted by Uta Larkey.

80 Selma to Marianne, 18 and 22 November 1938, Essen, OC.

81 This document, handwritten by Hanna and signed by Selma, reads: "I hereby authorize Miss Johanna Levy, fiancée of my son Kurt Steinberg (address Joseph-Haydn-Strasse 37) to act on his behalf regarding passport matters. Due to illness I am unable to do so. He is presently in protective custody. Selma Steinberg. Frankfurt am Main, November 26, 1938." FC.

82 Kurt to Marianne, 30 November 1938, Frankfurt am Main, OC.

83 Selma to Marianne, 29 November 1938, Essen, OC.

84 Kurt Riegner and Günter Friedländer, both leaders of the Jewish youth movement "Ring" in Berlin, part of the Association of German Jewish Youth (Bund deutsch-jüdischer Jugend or BDJJ), developed and led the group immigration project known as the Riegner Group. See Kurt Julio Riegner, *Transiciones. Mi biographia hasta 1938* (Buenos Aires: Edicion privada y limitada, 1991). As cited in Alfredo Jose Schwarcz, *Trotz allem...: Die deutschsprachigen Juden in Argentinien* (Cologne: Böhlau, 1995), 117.

85 Kurt credited Ernst Plaut with providing the "possibility for emigration to Argentina" in his letter to Marianne, 30 November 1938, Frankfurt am

Main. Kurt was very saddened by the news of Ernst Plaut's untimely death in England in 1945. Cf. letter from Kurt to Marianne and Arnold, 26 June 1945, Rishon le-Zion, OC.

86 Kurt to Marianne, 19 February 1939, Tel Aviv, OC.

87 Copy of letter from Jüdische Landarbeit GmBH Berlin to Kurt, 25 November 1938, Keynan Collection (henceforth KC). Fritz Schwarzschild also provided letters for others in need, such as Liesel Sternberg, the sister of Walter, who, together with his wife Hanna, had been in charge of the Essen Youth Center. Liesel Sternberg Collection, AR 4483, Alte Synagoge Archives, Essen. See also Ann Millin (USHMM historian) to the authors, 14 April 2008, Washington, DC, e-mail: "Letters were supplied by Jewish organizations as proof that a person had agreed to emigrate. The Gestapo gave released prisoners a limited amount of time to leave the country and followed up on each case... While some false papers were issued, it was not the case that Jewish officials were issuing a large number of false letters."

88 Hanna Levy Sella, "Bericht über meine Erlebnisse in der Nazi-Zeit," 1988, BR 517, Alte Synagoge Archives, Essen.

89 Berschel, *Bürokratie und Terror*, 256f.

90 Hanna erred in her report, stating that she needed a pre-dated passport "because the Argentinian consulate was closed down." Hanna Levy Sella, "Bericht über meine Erlebnisse in der Nazi-Zeit," 1988, BR 517, Alte Synagoge Archives, Essen.

91 Max Hermann Maier, "Auswandererhilfe in Frankfurt am Main, 1936–1938," written in 1961, Frankfurt am Main: Jewish Community Collection, Leo Baeck Institute Berlin, MF 314, 12. Also published in Kommission zur Erforschung der Geschichte der Frankfurter Juden (ed.), *Dokumente zur Geschichte der Frankfurter Juden*, 387.

92 Hanna Levy Sella, "Bericht über meine Erlebnisse in der Nazi-Zeit," 1988, BR 517, Alte Synagoge Archives, Essen.

93 Interview with Gideon Sella, 28 June 2006, Tel Aviv, conducted by Uta Larkey.

94 Hanna Levy Sella, "Bericht über meine Erlebnisse in der Nazi-Zeit," 1988, BR 517, Alte Synagoge Archives, Essen. The Thüringisches Hauptstaatsarchiv Weimar has a copy of the original receipt for Hanna's cable of 100 RM to Buchenwald. The documents also show that Selma sent an additional 10 RM to Buchenwald on 30 November 1938. The administration of KZ Buchenwald returned 109.35 RM to Selma on 18 February 1939, apparently retaining 65 Pfennig for processing fees. See Geldkarte in Prisoner files, Dr. Kurt Steinberg (Häftlingsnummer 24867), Konzentrationslager Buchenwald, Thüringisches Hauptstaatsarchiv, Weimar.

95 Kurt to Marianne, 19 February 1939, Tel Aviv, OC.

96 Harry Stein to Uta Larkey, 31 March 2006, Weimar, e-mail.

97 Hanna Levy Sella, "Bericht über meine Erlebnisse in der Nazi-Zeit," 1988, BR 517, Alte Synagoge Archives, Essen.

98 Kurt to Marianne, 9 February 1939, Tel Aviv, OC.

99 Interview with Gideon Sella, 28 June 2006, Tel Aviv, conducted by Uta Larkey.

100 Eyewitness Ms. M. remembered in 1988: "and then we emigrated to Argentina, on a ship. We were a group of 32 people. The youngest 17, the oldest about 24 or 25 of age, as was our revered leader, Dr. Riegner." As cited in Kruse and Schmitt, *Wir haben uns als Deutsche gefühlt*, 68.

101 Selma to Lotti, 29 November 1938, Essen, OC.

102 According to Gideon Sella, Hanna's brother Heinz emigrated to Argentina via Belgium in 1934–5; Hanna's sister Netty (nicknamed Moebbie) followed with her husband Richard Kahn in 1936, and Hanna's mother Sofie joined her two children in 1937.

103 Argentinian Foreign Minister Cantilo signed Secret Circular 11 on 12 July 1938. He ordered all Argentinian diplomats to refuse tourist or transit visas to any "undesirables" who had to leave their country of origin. Not mentioning the word "Jews," it was nevertheless clear that this order was issued as a response to the Evian Conference. Two weeks later, Decree 8972 provided the legal basis for further immigration restrictions.

104 Carlota Jackisch, "Einwanderungspolitik und öffentliche Meinung in Argentinien 1933–1945," in Karl Kohut and Patrik von zur Mühlen (eds.), *Alternative Lateinamerika: Das deutsche Exil in der Zeit des Nationalsozialismus* (Frankfurt am Main: Vervuert, 1994), 46. Cf. "Die Ausschiffungserlaubnis," *C.V. Zeitung*, 27/33 (18 August 1938).

105 Schwarcz, *Trotz allem*, 117.

106 Selma to Marianne, 3 January 1939, Essen, OC.

107 Kurt to Marianne, 19 February 1939, Tel Aviv, OC.

108 Selma to Lotti, 23 November 1938, Essen, FC.

109 Kurt to Marianne, 19 February, 1939, Tel Aviv, OC.

110 Kurt to Marianne, 14 December 1938, Essen, OC.

111 Richard Breitman and Alan Kraut, *American Refugee Policy and European Jewry, 1933–1945* (Bloomington and Indianapolis: Indiana University Press, 1988), 66.

112 Kurt to Marianne, 19 February 1939, Tel Aviv, OC. New York Congressman Bruce Barton was an outspoken opponent of "xenophobic laws." The German-Jewish newspaper *Aufbau* supported Barton's bid for the Senate and published his election advertisement under the title: "Vote for Men Whom We Trust," *Aufbau*, 6/44 (1 November 1940). Ultimately, Barton was not elected US Senator.

113 Hans Reichmann, *Deutscher Bürger und verfolgter Jude: Novemberpogrom und KZ Sachsenhausen 1937–1939* (Munich: Oldenbourg Wissenschaftsverlag, 1998), 261.

114 Selma to Marianne, 13 December 1938, Essen, OC.

115 Doris Meakin to Marianne, 14 June 1938, OC. "I shall be glad of an opportunity to repay all your kindness to me when I was in Germany." Doris visited the Steinberg family in 1933 in Altenessen.

116 Kurt to Marianne, 17 January 1939, Essen, OC.

117 Selma to Marianne, 3 January 1939, Essen, OC. Several relief organizations for German Jews were located at Woburn House, such as the Council for German Jewry and the German Jewish Aid Committee (in 1938 renamed the Jewish Refugee Committee).

118 A.J. Sherman, *Island Refuge: Britain and Refugees from the Third Reich* (Berkeley and Los Angeles: University of California Press, 1973), 214.

119 David S. Wyman, *The Abandonment of the Jews: America and the Holocaust 1941–1945* (New York: Pantheon Books, 1984), x.

120 Louise London, *Whitehall and the Jews, 1933–1948: British Immigration Policy, Jewish Refugees and the Holocaust* (Cambridge University Press, 2000), 99.

121 Following the Nuremberg Laws and German Jews' loss of German citizenship, the Reichsvertretung der deutschen Juden was forced to change its name to the Reichsvertretung der Juden in Deutschland (Reich Association of Jews in Germany).

122 As reproduced in Strauss (ed.), *Jewish Immigrants*, 492.

123 According to S. Adler-Rudel, the former secretary of the Reichsvertretung who emigrated to Palestine in 1936 and worked for the Council for German Jewry in London, by November 1938 5,500 refugees from Germany (Altreich) were registered with the Jewish Refugee Committee in London. From January to September 1939 this number almost quadrupled to 20,000. Adler-Rudel, *Jüdische Selbsthilfe*, 113. Cf. London, *Whitehall and the Jews*, 104. London mentions "11,000 German refugees from 1933–38."

124 London, *Whitehall and the Jews*, 109.

125 Sherman, *Island Refuge*, 196.

126 Marianne to Arnold, 14 November 1938, New York, OC.

127 London, *Whitehall and the Jews*, 115.

128 Selma to Lotti and Hans, 23 November 1938, Essen, FC.

129 Selma to Lotti, 29 November 1938, Essen, FC. Selma mistakenly wrote an "unlimited" visa.

130 Lotti and Hans to Marianne, 5 December 1938, Tel Aviv, OC.

131 Selma to Marianne, 3 January 1939, Essen, OC.

132 Hans Jacobi was not only the director but also the founder of the Emigration Counseling Office of the Hilfsverein in Cologne. Its primary goal was lending psychological and practical aid to Jews who were forced out of

Germany. Zvi Asaria, *Die Juden in Köln* (Cologne: Verlag J.P. Bachem, 1959), 344.

133 Ibid., 347.

134 Kurt to Marianne, 9 February 1939, Tel Aviv, OC. "After hours of waiting – you cannot imagine in your wildest dreams the crowds at each and every consulate these days – Dr. Hans Jacobi succeeded."

135 Bopf, *"Arisierung" in Köln*, 201ff.

136 Kurt to Marianne, 9 February 1939, Tel Aviv, OC.

137 Kurt, as it seems, took particular delight in the consul's statement: "Applicant Johanna Levy is to marry Dr. Steinberg." Kurt to Marianne, 17 January 1939, Essen, OC.

138 Interview with Marianne, 2 November 1988, IN 327, recorded at the Alte Synagoge Archives, Essen.

139 Hanna Levy Sella, "Bericht über meine Erlebnisse in der Nazi-Zeit," 1988, BR 517, Alte Synagoge Archives, Essen.

140 Kurt to Marianne, 19 February 1939, Tel Aviv, OC.

141 Avraham Barkai, "The Fateful Year 1938," in Walter H. Pehle (ed.), *November 1938: From "Kristallnacht" to Genocide*, trans. William Templer (New York and Oxford: Berg, 1991), 119f.

142 Kurt to Marianne, 19 February 1939, Tel Aviv, OC.

143 Barkai, *"Wehr Dich!"*, 355.

144 Kurt to Marianne, 19 February 1939, Tel Aviv, OC. While it is difficult to compare the value of currencies and other assets, the following numbers from Marianne's postwar restitution file might give a sense: The eleven silver spoons that Selma had to declare in 1939 were valued at 99 RM (126,50 DM in 1954). See Marianne's restitution file, OC. Another source states that the average income of an orchestra musician in a mid-town German theater was between 220 and 290 RM a month at this time. See Barbara von der Lühe, *Die Musik war unsere Rettung! Die deutschsprachigen Gründungsmitglieder des Palestine Orchestra* (Tübingen: Mohr Siebeck, 1998), 81.

145 Kurt to Lotti, Marianne and spouses, 26 June 1951, Rishon le-Zion, OC.

146 Selma to Marianne, 22 January 1939, Essen, OC.

147 Article IV of the 1 September 1938 anti-Jewish laws stated that foreign Jews who had settled in Italy after 1 January 1919 would have to leave within six months. If not, they would be prosecuted and expelled. Cf. *Jüdische Rundschau*, 43/71 (6 September 1938).

148 This was the *Unbedenklichkeitsbescheinigung*, a certificate verifying that the recipient had no outstanding financial obligations.

149 Kurt to Marianne, 28 January 1939, Milan, OC.

150 Kurt to several family members in Germany, Palestine and the United States, 28 January 1939, Milan, OC.

6 New beginnings in Palestine, 1935–1939: Lotti and Kurt

1 Julius to Lotti and Hans, 9 December 1938, Cologne, KC. Cf. Becker-Jákli, *Das jüdische Krankenhaus*, 243, 252, 464. Karl Kaiser-Blüth had been a member of the board of the Cologne Jewish community since 1931 and a member of the board of trustees of the Jewish hospital in Cologne, the Israelitsches Asyl.

2 Michael Keynan (Hans and Lotti's son) to Rebecca Boehling, 24 April 2005, e-mail. This organization, founded in 1912, prepared young German-Jewish people for life in Palestine, including Hebrew lessons, classes on Jewish history and tradition, and life on a *kibbutz*. Cf. Walter Laqueur, *Generation Exodus: The Fate of Young Jewish Refugees from Nazi Germany* (Hanover, N.H. and London: Brandeis University Press, 2001), 5.

3 Michael Keynan to Uta Larkey, 10 March 2009, e-mail. Hans earned his Diplom Ingenieur degree in Germany (Dipl. Ing.).

4 The contract was signed by MAN representatives and Hans Kaiser-Blüth on 4 March 1935 in Nuremberg. Copy of MAN contract provided by Gabriele Mierzwa, Museum und Historisches Archiv (VMM), manroland, Augsburg, 21 April 2009.

5 Interview with Michael Keynan, 29 June 2006, Tel Aviv, conducted by Uta Larkey. A family picture shows Lotti and Hans together in November 1934.

6 Interview with Alicia Frohmann, 27 April 2005, Miami, Florida, conducted by Rebecca Boehling.

7 Heiner Frohmann to Lotti, 21 February 1935, Erlangen, FC.

8 Ibid.

9 Flora and Julius Kaiser-Blüth to Lotti and Hans, 9 December 1938, Cologne, KC.

10 Interview with Marianne Bachrach Luedeking, 10 November 2006, Miami, Florida, conducted by Rebecca Boehling.

11 Interview with Lotti, 2 November 1988, IN 291, recorded at the Alte Synagoge Archives, Essen.

12 PHILO-Atlas, *Handbuch*, 142.

13 Due to several regulations the exchange rate had increasingly worsened: In 1933 LP 1,000 equaled about 12,500 RM, in 1937 20,000 RM and from late 1938 until September 1939 40,000 RM. See Barkai, *From Boycott to Annihilation*, 101.

14 In 1936 the annual income in Germany of a lawyer was about 10,800 RM, and that of a doctor about 12,564 RM. See Kater, *Doctors Under Hitler*, 33.

15 This agreement originated in a private initiative between Sam Cohen, the director of Hanotea Ltd. (an investment company for citrus orchards and equipment) in Palestine and the Reich Economics Ministry. For more information see Edwin Black, *The Transfer Agreement: The Dramatic*

Story of the Pact between the Third Reich and Jewish Palestine (New York: Carroll & Graf Publishers, 2001).

16 On 7 August 1933 representatives of the Jewish Agency for Palestine, the German Zionist Federation (ZVfD) and the Reich Economics Ministry signed the Ha'avarah Agreement. See Barkai, *Hoffnung und Untergang*, 167.

17 Juliane Wetzel, "Auswanderung aus Deutschland," in Benz (ed.), *Die Juden in Deutschland*, 464.

18 The Jewish-owned banks, Warburg in Hamburg and Wasserman in Berlin, acted on behalf of the Paltreu. Corresponding to the Paltreu was the Ha'avarah Trust and Transfer Office Ltd. in Tel Aviv. Cf. Black, *Transfer Agreement*, 249.

19 Francis Nicosia, *The Third Reich and the Palestine Question* (Austin: University of Texas Press, 1985), 47.

20 Lotti to Marianne, 17 June 1938, Tel Aviv, OC.

21 Wetzel, "Auswanderung aus Deutschland," 467.

22 Friedländer, *Nazi Germany and the Jews*, 63.

23 Yoav Gelber and Walter Goldstern, *Vertreibung und Emigration deutschsprachiger Ingenieure nach Palästina 1933–1945* (Düsseldorf: VDI Verlag, 1988), 76.

24 Interview with Michael Keynan, 29 June 2006, Tel Aviv, conducted by Uta Larkey.

25 Gelber and Goldstern, *Vertreibung und Emigration*, 76.

26 Marianne's Notebook, 31 December 1935, Bern, OC.

27 Werner Feilchenfeld, Dolf Michaelis and Ludwig Pinner, *Haavara-Transfer nach Palästina und Einwanderung deutscher Juden 1933–1939* (Tübingen: J.C.B. Mohr, 1972), 44.

28 Ibid., 51. Ha'avarah Ltd. granted a "bonification" to the importing companies in Palestine, a certain sum that was deducted from the asking price for imported goods. This lowered the price of German goods, which then could be offered at a competitive price in Palestine. After their arrival, the importing companies paid the net difference to Ha'avarah Ltd.

29 Ibid., 90. In 1939, however, the German-Jewish immigration rate climbed to 52 percent, an all-time high.

30 Friedländer, *Nazi Germany and the Jews*, 63. One-third of Jews from Germany emigrated to Palestine on a Capitalist Certificate. See Richarz (ed.), *Jewish Life in Germany*, 34f.

31 Samih K. Farsoun and Christina Zacharia, *Palestine and the Palestinians* (Boulder, Colo.: Westview Press, 1997), 76.

32 Joachin Schlör, *Endlich im gelobten Land? Deutsche Juden unterwegs in eine neue Heimat* (Berlin: Aufbau Verlag, 2003), 121.

33 Ibid., 76. About 85 percent of Jews lived in the three major urban centers: Tel Aviv–Jaffa, Jerusalem and Haifa.

34 Farsoun and Zacharia, *Palestine and the Palestinians*, 78. For a critical analysis of the foundation of Tel Aviv see Mark LeVine, *Overthrowing Geography: Jaffa, Tel Aviv and the Struggle for Palestine 1880–1948* (Berkeley and Los Angeles: University of California Press, 2005), 60ff.

35 Gideon Greif, Colin McPherson and Laurence Weinbaum (eds.), *Die Jeckes: Deutsche Juden aus Israel erzählen* (Cologne: Böhlau, 2000), 30.

36 Interview with Lotti, 2 November 1988, IN 291, recorded at the Alte Synagoge Archives, Essen.

37 Ibid.

38 Hitachdut Olej Germania (Association of German Immigrants) was founded in 1932 in Palestine as an immigrants' aid organization.

39 The Jewish Agency for Palestine was founded by Jewish leaders in Palestine, among them Chaim Weizman, as a representational body for Jews in Palestine. It was formally recognized in 1929 under Article 4 of the British mandate for Palestine. It was to be a "public body for the purpose of advising and cooperating with the Administration of Palestine in such economic, social and other matters as may affect the establishment of the Jewish national home and the interests of the Jewish population in Palestine." See http://avalon.law.yale.edu/20th_century/palmanda.asp#art4 (accessed 21 November 2009). The Jewish Agency also administered the Palestine Immigration Office (Palästina Amt) in different German cities.

40 Gerda Luft, *Heimkehr ins Unbekannte: Eine Darstellung der Einwanderung von Juden aus Deutschland nach Palästina 1933–39* (Wuppertal: Peter Hammer Verlag, 1977), 120. Luft emigrated to Palestine in 1924 and was the Palestinian correspondent for the *Jüdische Rundschau*. She was the first wife of Chaim Arlosoroff, one of the initiators of the Ha'avarah Agreement.

41 They rented from Toni Roer Rothschild, Lotti's first cousin, and her husband Richard, who had emigrated to Palestine in 1934.

42 Marianne's Notebook, 4 October 1935, Düsseldorf, OC. Mussolini's army invaded Abyssinia (Ethiopia) on 3 October 1935.

43 Lotti to Marianne, 1 October 1935, Tel Aviv, OC.

44 Marianne to Lotti, 2 March 1936, Essen-Altenessen, OC.

45 Lotti to Marianne, 1 October 1935, Tel Aviv, OC.

46 Techina, similar to tahini, is a flavored sesame paste essential for many Middle Eastern dishes.

47 Greif, McPherson and Weinbaum (eds.), *Jeckes*, 32ff.

48 Lotti to Marianne, 1 October 1935, Tel Aviv, OC.

49 Zamenhoff Street, where Hans and Lotti lived, is today a leafy residential street in the center of busy Tel Aviv, off Dizengoff Square. Tel Aviv, also called the "White City," became in 2003 a UNESCO World Heritage Site for its 1930s Bauhaus or International architectural style.

50 Schreiber, "Die Familie Steinberg–Kaufmann," 7.

51 Interview with Lotti, 2 November 1988, IN 291, recorded at the Alte Synagoge Archives, Essen.

52 Zeew (Wolfgang) Neufeld to Uta Larkey, 10 July 2008, Tel Aviv, e-mail. He died a few months later, at age 85, in December 2008.

53 The Arab Higher Committee (AHC) replaced the Palestine Arab Congress in 1936. The AHC was the central political organ and representative of Palestinian Arabs. Cf. Farsoun and Zacharia, *Palestine and the Palestinians*, 106.

54 Abraham Edelheit, *The Yishuv in the Shadow of the Holocaust: Zionist Politics and Rescue Aliya, 1933–1939* (Boulder, Colo.: Westview Press, 1996), 131.

55 "Blutige Unruhen in Jaffa," *Jüdische Rundschau*, 41/32 (21 April 1936).

56 "Weiterer Araberterror," *Jüdische Rundschau*, 41/46 (9 June 1936).

57 Interview with Lotti, 2 November 1988, IN 291, recorded at the Alte Synagoge Archives, Essen.

58 Selma to Marianne, 8 January 1939, Essen, OC.

59 Lotti did not mention this visit in her 1988 interview, but Michael, her son, found postcards sent to Selma in Palestine from her loved ones in Germany at this time. Michael Keynan to Rebecca Boehling, 24 April 2005, e-mail.

60 Alicia Frohmann stressed the pain and regret her mother Lotti experienced over this "lost opportunity" to have saved her mother Selma. Interview with Alicia Frohmann, 27 April 2005, Miami, Florida, conducted by Rebecca Boehling. Michael Keynan mentioned in his 2006 interview that as a child he often asked his parents why they had not locked up his grandparents, "all three of them," in a bathroom during their respective visits in Palestine. Interview with Michael Keynan, 29 June 2006, Tel Aviv, conducted by Uta Larkey.

61 The Zionist Congress supported the partition idea but disagreed with the proposed border. The AHC rejected the partition idea altogether. See Nicosia, *The Third Reich and the Palestine Question*, 111.

62 The question of Palestine as "a land twice promised" is still debated by historians. The answers depend on their interpretation of the McMahon–Hussein correspondence (1915) and the Balfour Declaration (1917). Whether or not Palestine was indeed twice promised, the British government clearly sent mixed messages and, arguably, in the midst of fighting a world war and trying to win over diverse allies, made pragmatic and contradictory commitments.

63 *Jüdische Rundschau*, 43/59 (26 July 1938).

64 "Die Gefahr versäumter Gelegenheiten," *Jüdische Rundschau*, 43/60 (29 July 1938).

65 Chaim and Lucie to Lotti, 10 August 1938, Stettin, FC. Last name(s) and envelope missing.

66 Johanna Steinberg Moses to Lotti, 17 June 1938, Hanover, FC.

67 One exception is the mention of her canceled vacation trip to Cyprus "due to the extremely critical political situation... Taking trips here in the country is no pleasure right now." Lotti to Marianne, 30 September 1938, Tel Aviv, OC.

68 See letters from Lotti to Marianne, 6 April 1938, 1 July 1938, and 16 August 1938, Tel Aviv, OC.

69 Lotti to Marianne, 1 July 1938, Tel Aviv, OC.

70 Johanna Steinberg Moses to Lotti, 17 June 1938, Hanover, FC. Johanna wrote: "I was very pleased to hear that your practice is doing so well. You are a hard-working, courageous woman."

71 Interview with Michael Keynan, 29 June 2006, Tel Aviv, conducted by Uta Larkey.

72 Lotti to Marianne, 6 April 1938, Tel Aviv, OC.

73 Luft, *Heimkehr ins Unbekannte*, 47f. Luft noted that among her more than a hundred German-Jewish interview partners, only two wealthy immigrants were able to maintain their standard of living.

74 Feilchenfeld, Michaelis and Pinner (eds.), *Haavara-Transfer*, 45.

75 The Interior Ministry was committed to increased Jewish emigration from Germany to Palestine. While the Reich Economics Ministry was very much in favor of the continuation of the terms of the initial agreement, the Foreign Office cautioned against further collaboration with Zionist leaders after the 1936 Arab revolts. The Arab Chamber of Commerce had requested a revision of the Ha'avarah Agreement in a note to the German Consulate. For more information on the specifics of this conflict, see Nicosia, *The Third Reich and the Palestine Question*, 126–40 and Appendix 9.

76 Feilchenfeld, Michaelis and Pinner (eds.), *Haavara-Transfer*, 51f.

77 Ibid., 69f.

78 Ibid., 45. Presumably it took a while for these changed conditions to have an impact on the actual transfer.

79 Hans to Marianne, 1 October 1938, Tel Aviv, OC.

80 Luft, *Heimkehr ins Unbekannte*, 118. Cf. Gelber und Goldstern, *Vertreibung und Emigration*, 116. The Organization for Enforcing the Hebrew Language, supported by several Hebrew-language papers and other publications, actively encouraged the use of Hebrew, sometimes to a fault. The immigrants from Germany deeply resented the boycott of the German language in parts of the Yishuv and assured their opponents that they spoke the language of Goethe, not Hitler.

81 The etymology of this originally derogatory, teasing term coined in the 1930s to describe German immigrants is still debated. Some relate it to the German custom of always wearing a jacket, or *Jacke*, no matter what the climate or circumstances. See Gabriele Koppel, *Heimisch werden – Lebenswege deutscher Juden in Palästina* (Hamburg: Europäische Verlagsanstalt,

2000), 8. Others attribute the term to a derivation of a word for "joker," a *Geck* or a *Jeck*. See Shlomo Erel (ed.), *Jeckes erzählen: Aus dem Leben deutschsprachiger Einwanderer in Israel* (Vienna: LIT Verlag, 2004), 410. Tom Segev and Gideon Greif explain that the term is actually a Hebrew acronym meaning "block-headed Jew" (Jehudi Kshe Havana). See Tom Segev, *The Seventh Million: The Israelis and the Holocaust* (New York: Henry Holt and Co., 2000). Cf. Greif, McPherson and Weinbaum (eds.), *Jeckes*. German Jews were often perceived as naïve, unwilling or unable to adapt to a Middle Eastern lifestyle, always proper and hard-working. See Martina Kliner-Fruck, *"Es ging ja ums Überleben": Jüdische Frauen zwischen Nazi-Deutschland, Emigration nach Palästina und ihrer Rückkehr* (Frankfurt am Main: Campus Verlag, 1995), 132.

82 Luft, *Heimkehr ins Unbekannte*, 120f.

83 Kliner-Fruck, *"Es ging ja ums Überleben,"* 153.

84 Interview with Michael Keynan, 29 June 2006, Tel Aviv, conducted by Uta Larkey.

85 Hans to Marianne, 1 October 1938, Tel Aviv, OC.

86 Lotti to Marianne, 30 September 1938, Tel Aviv, OC.

87 Hans to Marianne, 1 October 1938, Tel Aviv, OC.

88 Lotti to Marianne, 17 October 1938, Haifa, OC.

89 Lotti to Marianne, 18 October 1938, Haifa. OC.

90 Lotti to Marianne, 25 October 1938, Tel Aviv, OC.

91 Selma to Marianne, 6 November 1938, Essen, OC.

92 Lotti to Marianne, 5 December 1938, Tel Aviv. OC.

93 Lotti and Hans to Marianne, 5 December 1938, Tel Aviv, OC.

94 Ibid.

95 Kurt to Marianne, 9 February 1939, Tel Aviv, OC.

96 Selma to Marianne, 22 November 1938, Essen and Lotti to Marianne, 5 December 1938, Tel Aviv, OC.

97 As quoted by Lotti in letter to Marianne, 5 December 1938, Tel Aviv, OC.

98 Ibid.

99 For more information about Bell, see Chapter 5.

100 As quoted by Kurt in letter to relatives in the United States and Germany, 9 February 1939, Tel Aviv, OC.

101 Kurt to relatives in the United States and Germany, 9 February 1939, Tel Aviv, OC.

102 Interview with Gideon Sella, 28 June 2006, Tel Aviv, conducted by Uta Larkey.

103 Kurt to several family members in the United States and Germany, 9 February 1939, Tel Aviv, OC.

104 Kurt and Hanna to Marianne, 3 May 1939, Tel Aviv, OC.

105 Kurt to Marianne, 3 May 1939, Tel Aviv, OC.

106 Kurt, Lotti and Ernst to Marianne, 22 May 1939, Tel Aviv, OC.

107 Ernst's registration number was 10327. Kurt to Marianne, 3 May 1939, Tel Aviv, OC.

108 Letter from Marianne to Arnold, 22 March 1939. She mentioned that Kurt worked as a *poël*, which she translated as *Landarbeiter* (farm worker).

109 Interview with Gideon Sella, 28 June 2006, Tel Aviv, conducted by Uta Larkey. *Kibbutzim* and *moshavim* are the plural forms.

110 Interview with Lotti, 2 November 1988, IN 291, recorded at the Alte Synagoge Archives, Essen.

111 Kurt to Marianne, 3 May 1939, Tel Aviv, OC.

112 Ibid.

113 Lotti to Marianne, 30 April 1939, Tel Aviv, OC.

114 Kurt to Marianne, 9 February 1939, Tel Aviv, OC.

115 Kurt to Marianne, 19 February 1939, Tel Aviv, OC.

116 Kurt to Marianne, 3 May 1939, Tel Aviv, OC.

117 For the text of the 1939 White Paper, see http://avalon.law.yale.edu/ 20th_century/brwh1939.asp (accessed 2 January 2010).

118 Lotti to Marianne, 30 April 1939, Tel Aviv, OC.

119 Kurt to Selma and Henny, 3 June 1939, Tel Aviv, OC.

120 Lotti to Marianne, 28 May 1939, Tel Aviv. Sarafand was the name of an Arab village about 2 miles from Rishon le-Zion where Kurt and Hanna moved.

121 Kurt to Marianne, 14 June 1939, Tel Aviv, OC.

122 Kurt to Marianne, 10 July 1939, Tel Aviv, OC.

123 Lotti to Marianne, 28 May 1939, Tel Aviv, OC.

124 Hans to Marianne, 30 April 1939, Tel Aviv, OC.

125 Luft, *Heimkehr ins Unbekannte*, 48.

126 Even though Selma urged Kurt in almost every letter from October 1939 to March 1940 to arrange for the transport of the container with his furniture and other belongings from Antwerp to Tel Aviv, at times of war this was very unlikely.

127 Selma to Kurt and Hanna, 20 July 1939, Cologne, OC.

128 Kurt to Marianne, 3 May 1939 and 10 July 1939, Tel Aviv, OC. Kurt confirmed in May that he had received LP 8,500 and LP 6,345 from Marianne and then in July the receipt of LP 300 and $1,150 from her. Although these numbers seem very high, they are what Kurt claimed.

129 Kurt to Marianne, 10 July 1939, Tel Aviv, OC.

130 Hershel and Abraham Edelheit (eds.), *History of Zionism: A Handbook and Dictionary* (Boulder, Colo.: Westview Press 2000), 525. For the text of the British White Paper of 1939, see http://avalon.law.yale.edu/20th_ century/brwh1939.asp (accessed 21 November 2009).

131 Kurt to Marianne, 22 May 1939, Tel Aviv, OC. The Hatikvah (Hope), written in the 1880s, expresses the ancient hope of the Jewish people to be

a free people in the Land of Israel. The Hatikvah first became the unofficial anthem of the Zionist movement in the late 1880s and later the national anthem of the State of Israel after it was founded in 1948.

132 Black, *Transfer Agreement*, 287.

133 Edelheit, *The Yishuv*, 21f.

134 Segev, *The Seventh Million*, 16.

135 Kurt and Hanna to Marianne, 14 June 1939, Tel Aviv, OC.

136 Feilchenfeld, Michaelis and Pinner (eds.), *Haavara-Transfer*, 91.

137 Nicosia, *The Third Reich and the Palestine Question*, 160ff.

138 Hans to Marianne, 30 April 1939, Tel Aviv, OC.

139 Edelheit (eds.), *History of Zionism*, 243. In 1939 Constantia in Romania became one of the most significant disembarkation harbors for clandestine immigration operations to Palestine. Cf. Dalia Ofer, *Escaping the Holocaust: Illegal Immigration to the Land of Israel, 1939–1944*. Studies in Jewish History Series (New York: Oxford University Press, 1990), 77ff. The *Aufbau* in the United States also reported on the "tragedies at the Palestine coast," mentioning in particular the *Assimi*. The ship was prevented from landing and sent back to sea with more than 400 passengers and without food and water on board. Cf. *Aufbau*, 5/8 (1 May 1939).

140 Hans to Marianne in the United States, parents and in-laws in Essen and Cologne, 10 June 1939, Tel Aviv, OC.

141 Lotti and Hans to Marianne in the United States and relatives in Essen and Cologne, 10 June 1939, Tel Aviv, OC.

142 Ernst Kaiser-Blüth's addendum to Marianne in Hans' letter to all relatives in Essen, Cologne and New York, 18 June 1939, Tel Aviv.

143 Hans to family members in Essen and Cologne, 10 June 1939, Tel Aviv, OC.

144 According to Jewish tradition, male babies are circumcised on the eighth day after birth.

145 Hans to relatives in Essen, Cologne and New York, 18 June 1939, Tel Aviv, OC.

146 Kurt to Marianne, 10 July 1939, Tel Aviv, OC.

147 Flora to Lotti and Hans, 29 April 1939, Cologne, KC.

148 Lotti and Hans to Marianne, 25 September 1939, OC. Original in English.

149 Lotti to Marianne, 28 May 1939, Tel Aviv, OC.

150 Ibid.

151 Interview with Michael Keynan, 29 June 2006, Tel Aviv, conducted by Uta Larkey.

152 Lotti to Marianne, 25 July 1939, Tel Aviv, OC.

153 Feilchenfeld, Michaelis and Pinner (eds.), *Haavara-Transfer*, 67.

154 Kurt to Marianne, 10 July 1939, Tel Aviv, OC.

155 Selma to Marianne, 6 November 1938, Essen, OC.

156 Lotti to Marianne, 25 July 1939, Tel Aviv, OC.

157 Hans to Marianne, 30 September 1939, Tel Aviv, OC. The Carstanjen family was closely connected to MAN's history: Max (1856–1934) was a director of MAN and his son Richard (born 1901) followed in his footsteps. Richard, a director of MAN in the late 1930s, was appointed to the board of directors in 1950. Gabriele Mierzwa, Museum und Historisches Archiv (VMM) Augsburg to Uta Larkey, 24 April 2009, e-mail.

158 Interview with Michael Keynan, 29 June 2006, Tel Aviv, conducted by Uta Larkey.

159 Ibid.

160 Hans to Marianne, 30 September 1939, OC. Original in English.

161 Interview with Michael Keynan, 29 June 2006, Tel Aviv, conducted by Uta Larkey. On 23 August 1939 Nazi Germany and the Soviet Union signed a neutrality pact, the Molotov–Ribbentrop Agreement.

162 Kurt to Marianne, 6 September 1939, Tel Aviv, OC. Original in English.

163 Hans to Marianne, 2 January 1940, Tel Aviv, OC.

164 Contract signed by MAN representatives and Hans Kaiser-Blüth on 4 March 1935 in Nuremberg. Copy of contract sent to Uta Larkey by Gabriele Mierzwa, Museum und Historisches Archiv (VMM) Augsburg, 21 April 2009.

165 Kurt to Marianne, 6 September 1939, Tel Aviv, OC. Dr. Chaim Weizmann (1874–1952) was the president of the World Zionist Organization from 1935 to 1946 and would become the first president of the State of Israel in 1948.

166 *Aufbau*, 5/18 (1 October 1939).

167 Kurt to Marianne, 6 September 1939, Tel Aviv, OC. Original in English.

168 Kurt to Marianne, 29 January 1941, Rishon le-Zion, Sella Collection (henceforth SC).

169 Greif, McPherson and Weinbaum (eds.), *Jeckes*, 42.

170 Ibid.

171 Kurt to Marianne, 11 May 1940, Rishon le-Zion, OC.

172 Kurt to Marianne, 18 August 1940, Rishon le-Zion, OC. Kurt uses this term in English.

173 Ibid.

174 Marianne to Arnold, 11 June 1940, Tewksbury, Massachusetts, OC. Marianne was very worried that Kurt and Hanna lived so close to a British army base that they might be in danger of getting bombed: "The idea of my people living in Palestine with the Mediterranean becoming a battlefield now does not make me very cheerful." Original in English.

175 "Angriff auf Tel Aviv," *Aufbau*, 6/37 (13 September 1940). This air strike resulted in 113 deaths and 151 people injured.

176 Kurt to Marianne, 12 January 1940, Tel Aviv, OC.

7 Rescuing loved ones trapped in Nazi Germany, 1939-1942

1 Selma to Marianne, 22 January 1939, Essen, OC.
2 Selma to Marianne, 2 February 1939, Essen, OC.
3 The title of an article in the *Israelitisches Familienblatt* from 15 April 1937, "Children Become Letters," became a standard saying. A letter-writer from Wetzlar wrote his relatives in Palestine in 1937: "People become letters …" See Doetzer, *"Aus Menschen werden Briefe,"* 1.
4 Benz (ed.), *Die Juden in Deutschland*, 734.
5 Kaplan, *Between Dignity and Despair*, 143.
6 Selma's sister Paula had died at the age of 55 in 1931. Karl and she were the parents of Moritz Kaufmann, who together with his wife had emigrated to the Netherlands in March 1938.
7 The Law on Renting Arrangements with Jews from 30 April 1939 eliminated basic tenants' rights for Jews, allowed non-Jewish landlords to evict their Jewish tenants and provided the legal basis for the concentration of Jews in so-called "Jew houses" (*Judenhäuser*). See RGBl. I, 846.
8 Selma to Marianne, 1 May 1939, Essen, OC. Cf. Marianne's restitution files, OC.
9 Selma to Lotti, 21 March 1939, Essen, FC.
10 Selma to Marianne, 1 May 1939, Essen, OC.
11 Kurt to Marianne, 3 May 1939, Tel Aviv, OC.
12 Selma to Marianne, 6 November 1938, Essen, OC.
13 Selma to Lotti, 21 March 1939, Essen, FC.
14 Selma to Marianne, 18 June 1939, Essen, OC.
15 Ibid.
16 Decree on Registration of Jewish Assets, 21 February 1939, RGBl. I, 282. Cf. Blau, *Ausnahmerecht*, 66.
17 Marianne's restitution files, OC. Since Henny had never had her own independent household, these assets were all attributed to Selma as Alex's widow. The Essen restitution court in 1954 estimated the value to have been 340 RM or $850 in 1939. Selma instead received the equivalent of about $102 in 1939.
18 Asaria, *Die Juden in Köln*, 358f.
19 Marianne's restitution files, OC.
20 Selma and Henny to Marianne, 18 June 1939, Essen, OC.
21 Selma and Henny to Marianne, 2 October 1939, Drove, OC.
22 Selma and Henny to Marianne, 1 May 1939, Essen, OC.
23 Kurt to Marianne, 22–8 May 1939, Tel Aviv, OC.
24 "Die neue Schedule," *Jüdisches Nachrichtenblatt* (Vienna), 49/1 (20 June 1939). The mandate government's June-to-September schedule allowed

for a total of 7,800 certificates, but the number of anticipated certificates specifically for immigrants from Germany was not publicized.

25 Kurt to Selma, Henny and Onkel Hermann, Tel Aviv, 12 August 1939, OC.

26 Feilchenfeld, Michaelis and Pinner (eds.), *Haavara-Transfer*, 90.

27 Flora to Marianne, 2 September 1939, Cologne, OC.

28 Julius to Marianne, 5 September 1939, Cologne, OC.

29 Selma and Henny to Kurt and Lotti, 4 September 1939, Cologne, SC.

30 The German-Jewish newspaper *Aufbau*, published in New York, informed its readers on 1 October 1939 that postal connections to Germany had been restricted but were maintained by liners from neutral countries. The paper advised directing correspondence through acquaintances in neutral countries, such as Belgium, the Netherlands and Italy. On 15 October 1939 *Aufbau* reported that mail had been increasingly delayed.

31 Moritz Kaufmann to Kurt, 16 September and 1 November 1939, Amstelveen, SC, and 20 November 1939, FC.

32 Selma to Sofie Levy, undated, presumably late November 1940, Cologne, FC.

33 Selma to Marianne, 19 September 1939, Cologne, OC.

34 Ibid.

35 Blau, *Ausnahmerecht*, 79.

36 Flora to Lotti and Hans, 29 April 1939, Cologne, KC.

37 Selma to Marianne, 23 October 1939, Cologne. Thekla's daughter Carola had married Salo Weindling, and both emigrated to the United States in July 1939. Cf. Carola and Salo Weindling in Philadelphia to Frau Wirsbitzki, 19 January 1986, AR 10426, Alte Synagoge Archives, Essen. Also located at the Leo Baeck Institute, New York, MF 642.

38 Selma to Kurt and Lotti, 4 September 1939, Cologne, SC.

39 Kaplan, *Between Dignity and Despair*, 151.

40 Blau, *Ausnahmerecht*, 84. Decree of 4 July 1940.

41 Marianne to Kurt, Lotti *et al.*, 11 December 1939, Tewksbury, Massachusetts, OC. Original in English.

42 Selma to Marianne, 23 October 1939, Cologne, OC.

43 Lotti to Marianne, 19 September 1939, Tel Aviv, OC. Original in English.

44 Selma to Marianne, 23 October 1939, Cologne, OC.

45 Kurt to US consulate in Jerusalem, 11 November 1939, Tel Aviv, OC. Original in English.

46 US consulate, Jerusalem to Kurt, 16 April 1940. As cited in letter from Kurt to Marianne, Tel Aviv, 11 May 1940, OC. Original in English.

47 Kurt to Marianne, 11 May 1940, Tel Aviv, OC. Kurt must have received the notification that his registration number was up between January and May 1940.

48 Wetzel, "Auswanderung aus Deutschland," 485.

49 Bat-Ami Zucker, *In Search of Refuge: Jews and US Consuls in Nazi Germany 1933–1941* (London and Portland, Oreg.: Vallentine Mitchell, 2001), 33ff.

50 Ibid., 2ff., 35, 47, 172, 178f. Approximately two-thirds of the German applicants from 1933 to 1941 were Jews.

51 Ibid., 4.

52 Ibid., 111. Cf. Dwork and van Pelt, *Flight*,145f.

53 Zucker, *In Search of Refuge*, 145.

54 Ibid., 143ff., 168.

55 Ibid., 96f.

56 Ibid., 100f. and 178. Reputed to be anti-Semitic, Assistant Secretary of State Breckinridge Long and Visa Division Chief Avra M. Warren were particularly restrictive in their views toward Jewish immigration to the United States, views they shared with other State Department and, in particular, consular officials. See also Rafael Medoff, *Blowing the Whistle on Genocide: Josiah E. DuBois, Jr. and the Struggle for a US Response to the Holocaust* (West Lafayette, Ind.: Purdue University Press, 2009), 22f.

57 Zucker, *In Search of Refuge*, 172f. Polls in the United States in the late 1930s showed that 60 percent of Americans held that Jews had "objectionable qualities," close to half thought Jews held "too much power" in the United States and 20 percent claimed to "sympathize with an anti-Semitic campaign." Fewer than 9 percent supported changing the immigration system to allow more refugees into the country.

58 Ibid., 102f. and 154.

59 Ibid., 177. This was also known to be the case with the consulate in Hamburg, unlike Berlin or, after the *Anschluss* of Austria in March 1938, Vienna.

60 Dwork and van Pelt, *Flight*, 147.

61 Zucker, *In Search of Refuge*, 44f.

62 Selma and Henny to Kurt and Lotti, 14 July 1940, Cologne, OC.

63 Blau, *Ausnahmerecht*, 84. Decree of the Reich Postal Minister, 29 July 1940.

64 Kurt to Marianne, 18 August 1940, Rishon le-Zion, OC.

65 Kurt to Marianne, 18 August 1940, Rishon le-Zion, OC.

66 Marianne's Notebook, Camp Berkshire, 23 August 1940, OC. Original in English, as were almost all of Marianne's entries once she got settled in the United States.

67 Sworn Statement of Marianne Steinberg Ostrand regarding her income from July 1938 until the end of 1959. Marianne's restitution files, OC.

68 Marianne's Notebook, Camp Berkshire, 6 and 12 July 1940, OC.

69 Ibid., 16 December 1939, Tewksbury, Massachusetts, OC. See also Selma's comments about Arnold's job problems, Selma to children, 30 June 1940,

Cologne, and Marianne to Kurt and Lotti, New York, undated, presumably fall 1940, OC.

70 Marianne's Notebook, Camp Berkshire, 23 August 1940, OC.

71 Arnold to Marianne, 7 January 1941, New York, OC. Original in English.

72 Marianne and Arnold to Kurt and Hanna, 27 September 1944, New York, OC.

73 Marianne to Hilde(gard) Winkler in Switzerland, 27 August 1941, New York, OC. See also Marianne to Kurt *et al.*, 27 March 1941, OC.

74 Selma to Marianne and Arnold, 18 February 1941, Cologne, SC.

75 Marianne to Kurt and Lotti, 27 March 1941, New York, SC. Original in English.

76 Marianne to Selma and Henny, 29 March 1941, New York, OC. Trude was apparently her friend and colleague from the Israelitisches Asyl, Trude Löwenstein, who, together with her husband, had emigrated to the United States in mid 1939.

77 Kurt to Marianne, 13 May 1941, Rishon le-Zion, SC.

78 Marianne to Kurt and Lotti, 12 July 1941, New York, OC.

79 Selma to Marianne, 23 March 1941, Cologne, OC.

80 The outbreak of World War II restricted the international business that German shipping lines could conduct, and German emigrants had to book their passages with non-German lines, which charged foreign currency. See "Ueber Lissabon nach Uebersee," *Jüdisches Nachrichtenblatt*, 31 December 1940, 105/1.

81 When in 1939 the Nazis dissolved the Hilfsverein, the Jewish Self-Help Agency, it officially became the Emigration Department of the Reich Association of Jews in Germany. However, Jews in Germany kept referring to it as the Hilfsverein.

82 Selma to Marianne and Arnold, 23 March 1941, Cologne, OC.

83 Julius to Marianne, 24 March 1941, Cologne, OC.

84 Selma to Marianne, undated, end of February 1941, Cologne, SC.

85 Flora to Marianne, 24 March 1941, Cologne, OC.

86 Selma to Marianne, 23 March 1941, Cologne, OC.

87 *Chronik des Amtes Inden*, Rathaus Inden, 1941. Excerpts cited in essay by Bernd Hahne, *Entrechtung, Vertreibung,Vernichtung 1933–1945*, www. duereninfo.de/AGV/VI.pdf (accessed 24 January 2010).

88 Selma to Marianne, undated, at the end of February 1941, Cologne, SC.

89 Lotti and Kurt to Marianne, 23 May 1941, Tel Aviv, SC.

90 Selma to Marianne, 23 March 1941, Cologne, OC.

91 Marianne to Lotti, 1 May 1941, New York, OC. Original in English.

92 Marianne to the Honorable American Consul in Stuttgart (carbon copy), 17 May 1941, New York, OC. Original in English.

93 Copies of the 17 May 1941 affidavit and accompanying materials, OC. Marianne submitted her Declaration of Intent citizenship papers on 7 September 1938.

94 Marianne to Selma and Henny, 19 May 1941, New York, OC.

95 Ibid.

96 Marianne to Kurt and Lotti, 4 June 1941, New York, SC. Original in English.

97 Lotti to Marianne, 25 May 1941, Tel Aviv, OC.

98 Hans to Marianne, 25 May 1941, Tel Aviv, OC.

99 Kurt to Marianne and Arnold, 13 May 1941, Rishon le-Zion, SC.

100 Ibid.

101 Selma to Sofie Levy, 13 May 1941, Cologne, SC.

102 Joseph Walk, *Das Sonderrecht für die Juden im NS Staat*, 2nd edn. (Heidelberg: C.F. Müller Verlag, 1996), 341. The housing department of the Cologne Jewish community sent out a circular on 12 May 1941 relaying to their community the Nazi authorities' decision that "all Jewish houses … in the western suburbs have to be vacated." See Asaria, *Die Juden in Köln*, 366ff.

103 Marianne to Lotti and Kurt, 12 July 1941, New York, OC. Original in English. Selma's letter to Marianne is not extant.

104 Marianne's restitution file, OC.

105 Berschel, *Bürokratie und Terror*, 315f.

106 Flora to Hans and Lotti, 13 January 1939, Cologne, KC.

107 Marianne to siblings, 12 July 1941, New York, OC. Original in English.

108 Heinrich Böll, *Die Juden von Drove, Köln und das rheinische Judentum*, Festschrift Germania Judaica 1959–84 (Cologne: Bachem Verlag 1984), 487. Ernest Kaufman generously made his own personal translation of Böll's article available to the authors.

109 "Das Rheinland unter Bomben," *Aufbau*, 25 July 1941, 5/30.

110 Selma to children, 5 August 1941, Cologne, SC.

111 "Der Schlag gegen die Einwanderung," *Aufbau*, 18 July 1941, 7/29.

112 "Die Ausfüllung der neuen Affidavitformulare," *Aufbau*, 11 July 1941, 7/28.

113 "Schlag gegen Unschuldige," *Aufbau*, 11 July 1941, 7/28.

114 *Jüdisches Nachrichtenblatt* (Berlin), 17 October 1941.

115 Marianne to Selma and Henny, undated, early August 1941, New York, OC.

116 Marianne to Selma and Henny, 29 August 1941, New York, OC.

117 Marianne to Selma and Henny, 25 September 1941, New York, OC.

118 Marianne to all in Palestine, 25 September 1941, New York, SC.

119 Selma to Lotti and Hans, 3 October 1941, Cologne, SC.

120 Kurt to Marianne, 14 June 1939, Cologne, OC. Of the two acquaintances, Alice Sternberg was able to survive and emigrate to the United States, while Max Frank, who had lived in the same building with the Kaufmann–Steinberg family in Altenessen, is listed as "perished." http://resources.ushmm.org/stlouis/passenger_list.php (accessed 4 February 2010).

121 Selma to Lotti and Hans, 3 October 1941, Cologne, SC.

122 Selma to Marianne, 9 October 1941, Cologne, OC.

123 Wolf Gruner, "Von der Kollektivausweisung zur Deportation," in Birthe Kundrus and Beate Meyer (eds.), *Die Deportation der Juden aus Deutschland: Pläne, Praxis, Reaktionen 1938–1945* (Göttingen: Wallstein, 2004), 54.

124 Selma to Lotti and Hans, 3 October 1941, Cologne, SC.

125 Bertha Lachs' daughter Martha and son-in-law Walter Haase were transported to a collection point in Düren on 3 October 1941. They arrived in Theresienstadt on transport VII-2 on 25 July 1942. According to www.holocaust.cz, Bertha's last residence before deportation was Villa Buth in Kirchberg (accessed 23 January 2010).

126 Selma to Herta, 14 October 1941, Cologne, OC.

127 The Reich Security Main Office (RSHA) issued this decree on 24 October 1941. See Walk, *Sonderrecht*, 353.

128 Herta Poth to Marianne, 8 September 1947, Essen, OC.

129 Blau, *Ausnahmerecht*, 89. This police order, issued on 1 September, went into effect on 19 September 1941.

130 Selma to children, 1 September 1941, SC. Cf. E. Dominicus, *Chronik des Amtsbezirkes Nörvenich 1932–1946*, 2nd edn., 81, as cited in: www.geschichtswerkstatt-dueren.de (accessed 23 January 2010).

131 Selma to children, 1 September 1941, Cologne, SC.

132 Blau, *Ausnahmerecht*, 89. These measures helped facilitate the Nazis' deportation of the Jews.

133 Kaplan, *Between Dignity and Despair*, 157ff.

134 Ibid., 150.

135 *Kölnische Zeitung*, 13 September 1941, as cited in: Asaria, *Die Juden in Köln*, 367. Cf. Peter Longerich, *"Davon haben wir nichts gewusst": Die Deutschen und die Judenverfolgung 1933–1945* (Munich: Siedler Verlag, 2006), 165.

136 Flora to Marianne *et al.* 3 October 1941, Cologne, SC.

137 Kurt and Hanna to Marianne and Arnold, 9 July 1941, Rishon le-Zion, OC.

138 Marianne to Kurt and Lotti, 22 August 1941, New York, OC. Original in English.

139 Armin and Renate Schmid, *Im Labyrinth der Paragraphen: Die Geschichte einer gescheiterten Emigration* (Frankfurt am Main: Fischer Taschenbuch Verlag, 1993), 61. The Schmids report that Cuba required up to $1,500 as proof of intent and $50 as a landing fee, so that no refugees would become a burden to the state if their transit lasted longer than expected. There was a run on Cuban visas after the United States closed its consulates in Germany and German-occupied lands, with some 35,000 visas issued from September to November 1941, without nearly enough ships available, whether in neutral Barcelona or Lisbon, to transport all the refugees with visas.

140 Marianne to Kurt and Lotti, 22 August 1941, New York, OC. Original in English.

141 Marianne to Kurt and Lotti, 22 August 1941, New York, OC. Original in English.

142 Kurt to Marianne, 12 August 1941, Rishon le-Zion, SC.

143 Lotti to Marianne, 6 December 1941, Tel Aviv, OC.

144 Marianne to Hildegard Winkler, New York, 27 August 1941, OC.

145 Hildegard Winkler to Marianne, 5 November 1941, Bern, OC.

146 Marianne to Selma and Tante Henny, 31 November 1941, New York, OC.

147 Selma and Henny to children, 8 and 15 November 1941, Cologne, OC. Selma's last telegram to Marianne was dated 9 October 1941.

148 Marianne to Selma and Henny, 3 October 1941, New York, OC. Marianne suspected Selma would be in Cuba for two to three months.

149 Selma to children, 15 November 1941, Cologne, OC.

150 Arnold and Marianne to Lotti and Hans, 31 October 1941, New York, OC.

151 Kurt to Marianne and Arnold, 18 January 1942, Rishon le-Zion, OC.

152 Selma to children, 8 and 15 and 27 November 1941, Cologne, OC.

153 "Die Ausreise aus Deutschland," *Aufbau*, 7/49 (5 December 1941). The Nazis were associated with brown in contrast to the red of communism. SA storm-troopers wore brown shirts and the Nazi Party headquarters was named the "Brown House."

154 Kurt to Marianne and Arnold, 18 January 1942, Rishon le-Zion, OC. Original in English.

155 On 1 October 1941 Himmler announced a secret order that effectively prevented any further emigration from Germany "in light of dangers during wartime and the possibilities in the east." See Kulka and Jäckel, *Geheime Stimmungsberichten*, 640. On 23 October 1941 the Reich Security Main Office (RSHA) decreed: "The emigration of Jews from Germany is prohibited for the duration of the war, no exceptions." See Walk, *Sonderrecht*, 353.

156 Gruner, "Kollektivausweisung," 54f.

157 Christopher Browning, *The Origins of the Final Solution: The Evolution of Nazi Jewish Policy September 1939–March 1942* (Lincoln, Nebr.: University of Nebraska Press, 2004), 373.

158 Selma to Sofie Levy, 3 May 1942, Cologne-Müngersdorf, OC.

159 "Kommt die Auswanderung zu vollem Stillstand?" *Aufbau*, 7/52 (26 December 1941).

160 Dwork and van Pelt, *Flight*, 260. Between September 1939 and June 1945 23 million civilian messages were sent via the International Red Cross. See www.icrc.org/ihl.nsf/COM/380–600029?OpenDocument (accessed 19 December 2009).

161 Kurt to Marianne and Arnold, 3 May 1942 and 1 July 1942, Rishon le-Zion, SC. See also Red Cross messages from Selma and her sisters that Marianne received in 1942 and copies of Marianne's Red Cross message replies to each message received, OC.

162 See copies of Kurt's Red Cross messages to Selma and her sisters from the summer of 1942, SC.

163 Marianne to siblings, 24 July 1942, New York, OC. Original in English.

164 Ibid.

165 Kurt to Marianne and Arnold, 1 July 1942, Rishon le-Zion, SC. Original in English.

166 Red Cross messages from Selma and her sisters received by Marianne in 1942 along with copies of Marianne's Red Cross message replies, OC.

167 Selma to Moritz Kaufmann, 1 June 1942, Cologne-Müngersdorf, SC.

168 Selma to Herta Poth, 14 January 1942, Cologne, OC.

169 Selma to Kurt, 8 January 1942, Cologne, OC.

170 Selma to Moritz Kaufmann, 1 June 1942, Cologne-Müngersdorf, SC.

171 Selma and Henny to Herta Poth, 12 February 1942, Cologne, OC.

172 Ibid.

173 Selma to Herta Poth, 3 March 1942, Cologne, OC.

174 Kaplan, *Between Dignity and Despair*, 155. The barracks were built for Russian prisoners of war during World War I.

175 Selma to Sofie Levy, 3 May 1942, Cologne, FC.

176 Siegfried Wollenberg, 19 January 1942, Cologne-Müngersdorf. Postcard reproduced in: Asaria, *Die Juden in Köln*, 363.

177 Ibid., 386.

178 Max Schönenberg, a detainee at the Cologne-Müngersdorf collection point, 15 March 1942. His letter cited in Becker-Jákli, *Das jüdische Krankenhaus*, 334.

179 Selma to Sofie Levy, 3 May 1942, Cologne-Müngersdorf, FC. Selma refers here to Else and Leo Kaufmann from Drove, Thekla and Leopold Heumann from Linnich, and Martha and Walter Haase from Düren. Martha's mother, Bertha (Kaufmann) Lachs, was later deported to Theresienstadt.

180 Miroslav Kárný, "Theresienstadt 1941–1945," in Institut Theresienstädter Initiative (ed.), *Theresienstädter Gedenkbuch, Die Opfer der Judentransporte aus Deutschland nach Theresienstadt* (Prague: Verlag Academia, 2000), 20. Theresienstadt, or Terezín in Czech, was built in the late eighteenth century as a fortress on the northern border of the Austro-Hungarian empire. The Nazis forced the 4,000 Gentile Czech residents out of their homes to implement their plan of establishing a full-scale ghetto/concentration camp after January 1942.

181 Longerich, *"Nichts gewusst,"* 10ff. Longerich summarizes the arguments of different historians as to what Germans knew about the deportations. He includes the views of Marlis Steiner, Ian Kershaw, Otto Dov Kulka, David Bankier, Robert Gellately, Frank Bajohr and Hans Mommsen.

182 David Bankier, *The Germans and the Final Solution: Public Opinion under Nazism* (Oxford: Blackwell, 1992), 101ff.

183 Kaplan, *Between Dignity and Despair*, 194f.

184 Sibylle Tiedemann, "Frauenleben 1933–1945," unpublished prospectus for documentary film *Kinderland ist abgebrannt*, 1995, 11.

185 Kaplan, *Between Dignity and Despair*, 180f.

186 Konrad Kwiet, "Von der Ghettoisierung zur Deportation," in Benz (ed.), *Die Juden in Deutschland*, 651ff.

187 Lotti to Marianne, 3 June 1945, Tel Aviv, OC.

188 Flora's note evoking her deceased father on back of photograph of the tombstone of her father, David Palm (1818–1911), 13 May 1941, Cologne, KC.

189 Selma to Herta Poth, 5 May 1942, Cologne-Müngersdorf, OC.

190 Herta to Marianne, 8 September 1947, Essen, OC.

191 Becker-Jákli, *Das jüdische Krankenhaus*, 335. The estimated number of deaths was 500, with 5,000 people injured. Over 45,000 people lost their homes.

192 Interview with Inge Goldschmidt Oppenheimer. Interview code 11370, Shoah Foundation Institute, University of Southern California.

193 Onkel Hermann died on 28 October 1941 and his sister Johanna Moses on 6 December 1941.

194 Asaria, *Die Juden in Köln*, 387f.

195 Karl to Moritz Kaufmann, 1 June 1942, Cologne-Müngersdorf, SC. Moritz apparently still lived at his old address in the Netherlands at this point. He was deported from Westerbork to Theresienstadt on 4 September 1944 and, three weeks later, from there to his death at Auschwitz-Birkenau. See www.bundesarchiv.de/gedenkbuch (accessed 23 January 2010). His wife Bertl survived and emigrated to the United States.

196 Selma and Henny to Moritz Kaufmann, 1 June 1942, Cologne-Müngersdorf, SC.

197 Selma to Herta Poth, undated but presumably 14 June 1942, Cologne-Müngersdorf, Marianne Ostrand Collection, AR 5823, Leo Baeck Institute, New York. Selma signed the postcard "Sofie." Perhaps it was Selma's way of trying to have someone let Sofie Levy know that she had been deported to Theresienstadt, in the hope that from Argentina Sofie would inform Selma's children in Palestine.

8 Wartime rumors and postwar revelations

1 Kurt to Marianne and Arnold, 23 November 1942, Rishon le-Zion, OC. Original in English. Ernst Roer was the brother of Toni Roer Rothschild. Ernst was sent with his wife from the Holbeckshof collection point in Essen-Steele to Düsseldorf and then deported to Theresienstadt on 21 July

1942. The Rothschilds emigrated to Palestine in 1934 and rented a room to Lotti and Hans after their arrival there. See Kaufmann family tree, OC.

2 Lotti and Hans to Marianne, 10 January 1943, Tel Aviv, OC.

3 Hans to Marianne and Arnold, 12 January 1943, Tel Aviv.

4 Walter to Liesel Sternberg, Viña del Mar/Chile, 27 September 1942, AR 921, Alte Synagoge Archives, Essen.

5 Bundesarchiv (ed.), *Gedenkbuch: Opfer der Verfolgung der Juden unter der nationalsozialistischen Gewaltherrschaft in Deutschland (1933–1945)*, 2nd edn. (Koblenz, 2006). For an updated on-line version, see www.bundesarchiv. de/gedenkbuch/directory.html?id=975900&submit=1&page=1&maxview= 50&offset=0 (accessed 12 April 2010).

6 Dieter Corbach, *6:00 ab Messe Köln-Deutz: Deportationen 1938–1945* (Cologne: Scriba Buch- und Musikverlag, 1999), 26f. Cf. Berschel, *Bürokratie und Terror*, 391f.

7 Marianne's restitution files, OC.

8 Barkai, *From Boycott to Annihilation*, 180f.

9 Michael Zimmermann, "Eine Deportation nach Theresienstadt: Zur Rolle des Banalen bei der Durchsetzung des Monströsen," in Miroslav Kárný, Margita Kárná and Raimund Kemper (eds.), *Theresienstädter Studien und Dokumente* (Prague: Academia, 1994), 60ff.

10 Isidor Caro was the last rabbi of the Orthodox community "Adass Jeschurun" in Cologne. He died on 28 August 1943 in Theresienstadt.

11 Corbach, *6:00 ab Messe Köln-Deutz*, 26ff.

12 Ibid., 53f.

13 Ibid., 51.

14 Asaria, *Die Juden in Köln*, 388.

15 Corbach, *6:00 ab Messe Köln-Deutz*, 54.

16 Klara Caro, "Stärker als das Schwert, Erinnerungen," typewritten manuscript, MM14, 5, Leo Baeck Institute, New York. Cf. Alfred Gottwaldt and Diana Schulle, *Die "Judendeportationen" aus dem Deutschen Reich 1941–1945* (Wiesbaden: Marixverlag, 2005), 292.

17 Kárný, "Theresienstadt 1941–1945," 21. According to Kárný, numerous Jews had also signed "home purchase contracts" and paid for what they believed guaranteed them a place in a retirement home. Cf. Federica Spitzer and Ruth Weisz, *Theresienstadt: Aufzeichnungen* (Berlin: Metropol Verlag, 1997), 31. Cf. H.G. Adler, *Theresienstadt 1941–1945: Das Antlitz einer Zwangsgemeinschaft* (Tübingen: J.C.B. Mohr, 1960), 108.

18 In 1943–44 a single track was built from the railroad station at Bauschowitz to the center of the ghetto.

19 Resi Weglein, *Als Krankenschwester im KZ Theresienstadt: Erinnerungen einer Ulmer Jüdin* (Stuttgart: Silberburg-Verlag, 1990), 26. Cf. Adler, *Theresienstadt*, 267f.

20 This was most likely the so-called Dresden barrack, where mostly older women were housed.

21 Caro, "Erinnerungen," 5.

22 *Ubikationen* is an Austrian term used for this type of living quarters, historically connected with military barracks.

23 Kárný, "Theresienstadt 1941–1945," 21.

24 Philip Manes, *Als ob's ein Leben wär: Tatsachenbericht Theresienstadt 1942–1944* (Berlin: Ullstein, 2005), 44.

25 Selma, Henny and Emma were on Transport III-1 (III indicated the departure city of Cologne; 1 that this was the first transport from Cologne to Theresienstadt). Selma's individual transport number was 652, Henny's 651 and Emma's 653. See www.holocaust.cz/cz2/eng/victims/victims (accessed 13 March 2011). Cf. Corbach, *6:00 ab Messe Köln-Deutz*, 463 and 487.

26 Manes, *Als ob's ein Leben wär*, 44f.

27 Anita Tarsi, "Das Schicksal der alten Frauen in Theresienstadt," in Miroslav Kárný, Margita Kárná and Raimund Kemper (eds.), *Theresienstädter Studien und Dokumente* (Prague: Academia, 1998), 105. Anita Tarsi served until 2009 as the director of Beit Theresienstadt Archive and Holocaust Museum in Israel.

28 Kárný, "Theresienstadt 1941–1945," 20.

29 Tarsi, "Schicksal," 116.

30 Adler, *Theresienstadt*, 693.

31 Kárný, "Theresienstadt 1941–1945," 40.

32 Between April and September 1942 the number of inmates quadrupled, and the mortality rate rose fifteen-fold. See ibid., 20.

33 Herta Poth to Marianne, 8 September 1947, Essen, OC. Herta observed Emma's "fragile health" and Henny's "emotional vulnerability" when visiting the sisters in Cologne-Müngersdorf before their deportation.

34 Cf. Kárný, "Theresienstadt 1941–1945," 20. Cf. Adler, *Theresienstadt*, 109.

35 Tarsi, "Schicksal," 114.

36 Anna Hájková, "Strukturen weiblichen Verhaltens in Theresienstadt," in Gisela Bock (ed.), *Genozid und Geschlecht* (Frankfurt am Main: Campus Verlag, 2005), 209.

37 Klara Caro to Lotti and Hans, undated, as related by Kurt in his letter to Marianne, 26 June 1945, Rishon le-Zion, OC. Original in English.

38 Adler, *Theresienstadt*, 104.

39 Tarsi, "Schicksal," 123f. Cf. Klara Caro to Lotti and Hans, undated but presumably mid 1945, as reproduced by Kurt in his letter to Marianne, 26 June 1945, Rishon le-Zion, OC. Original in English.

40 Spitzer and Weisz, *Theresienstadt*, 41.

41 Klara Caro to Lotti and Hans, undated, as related by Kurt in his letter to Marianne, 26 June 1945, Rishon le-Zion, OC.

42 Tagesbefehl Nr. 125, 14 May 1942, Památník Terezín, A10/94, Theresienstadt Archives, Terezín, Czech Republic. Similar to the "Jewish Councils" in other ghettos and camps, the Council of Elders was put in the impossible position of having to run the internal affairs of the ghetto/camp as dictated by the Nazi administration, providing deportation lists and, generally, being caught between a rock and a hard place.

43 Ibid.

44 Tagesbefehl Nr. 213, 16 September 1942, Památník Terezín, A3241, Theresienstadt Archives, Terezín, Czech Republic.

45 Most of these exchanged German nationals were members of the Temple Society or Templars – a Protestant sect – that began to settle in Palestine in the late nineteenth century. At the outbreak of World War II the British mandate government interned them; many of whom were indeed proponents of Nazi ideology, as "enemy nationals." The Templars were expelled to Australia or exchanged for Jewish citizens of Palestine who had fallen into German hands. See Rockman, *None of Them Were Heroes*. Cf. Yad Vashem ed., *From Bergen-Belsen to Freedom: The Story of the Exchange of Jewish Inmates of Bergen-Belsen with German Templars from Palestine*, Proceedings of the Symposium in Memory of Dr. Haim Pazner (Jerusalem: Yad Vashem 1986).

46 "Rescue," in Laqueur and Tydor Baumel (eds.), *Holocaust Encyclopedia*, 536. Cf. David S. Wyman and Charles H. Rosenzveig, *The World Reacts to the Holocaust* (Baltimore: Johns Hopkins University Press, 1996), 848.

47 Hans to Marianne and Arnold, 12 January 1943, Tel Aviv, OC.

48 Marianne to siblings in Palestine, 4 February 1943, New York, SC.

49 Kurt to Marianne and Arnold, 1 July 1942. Marianne Bachrach Steinberg was Alex's mother, their grandmother. Original in English.

50 Ibid.

51 Marianne to Kurt and Hanna, 24 July 1942, New York, OC. Original in English.

52 Marianne to Kurt and Hanna, 27 September 1944, New York, OC. Original in English.

53 Arnold to Kurt and Hanna, 27 September 1944, New York, OC.

54 Marianne to Kurt and Hanna, 6 January 1946, New York, OC. See also Marianne to Lotti, 14 and 20 February 1946, OC.

55 Lotti to Marianne, 12 January 1944, Tel Aviv, OC.

56 Kurt to Marianne, 13 August 1944, Rishon le-Zion, OC. Original in English.

57 Lotti to Marianne, 13 December 1944, Tel Aviv, OC. Lotti and Hans divorced on 12 December 1944.

58 Marianne to all in Palestine, 29 November 1943, New York, OC. Original in English.

59 Marianne to all in Palestine, 4 February 1943, New York, SC.

60 Kurt to Marianne, 20 December 1943, Rishon le-Zion, OC. Original in English.

61 Lotti to Marianne, 19 June 1944, Tel Aviv, OC. See also Hans to Marianne and Arnold, 1 March 1945, Tel Aviv, OC.

62 Lotti to Marianne, Arnold and Thomas, 19 July 1944, Tel Aviv, OC. Paula, Leo and Eva Schwarzschild were probably related to the Fritz Schwarzschild who had signed the fraudulent letter Hanna used to expedite Kurt's release from Buchenwald. Mirjam Bolle, who worked for the Jewish Council in Amsterdam, and her family were on the same exchange. See Mirjam Bolle, *"Ich weiss, dieser Brief wird dich nie erreichen," Tagebuchbriefe aus Amsterdam, Westerbork und Bergen-Belsen* (Berlin: Eichborn, 2006).

63 Simon Heinrich Herrmann, "Austauschlager Bergen-Belsen," *Aufbau*, 11/10–13 (9–30 March 1945).

64 Kurt to Marianne, 13 August 1944, Rishon le-Zion, OC. Original in English.

65 Lotti to Marianne, 19 July1944, Tel Aviv, OC.

66 Kurt to Marianne, 13 August 1944, Rishon le-Zion, OC. Original in English.

67 Ibid.

68 Kurt to Marianne and Arnold, 10 December 1944, Rishon le-Zion, OC. Original in English.

69 Ibid.

70 Marianne to Hanna and Kurt, 10 May 1945, New York, OC. Application form 633 Petition for Issuance of Immigration Visa.

71 Yehuda Bauer, *Jews for Sale? Nazi–Jewish Negotiations 1933–1945* (New Haven, London: Yale University Press, 1994), 230. Bauer corrects the notion of "exchange" rather than a financial transaction in this fittingly titled book.

72 Himmler wanted a guarantee that these Jews would not go to Palestine, because Germany did not want to estrange the Arabs. Ibid., 230.

73 Lotti to Marianne, 15 April 1945, Tel Aviv, OC.

74 Adler, *Theresienstadt*, 200f.

75 "Befreite aus Theresienstadt, erste Liste der in der Schweiz Eingetroffenen," *Aufbau*, 11/7 (16 February 1945).

76 "Rettungsland Schweiz," *Aufbau*, 23 February 1945, 11/8.

77 "US Visa für Theresienstadt-Flüchtlinge in der Schweiz," *Aufbau*, 23 February 1945, 11/8.

78 Marianne to Kurt and Lotti, 27 February 1945, New York. Original in English.

79 Kurt to Marianne, 5 March 1945, Sarafand, OC. Original in English.

80 Marianne and Arnold to Kurt and Lotti, 27 September 1944, New York, OC.

81 Marianne to Lotti, 25 April 1945, New York, OC.

82 Ibid.

83 Marianne and Arnold to Kurt and Hanna, 27 September 1944, New York, OC. Original in English.

84 Kurt to Marianne and Arnold, 4 April 1945, Rishon le-Zion, OC. Original in English.

85 Arnold and Marianne to Hanna and Kurt, 10 May 1945, New York, SC. Original in English.

86 Kurt to Marianne and Arnold, 4 April 1945, Rishon le-Zion, OC. Original in English.

87 Kurt to Hilde and Ernst Plaut, 6 May 1945, Rishon le-Zion. SC. Original in English.

88 Lotti to Marianne and Arnold, 15 April 1945, Tel Aviv, OC. Caro's quotation was written in English.

89 Kurt to Marianne, 26 June 1945, Rishon le-Zion. Kurt copied and passed on to his sister what Klara Caro had written to Lotti and Hans.

90 Lotti to Marianne and Arnold, 15 April 1945, Tel Aviv, OC.

91 Lotti to Marianne, 3 June 1945, Tel Aviv, OC.

92 Marianne to Lotti, 13 June 1945, New York, OC. Original in English.

93 Ibid.

94 Kurt to Marianne and Arnold, 6 October 1945, Sarafand, OC. Original in English.

95 Moritz Schweizer to Marianne, 31 March 1946, Amsterdam, OC. He took Marianne to her ship in Rotterdam when she immigrated to the United States in June 1938. They had not been in contact with each other until his own immigration to the United States.

96 For the search notice, see *Aufbau*, 12/9 (1 March 1946).

97 For the death notice, see *Aufbau*, 13/18 (2 May 1947).

98 Kurt to Marianne, Arnold and Thomas, 23 June 1946, Rishon le-Zion, OC.

99 Marianne to Hanna and Kurt, 26 September 1946, New York, OC. Original in English.

100 Kurt to Marianne and Arnold, 9 October 1948, Rishon le-Zion, OC.

101 Rada židovských nabožexských obcí v českých Čechách a na Moravě.

102 United Restitution Office of the Association of Jews from Central Europe to Kurt Steinberg, 24 December 1950, File: Steinberg 2150/31, Prague, OC.

103 Kurt to Marianne, undated (presumably 1953), Rishon le-Zion, OC.

104 Kurt to Marianne and Arnold, 26 May 1955, Arolsen, OC.

105 Miroslav Kárný, "Das Schicksal der Theresienstädter Osttransporte im Sommer und Herbst 1942," *Judaica Bohemiae* XXIV/2 (Prague: Státní židovské muzeum, 1988), 82.

106 Ibid. About 85 percent of the deported inmates were older than 60.

107 Ibid., 95.

108 Adler, *Theresienstadt*, 123.

109 Gottwaldt and Schulle, Die *"Judendeportationen,"* 226.

110 Adler, *Theresienstadt*, 694. Cf. Karel Lagus and Josef Polak, *Mesto za mrizemi (City behind Bars)* (Prague, 1964), 347, as cited in Kárný, "Schicksal," 82.

111 www.holocaust.cz/cz2/eng/victims/victims (accessed 13 March 2011). The Central Database of Shoah Victims at Yad Vashem in Jerusalem lists the names of Selma Steinberg, and Henriette and Emma Kaufmann. Marianne submitted a Page of Testimony for her mother in 1994, assuming she was deported to Maly Trostinec. The information on Henny and Emma is based on the Bundesarchiv (ed.), *Gedenkbuch*, 1st edn. (Koblenz 1986). This *Memorial Book* of the Federal Archives in Germany from 1986 lists both as deported to Minsk, which was the ghetto closest to Maly Trostinec. The latest edition of the *Memorial Book* from 2007 (now on-line), however, lists Treblinka as the final destination for all three sisters: www.bundesarchiv. de/gedenkbuch/directory.html (accessed 4 April 2010). This information has not yet been updated in the registry at Yad Vashem.

112 Ausschuß für Arbeiter-Wohlfahrt, Berlin to Erna Karsen, 18 March 1947, Berlin.

113 Herta Poth to Marianne, 8 September 1947 Essen, OC.

9 Epilogue

1 Lotti to Herta Poth, November 1971, Buenos, Aires FC. *Requiem* returned to Lotti after Herta's death circa 1979. Lotti's father, Alex, born in 1866, would have actually been 105 in November 1971.

2 Interview with Alicia Frohmann, 7 April 2010, Washington, DC, conducted by Rebecca Boehling.

3 Lotti had not been able to get a visa to Argentina but was able to get one to Uruguay and thus flew there. Interview with Alicia Frohmann, 27 April 2005, Miami, Florida, conducted by Rebecca Boehling.

4 Interview with Lotti, 2 November 1988, IN 291, recorded at the Alte Synagoge Archives, Essen.

5 See the special German law passed in 1955 to reinstate the citizenship of those denied it by the Nazi regime: Gesetz zur Regelung von Fragen der Staatsangehörigkeit vom 22. Februar 1955.

6 Interview with Alicia Frohmann, 27 April 2005, Miami, Florida, and 7 April 2010, Washington, DC, conducted by Rebecca Boehling. Cf. interview with Lotti, 2 November 1988, IN 291, recorded at the Alte Synagoge Archives, Essen.

7 Interview with Alicia Frohmann, 27 April 2005, Miami, Florida, and 7 April 2010, Washington, DC, conducted by Rebecca Boehling. See photograph in Chapter 2.

8 Marianne to Kurt and Lotti, 6 April 1946, New York, OC. A *Schmeichelkatze* is someone who flatters as a form of cajoling. *Ringel Rangel Rosen* is the equivalent of *Ring around the Rosies* and *Tut dem Kindchen nichts mehr weh* translates as "That doesn't hurt the little child." Original letter in English.

9 Interviews with Thomas Ostrand, 6 April 2006, Metuchen, New Jersey, and with Suzanne Ostrand-Rosenberg, 3 May 2006, Baltimore, Maryland, conducted by Rebecca Boehling and Uta Larkey.

10 Marianne's restitution file, OC. See also New Jersey State Board of Medical Examiners to Marianne Steinberg Ostrand, MD, 11 December 1952 and 20 September 1957, Trenton, New Jersey, OC. Marianne was required to complete two new internships in New Jersey. Neither her *Asyl* internship in 1937–8 nor the one at Tewksbury State Hospital in 1940 were recognized in New Jersey. She had been denied various internships in New York in 1939 because the hospitals had no provisions for female interns. At Englewood Hospital in New Jersey this also presented a problem, which was resolved in the late 1950s, however, when she was housed with the nurses.

11 On 11 May 1955 Marianne Ostrand wrote the Herr Innenminister in Düsseldorf: "Ich bitte nun mehr die Bestallungsurkunde auszustellen" ("I request that my medical license finally be issued"). Marianne's restitution file, Columbia, Maryland, OC. On 8 August 1955 the Interior Ministry North Rhine-Westphalia recognized her certification as a medical doctor in Germany, as of 31 March 1938. Marianne Ostrand Collection, AR 5823, Leo Baeck Institute, New York.

12 Kurt to Marianne and Arnold, 26 May 1955, Arolsen, OC.

13 Kurt to Lotti, 1 November 1955, Arolsen, and Marianne to Marianne Luedeking, 24 November 1955, Tenafly, New Jersey, OC.

14 Marianne to Marianne Luedeking, 24 November 1955, Tenafly, New Jersey, OC. Original in English.

15 Englewood Hospital Association to New Jersey Board of Medical Examiners, 11 September 1957, Englewood, New Jersey, OC.

16 Interview with Alicia Frohmann, 2 October 2005, Miami, Florida, conducted by Rebecca Boehling. Interviews with Thomas Ostrand, 6 April 2006, Metuchen, New Jersey and with Suzanne Ostrand-Rosenberg, 3 May 2006, Baltimore, Maryland, conducted by Rebecca Boehling and Uta Larkey.

17 Marianne Ostrand Collection, AR 5823, Leo Baeck Institute, New York.

18 Kurt to Marianne and Arnold, 24 January 1951, Tel Aviv, OC.

19 Interview with Marianne, 2 November 1988, IN 327, recorded at the Alte Synagoge Archives, Essen. Marianne was convinced that Kurt's premature death was due to "severe cardiovascular disease," which she attributed to his "incarceration in the concentration camp in 1938."

20 Interview with Gideon Sella, 28 June 2006, Tel Aviv, conducted by Uta Larkey.

21 Kurt to Marianne and Lotti, 28 July 1951, Tel Aviv, OC.

22 Hanna to Marianne, 9 December 1954, Tel Aviv, OC. Cf. Kurt to Marianne and Arnold, 5 January 1957, Arolsen, OC.

23 The ITS archive is located in Bad Arolsen (called Arolsen until 1997), Germany, and until November 2007, when the US Holocaust Memorial Museum-led effort to open the ITS collection succeeded, it was the largest closed Holocaust archive in the world: www.ushmm.org (accessed 3 April 2010).

24 Kurt to Lotti and Heiner, 15 July 1956 and 9 June 1957, Arolsen, FC.

25 Kurt to Lotti and Heiner, 15 July 1956, Arolsen, FC.

26 Ibid.

27 Kurt to Lotti and Heiner, 1 November 1955, Arolsen, FC.

28 See Kurt to Marianne, 5 January 1957, Arolsen, OC.

29 Kurt to Marianne and Arnold, 13 March 1957, Arolsen, and Marianne to Kurt, 19 January 1957, Tenafly, New Jersey, OC.

30 Interview with Gideon Sella, 28 June 2006, Tel Aviv, conducted by Uta Larkey.

BIBLIOGRAPHY

Primary sources

Archives and library special collections

Alte Synagoge Archives, Essen, Germany

Correspondence with the Archive

BR 164–165 Charlotte Steinberg Frohmann, 11 May 1984.
BR 205 Otto Grausz, 22 May 1987.
BR 241 Walter Hoffmann, 29 October 1989.
BR 422 Gerhard Orgler, 19 May 1981.
BR 507 Inge Schweizer, 19 May 1981.
BR 517 Hanna Levy Sella, "Bericht über meine Erlebnisse in der Nazi-Zeit,"
    1988.

Documents

AR 921 Walter Sternberg Collection.
AR 4483 Liesel Sternberg Collection.
AR 1179–1180 *Jüdisches Gemeindeblatt für den Synagogenbezirk Essen.*
AR 102466 Alex Steinberg, Marriage license Nr. 217, Alexander Steinberg and
    Selma Kaufmann, Altenessen Standesamt, 15 September 1905.

Interviews

IN 291 Charlotte Steinberg Frohmann, 2 November 1988.
IN 327 Marianne Steinberg Ostrand, 2 November 1988.

Houghton Library, Harvard University, Cambridge, Massachusetts

Harry Kaufman, "Mein Leben in Deutschland vor und nach Januar 1933," in *Life in Germany Contest* (bMS Ger91), 1940, Houghton Library, Harvard University.

Leo Baeck Institute, Berlin, Germany

MF 314 Max Hermann Maier, "Auswandererhilfe in Frankfurt am Main, 1936–1938." Written in 1961. Frankfurt am Main: Jewish Community Collection.

Leo Baeck Institute, New York, USA

AR 5823 Marianne Ostrand Collection.
AR 10426 and MF 642 Correspondence Carola and Salo Weindling.
MM14 Klara Caro, "Stärker als das Schwert, Erinnerungen," typewritten manuscript.

MAN Company Archives, Augsburg, Germany

Contract between MAN representatives and Hans Kaiser-Blüth, 4 March 1935, Nuremberg.

Museum und Historisches Archiv (VMM), manroland AG, Augsburg

Copy of MAN contract with Hans-Kaiser Blüth, 4 March 1935, Nuremberg.

Nordrhein-Westfälisches Hauptstaatsarchiv (HStA Düsseldorf), Germany

RW 58-Nr. 28854 Gestapo Files, Kurt Alfred Steinberg.

Shoah Foundation Institute, University of Southern California

Interview code 11370. Interview with Inge Goldschmidt Oppenheimer.

Stadtarchiv Essen, Germany

Adressbücher Altenessen, 1905 and 1908.
Adressbücher Essen.

Theresienstadt Archives, Památník Terezín, Czech Republic

A10/94 Tagesbefehl Nr. 125, 14 May 1942, Památník Terezín.
A3241 Tagesbefehl Nr. 213, 16 September 1942, Památník Terezín.

Thüringisches Hauptstaatsarchiv (HStA), Weimar, Germany

Prisoner files. Dr. Kurt Steinberg (Häftlingsnummer 24867), Geldkarte, Konzentrationslager Buchenwald.

United States Holocaust Memorial Museum (USHMM) Archives, Washington, DC

Kurt Steinberg's official correspondence as an employee of the Centralverein in Hamm, Essen and Frankfurt am Main, 1932–8. Records of the Centralverein deutscher Staatsbürger jüdischen Glaubens, Berlin (Central Association of German Citizens of Jewish Faith), Fond 721, Record Group-11.001M.31, reel 338–1547, 1550, 1556, 1573 and reel 133–2880.

Yad Vashem Archives, Jerusalem, Israel

Final report on "The Microfilm Project Carried Out for Yad Vashem Memorial Authority at the International Tracing Service at Arolsen, Germany," by Kurt Sella.
Pages of Testimony, Selma Steinberg, Henriette and Emma Kaufmann.

Government documents and periodicals

Allgemeine Zeitung des Judentums.
Aufbau.
Bundesarchiv Deutschlands (ed.) *Gedenkbuch: Opfer der Verfolgung der Juden unter der Nationalsozialistischen Gewaltherrschaft in Deutschland (1933–1945).* Koblenz: Bundesarchiv, 1st edn. 1986 and 2nd edn. 2006 (on-line after 2007).
C.V. Zeitung.
Israelitisches Familienblatt.
Jüdisches Gemeindeblatt für den Synagogenbezirk Essen.
Jüdisches Nachrichtenblatt (Berlin).
Jüdisches Nachrichtenblatt (Vienna).
Jüdische Rundschau.
Kölnische Zeitung.
Ministerialblatt 1938.
New York Times.
Reichsgesetzblatt 1933–1945 (RGBl.).

Interviews of Kaufmann–Steinberg family members by both authors

Marianne Bachrach Luedeking, Miami, Florida. 10 November 2006.
Alicia Frohmann, Miami, Florida 27 April 2005 and Washington, DC. 7 April 2010.
Ernest Kaufman, Lumberton, New Jersey. 29 March 2005, 11 May 2005 and 8 May 2008.
Michael Keynan, Tel Aviv, Israel. 29 June 2006 and 27 December 2007.
Arnold Ostrand, Columbia, Maryland. 18 February 2004.

Thomas Ostrand, Metuchen, New Jersey. 6 April 2006.
Suzanne Ostrand-Rosenberg, Baltimore, Maryland. 3 May 2006, 23 April 2008, 6 and 9 June 2008 and 21 June 2010.
Gideon Sella, Tel Aviv, Israel. 28 June 2006 and 27 December 2007.

Private collections (and abbreviations)

Frohmann Collection (FC), Santiago, Chile.
Ernest Kaufman Collection, New Jersey, USA.
Keynan Collection (KC), Tel Aviv, Israel.
Ostrand Collection (OC), Columbia, Maryland, USA.
Hans-Jürgen Schreiber Collection, Essen, Germany.
Sella Collection (SC), Tel Aviv, Israel.

Other published primary sources

Allport, G.W., J.S. Bruner and E.M. Jandorf. "Personality under Social Catastrophe: Ninety Life-Histories of the Nazi Revolution." *Character and Personality: An International Psychological Quarterly.* 1941.
Grünebaum, Leo. "'Jews Not Welcome' in Hotels," in Margarete Limberg and Hubert Rübsaat (eds.). *Germans No More: Accounts of Jewish Everyday Life, 1933–1938.* Trans. Alan Nothnagle. New York and Oxford: Berghahn Books, 2006.
Institut Theresienstädter Initiative (ed.). *Theresienstädter Gedenkbuch: Die Opfer der Judentransporte aus Deutschland nach Theresienstadt, 1942–1945.* Prague: Academia, 2000.
Kommission zur Erforschung der Geschichte der Frankfurter Juden (ed.). *Dokumente zur Geschichte der Frankfurter Juden 1933–1945.* Frankfurt am Main: Verlag Waldemar Kramer, 1963.
Manes, Philip. *Als ob's ein Leben wär: Tatsachenbericht Theresienstadt 1942–1944.* Berlin: Ullstein, 2005.
Matthäus, Jürgen and Mark Roseman (eds.). *Jewish Responses to Persecution, 1933–38.* Lanham, Md.: Alta Mira Press in association with the United States Holocaust Memorial Museum, 2010.
PHILO-Atlas. *Handbuch für die jüdische Auswanderung.* Mainz: Philo Verlagsgesellschaft, 1998, repr. 1938 edn.
Reichmann, Hans. *Deutscher Bürger und verfolgter Jude: Novemberpogrom und KZ Sachsenhausen 1937–1939.* Munich: Oldenbourg Wissenschaftsverlag, 1998.
Spitzer, Federica and Ruth Weisz. *Theresienstadt: Aufzeichnungen.* Berlin: Metropol Verlag, 1997.

Strauss, Herbert (ed.). *Jewish Immigrants of the Nazi Period in the USA*, 6 vols. New York: K.G. Saur, 1992.

Walk, Joseph. *Das Sonderrecht für die Juden im NS Staat*, 2nd edn. Heidelberg: C.F. Müller Verlag, 1996.

Weglein, Resi. *Als Krankenschwester im KZ Theresienstadt: Erinnerungen einer Ulmer Jüdin*. Stuttgart: Silberburg-Verlag, 1990.

Unpublished manuscripts

Aebersold, Désirée and Sonja Stalder. "Da von dem Erwerb des Titels meine Zukunft abhängt." Unpublished licensing thesis (*Lizentiatsarbeit*) at the Institut für Soziologie, Schriftenreihe Kultursoziologie, University of Bern, 2000.

Gayle, Deborah. "A German-Jewish Family's Odyssey through the Holocaust." Paper in fulfillment of the requirements for History 751, November 2002, UMBC, Baltimore, Maryland.

Kaufman, Ernest. "Holocaust-Survivor or Escapee." Unpublished talk given on several occasions after 2002.

Schreiber, Hans-Jürgen. "Die Familie Loewenstein." Draft essay for study of the Jews of Altenessen, Essen, 2005.

"Die Familie Steinberg–Kaufmann." Draft essay for study of the Jews of Altenessen, Essen, 2005.

"Geschichte der Altenessener Jüdinnen und Juden." Unpublished ms., Essen, 1994.

"Übersicht über die Geschichte der Juden in Altenessen." Draft essay for study of the Jews of Altenessen, Essen, 2005.

Tiedemann, Sibylle. "Frauenleben 1933–1945." Unpublished prospectus for documentary film *Kinderland ist abgebrannt*, 1995.

Secondary sources (books and articles)

Adam, Uwe Dietrich. "How Spontaneous Was the Pogrom?" in Walter H. Pehle (ed.), *November 1938: From "Kristallnacht" to Genocide*. Trans. William Templer. New York and Oxford: Berg, 1991.

Adler, H.G. *Theresienstadt 1941–1945: Das Antlitz einer Zwangsgemeinschaft*. Tübingen: J.C.B. Mohr, 1960.

Adler-Rudel, S. *Jüdische Selbsthilfe unter dem Naziregime, 1933–1939*. Tübingen: J.C.B. Mohr, 1974.

Alte Synagoge (ed.). *Entrechtung und Selbsthilfe: Zur Geschichte der Juden in Essen unter dem Nationalsozialismus*. Studienreihe der Alten Synagoge, vol. IV. Essen: Klartext, 1994.

Jüdisches Leben in Essen 1800–1933. Studienreihe der Alten Synagoge, vol. 1. Essen: Klartext, 1993.

Anderson, Mark M. (ed.). *Hitler's Exiles: Personal Stories of the Flight from Nazi Germany to America.* New York: The New Press, 1998.

Asaria, Zvi. *Die Juden in Köln.* Cologne: Verlag J.P. Bachem, 1959.

Aschheim, Steven. "German History and German Jewry: Junctions, Boundaries and Interdependencies," in *In Times of Crisis: Essays on European Culture, Germans, and Jews.* Madison: University of Wisconsin Press, 2001.

Bajohr, Frank. *"Aryanisation" in Hamburg: The Economic Exclusion of Jews and the Confiscation of Their Property in Nazi Germany.* Trans. G. Wilke. New York and Oxford: Berghahn Books, 2002.

Bankier, David. *The Germans and the Final Solution: Public Opinion under Nazism.* Oxford: Blackwell, 1992.

(ed.). *Probing the Depths of German Antisemitism: German Society and the Persecution of the Jews, 1933–1941.* New York and Oxford: Berghahn Books, 2000.

Barkai, Avraham. "The Fateful Year 1938," in Walter H. Pehle (ed.). *November 1938: From "Kristallnacht" to Genocide.* Trans. William Templer. New York and Oxford: Berg, 1991.

From Boycott to Annihilation: The Economic Struggle of the Jews, 1933–1943. Trans. William Templer. Hanover, N.H. and London: University Press of New England, 1989.

Hoffnung und Untergang: Studien zur deutsch-jüdischen Geschichte des 19. und 20. Jahrhunderts. Hamburg: Hans Christians, 1998.

"Wehr Dich!" Der Centralverein deutscher Staatsbürger jüdischen Glaubens (C.V.) 1893–1938. Munich: C.H. Beck, 2002.

Bauer, Yehuda. *A History of the Holocaust,* rev. edn. Danbury, Conn.: Franklin Watts, 2001.

Jews for Sale? Nazi–Jewish Negotiations 1933–1945. New Haven, Conn. and London: Yale University Press. 1994.

Becker-Jákli, Barbara. *Das jüdische Krankenhaus in Köln: Die Geschichte des Israelitischen Asyls für Kranke und Altersschwache 1869 bis 1945.* Cologne: Emons Verlag, 2004.

Benz, Wolfgang (ed.). *Die Juden in Deutschland 1933–1945: Leben unter nationalsozialistischer Herrschaft,* 3rd edn. Munich: C.H. Beck, 1993.

"Der Rückfall in die Barbarei," in Walter H. Pehle (ed.). *Der Judenpogrom 1938: Von der "Reichskristallnacht" zum Völkermord.* Frankfurt am Main: Fischer Verlag, 1988.

Bergen, Doris L. *War and Genocide: A Concise History of the Holocaust.* Lanham, Md.: Rowman and Littlefield, 2003.

Berghahn, Marion. *Continental Britons: German-Jewish Refugees from Nazi Germany,* rev. edn. New York and Oxford: Berghahn Books, 2007.

Berschel, Holger. *Bürokratie und Terror: Das Judenreferat der Gestapo Düsseldorf 1935–1945*. Essen: Klartext, 2001.

Black, Edwin. *The Transfer Agreement: The Dramatic Story of the Pact between the Third Reich and Jewish Palestine*. New York: Carroll & Graf Publishers, 2001.

Blackbourn, David. *The Long Nineteenth Century: A History of Germany, 1780–1918*. New York: Oxford University Press, 1998.

Blau, Bruno. *Das Ausnahmerecht für die Juden in Deutschland, 1933–1945*, 3rd edn. Düsseldorf: Verlag Allgemeine Wochenzeitung der Juden in Deutschland, 1965.

Böll, Heinrich. *Die Juden von Drove, Köln und das rheinische Judentum*. Festschrift Germania Judaica 1959–84. Cologne: Bachem Verlag, 1984.

Bolle, Mirjam. *"Ich weiss, dieser Brief wird dich nie erreichen." Tagebuchbriefe aus Amsterdam, Westerbork und Bergen-Belsen*. Berlin: Eichborn, 2006.

Bopf, Britta. *"Arisierung" in Köln: Die wirtschaftliche Existenzvernichtung der Juden 1933–1945*. Cologne: Emons, 2004.

Breitman, Richard and Alan Kraut. *American Refugee Policy and European Jewry, 1933–1945*. Bloomington and Indianapolis: Indiana University Press, 1988.

Brenner, Michael, Stefi Jersch-Wenzel and Michael A. Meyer (eds.). *Deutsch-jüdische Geschichte in der Neuzeit*, vol. II: *Emanzipation und Akkulturation 1780–1871*. Munich: C.H. Beck, 2000.

Browning, Christopher. *The Origins of the Final Solution: The Evolution of Nazi Jewish Policy September 1939–March 1942*. Lincoln, Nebr.: University of Nebraska Press, 2004.

Browning, Christopher S., Richard S. Hollander and Nechama Tec (eds.). *Every Day Lasts a Year: A Jewish Family's Correspondence from Poland*. New York: Cambridge University Press, 2007.

Corbach, Dieter. *6:00 ab Messe Köln-Deutz: Deportationen 1938–1945*. Cologne: Scriba Buch- und Musikverlag, 1999.

Davie, Maurice R. *Refugees in America: Report of the Committee for the Study of Recent Immigration from Europe*. New York: Harper & Brothers Publishers, 1947.

Doerry, Martin. *My Wounded Heart: The Life of Lilli Jahn 1900–1944*. Trans. John Brownjohn. New York: Bloomsbury, 2004.

Doetzer, Oliver. *"Aus Menschen werden Briefe": Die Korrespondenz einer jüdischen Familie zwischen Verfolgung und Emigration 1933–1947*. Cologne: Böhlau Verlag, 2002.

Dominicus, E. *Chronik des Amtsbezirkes Nörvenich 1932–1946*, 2nd edn. As cited in: www.geschichtswerkstatt-dueren.de (accessed 23 January 2010).

Dwork, Deborah and Robert Jan van Pelt. *Flight from the Reich: Refugee Jews, 1933–1946*. New York and London: W.W. Norton, 2009.

Edelheit, Abraham. *The Yishuv in the Shadow of the Holocaust: Zionist Politics and Rescue Aliya, 1933–1939*. Boulder, Colo.: Westview Press, 1996.

Edelheit, Abraham and Hershel Edelheit (eds.). *History of Zionism: A Handbook and Dictionary*. Boulder, Colo.: Westview Press 2000.

Ellenson, David Harry. *After Emancipation: Jewish Religious Responses to Modernity*. Detroit: Wayne State University Press, 2004.

Erel, Shlomo (ed.). *Jeckes erzählen: Aus dem Leben deutschsprachiger Einwanderer in Israel*. Vienna: LIT Verlag, 2004.

Farsoun, Samih K. and Christina Zacharia. *Palestine and the Palestinians*. Boulder, Colo.: Westview Press, 1997.

Feilchenfeld, Werner, Dolf Michaelis and Ludwig Pinner (eds.). *Haavara-Transfer nach Palästina und Einwanderung deutscher Juden 1933–1939*. Tübingen: J.C.B. Mohr, 1972.

Fraenkel, Daniel. "Jewish Self-Defense under the Constraints of National Socialism: The Final Years of the Centralverein," in David Bankier (ed.). *Probing the Depths of German Antisemitism: German Society and the Persecution of the Jews, 1933–1941*. New York and Oxford: Berghahn Books, 2000.

"Nuremberg Laws," in Walter Laqueur (ed.). *The Holocaust Encyclopedia*. New Haven: Yale University Press, 2001.

Friedländer, Saul. *Nazi Germany and the Jews: The Years of Persecution, 1933–1939*, vol. 1. New York: HarperCollins, 1997.

Friedman, Jonathan C. *The Lion and the Star: Gentile–Jewish Relations in Three Hessian Communities, 1919–1945*. Lexington, Ky.: University Press of Kentucky, 1998.

Garbarini, Alexandra. *Numbered Days: Diaries and the Holocaust*. New Haven: Yale University Press, 2006.

Gelber, Yoav and Walter Goldstern. *Vertreibung und Emigration deutschsprachiger Ingenieure nach Palästina 1933–1945*. Düsseldorf: VDI Verlag, 1988.

Gottwaldt, Alfred and Diana Schulle. *Die "Judendeportationen" aus dem Deutschen Reich 1941–1945*. Wiesbaden: Marixverlag, 2005.

Greif, Gideon, Colin McPherson and Laurence Weinbaum (eds.). *Die Jeckes: Deutsche Juden aus Israel erzählen*. Cologne: Böhlau Verlag, 2000.

Gruner, Wolf. *Die Verfolgung und Ermordung der europäischen Juden durch das nationalsozialistische Deutschland 1933–1945*, vol. 1: *Deutsches Reich 1933–1937*. Munich: Oldenbourg Wissenschaftsverlag, 2008.

"Von der Kollektivausweisung zur Deportation," in Birthe Kundrus and Beate Meyer (eds.). *Die Deportation der Juden aus Deutschland: Pläne, Praxis, Reaktionen 1938–1945*. Göttingen: Wallstein, 2004.

Hacohen, Dvora. "British Immigration Policy to Palestine in the 1930s: Implications for Youth Aliyah." *Middle Eastern Studies*. 37/4, October 2001.

Hájková, Anna. "Strukturen weiblichen Verhaltens in Theresienstadt," in Gisela Bock (ed.). *Genozid und Geschlecht*. Frankfurt am Main: Campus Verlag, 2005.

Herbert, Ulrich. "Von der 'Reichskristallnacht' zum 'Holocaust': Der 9. November und das Ende des 'Radauantisemitismus'," in Thomas Hofmann, Hanno Loewy and Harry Stein (eds.). *Pogromnacht und Holocaust*. Cologne: Böhlau Verlag, 1994.

Heuberger, Rachel. *Hinaus aus dem Ghetto: Juden in Frankfurt am Main, 1800–1950*. Frankfurt am Main: Fischer Verlag, 1988.

Hilberg, Raul. *The Destruction of the European Jews*. Teaneck, N.J.: Holmes and Meier, 1985.

Hofmann, Thomas, Hanno Loewy and Harry Stein (eds.). *Pogromnacht und Holocaust*. Cologne: Böhlau Verlag, 1994.

Jackisch, Carlota. "Einwanderungspolitik und öffentliche Meinung in Argentinien 1933–1945," in Karl Kohut and Patrik von zur Mühlen (eds.). *Alternative Lateinamerika: Das deutsche Exil in der Zeit des Nationalsozialismus*. Frankfurt am Main: Vervuert, 1994.

Kampe, Norbert. "Jewish Emigration from Germany 1933–1942," in Herbert Strauss (ed.). *Jewish Immigrants of the Nazi Period in the USA*, vol. iv. New York: K.G. Saur, 1992.

Kaplan, Marion. "As Germans and as Jews in Imperial Germany," in Marion Kaplan (ed.). *Jewish Daily Life in Germany, 1618–1945*. New York: Oxford University Press, 2005.

Between Dignity and Despair: Jewish Life in Nazi Germany. New York: Oxford University Press, 1998.

The Making of the Jewish Middle Class: Women, Family and Identity in Imperial Germany. New York and Oxford: Oxford University Press, 1991.

(ed.). *Jewish Daily Life in Germany, 1618–1945*. New York: Oxford University Press, 2005.

Kárný, Miroslav. "Das Schicksal der Theresienstädter Osttransporte im Sommer und Herbst 1942." *Judaica Bohemiae*. xxiv/2. Prague: Státní židovské muzeum, 1988.

"Theresienstadt 1941–1945," in Institut Theresienstädter Initiative (ed.). *Theresienstädter Gedenkbuch, Die Opfer der Judentransporte aus Deutschland nach Theresienstadt*. Prague: Academia, 2000.

Kater, Michael. *Doctors under Hitler*. Chapel Hill and London: UNC Press, 1989.

Kingreen, Monica (ed.). *"Nach der Kristallnacht": Jüdisches Leben und antijüdische Politik in Frankfurt am Main 1938–1945*. Frankfurt am Main: Campus Verlag, 1999.

Kliner-Fruck, Martina. *"Es ging ja ums Überleben": Jüdische Frauen zwischen Nazi-Deutschland, Emigration nach Palästina und ihrer Rückkehr*. Frankfurt am Main: Campus Verlag, 1995.

Koppel, Gabriele. *Heimisch werden – Lebenswege deutscher Juden in Palästina*. Hamburg: Europäische Verlagsanstalt, 2000.

Kropat, Wolf-Arno. *"Reichskristallnacht": Der Judenpogrom vom 7. bis 10. November 1938 – Urheber, Täter, Hintergründe*. Wiesbaden: Kommission für die Geschichte der Juden in Hessen, 1997.

Kruse, A. and E. Schmitt. *Wir haben uns als Deutsche gefühlt: Lebensrückblick und Lebenssituationen jüdischer Emigranten und Lagerhäftlinge*. Darmstadt: Steinkopff, 2000.

Kulka, Otto Dov and Eberhard Jäckel. *Die Juden in den geheimen NS-Stimmungsberichten 1933–1945*. Düsseldorf: Droste Verlag, 2004.

Kundrus, Birthe and Beate Meyer (eds.). *Die Deportation der Juden aus Deutschland: Pläne, Praxis, Reaktionen 1938–1945*. Göttingen: Wallstein, 2004.

Kwiet, Konrad. "Von der Ghettoisierung zur Deportation," in Wolfgang Benz (ed.). *Die Juden in Deutschland 1933–1945: Leben unter nationalsozialistischer Herrschaft*. Munich: C.H. Beck, 1988.

Laqueur, Walter. *Generation Exodus: The Fate of Young Jewish Refugees from Nazi Germany*. Hanover, N. H. and London: Brandeis University Press, 2001.

Laqueur, Walter and Judith Tydor Baumel (eds.). *Holocaust Encyclopedia*. New Haven and London: Yale University Press, 2001.

Large, David Clay. *And the World Closed Its Doors: The Story of One Family Abandoned to the Holocaust*. New York: Basic Books, 2003.

LeVine, Mark. *Overthrowing Geography: Jaffa, Tel Aviv and the Struggle for Palestine 1880–1948*. Berkeley and Los Angeles: University of California Press, 2005.

London, Louise. *Whitehall and the Jews, 1933–1948: British Immigration Policy, Jewish Refugees and the Holocaust*. Cambridge University Press, 2000.

Longerich, Peter. *"Davon haben wir nichts gewusst": Die Deutschen und die Judenverfolgung 1933–1945*. Munich: Siedler Verlag, 2006.

Lowenstein, Steven M. "Das religiöse Leben," in Steven M. Lowenstein, Paul Mendes-Flohr, Peter Pulzer and Monika Richarz (eds.). *Deutsch-jüdische Geschichte in der Neuzeit*, vol. III: *Umstrittene Integration 1871–1918*. Munich: C. H. Beck, 1997.

"Jüdisches religiöses Leben in deutschen Dörfern. Regionale Unterschiede im 19. und frühen 20. Jahrhundert," in Monika Richarz and Reinhard Rürup (eds.). *Jüdisches Leben auf dem Lande*. Tübingen: Mohr Siebeck, 1997.

Lowenstein, Steven M., Paul Mendes-Flohr, Peter Pulzer and Monika Richarz (eds.). *Deutsch-jüdische Geschichte in der Neuzeit*, vol. III: *Umstrittene Integration 1871–1918*. Munich: C. H. Beck, 1997.

Luft, Gerda. *Heimkehr ins Unbekannte: Eine Darstellung der Einwanderung von Juden aus Deutschland nach Palästina 1933–39*. Wuppertal: Peter Hammer Verlag, 1977.

Maurer, Trudi. "From Everyday Life to a State of Emergency: Jews in Weimar and Nazi Germany," in Marion Kaplan (ed.). *Jewish Daily Life in Germany, 1618–1945*. New York: Oxford University Press, 2005.

Medoff, Rafael. *Blowing the Whistle on Genocide: Josiah E. DuBois, Jr. and the Struggle for a US Response to the Holocaust*. West Lafayette, Ind: Purdue University Press, 2009.

Meyer, Michael A. "Schlußbetrachtung," in Michael Brenno, Stefi Jersch-Wenzel and Michael A. Meyer (eds.). *Deutsch-jüdische Geschichte in der Neuzeit*, vol. II: *Emanzipation und Akkulturation 1780–1871*. Munich: C.H. Beck, 2000.

Nicosia, Francis. *The Third Reich and the Palestine Question*. Austin: University of Texas Press, 1985.

Ofer, Dalia. *Escaping the Holocaust: Illegal Immigration to the Land of Israel, 1939–1944*. Studies in Jewish History Series. New York: Oxford University Press, 1990.

Pulzer, Peter. *The Jews and the German State: The Political History of a Minority, 1848–1933*. Oxford: Blackwell, 1992.

"Rechtliche Gleichstellung und öffentliches Leben." Trans. Holger Fliessbach, in Steven M. Lowenstein, Paul Mendes-Flohr, Peter Pulzer and Monika Richarz (eds.). *Deutsch-jüdische Geschichte in der Neuzeit*, vol. III: *Umstrittene Integration 1871–1918*. Munich: C. H. Beck, 1997.

Quack, Sibylle. *Between Sorrow and Strength: Women Refugees of the Nazi Period*. Washington, DC: German Historical Institute, 1995.

Reinharz, Jehuda. *Fatherland or Promised Land: The Dilemma of the German Jew, 1893–1914*. Ann Arbor: University of Michigan Press, 1975.

Richarz, Monika (ed.). *Jewish Life in Germany: Memoirs from Three Centuries*. Trans. Stella P. Rosenfeld and Sidney Rosenfeld. Bloomington and Indianapolis: Indiana University Press, 1991.

Jüdisches Leben in Deutschland: Selbstzeugnisse zur Sozialgeschichte, 1918–1945, 3 vols. Stuttgart: Deutsche Verlags-Anstalt, 1982.

Richarz, Monika and Reinhard Rürup (eds.). *Jüdisches Leben auf dem Lande*. Tübingen: Mohr Siebeck, 1997.

Rockman, Chaim. *None of them Were Heroes: Letters between the Lines, 1938–1945*. Englewood, N.J.: Devora, 2003.

Roseman, Mark. *The Past in Hiding*. London: Penguin, 2000.

Schlör, Joachim. *Endlich im gelobten Land? Deutsche Juden unterwegs in eine neue Heimat*. Berlin: Aufbau Verlag, 2003.

Schmalhausen, Bernd. *Schicksale jüdischen Juristen aus Essen, 1933–1945*. Bottrup and Essen: Pomp, 1994.

Schmid, Armin and Renate Schmid. *Im Labyrinth der Paragraphen: Die Geschichte einer gescheiterten Emigration*. Frankfurt am Main: Fischer Taschenbuch Verlag, 1993.

Lost in a Labyrinth of Red Tape: The Story of an Immigration that Failed. Trans. Margot Bettauer Dembo. Evanston, Ill.: Northwestern University Press, 1996.

Scholz, A. and W. Burgdorf. "The Exodus of German Dermatologists and their Contributions to their Adopted Countries." *Clinics in Dermatology*. 23/5 (Sept.–Oct. 2005).

Schröter, Hermann. *Geschichte und Schicksal der Essener Juden. Gedenkbuch für die jüdischen Mitbürger der Stadt Essen.* Essen: Stadt Essen, 1980.

Schwarcz, Alfredo Jose. *Trotz allem...: Die deutschsprachigen Juden in Argentinien.* Cologne: Böhlau, 1995.

Segev, Tom. *The Seventh Million: The Israelis and the Holocaust.* New York: Henry Holt and Co., 2000.

Shapiro, Paul A. and Martin C. Dean. "Foreword," in *Confiscation of Jewish Property in Europe, 1933–1945: New Sources and Perspectives.* Proceedings of Symposium held at the United States Holocaust Memorial Museum Center for Advanced Holocaust Studies, Washington, January 2003. Washington, D.C.: United States Holocaust Memorial Museum, 2003.

Shealy, Gregory P. Review of W. Paul Strassmann, *The Strassmanns: Science, Politics, and Migration in Turbulent Times, 1793–1993.* New York: Berghahn Books, 2008. H-German, H-Net Reviews. May 2009. www.h-net.org/reviews/showrev.php?id=23651

Sherman, A.J. *Island Refuge: Britain and Refugees from the Third Reich.* Berkeley and Los Angeles: University of California Press, 1973.

Smith, Helmut Walser. *The Continuities of German History: Nation, Religion and Race across the Long Nineteenth Century.* New York: Cambridge University Press, 2008.

Sorkin, David. "Emancipation and Assimilation: Two Concepts and Their Application to the Study of German Jewish History." *Leo Baeck Institute Yearbook (LBIYB).* 35, 1990.

Stein, Harry. "Das Sonderlager im Konzentrationslager Buchenwald nach den Pogromen 1938," in Monica Kingreen (ed.). *"Nach der Kristallnacht": Jüdisches Leben und antijüdische Politik in Frankfurt am Main 1938–1945.* Frankfurt am Main: Campus Verlag, 1999.

Juden in Buchenwald 1937–1942. Buchenwald: Gedenkstätte Buchenwald, 1992.

Steinecke, Hartmut. "Einführung 1. Deutschland," in Jenny Aloni, *"Ich muss mir diese Zeit von der Seele schreiben...": Die Tagebücher 1935–1993: Deutschland–Palästina–Israel.* Paderborn: Ferdinand Schöningh, 2006.

Strauss, Herbert. "Jewish Emigration from Germany, Part 1." *Leo Baeck Institute Yearbook (LBIYB).* 1980.

Tarsi, Anita. "Das Schicksal der alten Frauen in Theresienstadt," in Miroslav Kárný, Margita Kárná and Raimund Kemper (eds.). *Theresienstädter Studien und Dokumente.* Prague: Academia, 1998.

Thalmann, Rita and Emmanuel Feinermann. *Crystal Night 9–10 November 1938*. Trans. Gilles Cremones. New York: Holocaust Library, 1972.

van Laak, Dirk. "Wenn einer ein Herz im Leibe hat, der läßt sich von einem deutschen Arzt behandeln: Die 'Entjudung' der Essener Wirtschaft von 1933 bis 1941," in Alte Synagoge (ed.). *Entrechtung und Selbsthilfe: Zur Geschichte der Juden in Essen unter dem Nationalsozialismus*. Studienreihe der Alten Synagoge, vol. IV. Essen: Klartext, 1994.

von der Lühe, Barbara. *Die Musik war unsere Rettung! Die deutschsprachigen Gründungsmitglieder des Palestine Orchestra*. Tübingen: Mohr Siebeck, 1998.

Wetzel, Juliane. "Auswanderung aus Deutschland," in Wolfgang Benz (ed.). *Die Juden in Deutschland 1933–1945: Leben unter nationalsozialistischer Herrschaft*, 3rd edn. Munich: C. H. Beck, 1993.

Weyers, Wolfgang. *Death of Medicine in Nazi Germany: Dermatology and Dermatopathology under the Swastika*. Lanham, Md.: Madison Books, 1998.

Wyman, David S. *The Abandonment of the Jews: America and the Holocaust 1941–1945*. New York: Pantheon Books, 1984.

Wyman, David S. and Charles H. Rosenzveig. *The World Reacts to the Holocaust*. Baltimore: Johns Hopkins University Press, 1996.

Yad Vashem (ed.). *From Bergen-Belsen to Freedom: The Story of the Exchange of Jewish Inmates of Bergen-Belsen with German Templars from Palestine*. Proceedings of the Symposium in Memory of Dr. Haim Pazner. Jerusalem: Yad Vashem, 1986.

Zimmermann, Michael. "Eine Deportation nach Theresienstadt: Zur Rolle des Banalen bei der Durchsetzung des Monströsen," in Miroslav Kárný, Margita Kárná and Raimund Kemper (eds.). *Theresienstädter Studien und Dokumente*. Prague: Academia, 1994.

"Die 'Reichskristallnacht' 1938 in Essen," in Alte Synagoge (ed.). *Entrechtung und Selbsthilfe: Zur Geschichte der Juden in Essen unter dem Nationalsozialismus*. Studienreihe der Alten Synagoge, vol. IV. Essen: Klartext, 1994.

"Zur Geschichte der Essener Juden im 19. und im ersten Drittel des 20. Jahrhunderts," in Alte Synagoge (ed.). *Jüdisches Leben in Essen 1800–1933*. Studienreihe der Alten Synagoge, vol. I. Essen: Klartext, 1993.

Zucker, Bat-Ami. *In Search of Refuge: Jews and US Consuls in Nazi Germany 1933–1941*. London and Portland, Oreg.: Vallentine Mitchell, 2001.

INDEX